Elite Youth Sport Policy and Management

Elite youth sport competitions have increased significantly in number in recent years, with the Youth Olympic Games representing the high point of this phenomenon. This book examines the global context within which elite youth sport has emerged and continues to grow. It explores elite youth sport policy across 15 countries, in Europe, the Americas, Africa and Asia, addressing the questions of how youth talent development is organised and why elite youth sport has become so popular.

Taking a comparative global perspective, the book analyses the growth in more systematic approaches to young athlete development and the increasing emphasis on early talent identification. It discusses the attitude of stakeholders (such as NGBs, governments and sponsors) towards elite youth sport, while also considering how, and the extent to which, young elite athletes' interests are protected and how the growth in elite youth sport affects a sport's development strategy.

Written by a team of internationally renowned researchers, *Elite Youth Sport Policy and Management: A comparative analysis* is fascinating reading for all students, scholars, managers, policy-makers and coaches with an interest in youth sport, elite sport development, talent identification and sports policy.

Elsa Kristiansen is Associate Professor at the University College of Southeast Norway and Visiting Professor at the Norwegian School of Sport Sciences. She has published over 40 articles and book chapters, the majority of which are in the areas of sport psychology (e.g. motivation, coping with organisational issues and media stress, coping with youth competitions) and sport event management (e.g. volunteerism, Youth Olympic Games, stakeholders involved in talent development).

Milena M. Parent is Associate Professor of Sport Management at the University of Ottawa and at the Norwegian School of Sport Sciences. Her expertise lies in sport event management and some recent publications include the *Routledge Handbook of Sports Event Management* (with J.-L. Chappelet, Routledge, 2015), *The Youth Olympic Games* (with D.V. Hanstad and B. Houlihan, Routledge, 2014), and *Managing Major Sports Events: Theory and practice* (with S. Smith-Swan, Routledge, 2013).

Barrie Houlihan is Professor of Sport Policy at Loughborough University, UK and Visiting Professor at the Norwegian School of Sport Sciences. He has authored or edited 20 books and authored over 60 journal articles. His most recent book is *Managing Elite Sport Systems: Research and practice* (edited with Svein S. Andersen and Lars Tore Ronglan, published by Routledge). He was the founding editor of the *International Journal of Sport Policy and Politics*.

Routledge Research in Sport Business and Management

Available in this series:

Elite Youth Sport Policy and Management

A comparative analysis

Edited by
Elsa Kristiansen, Milena M. Parent
and Barrie Houlihan

Routledge
Taylor & Francis Group
LONDON AND NEW YORK

First published 2017
by Routledge
2 Park Square, Milton Park, Abingdon, Oxon OX14 4RN

and by Routledge
711 Third Avenue, New York, NY 10017

Routledge is an imprint of the Taylor & Francis Group, an informa business

© 2017 Elsa Kristiansen, Milena M. Parent and Barrie Houlihan

British Library Cataloguing-in-Publication Data
A catalogue record for this book is available from the British Library

Library of Congress Cataloging in Publication Data
A catalog record for this book has been requested

ISBN: 978-1-138-88808-1 (hbk)
ISBN: 978-1-315-71370-0 (ebk)

Typeset in Sabon
by Saxon Graphics Ltd, Derby

Printed and bound by CPI Group (UK) Ltd, Croydon, CR0 4YY

Contents

Figures

Tables

Contributors

Verena Burk, Ph.D., is Senior Lecturer at the Institute of Sports Science, Department of Sport Economics, Sport Management and Sport Media Research at the University of Tübingen. Her research and teaching is focused on sport journalism, event management and national/international elite sport and she has published several publications in these fields. Since 2007 she has been a member of the Executive Committee of the International University Sport Federation (FISU).

Cora Burnett, Ph.D., is a Professor of the sociology of sport and Director of the University of Johannesburg, Olympic Studies Centre. Her expertise lies in the sport for development domain, Olympic studies and sociological research in Africa. Some recent publications include *Sport in Society: Issues and Controversies – A southern African edition* (with Jay Coakley, Van Schaiks, 2014), The significance of sports to sociology (in Joan Ferrante's adaptation – South African perspective, Cengage Learning, 2016).

Fernando Renato Cavichioli has a Doctorate in Education from the Methodist University of Piracicaba (UNIMED/2004) and post-doctoral qualification from the University of Coimbra (UC/ 2011) – Faculty of Sport Sciences and Physical Education. From 2014 he has been the Coordinator of the Program of Graduate Studies in Physical Education (PPGEDF) at the Federal University of Paraná.

Pippa Chapman is a Sports Researcher in the UK. She holds a Ph.D. in Elite Sport Policy from Loughborough University. She has experience lecturing at Brunel University and Loughborough University and has worked in the sport sector with England Netball, UK Sport and Women in Sport.

Pakianathan Chelladurai. Chelladurai, Distinguished Professor, Troy University, has received the Earle F. Zeigler Award from the North American Society for Sport Management, the Merit Award for Distinguished Service to Sport Management Education from the European Association of Sport Management (EASM), Sport Management Scholar

Lifetime Achievement Award from Southern Sport Management Association, and Letters of Law (LL.D., honorary degree) from the University of Western Ontario, Canada. EASM has named its most prestigious award the EASM Chelladurai Award.

Agnes Elling, Ph.D., is Senior Researcher at the Mulier Institute, centre for research on sports in society. Her research expertise includes the psycho-social well-being and social in/exclusionary mechanisms in (elite) sports biographies. She has published many books, reports and articles on talent development trajectories, education and psycho-social well-being in the Netherlands (often together with Niels Reijgersberg).

Vassil Girginov is Reader in Sport Management/Development at Brunel University London and Visiting Professor at the Russian International Olympic University and at the University of Johannesburg. His research interests, publications and industry experience are in the fields of Olympic movement, sport development, comparative management and policy analysis. Girginov's most recent publications include *Olympic Studies – 4* volume collection (Routledge, 2015), *Handbook of the London 2012 Olympic & Paralympic Games* (Vols 1 and 2), (Routledge, 2012–3), *Sport Management Cultures* (Routledge, 2011) and *Management of Sports Development* (Elsevier, 2008).

B. Christine Green is Professor and Director of the Sport+Development Lab at the University of Illinois. Her research examines the factors that facilitate or inhibit the development of sport at each level, and seeks to determine the separate, cumulative, and interactive effects of those factors within and across levels. She is a Research Fellow of the North American Society for Sport Management, and has served as an Editor of *Sport Management Review*, and as an Associate Editor for *Journal of Sport Management* and *Sport & Tourism*. Her work has been published in top journals in sport, leisure, and tourism, and has been funded in five countries. She was recently awarded the Earle F. Zeigler Award from the North American Society for Sport Management.

Matthew B. Greenberg is a Ph.D. student and member of the Sport+Development Lab at the University of Illinois. He earned his MS in Sports Business from New York University, and brings a wealth of experience in professional sport to his work. He has worked with Major League Baseball, the NBA, and served as Head of Sales and Marketing for Rule 1.02 Sports & Entertainment. He has also served as Head Wrestling Coach at Franklin & Marshall College. His current research examines governance and policy issues affecting athlete development at the university level.

Eunah Hong, Ph.D., is Assistant Professor of Sport Management & Administration at Ewha Womans University in Seoul, Republic of Korea.

Her expertise lies in human resource management (particularly match officials in sport) and leadership in sport organizations. Some recent publications include 'A Red Card for Women: Female Officials Ostracized in South Korean Football' (with M, C. Kim, 2016, *Asian Journal of Women's Studies*) and 'The development of Sport Policy and Management in South Korea' (with H. J. Won, 2015, *International Journal of Sport Policy and Politics*).

Barrie Houlihan is Professor of Sport Policy at Loughborough University, UK and Visiting Professor at the Norwegian School of Sport Sciences. He has authored or edited twenty books and authored over sixty journal articles. His most recent book is *Managing Elite Sport Systems: Research and Practice* (edited with Svein S. Andersen and Lars Tore Ronglan, published by Routledge). He is the Editor in Chief of the *International Journal of Sport Policy and Politics*.

Russell Hoye, Ph.D., is Professor and the Pro Vice-Chancellor for Research Development and Director of Sport at La Trobe University, Australia. His research interests are in corporate governance, public policy, volunteer management and the impact of sport on individuals and society. He has published more than fifty refereed journal articles on sport management and policy, has published seven books with colleagues, is the Editor of the Sport Management Series for Routledge and is a member of the editorial boards for *Sport Management Review*, the *International Journal of Sport Policy and Politics*, and the *Journal of Global Sport Management*.

Paul Jurbala is a Ph.D. candidate at Brock University where his research has focused on change implementation in community sport organizations. Formerly CEO of two provincial sport organizations, he has worked for the past decade as an independent consultant specializing in long-term athlete development and sport organization development, planning and evaluation. He is Director at the Knowledge at Sport for Life Society.

Elsa Kristiansen, Ph.D., is Associate Professor at the University College of Southeast Norway and Visiting Professor at the Norwegian School of Sport Science. She has published over 40 articles and book chapters, the majority of which are in the areas of sport psychology (e.g., motivation, coping with organizational issues and media stress, coping with youth competitions) and sport event management (e.g., volunteerism, Youth Olympic Games, stakeholders involved in talent development).

Fernando Marinho Mezzadri is Professor of Public Policy for Sport in the Department of Physical Education, and Vice Director of the Faculty of Biological Sciences at the Federal University of Paraná. He is also a Senior Researcher in the Centre for the Study of Sport, Leisure and Society at the

Federal University of Paraná, and is currently a visiting research Professor in the Faculty of Kinesiology and Physical Education at the University of Toronto and the author of five books.

Denis Musso has a background in Physical Education, Political Sciences and he specialized in Sport Management and Sport Law. Since 1991 and until 2013 he was Professor in INSEP Paris, the main elite sport centre in France and he was responsible for the Department of Management, Economics and Law. He has published widely both articles, reports and in books, especially on the status of the athlete and a professional sport. He is member of the team of the MEMOS programme and acts as Trainer Consultant in Sport Law and Sport Management.

Usha Sujit Nair, Ph.D., is an Associate Professor at the Lakshmibai National College of Physical Education, Thiruvananthapuram, India. Her publications include a chapter in Springer's 2013 *Comparative Sport Development Systems, Participation and Public Policy* edited by K. Kirstin and K. Petry and a chapter in Greenwood's 1994 *National Sports Policies: An International Handbook* edited by L. Chalip, A. Johnson, and L. Stachura.

Milena M. Parent, Ph.D., is Associate Professor of Sport Management at the University of Ottawa and at the Norwegian School of Sport Sciences. Her expertise lies in sport event management and some recent publications include *The Routledge Handbook of Sports Event Management* (with J.-L. Chappelet, Routledge, 2015), *The Youth Olympic Games* (with D.V. Hanstad and B. Houlihan, Routledge, 2014), and *Managing Major Sports Events: Theory and Practice* (with S. Smith-Swan, Routledge, 2013).

David Patterson, Ph.D., is the lead on the National Sport Federation Enhancement Initiative at the Canadian Olympic Committee. The project is designed to increase the organizational capacity of the 52 Olympic and Pan American Sport Federations in Canada. Prior to this role, he was the CEO of two different National Sport Federations in Canada. His field of expertise includes sport governance, long-term athlete development, development of sport officials and organizational development in sport organizations.

Karen Petry, Ph.D., is Deputy Head of the Institute of European Sport Development and Leisure Studies at the German Sport University in Cologne. She is responsible for the research activities in (European) Sport Policy and Sport Development. Karen has published several books and articles in these fields. Since 2002 she has been a board member (Vice President) of the European Network of Sport Science, Education and Employment (ENSSEE).

Niels Reijgersberg is Researcher at the Mulier Institute, centre for research on sports in society. His expertise includes physical education and talent development. He has published widely on talent development and education in the Netherlands (often together with Agnes Elling).

Michael P. Sam is a Senior Lecturer in the School of Physical Education, Sport and Exercise Sciences at the University of Otago (New Zealand). His research encompasses policy, politics and governance as they relate to the public administration/management of sport. Michael has published widely in both sport studies and parent discipline journals and has co-edited two books: *Sport in the City: Cultural Connections* (2011) and *Sport Policy in Small States* (2016).

Marcelo Moraes e Silva graduated in Physical Education. He has a master's degree in Education from the Federal University of Paraná – UFPR, a doctorate in Education at the UNICAMP. He also held post-doctoral training in Physical Education from the UFPR (2012–2014). He is Associate Professor at the Department of Physical Education UFPR, teaching classes at the undergraduate and graduate program in Physical Education. It operates on the following topics: Epistemology of Physical Education/Sports; Philosophy of Sport; History and Sociology of Sport; and Public Sport Policies.

Xiaoyan Xing, Ph.D., is Associate Professor of Sport Management at Capital University of P.E. & Sports, Beijing, China. Her research encompasses two areas: sport consumer behaviour and culture, and sport development in China. Her recent project delves into the participation and consumption behaviours of Chinese marathon runners.

Acknowledgements

We would like to thank Professor Dag Vidar Hanstad for initiating the project and supporting us throughout this endeavour, as well as the Department of Social and Cultural Studies (Norwegian School of Sport Sciences). We would also like to thank all our chapter contributors for making it the quality book it is and fostering critical thinking regarding elite youth sport worldwide.

Chapter 1

Introduction

Milena M. Parent, Elsa Kristiansen and Barrie Houlihan

The elite youth competition phenomenon is not new. A number of major sports have had junior world championships for over 30 years. For example, the International Association of Athletic Federations (IAAF) has had junior championships for age 19 and under men and women since 1986, Fédération Internationale de Football Association (FIFA) has had an under-16 men's world cup since 1985, and Fédération Internationale de Gymnastique's (FIG's) junior artistic championships have taken place since 1989 and are for females aged 13 to 15 and males aged 14 to 17. On the winter sports' side, the International Skating Union (ISU) has had junior figure skating championships since 1976, where skaters must be aged between 14 and 18 (or under 21 for men in pairs skating and ice dancing) and the International Ice Hockey Federation (IIHF) has had the under-20 men's junior world championships since 1974 and the under-18 since 1999.

What is new is the increasing presence of international youth multi-sport events and youth championships for women in traditionally male sports. For example, FINA (international aquatics association) has had world junior swimming championships (for 14–17 year old girls and 15–18 year old boys) since 2006. The IIHF has had its female under-18 world championships since 2008. The first Commonwealth Youth Games for athletes aged between 14 and 18 was in 2000, the first European Youth Sport Festival (athletes aged 13–18) was held in 1991, the first Australian Youth Olympic Festival (athletes aged 13–19) was held in 2001, and the first Youth Olympic Games (hereafter, YOG) for athletes aged 15–18 was held in 2010.

Explaining the growth in elite youth sport events is far from easy. Few youth events attract substantial sponsorship or interest from broadcasters and many youth events, such as the Commonwealth Youth Games and the YOG, are heavily subsidized by the host government. A possible explanation might be the persistence of the myth that hosting sports events increases sport participation despite the accumulation of evidence indicating that hosting sports events, even major events, does not result in significant or sustained new sport participation, although they can assist in sport participation retention and further progression/development in the sport system (Taks et al., 2014). If the impact is modest in the host country, then it is likely to be negligible elsewhere due to the lack of television coverage. The most plausible explanations are the desire by international federations to strengthen the development pathway for their young athletes by exposing them to more substantial competition at an early age and to better ensure the long-term commitment of young athletes to their sport. It might also be the case that, despite evidence to the contrary (Baker et al., 2009; Myer et al., 2015), there has been a strengthening in the belief among National Governing Bodies (NGBs) that ever earlier specialization is a prerequisite for eventual elite success (Hodges & Williams, 2012).

While the expansion in the opportunities for intense competition at a young age is not necessarily problematic, there are aspects of the growth in the number and popularity of elite youth sport events that prompt concern. The 1989 UN Convention on the Rights of the Child (CRC) was a watershed in modern thinking about childhood, as it "moved children and adolescents away from old-fashioned welfare and charity policies by turning needs into legal rights" (David, 2008, p. 108). Perhaps more importantly, the CRC reflected the acceptance that "the needs of the child justified an instrument in addition to the Universal Declaration of Human Rights" (Social Commission of the United Nations, quoted in Veerman, 1992, p. 57). What the CRC acknowledged was that children have distinctive developmental needs, which require the protection of the law. While the CRC provides a valuable reference point for an analysis of the involvement of children in elite sport, the Convention has its limitations. The primary limitation is that the focus and interpretation of the Convention has tended to be on young children (0–10 years) rather than on adolescents (10–19 years) and the "crucial phase of rapid biological and psychosocial changes, in which they need adequate support from their environment" (Desmet, 2012, p. 4). Furthermore, there is some concern that the CRC is out of date and has not kept up with changes in the lives of young people and developments in youth policies (of both governments and, one might add, of international sport organizations). These criticisms notwithstanding, the CRC remains the primary global reference point for assessing the extent to which the welfare interests of children and adolescents are protected and promoted. Many of the 42 articles of the Convention are relevant to young elite athletes with the following being of especial importance:

- Article 3: The best interests of the child must be a top priority in all decisions and actions that affect children.
- Article 12: Every child has the right to express their views, feelings and wishes in all matters affecting them, and to have their views considered and taken seriously.

- Article 19: Governments must do all they can to ensure that children are protected from all forms of violence, abuse, neglect and bad treatment by their parents or anyone else who looks after them.
- Article 28: Every child has the right to an education.
- Article 31: Every child has the right to relax, play and take part in a wide range of cultural and artistic activities.
- Article 32: Governments must protect children from economic exploitation and work that is dangerous or might harm their health, development or education.

The CRC highlights the importance of meeting the psycho-social developmental needs of young athletes and of maintaining an appropriate balance within their dual careers of academic progress and achievement on the one hand, and training and competition on the other. In recent years the need for government intervention to protect young athletes from physical and sexual abuse has been recognized in a number of countries (Donnelly, 1997; Farstad, 2007; McGeehan, 2013; Brackenridge et al., 2013). The problem of burnout has also attracted greater attention (Vitali et al., 2014; Mostafavifar et al., 2012; Myer et al., 2015), as has the need to manage more effectively the dual career ambitions of young athletes (Athletes to Business, 2011; Aquilina, 2013; De Knop et al., 1999; European Union, 2013; Henry, 2013). Despite the growing awareness of these issues, the momentum behind the expansion in the opportunities for youth to take part in intensely competitive sport appears to be gathering pace. The explicit, or in some cases tacit, support provided by governments for elite youth sport often stands in direct conflict with the public position of many governments, which emphasizes participation and gradual progression within sport so as to foster life-long involvement in sport and physical activity. In Canada, for example, there is the Canadian Sport For Life (CS4L) movement (see http://canadiansportforlife.ca/) and its associated Long-Term Athlete Development (LTAD) system (see http://canadiansport forlife.ca/learn-about-canadian-sport-life/ltad-stages) that Sport Canada required each NGB to follow. Still, a number of provinces have sport-focused schools, and the degree to which NGBs truly follow the LTAD system – versus paying lip-service to it and applying its principles only superficially or offloading such responsibilities to their provincial counterparts in order to get funding from Sport Canada – remains to be ascertained. Likewise, in Norway, the Norwegian Olympic and Paralympic Committee and Confederation of Sports (NIF) has required that all federations implement child protection measures. These were first developed as guidelines before becoming mandatory regulations. The intentions behind the regulation of children's sport are to ensure learning of a wide array of movements and skills for all children and to protect them from the negative effects of competition. For example, at the age of 11, lists of results, tables and rankings may be used for the first time, and the children may participate in regional competitions, where there is no need to meet a qualifying standard, in Norway, Scandinavia or other North Calotte group countries. In 2007, the regulations were modified to allow children to compete at national and international championships from the year they turn 13, previously the lower age limit for the European Youth Olympic Festival. Despite the concerns evident in Canada and Norway regarding the exposure of young people to intense competition, both countries, along with most other Western industrialized countries, have enthusiastically supported highly competitive youth sports events such as the YOG, with Norway, somewhat ironically, hosting the 2016 YOG.

The ethics of early involvement in elite-level sport is, however, only one of a number of issues prompted by the rapid increase in the number of elite competitions. A second issue relates to the management of the crowded competitive schedule for youth sport. As previously mentioned, young athletes typically must balance school and sports, as well as balancing attendance at events that will help them develop and events that are prestigious. Emerging events, such as the YOG, may not have the same level of prestige as other events, but national sport organizations are under pressure from their national Olympic committees to send good quality squads. For instance, snowboarders seem to still favor events with sponsors that pay over participating in the winter YOG. This particular event is also situated in a rather packed schedule – there are only so many days in the winter season. There is an increasing inter-organizational competition for market share in terms of number of athletes attending, potential sponsorship and broadcasting income, and youth/parents/families as spectators between individual international federations, as well as between the international federations and multi-sport event organizers, especially the International Olympic Committee (IOC). Whether the international sport system can sustain this growth remains uncertain.

A third issue concerns the cost to NGBs of sport and, for the YOG, to national Olympic committees of sending squads to international youth events. By adding new youth events, NGBs also see their already stretched resources further strained. Small national Olympic committees "forced" to attend the YOG in order to obtain much needed financial resources from the IOC and Olympic Solidarity may end up spending more than they receive. Furthermore, it is questionable whether young athletes can peak two, three or four times in a season. If they must now attend two youth multi-sport events (e.g., European Youth Sport Festival and YOG), plus their world junior championships, is it truly feasible to expect them to perform at their peak each time? Moreover, early talent identification systems not only impact the youth, but also their support team. Increasing the number of events to attend, for example, stretches parents' abilities to support their children, financially, emotionally, and materially. Finally, is it truly in the youth's long-term best interest to miss additional days of schooling to attend these new youth sport events? Despite these concerns, it has to be acknowledged that, in some countries (e.g., Kenya and Ethiopia), success in sport may be one of the few ways for poorer youth to improve their living standards.

Some researchers are already raising concerns over the growth of elite youth sport events, in particular the YOG. Wong (2011, p. 1839) warned that "by mirroring the adult games at the youth level, the IOC walks a fine line between celebrating what sport should be and succumbing to what has become a sporting model dominated by excessive competition."

Nevertheless, there seem to be some potentially positive outcomes from such events, be it learning what it means to attend a multi-sport event; fostering an awareness and appreciation of different cultures; solidifying a resolve to go to and/or win an Olympic Games or world championship medal; training of young volunteers, coaches and leaders; and returning the YOG to the Olympic Movement's roots and values (Gold & Gold, 2011; Hanstad, Parent, & Houlihan, 2014; Hanstad, Parent, & Kristiansen, 2013; Parent, Kristiansen, & MacIntosh, 2014a, 2014b; Parent et al., 2015).

The book

As is the case in much comparative research, most research utilizes a culturally narrow and often small sample drawn mainly from Western, industrialized countries. If insight is to be gained regarding areas of convergence and divergence in current policy and practice in international elite youth sport, then a larger and more representative sample is required.

Perceptions, norms and practices differ between countries and regions. As such, this book sets out to explore elite youth sport policy and management across 17 countries. It also examines a range of issues including: why elite youth sports events have become more common; the attitude of selected stakeholders (particularly NGBs and governments) towards the growth in elite youth sport; how the interests of young elite athletes are protected and who protects them; how elite development systems are adjusted to cater for the requirements of youth athletes; and how the growth in elite youth sport affects a sport's development strategy.

The aims of this book are to analyze:

- national public policy (organization, financing and regulation) for elite youth sport;
- the attitude of selected stakeholders (such as the media, government, NGBs, sponsors and school sport associations) towards the growth in elite youth sport;
- the management of elite youth athletes by selected NGBs of sport;

- the development of services for young athletes, both male and female, including coaching, education, post-competition career, lifestyle and financial support; and
- the impact of the growth in elite youth sport on national sport policy and the development strategy of selected sports.

While variations occur between countries, the chapters will provide a summary and analysis of the national sports system, which identifies the role of government in influencing and supporting the sport system and in shaping policy regarding the welfare of children in sport. The chapters will also offer an analysis of public policy, if any, in relation to elite youth sport; an outline of the prominence of elite youth sport using three or four sports as exemplars that include an early peak performance sport (e.g., figure skating, gymnastics or swimming/diving), a commercial team sport (e.g., football or ice hockey) and a major national sport or prominent Olympic sport in the country; the process of talent identification and development (e.g., the use of academies, centers of excellence, sports schools) and the extent to which it accommodates the needs of young people (educational, pastoral, social); the development of youth coaches/coaching practices designed for young athletes; the adaptation of other elements of the development process, such as the competition structure, to accommodate the interests of young people; and the identification of issues associated with the growth of elite youth sport, which might include organizational, financial and coaching capacity as well as (educational) career management and general welfare. Finally, each chapter will present a discussion of the future impact of the increasing emphasis on elite youth sport for the three or four focal sports and their talent identification and development systems.

Framework for analysis

One of the most significant outcomes of the recent body of comparative research into elite sports systems is the degree of convergence in national systems (Bergsgard et al., 2007; De Bosscher, 2007; De Bosscher et al., 2009; Houlihan & Green, 2008). De Bosscher (2007, p. 246) identified "increasing homogeneous elite sport development systems" and Bergsgard et al. (2007, p. 255) concluded that "elite sport systems and policies do converge." A high degree of convergence between overall elite systems might be explained by mimetic pressures, increased opportunities for policy learning and transfer, and possibly the limited range of policy options available to states that want elite sport success. However, at the junior level of the elite sport system, one would expect other influential policy sub-sectors, particularly child welfare, education and health, to limit the extent of convergence. Consequently, an important element in the analysis of the youth sport systems reported in this book is an assessment of the extent of similarity and convergence and the particular aspects of policy which provide the greatest evidence of convergence.

Houlihan (2012) argued that it was possible to identify seven dimensions of the policy process against which convergence can be assessed:

1 **Motives.** It is quite possible for governments or sports federations to share similar aspirations for youth sport and design similar elite youth sport systems yet have divergent motives. It may also be possible for convergence in motives to be accompanied by divergence in system design.

2 **Agenda and aspirations.** "Agenda" refers to presence of issues related to youth sport within the decision-making processes of government and the acceptance by government of a need to respond. Of course, even if there is noticeable convergence in the content of domestic political agendas, the response may be to do nothing. A positive response is usually expressed as an aspiration prior to action in the form of the allocation of resources and the design of processes/systems for policy delivery.

3 **Contextualizing discourse/ideology/values.** Contextualizing discourses range from the deeply rooted values and beliefs about competitive sport, education and the acceptable activities for young boys and girls, which are long-lasting structural constraints on policy, through to the more ephemeral ideas or fashions, such as a preference for fitness activities rather than doing sport, which can nonetheless impact on policy.

4 **Inputs** refer to the mix of resources (e.g., finance, expertise and administrative capacity) and the source of resources (whether from the public, commercial and/or not-for-profit sector) which enable youth sport policy responses by the government to be formulated.

5 **Implementation** refers to the selection of instruments, such as incentives, sanctions and marketing/promotion, and delivery mechanisms (via commercial providers, not-for profit clubs, schools, colleges and universities etc.) for the youth sport policy. It is often in relation to the selection of policy instruments that the clearest examples of convergence are found in analyses of overall elite sport systems.

6 **Momentum** refers to the intensity of commitment by powerful policy actors to the expressed aspirations and their continued commitment of resources beyond the initial phase of the policy process. Recent studies have shown how the level of commitment by national Olympic committees, NGBs and international federations to the YOG is highly variable (Skille & Houlihan, 2014).

7 **Impact** is, in many respects, the crucial dimension in any analysis of convergence and may be defined in terms of intended effects, that is, the extent to which change has been achieved in line with policy objectives for elite youth sport.

These seven dimensions will provide the framework for the analysis and comparison of the elite youth sport systems included in this collection. The intention will not only be to identify similarities and differences and consider evidence of convergence, but equally importantly to identify variation or evidence of differences and of widening differences (i.e. policy divergence). Given the variation in political systems, cultural contexts and economic wealth, the chapters that follow will provide a rich foundation for drawing conclusions about current trends in elite youth sport talent identification and development.

References

Aquilina, D. (2013) A study of the relationship between elite athletes' educational development and sporting performance, *The International Journal of the History of Sport*, 30(4), 374–392.

Athletes to Business (2011) Guidelines: Promoting Dual Careers in the EU, European Commission.

Baker, J., Cobley, S., & Fraser-Thomas, J. (2009) What do we know about early sport specialization? Not much!. *High Ability Studies*, 20(1), 77–89.

Bergsgard, N.A., Houlihan, B., Mangset, P., Nodland, S.I., & Rommetvedt, H. (2007) *Sport Policy; a comparative analysis of stability and change*, Oxford: Butterworth-Heinemann.

Brackenridge, C., Palmer-Felgate, S., Rhind, D., Hills, L., Kay, T., Tiivas, A., & Lindsay, I. (2013) *Child Exploitation and the FIFA World Cup: A review of risks and protective interventions*, Uxbridge, London: Brunel University.

David, P. (2008) The human rights of young athletes. In B. Houlihan (ed.) *Sport and society: A student introduction*, London: Sage.

De Bosscher, V. (2007) *Sport Policy Factors Leading to International Sporting Success*, Brussels: VUBPRESS.

De Bosscher, V., De Knop, P., van Bottenburg, M., Shibli, S., & Bingham, J. (2009) Explaining international sporting success: an international comparison of elite sport systems and policies in six countries, *Sport Management Review*, 12, 113–136.

Desmet, E. (2012) Implementing the Convention on the Rights of the Child for "youth": who and how?, *International Journal of Children's Rights*, 20(1), 3–23.

De Knop, P., Wylleman, P., Van Hoecke, J., De Martalaer, K., & Bollaert, L. (1999) A European approach to the management of the combination of academics and elite-level sport, *Perspectives: The Interdisciplinary series of Physical Education and Sport Science: School Sports and Competition*, 1, 49-62.

Donnelly, P. (1997) Child labour, sport labour: Applying child labour laws to sport, *International Review for the Sociology of Sport*, 32(4): 389–406.

EU Guidelines on Dual Careers of Athletes (2013) European Union. Retrieved from http://bookshop.europa.eu/en/
eu-guidelines-on-dual-careers-of-athletes-pbNC0213243/.

Farstad, S. (2007) "Protecting children's rights in sport: The use of minimum age," available from www.nottingham.ac.uk/hrlc/documents/publications/hrl commentary2007/childrensrightsinsport.pdf, accessed March 13, 2013.

Gold, J.R. & Gold, M.M. (2011) *Olympic Cities: City agendas, planning, and the world's games, 1896-2016* (2nd edn), London: Routledge.

Hanstad, D.V., Parent, M.M., & Houlihan, B. (Eds.). (2014) *The Youth Olympic Games*, London: Routledge.

Hanstad, D. V., Parent, M.M., & Kristiansen, E. (2013) The Youth Olympic Games: the best of the Olympics or a poor copy? *European Sport Management Quarterly*, *13*(3), 315–338.

Henry, I. (2013) Athlete Development, Athlete Rights and Athlete Welfare: A European Union Perspective, *The International Journal of the History of Sport*, *30*(4), 356–373.

Hodges L.J. & Williams A.M. (2012) *Skills Acquisition in Sport: Research, theory and practice*, London: Routledge.

Houlihan, B. (2012) Sport policy convergence: a framework for analysis, *European Sport Management Quarterly*, *12*(2), 111–135.

Houlihan, B. & Green, M. (2008) *Comparative Sport Development: Systems, structures and public policy*, Oxford: Butterworth-Heinemann.

Judge, L.W., Petersen, J., & Lydum, M. (2009). The Best Kept Secret in Sports : The 2010 Youth Olympic Games. *International Review for the Sociology of Sport*, *44*(2–3), 173–191.

Krieger, J. (2013) Fastest, highest, youngest? Analysing the athlete's experience of the Singapore Youth Olympic Games, *International Review for the Sociology of Sport*, *48*(6), 706–719. doi: 10.1177/1012690212451875

Kristiansen, E. (2015) Competing for culture: Young Olympians' narratives from the first winter Youth Olympic Games, *International Journal of Sport and Exercise Psychology*, *13*(1), 29–42.

McGeehan, N. (2013) Spinning Slavery: The role of the United States and UNICEF in the denial of justice for the child camel jockeys of the United Arab Emirates, *Journal of Human Rights Practice*, *5*(1): 96–124.

Mostafavifar, A.M., Best, T.M., & Myer, G.D. (2012) Early sport specialisation, does it lead to long-term problems?. *British Journal of Sports Medicine*, bjsports-2012.

Myer, G.D., Jayanthi, N., Difiori, J.P., Faigenbaum, A.D., Kiefer, A.W., Logerstedt, D., & Micheli, L.J. (2015) Sport Specialization, Part I Does Early Sports Specialization Increase Negative Outcomes and Reduce the Opportunity for Success in Young Athletes? *Sports Health: A Multidisciplinary Approach*, 1941738115598747.

Parent, M.M., Kristiansen, E., & MacIntosh, E.W. (2014a) Athletes' Experiences at the Youth Olympic Games: Perceptions, Stressors, and Discourse Paradox, *Event Management*, *18*(3), 303–324. doi: 10.3727/152599514X13989500765808

Parent, M.M., Kristiansen, E., & MacIntosh, E.W. (2014b) *Report on the Impact of the Youth Olympic Games on Young Athletes and Young Ambassadors* (p. 45). Ottawa, Canada: University of Ottawa.

Parent, M.M., Kristiansen, E., Skille, E.Å., & Hanstad, D.V. (2015) The sustainability of the Youth Olympic Games: Stakeholder networks and institutional perspectives,

International Review for the Sociology of Sport, 50(3), 326–348, doi: 10.1177/1012690213481467

Skille, E. & Houlihan, B. (2014) The contemporary context of elite youth sport: the role of national sport organisations in the UK and Norway. In D.V. Hanstad, M.M. Parent & B. Houlihan, *The Youth Olympic Games*, Abingdon: Routledge.

Taks, M., Misener, L., Chalip, L., & Green, B.C. (2014) *Leveraging Sport Events for Sport Development.* Paper presented at the Sport Canada Research Initiative Conference, Ottawa, Canada.

Veerman, P.E. (1992) *The Rights of the Child and the Changing Image of Childhood*, Dordrecht: Martinus Nijhoff Publishers.

Vitali, F., Bortoli, L., Bertinato, L., Robazza, C., & Schena, F. (2014) Motivational climate, resilience, and burnout in youth sport. *Sport Sciences for Health*, 11(1), 103–108.

Wong, D. (2011). The Youth Olympic Games: Past, Present and Future, *International Journal of the History of Sport*, 28(13), 1831–1851.

Part I

Europe

Chapter 2

England/United Kingdom[1]

Barrie Houlihan and Pippa Chapman

The national sports system and the role of government

In the most recent policy statement (Cabinet Office 2015, p. 7), the Prime Minister identified, as one of the three policy objectives, 'long term elite success' and noted that this objective would require 'examining how our investments in school sport, coaching and facilities can best support the identification and development of talent'. This prioritisation of elite success and effective talent identification can be found in a series of previous policy statements going back to the mid-1990s and the publication of *Sport: Raising the Game* (Department of National Heritage 1995). The acceptance by government of international sporting success as a strategic objective was supported by a series of distributional (funding), regulatory and organisational policies.

As is the case in many countries, the costs of developing elite athletes in most Olympic and Paralympic sports is borne by the government. Up until the early 1990s, the financial support provided from general taxation by the British government was modest (e.g. £62 million for the four-year cycle up to the Barcelona Olympic and Paralympic Games). However, the introduction of the National Lottery in 1994 resulted not only in a substantial increase in the funding (£172 million for the Sydney 2000 cycle, £394 million for the Beijing 2008 cycle and £379 million for the Rio de Janeiro cycle), but also a significant increase in the influence of government over policy within the country's national governing bodies of sport (NGBs). The allocation of funding became increasingly linked to specific requirements such as performance (medal) targets and to more general requirements such as organisational modernisation and the streamlining of talent pathways (Lusted & O'Gorman 2010; Green 2009). The regulatory interventions by government were, in part at least, designed to reinforce elite success. The introduction of a national curriculum for physical education in 1992 prioritised not only competitive sport, but also traditional British team sports. Although the emphasis on competitive sport was relaxed under the

Labour governments of 1997 to 2010, it was intensified with the election of a centre-right coalition in 2010 (Griggs & Ward 2012). The regulations which skewed the Physical Education (PE) curriculum towards competitive sport were coupled with a relaxation of the regulations determining who could deliver sport with many schools, especially primary schools, opting to employ cheaper coaches rather than the more expensive PE teachers (Griggs 2010).

The government interventions regarding finance and regulation of the content of the school PE curriculum was complemented by a substantial reform of the organisational framework within which elite sport and elite youth sport was coordinated. From 1972 to 1997 the main government agency responsible for sport at both the community and elite levels was the Sports Council, which had a modest budget that it distributed to over 100 different sports. In 1997, structural reform replaced the Sports Council with two new organisations – Sport England, primarily responsible for community sport, and UK Sport, responsible for delivering elite, especially Olympic, success. The restructuring was accompanied by a drastic reduction in the number of sports funded – around 30 at the elite Olympic and Paralympic level. Funding is currently channelled through the NGBs for Olympic and Paralympic sports on the basis of past medal performance and prospects of future medal success. The sums involved are substantial, with athletics receiving £26.8 million, cycling £30.5 million, rowing £32.6 million and boccia £3.7 million over the period 2013–17. Olympic and Paralympic sports are able to access the specialist (coaching, psychology, physiology and nutrition) services of the English Institute of Sport, as well as various specialist sports injury and medicine services and institutions. In summary, the sports system in the UK is well funded, has a sophisticated organisational infrastructure, and benefits from the policy stability resulting from the strong political support from all major political parties.

With regard to the protection of the welfare of children in sport, the broad context is set by the previously mentioned strong cross-party commitment to elite success and strong commitment from centre-right governments for competitive sport in schools from an early age. The most recent edition of the national curriculum for PE (Department for Education 2013, p. 2) states, with regard to children aged between five and seven years that: 'They should be able to engage in competitive (both against self and against others) and co-operative physical activities, in a range of increasingly challenging situations.' Children's welfare, in relation to the development of character, is considered to be well served by the emphasis on competitive sport: 'Opportunities to compete in sport and other activities build character and help to embed values such as fairness and respect' (DfE 2013, p. 1). The broad social and political encouragement for involvement in competitive sport from a young age is complemented by specific regulations regarding the protection of children. Prompted by evidence of the sexual abuse of young athletes by coaches in the 1990s (Brackenridge 1997) and reinforced by subsequent research exploring abusive training regimes (David 2005) and violence in youth sport (Brackenridge et al. 2010), a dedicated Child Protection in Sport Unit was established in England in 2001. Part of the role of the Unit, which is co-funded by the National Society for the Prevention of Cruelty to Children and Sport England, is to establish and promote standards for the protection of children in sport to which all NGBs would be expected to adhere. Since 1997, people wanting to coach young athletes (or work with young people in any capacity) have had to be vetted by the police. Since 2012, this function has been fulfilled by the Disclosure and Barring Service – an arm's-length government agency. 'Child-safeguarding' is, for almost all NGBs and clubs, a central element in their management structures and operational procedures (CPSU 2013). Child safeguarding standards are strongly reinforced by Sport England through its Charter Standard club accreditation programme.

Public policy in relation to elite youth sport

Public policy in relation to elite youth sport is a responsibility shared between two government agencies, Sport England and UK Sport. Talent identification and development (TID) as a specific strand of the process of developing elite athletes has been prominent in British elite sport policy since the establishment of the World Class Start and World Class Potential programmes in 1998. These programmes were funded and managed by Sport England and were designed to develop a more systematic approach for the identification and nurturing of young talent in order to form a foundation below the World Class Performance Programme (WCPP) (Houlihan & White 2002). These programmes were absorbed into the WCPP and responsibility for their management was transferred to UK Sport in 2006 (UK Sport 2012), after which, the three levels of the WCPP were known as Talent, Development and Podium.

In *A Sporting Future for All* (DCMS 2000, p. 15), there was a clear statement of intent by the government for NGBs to focus on talent: 'As part of our modernising partnerships, we will ask governing bodies to create a national talent development plan identifying pathways from grassroots of their sport to the international stage.' Furthermore, the Cunningham Report (2001, p. 5) identified that many sports were failing to support talented young people and stated: 'Developing talented youngsters should not be a matter of chance. It requires a well-structured sports-specific plan which links grassroots participation to international excellence by defining critical steps along the way.' The political salience of youth talent development continued to grow in the following years. Bloyce and Smith (2010, p. 144) stated that from the time London won the bid to host the 2012 Olympic and Paralympic Games, 'TID [became] a more obvious and central feature of the

ESD [elite sport development] policy in the UK.' The cumulative effect of government policy statements and the awarding of the Olympic Games to London was to embed the importance of TID firmly within the sport policy discourse. A more systematic approach was developed due to the pressures on sports agencies and NGBs to deliver medal success regularly in return for their public funding. Additional pressure has come from the intensification of international competition and the significant increase of investment in elite athlete development by many of the UK's competitors (Houlihan & Zheng 2013).

In addition to the pressures being placed on NGBs to improve their talent pathways as a means of delivering medal success, the government initiated a hierarchy of youth school sport events partly designed to reinforce the government's commitment to competitive sport and partly to provide an additional focus for talent development. The School Games and its predecessor, the UK School Games (UKSG), have been significant in the development of high-level competitive sport opportunities for school-aged children. Melville (2012, p. 8), in analysing the development of the UKSG, reported the comments of the former sports minister, Richard Caborn, who stated that his aim was to have an event that 'could provide talented young people with the experience they needed to perform well at high-profile multi-sport competitions'. The UKSG was incorporated into the Labour government's plans for achieving a legacy as a result of hosting the London 2012 Olympic and Paralympic Games: the government stated that the UKSG was 'designed to replicate the feel of major events such as the Olympic Games and Paralympic Games' (DCMS 2008, p. 22). The event was adapted following the election of the coalition government in 2010 and the new event, the School Games, began in 2012. The government stated: 'the School Games provides a framework for competitive school sport at school, district, county and national levels' (DCMS 2012, p. 3–4). Although both the UKSG and the School Games were significant innovations in the youth sport landscape, their significance in terms of elite youth sport was more ambiguous as both were more concerned with the promotion of competitive sport among young people than talent development (though see discussion of swimming below). If there was a significant contribution to TID from the School Games, it was to retain talented young people in sport, rather than advance them along the performance pathway.

At an organisational level, the identification and development of youth talent involves a network of partnerships and programmes across the country. NGBs receive funding through Sport England, which is responsible for supporting the development of the England Talent Pathway. Personnel within UK Sport offer advice and guidance on talent development, and both Sport England and UK Sport advise on the School Games, which is managed by a group of organisations including the Youth Sport Trust (YST). Youth elite sport is less self-contained than other elements of the sport policy sub-sector because it intersects with other policy areas, especially education, which sets the curriculum for physical education and makes recommendations about school management and priorities, but also health policy with regards to physical activity and welfare policy with regards to issues such as citizenship and volunteering.

The allocation of responsibility for the talent pathway between UK Sport and Sport England has changed over time. The situation was described by one senior official from a national non-government sports organisation as a 'turf war' about deciding how far up the performance pathway Sport England's responsibilities should reach, and conversely how far down the pathway UK Sport should operate (Chapman 2014). In 2006, the responsibility for the first two levels of the WCPP, known as 'talent' and 'development', was transferred from Sport England to UK Sport. This decision was taken because UK Sport began to plan their investment over two Olympic cycles and therefore there was a shift to include funding for those athletes expected to excel at an Olympic Games up to eight years away. According to one senior figure in British sport, this change allowed UK Sport to create 'a unified view of elite sport' (quoted in Chapman 2014, p.134). At the same time, responsibility for the English Institute of Sport (EIS) also transferred to UK Sport from Sport England (UK Sport 2012). However, despite greater clarity of responsibility between the two organisations, evidence of a 'turf war' re-emerged. In Sport England's 2008–2011 strategy, the organisation indicated talent was a priority, and the development of the England Talent Pathway began in 2009. However, this did not remove responsibility for talent from UK Sport, but rather UK Sport's work became more focused on programmes around talent transfer and fast-tracking of talented athletes. Although Sport England and UK Sport promoted the broad strategic framework for the development of youth TID programmes, the design and delivery of the programmes often involved a range of other policy actors who, to varying degrees, shared the priorities of the two government agencies.

The final element of public policy related to elite youth sport concerns the further and higher education sector. The government's Talented Athletes Scholarship Scheme (TASS) operates in partnership with NGBs and Further and Higher Education institutions to support young talented people across a wide range of sports. The aim of TASS is 'to help its athletes to balance academic life with training and competition as a performance athlete'.[2] TASS began in 2004, and there were 200 TASS-supported athletes in the British team at London 2012, 44 of whom won medals. UK Sport previously funded TASS, and UK Sport's primary objective of winning medals at the Olympic and Paralympic Games influenced the TASS programme and raised standards in terms of the athletes that the programme supports. However, from October 2014, funding of the programme shifted to Sport England, a change that was made in order to 'align it [TASS] with the funding already investing into talent development, and reflect Sport England's ambition to ensure the England talent system is open and accessible to everyone' (Sport England 2014). The TASS scheme continues to fill the places available on the programme each year because it works with NGBs rather than schools and nominated candidates have developed through club structures. In spite of the success achieved by TASS, a representative of government questioned whether TASS was able to identify and support the most talented young people who will actually achieve international success (Chapman 2014). Unlike schools, Higher Education Institutions (HEIs) have become an increasingly significant part of the elite sport landscape, although much of their role is complementing the developmental role of NGBs. However, given growing emphasis on dual-career athletes, both in the UK and internationally (Aquilina & Henry 2010), the significance of HEIs as part of the architecture of the upper end of youth TID policy implementation is likely to increase.

Youth sport examples

Swimming: an early peak sport

By comparison to other sports with similar physiological requirements such as track athletics, swimmers reach their peak about four or five years earlier, around the age of 22 for women and 24 for men with the time taken to reach peak performance being around eight years.[3] Although swimming has, for a number of years, been the most popular participation sport in England, with around 2.5 million people swimming at least once a week, it is only recently that elite-level performance has begun to achieve the ambitious goals set by the NGB. In the 2004 Olympic Games, Great Britain (GB) swimmers won just two bronze medals, but significantly increased their success in 2008 when the squad collected six medals (two gold, two silver and two bronze). Although the squad's performance in 2012 (one silver and two bronze) was considered disappointing, the performance at the 2015 World Swimming Championships (seven gold, one silver and six bronze medals) put GB in fifth place in the medals table and was considered to better reflect the quality of the current squad.

The balance between risks and rewards in identifying and developing young talent in swimming are distinctive insofar as it is a sport in which a single talented athlete can compete and be successful in multiple events at the Olympic Games and consequently make a substantial difference to the success of the sport and of the national team. At the 2012 Olympic Games, three US swimmers (Michael Phelps, Missy Franklin and Allison Schmitt) won a total of 16 medals, of which 11 were gold. These three athletes accounted for over half of the country's swimming medals (31 medals) and two-thirds of the 16 gold medals won by the United States. They also accounted for almost a quarter of the country's gold medals. The implication is that if a country has an effective TID programme for swimming, the rewards at the Olympic Games can be disproportionate. The search for a British Michael Phelps or Missy Franklin has proved to be a challenge, with Rebecca Adlington (two gold medals in 2008, two bronze in 2012) the only British swimmer to have achieved sustained Olympic success. Over the last ten years, British Swimming (the sport's NGB) has refined its TID system and sees the recent success of the GB squad in the 2015 World Championships as evidence of effectiveness. The most recent refinement of the TID strategy followed the relatively disappointing performance of British swimmers in 2012. The post-2012 review acknowledged the many successful elements of the TID programme and concluded that the core problem areas included 'the selection policy and the trials process, improved communication [with athletes] and further development of the performance planning and athlete monitoring regimes currently in place'.[4] The review also noted that Team GB had the highest number of finalists ever at an Olympic Games and that in addition to the three medallists there were 20 swimmers in fourth to eight places.

The British Swimming strategy published in 2013 (British Swimming 2013, p. 11) emphasised the importance to the NGB of elite-level success, which was to be achieved through a combination of a 'world class talent pathway ... based on a well-researched Long Term Athlete Development Model', '[w]orld [c]lass [c]oaches', and a 'quality competition programme ... ensuring competition is appropriate, meaningful and fun at all stages'. The successful delivery of the strategy depends to a large extent on close cooperation between GB Swimming and the four home countries (England, Scotland, Wales and Northern Ireland) swimming NGBs. British Swimming is responsible for the upper levels of talent development, the Podium and Podium Potential programmes, but it is the home country NGBs that are responsible for talent identification and the earlier stages of development – the Talent programme.

The School Games were also considered by the NGB to be an important aspect of the TID process, which was in contrast to most other NGBs. However, the foundation for TID across the UK is the extensive network of voluntary-run clubs, normally based in municipally-owned facilities, the vast majority of which have achieved accredited (or charter) status which includes extensive youth welfare requirements. The 1,151 clubs and the 190,000-plus membership have a primary focus on competition with inter-club events and district swimming galas being a regular element in the club calendar. It is at these events and galas that young talented swimmers are identified, often between the ages of 10 and 12, but sometimes younger. Talented club swimmers progress to the county elite squad development club where they will receive coaching and train for between 12 and 20 hours a week. The county squads, like the local clubs, take part in a structured competition programme which is age-graded from 10 years to 16 years. For example, the English County Championships have six age categories starting at 10/11 year olds through to 16 and over. The County events are an important talent identification opportunity for the home country NGBs and are the foundation for a hierarchy of competitions, each of which has a similar broad range of age-defined events. The next level of competition and selection from County competition is the Regional (age range 11/12 to 17 and over), followed by Home Nations (12/13 to 18 and over) and the British Summer Championships (13/14 to 19 and over). Entry criteria for each level of competition varies with each county and region being able to set their own qualifying standard for their respective competitions, but it is the position of the swimmer on the national rankings which is the key criterion for participation in the Home Nations and the British Summer Championships.

At County and Regional level young elite swimmers will be placed in one of a series of development squads based on ability and on age/physical development. Outstanding swimmers will be invited to join one of the two Intensive Training Centres (ITCs), at Bath and Loughborough, and attend specialist training camps which focused on technical development (e.g. pool turns or specific strokes). Swimmers at one of the two ITCs will be involved in full-time training and regular international competition. Swimmers at the ITCs will normally be in receipt of UK Sport funding and be on either the Podium programme (which is designed to support athletes with a strong chance of winning a medal at the next Olympics, i.e. within four years) or the Podium Potential programme (for those swimmers considered to be medal prospects within eight years, i.e. the next but one Olympics).

Football: a commercial team sport

Football is played by approximately 1.8 million people each week and over 3 million (aged 14 and over) play at least once a month. Although participation by girls and women lags behind many other European countries, there was a 5.3 per cent increase in participation between 2010/11 and 2014/15 at a time when male participation declined.[5] The growth in female participation has been paralleled by the increasing success of the women's national team (third place in the 2015 World Cup). While the men's national team has been less successful, the English Premier League continues to be the richest league in the world with an estimated income of £3.3 billion in the 2014–15 season. Power in English football is divided between the Football Association (FA) which is the NGB for the sport, the Premier League (PL) and the Football League (FL). Control of the national team, some competitions (the FA Cup) and non-professional community football rests with the FA, while the other two organisations are responsible for the professional leagues and some competitions. Although the FA has some involvement in talent identification and development due to its responsibility for the grassroots game, almost all youth TID is undertaken by the professional clubs through their academies (see Table 2.1).

All Premier League and Championship (the second highest professional division) clubs have academies, as well as some clubs in the lower divisions. The minimum age at which a player can join a football academy is nine years, although many clubs circumvent this FA regulation by organising development schemes designed to cater for younger players. The development schemes are less formal, although admission to the schemes is by invitation rather than being open to all. In addition, many clubs run open access developmental programmes. Chelsea FC, for example, runs over 200 Soccer schools each year for children as young as four years and up to 12 years. While the Soccer schools are seen as developmental, they are an important opportunity for talent identification.

Admission to an academy is a formal process which requires the child to sign a loose contract referred to as 'schoolboy forms'. Between the ages of nine and 16 the young players will have their progress reviewed on an annual or biennial basis with players being dropped from the academy at each review. Those who are still with the academy at the age of 16 are then assessed for progression to the club's youth training scheme with most clubs only offering around six to ten places each year. The small proportion that are offered a place on a club's youth training scheme receive a scholarship, are expected to relocate close to the club, and begin a period of much more intensive training which lasts between two and three years. For many clubs, the decision whether to offer a young player a professional contract is made at the age of 19, after which the successful youth players will play for the club's reserve team, under-21 team or the first team.

The support that players receive while at the academy is a mix of training, often two or three sessions during the week with competitive matches against other academy teams at the weekend. Matches are age-graded and those for the younger players are often eight-a-side with eleven-a-side matches played by those over 11 years. Clubs will often expect players to undertake further training in their own time. Most clubs will liaise with the young player's school, but often simply to try to influence the physical education and sports curriculum rather than to support the academic progress of the child. However, once players move into the youth training

Table 2.1 Expenditure and recruitment to England football academies, 2010

£66m	Annual expenditure on academies in English football: each Premier League club was estimated to invest £2m per annum
10,000	Boys registered at top clubs' academies and centres of excellence (aged 8–18)
1%	Estimated percentage of trainees who will play football for a living

Source: Adapted from Conn 2010, p.9

scheme aged 16, they are required by the Football Association to continue with their education on a part-time basis at a local college.

The current protocols by which academies operate are the outcome of a steady growth in concern about the exploitation of young players and the damage that their treatment may do to the young players and also to the image of the sport. In the 1970s, young players were seen 'as a form of cheap labour to carry out various tasks around the club which meant that their welfare and needs (particularly their educational and future career needs) were not routinely regarded as being particularly important by clubs, let alone seen as a major responsibility' (Platts & Smith 2009, p. 326). During the 1970s and 1980s, various initiatives were introduced by the FA and the Professional Footballers Association (PFA) to enhance the rights of young players. The most recent changes were those that introduced the Football Scholarship for players selected for the youth training schemes. Including the word scholarship in the title was an effort to emphasis the academic element of the contract. At around the same time, the late 1990s, the FA published the 'Charter for Quality' designed to improve the quality of young player development with the key proposal being the introduction of youth academies. The Charter stated that clubs would receive funding for their academy if they fulfilled certain criteria, one of which was to ensure that 'appropriate and adequate educational provision is available for each Academy player including primary, secondary, further and higher educational provision' (FA 1997, p. 4.7.1).

Although the FA and the PFA have established clear expectations about the general welfare and, especially, the educational welfare of young players the evidence suggests that the dominant culture within clubs generally and within youth academies in particular is not one that is supportive. Kelly and Waddington consider that young players were frequently socialised into 'an abusive and violent workplace' (2006, p. 149, quoted in Platts & Smith 2009). In relation to educational ambitions, Platts and Smith (2009, p. 336) conclude that 'there exists a widespread belief that a desire to do well academically is to accept they may have no future in football' and echo Parker's (2000, p. 67) assessment that 'education and schooling represented sub-cultural metaphors for occupational failure'.

Netball: a major national sport

England Netball was established in 1926 and is the NGB for one of the major team sports for girls and women. It has over 90,000 affiliated members and the number of participants almost doubled between 2004 and 2015. It is also estimated by the NGB that 'at least one million women and girls play netball every week'.[6] The sport is particularly strong among girls, as it is a traditional school sport in England. The growing popularity of the sport is matched by the recent success of the England team which won bronze medals at the 2010 Commonwealth Games and at the 2011 and 2015 International Netball Federation World Cup events.

In the 2013–17 strategic plan, the ambitions of the NGB for elite-level success were clearly stated. Among the strategic objectives were to: 'build a system that is aimed at sustaining a high level of performance'; 'build a culture of elite expectation and commitment all the way from the start of the Performance Pathway to the senior team'; and 'identify players and build teams with success at the World Netball Championships as primary focus' (England Netball 2013, p. 14). The popularity of the sport in the English school and higher education system provides a strong foundation on which a performance pathway can be built. Figure 2.1 describes the current performance pathway, which was introduced in 2013.

The foundation of the pathway is a network of Satellite Academies, managed by each County Netball Association and aimed at netball players aged from 11 to 14 years. The Satellite Academies organise about 15 training sessions each year, which are structured according to the NGB's training programme and are designed to teach young players 'how to train on their

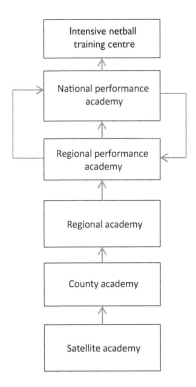

Figure 2.1 The England Netball Performance Pathway

Source: Adapted from England Netball 2013

own, and to understand, experience and practice some of the different components required in a training program'.[7] At this stage of the pathway, players are not required to interrupt their studies, as there would be no great distance to the nearest Academy and the training sessions are not held during school hours. The NGB has a comprehensive talent identification policy for each level identified in Figure 2.1 (England Netball 2014). The policy document specifies those responsible for talent identification at each level, the qualities that they should look for in the young athlete and the ethical principles on which talent selection is based. At the Satellite Academy level, talent identification is the responsibility of the County Selector, the County Academy Head Coach, and the Satellite Academy Head Coach. Selected players move on to the County Academy which is designed to provide training for young athletes aged between 14 and 16 with over 15 to 30 sessions a year. Delivered by Level 2 coaches, the aim is to provide around 14 to 16 hours a week of training (which would include strength and conditioning routines) and competition.

It is at the Regional Academy level that the training becomes significantly more intensive and that players begin taking part in national representative teams. The 20 or so under-17 years players selected for the each of the 18 Regional Academies are required to train up to eight hours per week throughout the year. At this level, some of the players will also be taking part in the National Academy, as they will be members of the England U17 squad. Part of the successful development of U17 players is the ability of the NGB to integrate training into the school routine. While this balance has been maintained in recent years, the latest performance strategy emphasises the need to intensify training if the England team is to compete with the three dominant countries in the sport, New Zealand, Australia and Jamaica. In parallel with the restructuring of the performance pathway, there has been a similar reorganisation of the competition pathway. There are two competition pathways, one focused on schools and the other on clubs and the academies. The National Schools Competition has a tiered structure beginning at local or county level and progressing to the national finals and comprises three age groups – under 14, 16 and 19. At the club level, there are under 14 and under 16 leagues, plus a 16–19 year olds open competition for clubs or schools. These various competitions not only provide opportunities for training, but also a further opportunity for the identification of players who can progress to the Regional Performance Academy.

Players selected for one of the nine Regional Performance Academies are under the age of 19 and are likely to be members of the national under-17 or under-19 squads. Training at this level is more intensive (17–19 hours per week) and a mix of squad training, individual training and competition. The National Academy is for U17 and U19 England squad players and comprises a series of training camps run throughout the year and is designed to meet the needs of players who are on the threshold of obtaining a place at one of the three Intensive Netball Training Centres (INTC). By the time a player reaches one of the INTCs, which accommodate about 15 players each, she is usually out of the junior ranks and part of the senior squad.

The popularity of the sport, the substantial funding received from Sport England (£25 million 2013–17, although no funding from UK Sport because the sport is not included in the Olympics) and the close integration of the sport with the education system has enabled the NGB to develop one of the more sophisticated talent identification and development strategies in the country. The close association between the sport and selective and fee-paying schools (see the list of schools that qualify for the national schools championships[8]) indicates not only the social selectivity of the sport at the higher competitive levels, but also the ability of the NGB to combine player development with a highly competitive education environment.

Discussion and conclusion

International sporting success, particularly at the summer Olympic Games, has been a high political priority since the mid-1990s. The ambition to be successful in international sport is reinforced by strong popular support and a deeply entrenched culture which values competitive sport, especially for the young, as a source of individual personal benefits and collective benefits. It is therefore not surprising that youth talent identification and development is an integral element of the broader elite sport system funded by government through Sport England and UK Sport. NGBs in receipt of government and lottery funding are required to develop talent pathways and complementary competition opportunities for young aspiring athletes. However, the prioritisation of elite success and the acknowledgement of the importance of youth talent development have, in general, taken place within a context of youth safeguarding and a concern to maintain the young athletes' dual career. Football, as noted above, is an exception insofar as the dominant culture within the youth academies challenges, if not undermines, the fine words of the Football Association. Given the very large number of young players who do not make it through to a professional contract, this is a serious problem the sport needs to address more forcefully if the FA is to live up to the rhetoric of 'caring' in its policy documents.

For most of the Olympic sports, the picture is, in some ways at least, more positive. Most Olympic and nationally important non-Olympic sports have successfully constructed their training systems around the educational needs of the young athletes: both swimming and netball are typical. However, there is an important caveat which concerns the skewed social demographics that has resulted or, more properly, has been reinforced. The British Olympic squad has been socially unrepresentative for a number of years.[9] While only 7 per cent of the population were educated at fee-paying schools in the 2008 Beijing Olympics, 50 per cent of GB gold medals were won by athletes educated privately. In 2012, 36 per cent of medallists were privately educated and 60 per cent of medal winners went to university. These figures are not surprising given that most private schools have excellent sport facilities and extensive after-school sports opportunities. In addition, the cost of supporting a child in a supposedly 'cheap' sport such as swimming can be prohibitive once the cost of travel for early morning training, weekend galas and specialist training camps is taken into account. As the case of England demonstrates, it is possible to have an elite youth sport system which takes child welfare seriously and which protects the longer-term career interest of the young athlete, but it comes at the cost of a socially unrepresentative national squad – unless of course the sport is football which has equally serious, but quite different, problems to address.

Notes

1   The United Kingdom refers to the four countries of England, Scotland, Wales and Northern Ireland and Great Britain refers to the three countries of England, Scotland and Wales. Confusingly, the Olympic squad is referred to as Great Britain or Team GB, but does include those athletes from Northern Ireland who choose to represent Great Britain rather than the Irish Republic.
2   www.tass.gov.uk/pages/about-us.html (accessed 23 June 2014).
3   www.swimmingscience.net/2015/08/age-of-swimming-peak-performance-trends-and-predictions-with-dr-sian-allen.html (accessed 15 March 2016).
4   www.pullbuoy.co.uk/news/british-swimming-reveals-review-findings (accessed 13 March 2016).
5   www.skysports.com/watch/tv-shows/sportswomen/news/10019792/girls-football-week-what-is-it-all-about (accessed 14 March 2016).
6   www.englandnetball.co.uk/About_England_Netball (accessed 11 March 2016).
7   www.englandnetball.co.uk/england/England_Performance_Pathway/Satellite_Academies (accessed 11 March 2016).
8   www.englandnetball.co.uk/competitions/2015-16/national-schools_107 accessed 11 March 2016).
9   www.suttontrust.com/newsarchive/third-british-olympic-winners-privately-educated/ (accessed 15 March 2016).

References

Aquilina, D. & Henry, I. (2010) Elite athletes and university education in Europe: a review of policy and practice in higher education in the European Union Member States, *International Journal of Sport Policy*, 2(1), 25–47.
Bloyce, D. & Smith, A. (2010) *Sport Policy and Development: An Introduction*, Abingdon: Routledge.
Brackenridge, C.H. (1997) 'He owned me basically': Women's experience of sexual abuse in sport, *International Review for the Sociology of Sport*, 32(2), 115–30.
Brackenridge, C., Fasting, K., Kirby, S., & Leahy, T. (2010) *Protecting Children from Violence in Sport*, Florence, Italy: Innocenti Publications.

British Swimming (2013) *A Vision for Swimming*, Loughborough: British Swimming.

Cabinet Office (2015) *Sporting Future: A new strategy for an active nation*, London: Cabinet Office.

Chapman, P. (2014) Policy stability in a time of turbulence: the case of elite sport policy in England/UK, unpublished PhD thesis, Loughborough: Loughborough University (http://dspace.lboro.ac.uk/2134.16219).

Child Protection in Sport Unit (2013) *Sport safeguarding children initiative: Mid-project progress report*, London: CPSU.

Conn, D. (2010) Arrested development, *Guardian newspaper*, Sport section, p.9.

Cunningham, J. (2001) *Elite Sports Funding Review: A report to the Prime Minister and Secretary of State for the Department for Culture*, Media and Sport, London: DCMS.

Department for Culture, Media and Sport (2000) *A Sporting Future for All*, London: DCMS.

Department for Culture, Media and Sport (2008) *Before, During and After: Making the most of the London 2012 Games*, London: DCMS.

Department for Culture, Media and Sport (2012) *School Games 2011/12 Statistical Release*, London: DCMS.

Department for Education (2013) *Physical education programmes of study: Key stages 1 and 2*, London: DfE.

Department of National Heritage (1995) *Sport: Raising the game*, London: DNH.

England Netball (2013) *England Netball's Executive Summary: Whole sport plan 2013-2017*, Hitchin: England Netball.

England Netball (2014) *Scouting, screening and selection*, Hitchin: England Netball.

Football Association (1997) A charter for quality, London: The FA.

Green, M. (2009) Podium or participation? Analysing policy priorities under changing modes of sport governance in the United Kingdom. *International Journal of Sport Policy*, 1(2), 121–144.

Griggs, G. (2010) For sale–primary physical education. £ 20 per hour or nearest offer. *Education 3–13*, 38(1), 39–46.

Griggs, G. & Ward, G. (2012) Physical Education in the UK: disconnections and reconnections, *The Curriculum Journal*, 23(2), 207–229.

Houlihan, B. & White, A. (2002) *The Politics of Sports Development: Development of Sport or Development Through Sport?* London: Routledge.

Houlihan, B. and Zheng, J. (2013) The Olympics and elite sport policy: Where will it all end? *International Journal of the History of Sport*, 30(4), 338–355.

Kelly, S. & Waddington, I. (2006) Abuse, intimidation and violence in aspects of managerial control in professional soccer in Britain and Ireland, *International Journal for the Sociology of Sport*, 41(2), 147–164.

Lusted, J. & O'Gorman, J. (2010) The impact of New Labour's modernisation agenda on the English grass-roots football workforce. *Managing Leisure*, 15(1–2), 140–154.

Melville, S. (2012) *The UK School Games and the competition structure of selected participating sports: a study of policy implementation*, https://dspace.lboro.ac.uk/2134/10805 accessed 07 March 2016.

Parker, A. (2000) Training for glory, schooling for failure: English professional football, traineeship and education provision, *Journal of Education and Work*, 13(1), 61–76.

Platts, C. & Smith, A. (2009) The education, rights and welfare of young people in professional football in England: Some implications of the White Paper on Sport, *International Journal of Sport Policy and Politics*, 1(3), 323–339.

Sport England (2014) 'Sport England supports next generation of sporting superstars' www.sportengland.org/media-centre/news/2014/march/25/sport-england-supports-next-generation-of-sporting-stars/, accessed 9 May 2014.

UK Sport (2012) *Annual Report and Accounts 2011/12*, London: The Stationery Office.

Chapter 3

The Netherlands

Agnes Elling and Niels Reijgersberg

Introduction

The Netherlands is a small, densely populated and rather prosperous country located on the coast of north-western Europe, with a population of about 16.7 million. With 4.8 million members in nearly 25,000 sport clubs, this organizational structure forms the heart of competitive sport participation in the Netherlands. The Dutch have a long sports tradition, both in terms of grassroots sports and elite sports performance. The average ranking of the Netherlands on the summer Olympic medal index since 1960 has been eighteenth position, with a lowest ranking in 1980 (thirtieth) and a highest in 2000 (eighth). Since 1996, the average ranking has been rather stable at around thirteenth position with a market share of 2 per cent of all Olympic medals (Dijk, De Bosscher & van Bottenburg, 2014).[1] Abroad, Dutch performance in elite sports is mainly related to the results and playing style of the men's national football team – 'brilliant orange' (Winner, 2000). Apart from football as the most prestigious, professional and globalized sport, Dutch athletes have performed especially well in swimming and speed skating. The Dutch Olympic committee and sports federation NOC*NSF initiated a focus sports policy in 2012, investing a relatively high budget share in only a few sports, a strategy that had been successfully implemented in several other countries since the 1980s (Van Bottenburg, Dijk & De Bosscher, 2014; NOC*NSF, 2012).[2] Such a budget differentiation was initiated to eventually effectuate the long-term top-ten ambition, which was formulated after the successful summer Olympic Games in Sydney 2000. NOC*NSF aims at a structural top-ten position in the world regarding elite sports performance for the Netherlands.

Elite sports policy and talent development

Possibly due to values related to Dutch Calvinism such as modesty and temperance (Lechner, 2008), compared to other countries such as Australia, England or France, the Netherlands was relatively late in identifying top-level sports as a sector of national importance. From the 1990s onwards, the Dutch government increasingly recognized the national importance of a professional national elite sports policy and system that legitimizes large financial investments (Ministry of VWS, 1999, 2008, 2011; see also Van Bottenburg et al., 2012). From a personal ambition of individual talents dependent on the elite sports climate within their sports club and sports federation (e.g. coaches, training facilities, competition), elite sports participation became an increasingly positively rewarded and facilitated primary-time investment for talented athletes. Being an athlete became a recognized job. Alongside the intensification of the search for national identity, the government increasingly legitimized its elite sports policy in terms of the contribution of top-level sports performances to national identity, pride and international prestige (Elling, Hilvoorde & Van den Dool, 2014). Since the end of the 1990s, the collective budget for elite sports from the national government and the national lottery has increased significantly, from €20 million in 1997 to €55 million in 2011. In 2012, however, for the first time, the total investments for elite sports somewhat decreased to around €52 million a year, and remained the same for the Olympic cycle 2013–2016 (Van Bottenburg et al., 2016).

The relatively succesful elite sports performances of the Dutch athletes in the last two decades illustrates the working of the 'global sporting arms race' (De Bosscher et al., 2008), where elite sports success increasingly becomes dependent on the (totalization) process of the elite sports investments of national systems instead of the characteristics of individual talented athletes (Heinilä, 1982; Oakley & Green, 2001). Countries have to invest increasingly more money to become/remain successful in winning (gold) medals; the 'price per medal' increased significantly (De Bosscher et al., 2015).

Talent recognition and development is regarded as one of the key factors for continuous elite sports success. Due to the dense network of sports clubs in the country, a relatively high quality of sport-specific training programmes for competitive coaches and local to national sports competition in most sports, initial talent selection and development is organized within local sports clubs. Since 1993, the financial conditions of already successful elite athletes have improved, as a special Fund for Elite Athletes was established, to secure them a minimum 'wage'. In addition, there was increased professionalism in the management of full-time training/ competition programmes and facilities for elite athletes in specific sports (National Training Centres). Furthermore, talent development also became more professionalized and centralized in the Netherlands (see also Van Bottenburg, 2009; Van Bottenburg et al., 2012; Van Heijden et al., 2012). Overall, talented athletes tend to train more at an earlier age, illustrating simultaneous development of intensification and rejuvenation of elite sports practices. Comparative Dutch data (Van Bottenburg et al., 2015) showed that current elite athletes had more training hours at the age of 15 compared to earlier cohorts, increasing from a mean of 11.5 hours per week in 2008 to 12.6 in 2015.

Simultaneously, a decrease was found in the group that trained a maximum of ten hours a week from 60 per cent in 2008 to 38 per cent in 2015. Furthermore, compared to 2011, in 2015, more elite sport directors affirm that their sport federation has a policy – based on scientific knowledge – regarding the structural recognition and development of talents, that their federation starts 'on time' with talent recognition and that there are enough specific talent coaches appointed.[3] However, nearly all elite sport directors also recognize a shortage of money as a major problem.

The initiation and development of elite sport schools

Athletes in most types of sports need to practice their sport for many hours over a long time period – e.g. a still often used mean is 10.000 hours over a period of ten years (Bloom, 1985; Starkes, 2000) – in order to be able to perform at the international top level. Since the hours of practice in sport will intensify during adolescence, the demands of elite sports make it difficult to balance both school and sport (Wylleman & Lavallee, 2004). Especially former communist countries such as Eastern European countries and China are known for state-run, centralized talent selection and development programmes from an early age (elite sport boarding schools; see Dennis & Grix, 2012 and Hong, 2008). Nowadays, many Western (European) countries have national programmes to facilitate increasingly younger talents to practice more hours and have amended mainstream educational laws and practices to accommodate their training regime (Elling et al., 2014b; Radtke & Coalter, 2007).

In 1991, the LOOT foundation was founded in the Netherlands, consisting of a group of six secondary schools – Topsport Talent Schools – to help talented athletes to better balance school obligations and elite sports ambitions. Over the years, the LOOT foundation grew towards a total of 30 regionally distributed Topsport Talent Schools in 2013/2014, supporting a total of around 3,000 young athletes with an official talent status (about 40 per cent of all status talents) and optimized individual support (Von Heijden et al., 2012; Reijgersberg & Elling, 2013; Van Rens et al., 2015). Similarly to mainstream secondary schools, Topsport Talent Schools are 'normal' schools, mainly attended by pupils without talent status.[4] But only accredited Topsport Talent Schools are legally allowed to reduce the national standard of at least 1,040 hours of education per year to 800 hours for pupils with an official talent status, for example by exemptions for specific courses such as physical education. Perhaps more important is that recognized talents receive individual support from a coordinator in creating a more flexible timetable and assisting them with requests for adjusted or delayed tests or the spreading of the final exam over two years. Such exceptions to the mainstream educational laws are especially beneficial for young talents with a high amount of training hours and for talents in structured talent programmes of sport organizations with many training hours during school hours, like professional football organizations and, since 2012, the centralized talent programmes of sport federations at national trainings centres. Although the majority of Dutch athletes eligible to attend a Topsport Talent School still attend mainstream secondary schools (Reijgersberg & Elling, 2013), with the ongoing professionalization of national talent programmes, coordinated by NOC*NSF, attending specific Topsport Talent Schools has become more compulsory for pupils when joining a national talent programme.

The results of a study about the effectiveness of Topsport Talent Schools concerning the elite sports success and school performance showed that former talents that had attended a Topsport Talent School achieved similar sport performance levels, and lower school performance levels than their counterparts that had attended mainstream secondary schools (Von Heijden et al., 2012; Van Rens et al., 2015). These results partly confirm other international research into elite sport schools (De Bosscher & De Croock, 2010; Emrich et al., 2009). The results can be partly explained as selection effects based on needs and motivations that could not all be controlled for in the analyses. Football talents and talents who are active in early specialization sports with high international competition (e.g., tennis, gymnastics) and with a relatively high sport performance level at an early age are more likely to attend a Topsport Talent School, although the chance of being eventually successful is relatively small for this group. Also talents choosing to attend a Topsport Talent School showed a higher sport motivation and a lower level of school motivation, which may be due to a selection effect before attending secondary school and/or develop during their secondary school career, since they are primarily supported in their elite sports career aspirations. Also in terms of self-regulating capacities that are positively related to becoming successful (Jonker et al., 2010) talents who are, for instance, very capable in structuring their tasks (i.e. time management) might be less likely to attend a Topsport Talent School, since they are less in need of the extra support offered. Furthermore, following the increased cultural acceptance of elite sports as an important societal practice, many mainstream secondary schools have invested in better support for talented athletes (Von Heijden et al., 2012). Nonetheless, a recent study showed that talents attending a Topsport Talent School are more satisfied with the support they received in combining school and sport (Van Bottenburg et al., 2015). However, talents are less satisfied with the support received in higher or vocational education institutions compared to secondary education. These studies among talents and studies among parents and coaches and other supporting professionals of talented athletes (Elling et al., 2013, 2014b) confirm the ongoing tensions between elite sports aspirations and the (increasing) demands from sport talent

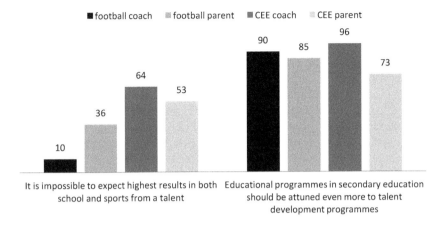

Figure 3.1 Opinions of coaches and parents from children in football programmes and at Centres for Elite sports and Education (CEE) about combining elite sports and school for sports talents, in % (completely) agree

programmes on the one hand and an educational development fitting the broader competencies and aspirations of talents on the other hand (see also Brettschneider, 1999; Elling et al., 2014a).

Increasingly, not only sports organizations (like professional football clubs or national training centres) but also talents themselves seem to demand the full cooperation of educational organizations in meeting their needs regarding their sports ambition. As shown in Figure 3.1, especially coaches at centres for elite sports and education regard the full-time talent development programmes as a clear priority, with all other obligations such as school having to accommodate the sports programme. A study among participants of the European Youth Olympic Festival (EYOF) 2013 in Utrecht showed that Dutch participants scored middle range on the support received compared to athletes from other European countries (n=30). The analysis showed that the variety of facilities available to enable the combining of school and sports is the most important factor in determining the overall satisfaction of student athletes with the support they receive. Such facilities correlate highly with the type of school: elite sports school more often offer more facilities than mainstream schools.

Centralization

In 2006, the NOC*NSF published a masterplan for talent development, with the main focus on more standardization, professionalization and centralization of talent selection and talent development over a longer time period to optimise the often difficult connection between the talent identification phase and senior elite sports participation (NOC*NSF, 2006).

In the following years, an important reallocation of budget and supervision took place with primary investment in the development of multi-year 'full-time' talent development programmes by national federations certified by NOC*NSF and in the establishment of national training centres, mainly located within four Centres for Elite Sports and Education (Amsterdam, Arnhem, Eindhoven and Heerenveen). Within these centres, high-quality sports facilities were supposed to be combined with flexible educational programmes (e.g., at Topsport Talent Schools for secondary education), housing and other supporting facilities and professionals (e.g., medical, psychological), all at near (cycling) distance. Also, specific full-time talent coaches were appointed to optimize the athletic and broader personal development of sport talents.

Since 2010, registration of official talents has become similar to the centralized registration system which allocated elite athletes to specific status groups (A, B or High Potential). Before 2010, there was no central registration and there were large regional differences in talent status designations, for example 'regional talents', that were awarded mainly by the local Olympic Networks. Currently, all talents with an international, national or 'promise' status are registered by NOC*NSF, although the status allotment still differs per sports federation (Reijgersberg & Elling, 2013; pp.14/15). According to one Topsport Talent School coordinator: 'Sportsfederations all use different criteria. Some are far too strict, indicating that potential talents do not receive enough suport.' This view was echoed by a talent coordinator for one sports federation who commented that: 'We think that talents need to comply to strict demands. In that way you can distinguish real talents. Giving such a status also has implications for making a choice for a specific training centre.'

Early specialization sports with many children practising these sports, such as gymnastics and swimming, are less generous with talent status acknowledgement compared to team sports such as basketball, handball, rugby and volleyball, which have far fewer youth practitioners, but are more dependent on having a sufficient number of same-age pupils for training. On the one hand, the central registration of talents is a clear objective tool for Topsport Talent Schools to differentiate between talents who may receive extra facilities and support and those who may not. On the other hand, the system appears to be more objective than it is and may give extra support to many talents who may not really need it, whereas other nonregistered talents may train many more hours and would benefit more from extra support in both sport and school performance (Von Heijden et al., 2012; Reijgersberg & Elling, 2013).

In the two last elite sport climate measurements in 2011 and 2015 (Van Bottenburg et al., 2015), elite athletes, coaches and technical directors of sports federations, were asked how they judge the influence of the clustering of training, education and housing in the centres for elite sports and education

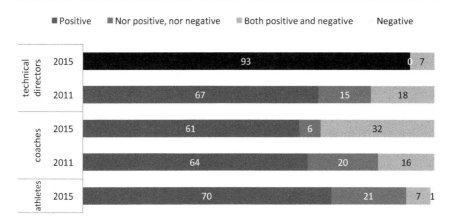

Figure 3.2 Judging the influence of the clustering of housing, education and training on the development of talents, by elite athletes, coaches and technical directors 2011, 2015, in %

(CEE) on the developments of talents. All groups were mainly positive, especially the technical directors (97 per cent), with coaches having become somewhat more ambivalent, also noticing negative influences (see Figure 3.2).

Positive outcomes mainly seem to relate to the enhancement of athletic performance resulting from optimizing the frequency and quality of training opportunities for a larger group of young sport talents. Technical directors recognize their return on investments regarding better performances (higher medal ranking) in international competitions. Coaches, however, may also notice possible negative consequences for several young talents regarding housing conditions, school–sport balance and psycho-emotional development that may also negatively affect sport performances. In another study, talent coaches and parents were asked about the evalution of the general development of sport talents, compared to peers (Elling et al., 2014). Here the CEE coaches were most convinced (92 per cent) that sport talents developed even better compared to peers. Most parents were also positive (70 per cent), with others regarding the development neutral (26 per cent) or negative (4 per cent). In the focus group discussions held at CEEs with different responsible professionals (coaches, education coordinators, life skill coaches, physiotherapists, account managers), several challenges were identified regarding creating and mantaining a pedagogically responsible environment for talents including:

- Balancing sports and educational/societal development – see above.
- The risk of overburdening the young athlete. The daily programme for talents following education is overfull, indicating that talents are nearly permanently exhausted and on the point of being overburdened.

- Juvenization (i.e. the lowering of the age at which talent development begins) requires an intensification of pedagogical support – talents nowadays may leave their family at a younger age to join a CEE (eg 13–15 years), which may not be justified for all children's psycho-social development; moreover housing conditions at CEEs are not always adequate for young children.
- Communication within the team of supporting actors and between talents, coaches and parents – especially coach–parent communication has been rather poorly structured at CEEs.
- Accountability – it is not always clear who is accountable for different developmental processes.
- After-care – the support for talents that have to leave a talent development programme (CEE) was generally regarded as requiring improvement.

Whereas most CEE coaches and parents agreed that the overall attention for pedagogically responsible talent development was sufficient, only one in three agreed with the statement that talents who have to leave the programme receive enough support (see Figure 3.3).

The focus groups discussions showed a general consensus that CEEs have a pedagogical responsibility and that talent development should be tailored to individual needs as much as possible. Safety, trust, balancing sports and broader educational, social, emotional development and stimulating (self) responsibility and positive coaching/communication, were deemed key concepts. The study also exposed, however, that pedagogically responsible development may at times contradict the hegemonic performance culture aimed at winning medals, that there isn't always enough embedded pedagogical expertise within the CEE teams and that a transparent system of recognizing and preventing problems with respect to the welfare of athletes is lacking. One coach commented on always prioritizing pedagogic responsibility: 'I don't think we are a medal factory. We do not work to gain medals at all costs, at the cost of a child... It doesn't mean one has to undermine sports performance, certainly not. But it should remain

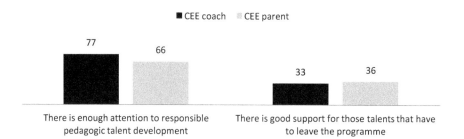

Figure 3.3 Evaluation of attention to pedagogic values, in % agree

responsible.' Another coach more clearly states that prioritizing sports includes making sacrifices with respect to pedagogical responsibilities:

> Athletes here at the CEE make choices and want to win a medal at the Olympic Games, EC's, WC's, that is the main goal. Of course this should happen in a pedagogically responsible manner, that may be clear. But sometimes you must do things that are less pedagogically responsible, but help towards that goal... You should push them in a kind of corsage... they have to give up part of their freedom to win that medal... Sometimes I decide for them that they should give up on a particular educational goal... which may lead to problems with the parents,... but there is no other choice.

Apart from the national trainings centres, mainly integrated within the four CEEs, there has been in more recent years an additional development to initiate regional training centres. This process is stimulated by several sports federations (e.g. athletics, badminton, cycling, sailing, speed skating, swimming, table tennis, volleyball). These regional training centres (RTC) are not centrally structured, supervised and financed like the NTCs, but are recognized by, and under the supervision of, their particular sports federation. RTCs are regarded as a necessary step between primary talent selection and development at sports clubs and the full-time talent development programmes at the CEE. Such developments illustrate further systematic involvement of national federations in early talent identification and development. Furthermore, apart from the Olympic ranking of Dutch elite athletes the performance of talents at global level are nowadays also monitored in light of the top-ten ambition. In January 2015, the Netherlands ranked ninth position at the global medal ranking of World Youth Championships within Olympic sports (Infostrada, 2015).

Talent development in swimming, football and speed skating

Swimming

Swimming is the fifth largest youth club sport in the Netherlands with about 75,000 youth members, of whom nearly 300 (0,4 per cent) have an official talent status. Dutch Olympic sporting success has traditionally been achieved in the water. The Sydney 2000 Olympic Games and Athens 2004 Olympic Games were very successful for the Dutch swimming team, with eight medals (five gold) and seven medals (two gold) respectively, due to extraordinary talented swimmers Inge de Bruijn and Pieter van den Hoogenband. New talents have always emerged due to a broad swimming culture (swimming is the most practiced (recreational) sport in the

Netherlands) and an extensive network of local swimming pools which have their own clubs and dedicated coaches. However, as a globalized, early specialization and quickly improving and innovating sport, the Dutch swimming federation KNZB and private top swimming initiatives deemed that radical measures were necessary to be less dependent on great individual talents, and optimize the system of talent identification and development, in order to double the inflow of talents in elite swimming programs and maintain the status as one of the leading swimming nations (KNZB, 2005; Volkers, 2003).

> The Dutch swimming building is based on several coincidental elements. The roof, elite swimming, is quite solid. We recognized that we should offer our talents another access route towards the top than via the clubs... The foundation of that building, the club culture, is in transition... I see the outlines of a new building. (Elite swimming manager, in Volkers, 2003)

Among the identified problems were the limited 'free' swimming time which constrained the opportunity for more training hours for talents and elite athletes, the shortage of top quality competition facilities and the limited number of professional talent coaches. Most swimming pools are small (25 instead of 50 metre) and dominated by recreational swimmers. Talent development within clubs was mainly dependent on highly committed volunteers. Furthermore, despite the highly praised Olympic successes of de Bruijn and Van den Hoogenband, the KNZB saw a decline in their membership from 2000 to 2008 (KNZB, 2009).

Two private professional initiatives had developed around the elite swimmers Van Hoogenband (Eindhoven) and De Bruijn (Amsterdam), with a third initiative in Dordrecht. However, talent development in swimming does not take place within commercial teams. Consequently, in 2006 the swimming federation established two NTCs and four RTCs in close cooperation with the existing professional structures (KNZB, 2005). Apart from the four accredited RTC talent programs, 13 Talent Centres are acknowledged as conforming to the required quality criteria and applying the multiannual training plan swimming and consequently receive intensive support from the federation. Similar to other sports, the national federation KNZB has taken a supporting and coordinating role in club-transcending and regional initiatives 'to help talents realise their ambitions' (KNZB, 2005). Central criteria for inflow to and outflow from the talent programs within swimming is competition performance, minimum amount of training hours (10–16 hours/week), full commitment and high elite sport ambitions (e.g. KNZB, 2010; 2014). Aspects of pleasure, safety, healthy physical and psycho-social development are not explicitly mentioned in the documents.

Football

The largest group of sport talents with an official talent status (n=1.400; about 20 per cent of all talents) are male football players (Reijgersberg & Elling, 2013). Different from most other sports, however, talent development in men's football is mainly organized by the Dutch Professional Football Organizations (PFOs), partly independent from the national football federation. Until 2005, all PFOs (then 38, currently 35) had their own youth academy. This was regarded as not effective enough with respect to 'real' talent production; most talents never became professional players and the quality of youth development was very different. In 2001, the Dutch football federation KNVB developed a quality mark for youth trainings. By 2005, a total of 14 different regional youth academies connected to one or more cooperating PFOs were certified by the football federation. In 2013 the KNVB initiated a new overall talent development plan, the Quality and Performance Programme, aimed at 'the complete football pyramid', including amateur clubs. Clubs can request an audit – by the KNVB and an independent management organization – for the certification of their youth development programme at four different levels (local, regional, national, international). Among a total of 62 audit aspects, several relate to child safety, for example the presence of enough medical support, pedagogic/didactic expertise, school progression and communication with parents (KNVB, 2013).

On the one hand, Dutch youth coaches and football academies traditionally have been rather successful in developing football talent that become professionals playing for Dutch clubs or abroad. Most clubs still strive towards 'educating' young football talents from their own academies to flow into their first teams. However, in recent decades, Dutch clubs have had more problems in keeping talents. Due to higher salaries abroad, young talents are often effectively scouted at an early age by international agents working for football organizations in, for example, England or Spain. Despite rules initiated by UEFA and FIFA, like the minimum contract age or the 'homegrown' rules, designed to end child trafficking by mala fide agents and PFOs (e.g., Scott, 2005; FIFA, 2010), these activities seem not to have decreased. Players and their families are contacted at younger ages and ways are found to avoid the rules. Many Dutch talents aged 15–18, or even younger, have moved abroad to 'big money' clubs like Barcelona and Arsenal, where, for example, their father was offered a small job, to avoid anti-child trafficking rules. A recent example is Bobby Adekanye, born in Nigeria and brought up in the Netherlands: he was scouted by Ajax at the age of 7 and was contracted by Barcelona – the La Masia academy – at the age of 12 in 2011 (Miserus, 2015; Verweij, 2015). Since Barcelona broke the FIFA under-age transfer rules, the club was sanctioned and Bobby and nine other young players were not allowed to play competitions until

January 2016. At the age of 15, Adekanye returned to the Netherlands to play a year on loan by the Dutch top club PSV Eindhoven. Both Ajax and PSV wanted to contract him for the 2015–2016 season, but Liverpool offered the best bid. He also played in the Dutch youth national team under 16. Football emigration abroad at a young age is mostly not successful, however. According to Bruma and Aké (2013), between 1988 and 2012, a total of 45 young talented players who had not yet played for the first team of their PFO went abroad, of whom only one played for the first team of their club. But young football talent trafficking is not only happening from the Netherlands abroad. Dutch clubs also recruit young foreign players, mainly from Africa or South America, but increasingly from Scandinavian and Eastern European countries, with often false promises to become football professionals. Compared to other Dutch sport talents, parents of football talents may be more inclined to stimulate a total focus on sports and regard school achievement as less important, both due to the potential of a professional football career and the higher proportion of parents with lower educational and socio-economic background and/or non-Western ethnicities. Among teachers at Topsport Talent Schools football talents are more negatively evaluated compared to other sports talents. They are more often regarded as 'spoiled' and having an attitude (Von Heijden et al., 2012). In addition, since football talents often come from lower class households, they may be more often stereotyped as less cognitively gifted, which is detrimental to school performance (cf. 'dumb jock stereotype'; Hartman, 2008; Winiger and White, 2008).

Speed skating

Compared to the Dutch football federation with more than 600,000 youth members and the Dutch Swimming federation with 75,000 youth members, speed skating is a relative small club sport among youth with less than 7,000 youth members, of whom about 350 (5 per cent) have an official talent status. However, speed skating is a very popular recreational sport in winter time and the most successful Olympic sport in history for the Netherlands. Especially in Sochi 2014, the Dutch speed skating team dominated by winning eight gold medals, with four 'clean sweeps' and a total of 23 medals out of all 36 speed skating medals (64 per cent). Another (bronze) medal was won in short track, which made a total of 24 medals, destroying the old record of 11 medals from Nagano 1998. Apart from a long speed skating tradition and the relative poor international competition, the success of the Dutch can also be ascribed to a functional talent development system. Like with most sports, talent identification and development traditionally took place mainly within local skating clubs and the eight rather independent regional skating federations of the national skating federation KNSB. Nowadays, all elite skaters are fully professional, skating for commercial teams.

Professionalization of Dutch elite speed skating started in 1995, when Rintje Ritsema started his own sponsored team, outside of the Dutch skating federations national team ('kernploeg'). Until the 2001–2002 season, skaters from commercial teams competed with skaters from the federation's national teams for selection for international competitions. Since 2002, the KNSB broke up their own national senior selection and only sent skaters from commercial teams. Due to extra financial investments and extra national competition between commercial teams and despite continuing conflicts between the commercial teams and the federation, Dutch elite speed skating has further professionalized and improved, culminating in the Olympic gold medal success in Sochi 2014. However, the rapid improvements at the top also have led to an increasing gap with talent development at club/regional/federation level that has not improved at the same pace, as Bogerd (2010) concluded, based on interviews with representatives from commercial and federation coaches, managers and (talented) top skaters. Many recognized both a gap between the quality of talent selection and development at club/regional level and the national trainings centre (NTC), 'Young Orange', and between the NTC and the commercial teams, with the results that many young talents have been 'wasted', for example by overburdening. In 2013, the Dutch speed skating federation KNSB published their new strategic plan concerning the optimization of talent development, by initiating five to six autonomous Regional Trainings Centres (RTCs) spread over the country, accredited by the national federation. Different to most other federations, the KNSB plans to end centralized talent development within the NTC. After successful talent development in the region, talents should be able to make the step towards commercial teams. The concept of the RTCs is based on the existing NTCs under the direction of NOC*NSF, including the appointment of full-time talent coaches, medical, educational and psychosocial support, but lacks similar financial support. Funding should be mainly sought by local governments, sponsors and/or the skaters themselves (Schaatsacademie Haarlem, 2014; Straatmeijer, Elling & Reijgersberg, 2015). And although the initiation of different RTCs instead of one NTC can be regarded as a kind of decentralization, within the KNSB it simultaneously can be regarded as an increasing centralization of overall talent development, since it reduces the influence of the eight autonomous regional federations.

Conclusion

The different financial and structural investments in the Dutch field of elite sports concerning talent development (e.g., registration, centralization, professionalization, coaches and other educational/medical/social support) have definitely improved possibilities for more young people, in specific sports, to develop their sporting talents with the potential of a future career as an elite athlete. Furthermore, the athletic outcomes also seem to be promising with regard to both keeping in step with global developments in elite sports and the ambition to join the top-ten most successful sporting countries. However, the positive quantitative and qualitative developments regarding sport talent development in the Netherlands also have a darker side. Since winning more gold medals to reach a world top-ten position in international sporting success at senior level is the ultimate policy goal and professionals working in this field (e.g. talent coaches) are in the end assessed on whether they produce better athletes instead of contributing to the talent's wellbeing, the welfare of these talented children sometimes seems to lose priority. In tackling problems, for example with respect to balancing elite sports with education, 'it is always education that has to give in, since the elite sports system won't do it', as stated by a CEE education-coordinator. This means in the end that for an increasing group of young athletes the identity development is becoming more one dimensional, which increases the chance of problems when they are forced to quit, which is still the case for most talents since 'there is simply not enough room at the top...' (Ingham et al., 1999, p.246; see also Luijt et al., 2009; Oldenziel, Gagné and Gulbin, 2003). Moreover, the increased centralized structures and normative training and lifestyle scripts that are imposed do not always seem to fit the 'talent central' idea, that is often also mentioned as a key principle in policy documents. Especially in a small country like the Netherlands that cannot afford talents to be 'wasted', there should be enough space for talented and elite athletes to develop outside confined systems (Van Bottenburg et al., 2012).

There seems to have been a silent revolution within the sports sector and in society at large, that pursuing elite sports performance, that until recently was despised or devalued in large parts of the country including the national government, only seems to be regarded as a good thing without questioning possible risks and for talent's welfare and healthy, psychysocial development. Since the Netherlands is a small country, we should be extra careful with our talents, not only to be most effective in winning medals, but also to be careful in managing the human capital of this group. Where the Dutch are known to be rather expressive in showing moral superiority to unacceptable violation of human dignity elsewhere in the world, (including in sports, e.g. talent development in countries like China), critical notes on our own systems – whether internal or external, even by international human rights organizations – tend to be met with skepticism. Interestingly, but also worryingly, the Dutch national government seemed to have been more interested in increasing international prestige through higher international elite sports performance and has not invested equally in a critical, independent monitoring of the general welfare of sport talents, both during and after their sports career.

Notes

1   From 1960–1996 the Netherlands performed even better in the Paralympic Games with a top 10 position. However since 1996 Paralympic medal performance declined rapidly (position 27 in 2004) until London 2012 where the Dutch Paralympic team reached tenth position, reclaiming again.
2   Since 1948, 96 percent of all Olympic medals by Dutch athletes were won in only eight different sports: equestrian, field hockey, judo, rowing, sailing, speed skating and swimming.
3   Top coaches regard the age of 12 as the mean optimum age to start talent recognition in their sport; among elite sport directors the mean optimum age is 11 years. Three to four out of ten of these coaches and managers mentioned an optimum selection age under 12 years (Source: data Elite sports climate measurement 2015).
4   Topsport Talent Schools on average have 2.100 pupils, of which most schools have between 50–100 (41 per cent) or more than 100 (41 per cent) pupils with an a official sports talent status (Reijgersberg & Elling, 2013, p.21).

References

Bloom B.S. (1985) *Developing Talent in Young People*. NY: Ballantine.
Bogerd, J.A. (2010) *Twee kanten van de medaille. Sleutelfiguren uit de schaatssport over de gevolgen van de ontwikkeling van de merkenteams voor het topsportklimaat van het langebaanschaatsen en talentontwikkeling in het bijzonder*. Master thesis. Utrecht: Utrecht University (Faculty of Law, Economics and Governance).
Bottenburg, M. van (2009) *Op jacht naar goud. Het topsportklimaat in Nederland 1998-2008*. Nieuwegein: Arko Sports Media.
Bottenburg, M. van, Dijk, B., Elling, A., & Reijgersberg, N. (2012) *Bloed, zweet en tranen – en een moment van glorie. 3-meting topsportklimaat in Nederland*. Nieuwegein: Arko Sports Media.
Bottenburg, M. van, Dijk, B., Elling, A., Dool, R. van den & Reijgersberg, N. (2015). *Topsportklimaat 4-meting*. [Main results] Utrecht: Universiteit Utrecht /Mulier Instituut.
Bottenburg, M. van, Dijk, B., Elling, A., Dool, R. van den & Reijgersberg, N. (2016, in progress). *Topsportklimaat 4-meting*. Utrecht: Universiteit Utrecht.
Brettschneider WD (1999). Risks and opportunities: Adolescents in top-level sport growing up with the pressure of school and training. *European Physical Education Review*, 5, 121–133.
Bruma J. & Aké, N. (2013) Jonge voetbaltalenten zijn het beste af in Nederland. Buitenlands geld blijkt niet zaligmakend. *The Post online*, 13-07-2013.
De Bosscher V., Bingham, J., Shibli, S., Van Bottenburg, M. and De Knop, P. (2008) *The Global Sporting Arms Race: An international comparative study on sports policy factors leading to international sporting success*. Oxford: Meyer & Meyer.
De Bosscher, V. & De Croock, S. (2010) De effectiviteit van de topsportscholen in Vlaanderen: een vergelijking van het loopbaantraject van topsporters al dan niet in een context van een topsportschool. Brussel: Vrije Universiteit Brussel.

De Bosscher, V., Shibil, S., Westerbeek, H. & Bottenburg, M. van (2015) Successful Elite Sport Policies: An international comparison of the Sports Policy factors Leading to International Sporting Success (SPLISS 2.0) in 15 nations. Aachen: Meyer & Meyer Verlag.

Dennis, M. & Grix, J. (2012) Sport under communism: Behind the East German 'miracle'. *International Journal of Sports Science and Coaching*, 7(4), 721–726.

Dijk, B. De Bosscher, V and Bottenburg, M. van (2014) Topsportbeleid in relatie tot prestaties. In A. Tiessen-Raaphorst (red.) *Rapportage Sport 2014* (pp. 224–247). Den Haag: Sociaal en Cultureel Planbureau.

Elling, A. Hilvoorde, I. van & Dool, R. van den (2014a) Creating or awakening national pride through sporting success: A longitudinal study on macro effects in the Netherlands. *International Review for the Sociology of Sport*, 49(2), 129–151.

Elling, A., Otterloo, M. van & Hakkers, S. (2014b) *EYOF participants on EYOF and combining elite sports & education*. Utrecht: Mulier Instituut.

Elling, A., Rijgersberg, N. & Hakkers, S. (2013) Talenten in balans?! Talentcoaches en talentouders over *pedagogisch verantwoorde ontwikkeling van jonge sporttalenten*. Utrecht: Mulier instituut.

Elling, A., Reijgersberg, N., Hakkers, S. & Koolmees, R. (2014b) *Een kwetsbare balans: talentcoaches en andere CTO-actoren over pedagogisch verantwoorde talentontwikkeling*. Utrecht: Mulier Instituut

Emrich, E., Fröhlich, M., Klein, M. and Pitsch, W. (2009) Evaluation of the elite schools of sport. *International Review for the Sociology of Sport*, 44(2), 151–171.

FIFA (2010) Revolutionary moment in football: Transfer Matching System becomes mandatory. FIFA.com, 29 September 2010.

Hartmann D (2008) High school sports participation and educational attainment: Recognizing, assessing, and utilizing the relationship. University of Minnesota/ LA84 Foundation.

Heijden, A. von, Elling, A. Rijgersberg, N., Hakkers, S., Rens F. van & Wisse, E. (2012) *Evaluatie topsport talentscholen*. Nieuwegein: Arko Sports Media.

Heinilä, K. (1982) The Totalization Process in International Sport. Toward a theory of the totalization of competition in top-level sport. Sportwissenschaft, 12(3), 235–254.

Hong, F. (2008) China. In B. Houlihan and M. Green (eds.) Comparative elite sport development: Systems, structures and public policy (pp. 26–52). Oxford: Butterworth-Heinemann.

Infostrada/NOC*NSF (2015) Top 10 Wereld Junior Kampioenschappen 2014. Table available at https://www.volksgezondheidenzorg.info/sport/kern indicatoren/presteren#node-talentontwikkeling

Ingham, A.G., Blissner, B.J. & Wells Davidson, K. (1999) The expendable prolympic self: Going beyond the boundaries of the sociology and psychology of sport. *Sociology of Sport Journal*, 16, 236–268.

Jonker L., Elferink-Gemser, M.T. and Visscher, C. (2010) Differences in self-regulatory skills among talented athletes: The significance of competitive level and type of sport. *Journal of Sport Sciences* 28: 901–908.

KNSB (2012) *Verbindend naar de Top*. Utrecht: KNSB.

KNSB (2013) *Beleidsplan Ontwikkeling Regionale Talenten Centra (RTC)*. Utrecht: Koninklijke Nederlandse Schaatsenrijders Bond.

KNVB (nd) *Regionale voetbaltraining*. Zeist: KNVB.

KNVB (2013) *Informatie Kwaliteit & Performance Programma Jeugdopleidingen*. Zeist: KNVB.

KNZB (2005) *Topzwemmen in uitvoering*. Nieuwegein: KNZB.

KNZB (2009) *Waterkracht 2012*. Nieuwegein: KNZB.

KNZB (2010) In- en uitstroomprocedure voor regionale trainingscentra (RTC) en nationale trainingscentra (NTC). Nieuwegein: KNZB.

KNZB (2014). *Beleid TOPzwemmen Nederland 2014-2016*. Nieuwegein: KNZB.

Lechner, F.J. (2008) *The Netherlands. Globalization and National Identity*. New York/London: Routledge Taylor & Francis Group.

Luijt, R., Reijgersberg, N. & Elling, A. (2009) Alles voor de sport!? (Gestopte) topsporttalenten en hun *ouders over investeringen, opbrengsten en offers*. Nieuwegein/ 's-Hertogenbosch: Arko Sports Media/ W.J.H. Mulier Instituut.

Oakley, B. & M. Green (2001) The Production of Olympic Champions: International Perspectives on Elite Sport Development Systems. *European Journal for Sport Management*, 8(1), 83–105.

Oldenziel, K., Gagné, F. & Gulbin, J. (2003) *How do elite athletes develop? A look through the 'rear-view mirror:' A preliminary report from the national athlete development survey (NADS)*. Canberra: Australian Sports Commission.

Miserus, M. (2015) Als jong voetbaltalent naar het buitenland: Bobby's droom bij Barcelona is nu voorbij. *de Volkskrant*, 10 April 2015.

NOC*NSF (2006) *Talent Centraal. Masterplan Talentontwikkeling 2006-2010*. Arnhem: NOC*NSF.

Ministerie van VWS (2008) *De kracht van sport*. Den Haag: Ministerie van VWS.

NOC*NSF (2010) *Nederland in de top 10*. Arnhem: NOC*NSF.

NOC*NSF (2012) *Sportagenda 2016*. Arnhem: NOC*NSF. (English summary available)

Radtke, S. and Coalter, F. (2007) Sports schools: An international review. Stirling: University of Stirling Reijgersberg, N. & Elling, A. (2013) *Evaluatie van de beleidsregel voor Topsport Talentscholen*. Utrecht: Mulier instituut.

Rens, F. van, Elling, A. & Reijgersberg, N. (2015) Topsport Talent Schools in the Netherlands: A retrospective analysis of the effect on performance in sport and education. *International Review for the Sociology of Sport*, 50(1): 64–82.

Schaatsacademie Haarlem (2014). *Schaatsacademie Haarlem: Talentontwikkeling binnen een professioneel topsportkader*. Haarlem.

Scott, M. (2005) UEFA taking on child traffickers. *The Guardian*, 14 December 2005.

Starkes, J. (2000) The road to expertise: Is practice the only determinant? *International Journal of Sport Psychology*, 31: 431–451.

Straatmeijer, J., Elling, A. & Reijgersberg, N. (2015) *RTC schaatsen in Tilburg. Onderzoek naar de haalbaarheid van een regionaal talenten centrum schaatsen in Tilburg*. Utrecht: Mulier Instituut.

Verweij, J. (2015) Toptalent Adekanye tekent meerjarig contract op Anfield. *Voetbal International*, 2 July 2015.

Volkers, J. (2003) Wachten op het nieuwe zwemtalent. *de Volkskrant*, 13 December 2004.

Winiger, S. and White, T. (2008) The Dumb Jock Stereotype: To What Extent Do Student-Athletes Feel the Stereotype? *Journal for the Study of Sports and Athletes in Education* 2: 227–237.

Winner, D. (2000) *Brilliant Orange: The Neurotic Genius of Dutch Football.* London: Bloomsbury.

Wylleman, P. and Lavallee, D. (2004) A developmental perspective on transitions faced by athletes. In M. Weiss (Ed.) *Developmental sport and exercise psychology: A lifespan perspective* (pp. 507–527). Morgantown, WV: Fitness Information Technology.

Chapter 4

Germany

Verena Burk and Karen Petry

Introduction

The actual situation of German elite youth sport is closely related to the social changes taking place in Germany. The demographic trend in Germany is leading to fewer children and young people engaging in sporting activity and becoming part of the elite youth sport system. In addition to sport offers, there are a wide range of alternative leisure facilities available (such as the media) and the changes in the educational policy created by the introduction of the eight-year high school, reducing the number of years at *Gymnasium* (upper secondary school) from nine to eight years and all-day school, are certainly having an impact on the leisure time of young children and young people (Deutscher Olympischer Sportbund, 2013).

Creating social conditions that support elite youth sport calls for political management and intervention, which is evident in Germany, but only to some extent. Neither political party policy sports programs nor the government institutions responsible for sport indicate that top-level sport has been accorded a particular priority which, in part, reflects the deeply embedded principle of the autonomy of sport that is embodied in the differentiated structures that exist for the self-administration of sport. In general, Germany is less interventionist in sport, including elite sport, than many other countries.

The situation with elite youth sport in Germany is marked in particular by a high degree of fragmentation and a system of different competencies of governmental and non-governmental organizations. In the *Elite Youth Sport Concept 2020*, which was adopted in 2013 by the General Assembly of the German Olympic Sports Confederation (DOSB), the DOSB mentioned the failure to adopt a systematic approach to talent identification and talent development in junior sport. Instead, the focus is placed on short-term success and early specialization rather than on offering diverse, basic training in motor skills. A lack of motivation among young athletes transitioning into top-level sport is also identified as one of the reasons why the situation in Germany is deteriorating by international standards (Deutscher Olympischer Sportbund, 2013).

The increase in competitions owing to the introduction of new international formats in youth sport is another contributing factor. The respective federations determine the importance of these competitions, i.e. they decide whether these competitions serve as selection processes for squad athletes.

Elite youth sport structure in Germany

The organization of sport in Germany is oriented to the principles of the autonomy of sport, subsidiarity and cooperation based on the spirit of partnership. These principles, like the federal structure of the state and administration, are the result of historical learning processes that extend beyond sport. They are a natural part of the landscape and are therefore extremely resistant to all types of reform endeavors. The organizational structure of the sport system is shaped, to a large extent, by the federal structure that is characteristic of the Federal Republic of Germany and which is a feature of both public sports administration and the structures of autonomous civic or self-administration of sport. The organizational structure of sport at the federal level has two distinct pillars: one of public administration and a two-tier pillar of autonomous or self-administration of sport. Non-profit sport clubs offer a range of sport programs to the population and there are more than 91,000 non-profit sport clubs in existence (Breuer & Feiler, 2013).

In the public administration of sport, both the Federal Government (through the Federal Ministry of the Interior) and the 16 federal states (for instance, via their Ministries of Culture or the Interior) have joint responsibility for sport in their area. There are consequently no independent specialist Ministries of Sports. Responsibility for top-level sport in general, however, lies with the Federal Ministry of the Interior operating as the specialized department. The latter plays the leading role in the area of state support for elite youth sport. It also coordinates the activities of the other federal ministries that have specific responsibilities in the area of top-level sport, for instance, supporting top-level sport in the Federal Armed Forces (Petry, Steinbach, & Burk, 2008).

However, sport issues at the local government level are the responsibility of specialist sports offices. As a result of the country's federal structure, these public structures do not constitute a hierarchically integrated, top-to-bottom system. Rather, the individual ministries operate, by and large, independently although they do, at the regional level, coordinate their activities as part of the Conference of Ministers of Sports of the regions. The situation is different with regard to the self-administered autonomous sport sector: clubs are organized (into governing bodies) both at the level of specific disciplines (e.g., they are member of the German Athletics Federation) and at the level of multiple sports (they are all members of the regional sport confederation) (Petry & Hallmann, 2013).

The Federal Ministry of Family Affairs, Senior Citizens, Women and Youth (BMFSFJ) supports sport for children and young people. The Federal Government's plan for children and young people envisages supporting the so-called free and public youth welfare organizations. It appropriates funds mainly for the German Sports Youth, although it also supports other youth associations belonging to the various sport federations, two bilateral youth offices (Franco-German Youth Office and the German-Polish Youth Office) and the implementation of the Federal Youth Sport Games.

The German Sports Youth is the umbrella federation of youth organizations belonging to the German Olympic Sports Confederation. It focuses, in particular, on working with children and young people. The German Sports Youth harnesses the interests of more than 10 million young people under the age of 27. They are organized in sport clubs in 16 regional sports youth organizations, 53 youth organizations of the national federations, and 10 youth organizations of the federations entrusted with special tasks (Bundesministerium des Innern, 2014).

Elite youth sport system, talent identification, development and support

Since the merger of the German Sport Confederation (DSB) and the National Olympic Committee (NOC) in May 2006, the German Olympic Sports Confederation (DOSB) has represented the interests of its member organizations as the sole umbrella organization. The DOSB has 98 member organizations comprising 27.8 million members including people who are members of two or more sport clubs. The member organizations of the DOSB unite 16 regional sport confederations/federations, 62 national federations (34 Olympic and 28 non-Olympic federations) and 20 sport federations entrusted with special tasks (e.g. German Olympic Society, German Association of Physical Education Teachers) (Petry & Hallmann, 2013).

As a rule, athletes begin their careers in Olympic and non-Olympic clubs. In fact, they need to become a member of a sports club in order to compete in sporting competitions in the first place. Clubs can represent a training base and there is a lot of cooperation between the athletes' home clubs and supplementary training bases, particularly in the area of sport for children and young people. The situation of training bases envisages offering athletes high-quality training across sports clubs. The most promising young athletes are appointed to the regional squads (D-squads) or federal squads (C-squads) based on predefined criteria. The age of team members differs considerably among different types of sport.

The DOSB's High Performance Division and the equivalent structures at the regional level (Regional Performance Committee) play a guiding and coordinating role in elite youth sport development. The High Performance Sports Division is responsible for managing and coordinating top-level sport within the DOSB. It launches initiatives for the development of strategic plans and makes declarations of principle regarding performance sport for athletes and top-level sport. The DOSB adopted the *Elite Youth Sport Concept 2020* in 2013 with a view to developing a more systematic approach. The concept involves, by and large, creating a binding framework for the regulation of competencies and responsibilities (Deutscher Olympischer Sportbund, 2013). This general concept applies to all Olympic and non-Olympic sport disciplines that are organized under the umbrella of the DOSB. However, it does not include the Paralympic sport disciplines as they come under the organizational structure of the German Paralympic Committee.

It is apparent that although the DOSB assumes overall responsibility for the development of elite youth sport in Germany, the main organizational tasks are, by and large, incumbent upon the individual sport federations.

Talent identification and development

With regard to talent identification in German elite sport, it has not been possible to transfer the advantages of talent identification in the German Democratic Republic (GDR) into the new common social system since the unification of the two German nations in 1990.

In its *Elite Youth Sport Concept 2020*, the DOSB speaks about "the lack of a system and all-sport coordination of talent identification" (Deutscher Olympischer Sportbund, 2013, p. 6) which leads to major deficits with the world elite in some sports that are hard to overcome. To meet these shortcomings, the DOSB *Elite Youth Sport Concept 2020* intends to provide practical checks in all sporting disciplines. This means children under the age of 10 are checked for their motion behavior and their motor abilities using validated testing procedures. Based on their test results, talented children are referred to appropriate sport programs in clubs and associations. Elementary schools, clubs and sports federations of cities, counties and states are important partners. Since the stages of elite youth sport are based on school age, cooperation between schools and clubs is crucial for a successful talent identification and talent promotion system. To ensure there is a broad base in elite youth sport, it is necessary to get children and adolescents enthusiastic about elite sport, to encourage them to make an ongoing commitment and most of all, if possible, to integrate as many talented young athletes as possible into the high-performance structures of clubs and associations. In order to make this possible, nationwide cooperation programs have been established between sport clubs and schools in all federal states (Deutscher Olympischer Sportbund, 2013). In cooperation with schools and clubs, training groups in different sports and skill levels are offered. The aim is to attract children and young people to the sport, foster lifelong sports participation and to pave the way towards club sports. Sports clubs reach these potential members by offering a full day-care in schools complemented by sport-based activities. For example, voluntary sports associations train of so-called student mentors in selected sports.

At the same time, special talent tests, promotion measures and training courses represent a common recruitment process in the individual sport disciplines. These come under the remit of the umbrella organizations and their regional specialist associations. Talented children and young people are identified on the basis of testing procedures adapted to the specific requirements of each individual sport. Furthermore, performance in competitions is still a key criterion of practice-oriented talent identification. It most closely approximates the complexity of the requirements profile of each individual sport and the required psychological profile. This explains why talent identification based on specific competition formats of clubs and associations is the most widespread. In the German Gymnastics Federation (hereinafter referred to as DTB), for example, nationwide standardized competition-format tests for talent identification are performed by the regional gymnastics talent schools in order to add children over the age of 6–8 to the squad of the gymnastics talent schools. Suitable locations for talent identification are kindergartens, preschools, elementary schools (first grade) as well as club parties or sport parties. Athletic, technical and coordination tests are carried out for participants who score a maximum of five points in each test. The standard score for being included in a DTB gymnastics talent school is 60 per cent (Deutscher Turner-Bund, 2006). The German Athletics Federation (hereinafter referred to as DLV) has developed ongoing cooperation between schools, clubs and Olympic training facilities for talent identification purposes. As a result, the DLV collaborates with its regional associations. Moreover, in addition to the Federal Youth Games, competitions called "Young people training for the Olympics" or the two-stage DLV youth athletics badge are used for talent identification purposes. In addition, German Athletics Federation hosted events, such as the "Action Day for children athletics," pursue the goal of talent identification. The action program for youth athletics was established in the spring of 1998. It recommends practical methods on how running, jumping and throwing can be organized in a motivating fashion as basic exercise patterns for children.

When children are recognized as talents and decide to pursue a career in elite sport, they go through the multiple training stages of the sport federations, namely basic, development, follow-up and high-performance sport training (cf. Figure 4.1). Sport-specific appropriate adjustments can be made. Training intervals and contents are not only oriented towards the relevant stage of the training process and age, but also towards squad status (Deutscher Olympischer Sportbund, 2015a). The D-squad of the regional specialist associations forms the first official stage of the German squad system. In order to be admitted to the D-squad, athletes need to take part in basic club training throughout the year. The DC-squad includes several athletes from the D-squad who were selected by the umbrella organizations because of their potential in elite sport. As a state squad member, the athlete is under the support program of the state but can be integrated into the support measures of the umbrella organizations. The C-squad is the national youth squad of an umbrella organization. It follows the age regulations in the respective sport and includes athletes with medium- to long-term prospects of success in international high-performance sport. Athletes who have exceeded the age limit of the C-squad in their sport yet meet the sport-specific performance criteria of their umbrella organization are incorporated into the B-squad. At this point, an athlete has to meet the requirement of offering the medium-term prospect of success in international high-performance sport. The A-squad includes athletes who belong to the world elite because of the performances they have achieved (for example, in the Olympic Games, World Championships, European Championships). In general, A-squad membership is recognized as well as the B-, C- and D/C-squads for a period of one year. In September 2015, according to the DOSB, 5,488 athletes belonging to the member associations of the DOSB (Olympic/non-Olympic sports) had the status of a national A, B, or C-squad member (Deutscher Olympischer Sportbund, 2015b).

Support for young athletes

The successful involvement of young high-performance athletes is based on time-related factors which are the result of high training capacities and frequent absence from school because of training camps and competitions. In order to enable athletes to cope with this serious difficulty, a number of benefits have already been institutionalized for athletes involved in elite youth sport. The national umbrella organizations are provided with resources to finance a series of educational and professional measures and funding institutions. At the 19 Olympic training centers, career guidance officers give guidance on the coordination of athletics and education in order to ensure athletes have a career after they complete their athletic career. Elite sport schools are partnering with the Olympic training centers and are equipped with a boarding school. In 2014, 43 of these combined systems consisting of around 110 schools with 11.500 participants had already been established, 22 of which were in West German states, 18 of which were in East German states and three of which were in Berlin. Twenty-nine elite sport schools focused on summer sports, seven focused on winter sports and another seven covered both summer and winter sports (Deutscher Olympischer Sportbund, 2015c).

The overall system of support for talented young athletes consists of several sub-systems which aim to make it possible for young and adult top-level athletes to pursue a dual career within and outside top-level sport.

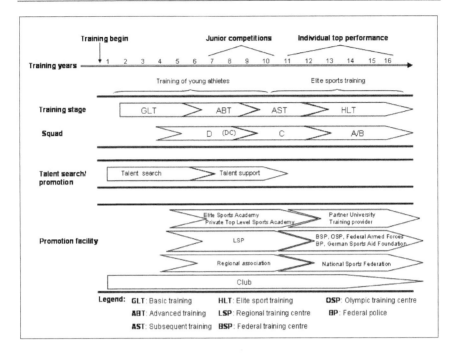

Figure 4.1 Model of training and performance (Deutscher Sportbund, 2006)

Training stages, squad membership and support systems need to be coordinated in a targeted way as part of talent support.

The situation of coaches for young athletes

Coaches are important partners for young athletes and are actually the persons they rely on most, in addition to their parents and teachers. In the German sport system, a distinction is made between coaches who identify talent and coaches who deal with young athletes. Coaches who identify talent are tasked with identifying talented young athletes across all sport disciplines by carrying out practical checks and systematic talent tests on children attending elementary school, encouraging them to join sport clubs. By contrast, coaches dealing with young athletes are the people who actually work with them. Generally speaking, they are employed by clubs or regional sport federations. The employment contracts for coaches vary greatly (there are voluntary, part-time and full-time contracts) although the vast majority of employment contracts are short-term contracts offering few career opportunities for the future. There are continual changes of coaches from training centers and from talent promotion programs to professional sport. The DOSB is undertaking serious efforts to enhance the recognition of coach as a profession in society and to raise coaches' pay. Training of coaches in Germany is regulated by the general guidelines on qualifications issued by the DOSB. In order to ensure that the quality of coaching and training is consistent throughout the country and across all performance levels, initial and advanced training for coaches in all the sports federations is structured in a four-tier coaching system, the uppermost tier being the training course at the DOSB's Coaches' Academy in Cologne leading to the qualification of state-certified "qualified coach." Both voluntary and full-time coaches work at the training centers. In addition, regional and national coaches employed on a full-time basis normally coordinate the training process at regional and national level. They also coach the relevant selections and supervise training courses run by the sport federations.

There were a total of 160,000 licensed coaches working in top-level sport in 2008 (Deutscher Olympischer Sportbund, 2010). The National Sports Federations are responsible for training coaches involved in elite youth sports, which means that overall the quality of training tends to vary greatly.

In order to shed more light on the complex situation that prevails in elite youth sport in Germany, focus will be placed on the following: the early peak performance sport of gymnastics, the team sport of basketball and the prominent Olympic sport of athletics.

Elite youth sport structure and development in selected sports

Gymnastics

The German Gymnastics Federation (DTB) is the second-largest Olympic top-level sport federation in Germany based on the number of members after the German Football Association (which has a total of 6.85 million members). It is worth noting – even in sport for children and adolescents – that the number of young female members is higher than the number of male members (cf. table 4.1). In 2014, children and adolescents under the age of 18 accounted for around 40 percent of the total number of members of the DTB engaging in gymnastics in around 20,380 clubs (Deutscher Olympischer Sportbund, 2014).

The DTB had developed a national concept for top-level sport structure in the Olympic disciplines as far back as 2004. The objective of the concept is to provide professional training for talented young gymnasts competing in top-level Olympic sports by establishing a system of diverse, nationwide structural elements and by combining the squads of the national team. The DTB has set standards in its concept that are intended to safeguard optimum promotion such as standardized training content and methods of talent identification, relevant qualifications for coaches, support measures for the athletes during and outside training as well as a coordinated marketing concept.

Table 4.1 Number of children and young people under the age of 18 who were
members of the DTB – broken down by age group and gender (Deutscher
Olympischer Sportbund, 2014)

Age groups	Male	Female	Total
Under 6	299,415	349,481	648,896
7–14 year-olds	332,383	608,975	941,358
15–18 year-olds	88,571	184,275	457,121
Total number of children and adolescents under 18	720,369	1,142,731	2,047,375
Total number of DTB members	1,567,908	3,450,911	5,018,819

There are three structural elements to talent promotion in the German
Gymnastics Federation: The bottom tier consists of DTB schools for talented
young gymnasts. These are elite sport facilities for children under the age of
5/6 and 10 (artistic gymnastics/rhythmic sport gymnastics) and for children
under the age of 7 and 10 respectively (trampoline gymnastics). The schools
for talented young gymnasts are financed with public funds (inter alia, local
authorities, if applicable, federal states), sport clubs, gymnastics districts,
sponsors, parents' contributions and donations. A seal (i.e. accreditation) is
issued for a period of four years (Deutscher Turner-Bund, 2004). In 2015,
the number of schools included 18 schools for rhythmic sport gymnastics,
ten for trampoline gymnastics, 28 for artistic gymnastics for male athletes
and 46 artistic gymnastics for female athletes. Children who have been
identified as talented young athletes undergo thorough basic training while
specializing simultaneously in artistic gymnastics, trampoline gymnastics or
in rhythmic sport gymnastics, thus launching their career in elite sports. The
aim is to increase the number of talented young gymnasts who have
undergone training (Deutscher Turner-Bund, n.d.). Training sessions at
these schools are carried out on the basis of scientific training schedules in
three age groups (under 6: 4 to 6 hours per week; 7–8 year-old: 6 to 12
hours per week; 9–10 year-old: 12 to 18 hours per week) (Deutscher Turner-
Bund, 2004). Once they have completed their education at elementary
school, talented young gymnasts are referred to a DTB gymnastics center or
– if they show special talent – to a federal training base.

Gymnastics centers have schools for talented young gymnasts run by the
DTB and look after additional schools for talented young gymnasts assigned
to them. The gymnastics centers are run by a full-time coach who holds an
A-license. In addition, the gymnastics centers have an educational support
concept and cooperate with a sports intermediate secondary school, a sport
higher secondary school/elite school and a partner school/special sports
school (Deutscher Turner-Bund, 2004). The Olympic bases support the
athletes at the gymnastics centers by providing medical care and
physiotherapy as well as career guidance. In 2015, the total number of

gymnastics centers was 17 (8 for artistic gymnastics for female athletes and 6 for male athletes, 3 for rhythmic sport gymnastics).

By contrast, the federal bases are facilities offering athletes who are likely to reach the finals and win a medal in international competitions optimum training conditions. The athletes are admitted to the federal bases depending on their sporting discipline, age and level of performance. The federal bases are financed exclusively by public funds; the DTB can also appropriate funds. In addition, federal bases need to have a boarding school or an adequate facility that has a professional support concept (Deutscher Turner-Bund, 2004). As of 2015, the DTB will be running a total of 14 federal bases for the Olympic disciplines artistic gymnastics for men (6) and artistic gymnastics for women (3), trampoline gymnastics and rhythmic sport gymnastics (5). In addition, there are three federal bases that cater specifically for talented young athletes.

Basketball

In 2014, the German Basketball Federation (hereinafter referred to as DBB) had a total of 92,585 members under the age of 18 who were members of 2,128 basketball clubs and departments (cf. Table 4.2). This accounts for around 48 percent of all members of the DBB (Deutscher Olympischer Sportbund, 2014).

In its elite youth sport program, the DBB bases its training concept on the ongoing promotion of talented basketball players based on their age and development. As such, training content and performance criteria are allocated to the different age groups, development and squad levels. The objective is "to attract more talent to engage in top-level sport and above all to ensure talented athletes make a long-term commitment to top-level sport in the interest of offering them long-term career opportunities and career development" (Deutscher Basketball Bund, 2014a, p. 3).

Talent identification and promotion within the DBB begins with targeted identification at the level of clubs and regional associations. The "Promising Talent" project in which talented young athletes under the age of 13 are

Table 4.2 Number of children and young people under the age of 18 who were members of the DBB – broken down by age group and gender (Deutscher Olympischer Sportbund, 2014)

Age groups	Male	Female	Total
Under 6	1,956	1,239	3,195
7–14 year-olds	38,403	15,024	53,427
15–18 year-olds	25,993	9,970	35,963
Total number of children and adolescents under 18	66,352	26,233	92,585
Total number of DBB members	140,344	51,820	192,164

selected by federal coaches when they compete with teams of talented athletes from all the federal states is an important component of talent inspection. The talented young athletes identified are integrated into the DBB squad structure and also into the national youth teams based on their age. The DBB organizes federal youth camps, performance camps and try-outs in the various age groups as identification and allocation measures. The Junior Basketball Leagues for young males and females represent additional talent identification and talent development platforms.

A range of institutions are involved in looking after talented young basketball players based on the spirit of partnership. They include clubs offering performance-based and age-based training for competitive basketball matches and training as well as highly-trained coaches. Training bases are instrumental in providing professional guidance for talented young athletes. Central funding is provided for talented young female athletes in the DBB.

In 2015, there were two performance bases for young female athletes funded exclusively by the DBB. Both training bases cooperate with elite sport clubs in the vicinity, provide boarding school accommodation or assisted accommodation facilities, cooperate with schools (elite sport schools, sport partner schools) and have established a competitive and league structure (Deutscher Basketball Bund, 2014b).

Training at training bases for young male athletes is organized on a decentralized basis and was implemented at a total of 28 training bases in 2014. In addition, six clubs run by federal coaches in the regional vicinity were included in the training measures (Deutscher Basketball Bund, 2014b). The training bases for young male athletes who are members of the DBB receive funding from the Federal Government. In addition, clubs have the option of applying for the seal "Performance base for talented young athletes of the German Basketball Federation" through their regional sport federations. The seal is issued for a period of four years; no funding is provided by the DBB or the Federal Government.

Athletics

In 2014, the German Athletics Federation (DLV) had a total of 335,257 children and young people under the age of 18 who were members of the more than 7,700 clubs and departments (cf. Table 4.3). That figure represents approximately 40 per cent of the total membership (Deutscher Olympischer Sportbund, 2014).

The "Strategies for improving the development of young talent in the DLV," which were adopted in October 2008 and are still in operation today, are based – as in practically all other sport disciplines – on the relevant age group and the existing squad structure. The objective is the long-term development of athletes who are to be internationally competitive at adult

Table 4.3 Number of children and young people under the age of 18 who were members of the DLV – broken down by age group and gender (Deutscher Olympischer Sportbund, 2014)

Age groups	Male	Female	Total
Under 6	19,902	20,052	39,954
7–14 year-olds	98,966	117,534	216,500
15–18 year-olds	36,330	42,473	78,803
Total number of children and adolescents under 18	155,198	180,059	335,257
Total number of DLV members	412,651	422,236	834,887

level. According to the DLV, this objective can only be achieved by the right amount of proper training, with special priority being given to the athlete/coach team. Additional factors (e.g. dual career) need to be optimized in order to make this development possible (Deutscher Leichathletik-Verband, 2008).

The individual regional federations are responsible for squad athletes. As a rule, D-squad includes athletes belonging to the age groups of 14- to 17-year-olds who are appointed on the basis of age-related performance criteria and assessment by disciplinary coaches belonging to the regional federations. In addition to training at their home club, they are offered 14-day squad training sessions in which the best-performing athletes of the regional federation compete. The D/C squad is the transition squad of the regional and federal federation. It includes athletes in the age group of 15 to 17 years taking part in central training measures of the DLV who show potential for reaching the C-squad. Their C-squad is the federal young athletes squad of the DLV. It comprises athletes offering maximum development potential who are preparing to compete in international competitions for young athletes. Admission to the C-squad is based on performance and placings. The B-squad can be construed as the next squad for athletes who have clear prospects of reaching international performance in the foreseeable future. Here too, admission is based on performance and placings. The junior elite team of the DLV includes athletes from the group of younger B-squad athletes. Athletes who won a medal in the Under 23 European Championships and who are predicted to compete in the European Championships in the short term, in the World Championships or the Olympics in the medium term are admitted to the squad for promising young athletes.

The A-squad includes members of the German national athletics team and is made up of athletes who represent their sport based on their performance and their extraordinary prospects of success in the international arena.

Depending on the level of performance and what squad they belong to, the athletes do not just train with their home coaches in athletics clubs and departments but also at the regional and federal bases. At federal level, the

DLV has over 17 federal bases offering optimum training conditions in terms of structure and human resources in selected track and field disciplines. So-called framework training schemes for basic and development training provide the basis for training section.

Additional factors to support elite youth sport

In addition to talent search, talent promotion, and various support services (e.g., provided by the educational system and service providers), there are additional factors that facilitate the development of young athletes in high-performance sports in Germany. Among others, these services are provided by the competition system and by the professional team sport leagues, which will be discussed in the following.

The competition system in Germany

Competitions within the associations are staged in Olympic and non-Olympic sports nationwide throughout the year. The competition system is structured hierarchically, ranging from children and junior to adult and senior competitions. Furthermore, the system is divided into performance categories, of which local competitions form the basis. Through these qualification systems, it is possible to advance to national competition levels. A typical competition structure, evident for most sport associations in Germany, begins at the lowest level of club championships, followed by county, district, state, and regional championships (e.g., Southern German Championships, Northern German Championships) and German Championships.

The German Athletics Federation, for example, offers a total of seven different age group championships for children and young people (male/ female): Under 8 (7/6 years), Under 10 (9/8 years), Under 12 (11/10 years), Under 14 (13/12 years), Under 16 (15/14 years), Under 18 (17/16 years), and Under 20 (19/18 years). German championships only take place in the Under 16, Under 18, and Under 20 age groups. In the other age groups, championships are offered at the level of state associations. In addition, athletics team competitions for children are hosted for the age groups Under 8, Under 10, and Under 12. These competitions offer a choice between 35 different disciplines in athletics events, which are geared towards introducing the children to the disciplines in youth athletics.

There is a large differentiation in the children and youth competition systems particularly in team sports. For basketball, the state associations offer league structures for the age groups Under 8's to Under 18. At national level, a National Talent Basketball League (NBBL) was established in the season 2006/07 to support talented young German high-performance athletes in the age group Under 19 (male). In addition, in the season 2009/2010, a national basketball youth league (JBBL) was launched for the age group

Under 16 (male). Furthermore, the German Basketball League hosts German youth championships for the age groups Under 14 to Under 18.

School competitions are also organized alongside those organized by the associations. The Federal Youth Games take place at schools, are oriented more to sport for all, and are geared for school children achieving an average athletic performance. Even children with poor athletic skills are given the opportunity to experience a sense of achievement in sport competition. The Federal Youth Games are aimed at introducing children in younger age groups to basic forms of sport without focusing on early specialization. The Games comprise gymnastics, athletics, and swimming.

The nationwide school sport competition called "Young People training for the Olympic Games" was first staged in 1969 and is the largest school sport competition in the world with around 800,000 participants (Deutsche Schulsportstiftung, 2015). It was modeled after the national "research at school" competition "Young scientists," while the children and youth Spartakiades sporting events that took place in the former GDR may have also had some influence. The range of competitions is advertised each year and competitions are held separately for girls and boys in 17 different sports. School team competition is based on a nationally uniform competition system, consisting of five age group dependent competition categories that are open to all schools in the 16 German federal states. There are elimination rounds at county, district, and state levels, culminating in the national finals in which participants compete for the national title. The aim of the competition is to foster school sports, introducing children to more performance-oriented sports, and to lay the foundations for lifelong involvement in sporting activities. It has furthermore explored new avenues in terms of concept in that it now also increasingly integrates talent selection and support for high-performance sports.

The role of professional leagues

Alongside associations and schools, professional team sport leagues in Germany are heavily involved in supporting, funding, and developing young athletes. After the disappointing UEFA European Football Championships in 2000, the German Football Association made it an obligatory requirement for all National German Football League clubs (first and second league) to create intensive training centers for talented young football players. Meeting specific requirements is now necessary in order to attain the annual league license. Training center grounds, for instance, need to have at least four football fields and in winter alternative access to a nearby indoor field. There are also guidelines for coaches and coaching support staff as well as for medical, physiotherapeutic, pedagogical, and psychological support. Looking more closely at the financial investment, it becomes evident how important talent development has become for the league clubs: in the season

2014/2015, the overall investment by licensed football clubs in their intensive training centers for talented young athletes exceeded one billion euro (Deutsche Fußball-Liga, 2015).

The German Basketball League has a complex talent training concept. An important cornerstone of this concept is the training and education fund, which is made up of financial resources supplied by the clubs from the top three leagues (Beko BBL, ProA, and ProB). All clubs make basic annual payments along with variable payments based on their transfer activities within their respective leagues. Thus, additional resources can be provided for talent development and support, for instance, to finance cross-club projects (such as school projects), support for full-time youth coaches as well as payment of training bonuses (for clubs as reimbursement for the financial expenses incurred by fostering talented young players) (Beko Basketball-Bundesliga, 2015).

Conclusion

Growing dissatisfaction has manifested itself in top-level sports and youth sport in Germany in recent years and criticism has been voiced repeatedly by many stakeholders. They criticize, inter alia, that sport science in general and training science in particular has had less and less of an input in elite sport in the past 20 years, that the conditions for combining a professional career with top-level sport are far from ideal, that athletes do not have sufficient pension arrangements upon completion of their sporting career and that the promotion measures implemented by the Federal Government and the federal states are of little or no benefit for athletes and are being leveraged with little or no effect. However, the considerable expansion of programs aimed at promoting talented young athletes and talent search in Germany has not yet led to any major increase in success stories in elite sport. Emrich and Güllich (2008, p. 421) say: "Selection decisions in the system promoting talented young athletes that are based mainly on recent performance and successes are only sustainable in the short term."

More government responsibility and coordination is being called for in order to improve the situation (Hottenrott & Braumann, 2015). It is also necessary to give training and talent promotion programs a more individual focus and to focus more on creativity and flexibility in dealing with young athletes instead of adopting a standardized approach.

Furthermore, the aspect of a holistic career development is of utmost importance in Germany, as there is a general lack of psycho-social support for young athletes. It is specifically the social circumstances of young athletes that tend to be disregarded in their career planning. The particularly high number of drop-outs among young athletes transitioning to top-level sports owing to the inability to reconcile a career in elite sports with educational-vocational training is also proving to be an obstacle to the development of young athletes in Germany.

References

Beko Basketball-Bundesliga (2015). *Ausbildungsfond.* Retrieved from www.beko-bbl.de/de/nachwuchs/ausbildungsfonds/allgemeine-infos/

Breuer, C., & Feiler, S. (2013). Sportvereine in Deutschland – ein Überblick. In C. Breuer (Ed.), *Sportentwicklungsbericht 2011/2012. Analyse zur Situation der Sportvereine in Deutschland.* Köln: Sportverlag Strauß.

Bundesministerium des Innern (2014). *13. Sportbericht der Bundesregierung.* Berlin: Bundesministerium des Innern.

Deutsche Fußball-Liga (2015). *Qualität durch Lizenzierung: Die Nachwuchsförderung in der Bundesliga.* Retrieved from www.bundesliga.de/de/liga/news/qualitaet-durch-lizenzierung-nachwuchsfoerderung-der-bundesliga-dfl-deutsche-fussball-liga.jsp

Deutsche Schulsportstiftung (2015). *Jugend trainiert für Olympia – Daten und Fakten.* Retrieved from www.jtfo.de/daten_und_fakten/

Deutscher Basketball Bund (2014a). *Leistungssportstruktur und Fördermaßnahmen für DBB-Kaderathletinnen und -athleten.* Hagen: Deutscher Basketball Bund.

Deutscher Basketball Bund (2014b). *Stützpunktkonzept.* Hagen: Deutscher Basketball Bund.

Deutscher Leichtathletik-Verband (2008). *Strategien zur Verbesserung der Nachwuchsentwicklung im Deutschen Leichtathletik-Verband:* Darmstadt: DLV.

Deutscher Olympischer Sportbund (2010). Qualifizierungsbericht der Sport-organisationen. Frankfurt a.M.: DOSB.

Deutscher Olympischer Sportbund (2013). *Nachwuchsleistungssportkonzept 2020.* Frankfurt a.M.: DOSB.

Deutscher Olympischer Sportbund (2014). *Bestandserhebung 2014.* Frankfurt a.M.: DOSB.

Deutscher Olympischer Sportbund (2015a). *Anpassung der Kadersystematik zum 01.01.2015.* Neu-Isenburg: DOSB.

Deutscher Olympischer Sportbund (2015b). *Kaderzahlen je Kader und Verband/ Sportart.* Neu-Isenburg: DOSB.

Deutscher Olympischer Sportbund (2015c). *„Eliteschule des Sports": Daten, Zahlen, Fakten.* Retrieved from www.dosb.de/de/eliteschule-des-sports/hintergrund/

Deutscher Sportbund (2006). *Nachwuchsleistungssportkonzept 2012. Leitlinien zur Entwicklung des Nachwuchsleistungssports.* Frankfurt a.M.: DSB.

Deutscher Turner-Bund (2004). *Olympischer Spitzensport 2012.* Frankfurt a.M.: DTB.

Deutscher Turner-Bund (2006). *DTB-Aufnahmetest für DTB-Turn-Talentschulen.* Frankfurt a.M.: DTB.

Deutscher Turner-Bund (n.d.). *Das Prädikat DTB-Turn-Talentschule.* Frankfurt a.M.: DTB.

Emrich, E., & Güllich, A. (2008). Leistungssport im Kinder- und Jugendalter. In W. Schmidt (Ed.), *Zweiter Deutscher Kinder- und Jugendsportbericht* (pp. 409–426). Schorndorf: Hofmann Verlag.

Hottenrott, K., & Braumann, K.-M. (2015). Aktuelle Situation im deutschen Spitzensport. Eine notwendige Diskussion. *Sportwissenschaft*, *45*(3), 111–115.

Petry, K., & Hallmann, K. (2013). Germany. In K. Hallmann & K. Petry (Eds.), *Comparative sport development: systems, participation and public policy* (pp. 75–86). New York: Springer International Press.

Petry, K., Steinbach, D., & Burk, V. (2008). Elite Sport Development in Germany: Systems, Structures and Public Policy. In B. Houlihan & M. Green (Eds.), *Comparative Elite Sports Development* (pp. 114–146). London: Butterworth-Heinemann.

Chapter 5

Russia

Vassil Girginov

Analyses of Russian sport policy are rare and while Russian experts have hardly ever seriously ventured into this field, attempts by Western commentators to produce explanations have suffered from ideological blindness about the role of sport in society and its exploitation by the communist (in the past) or the authoritarian (currently) state. Several years after the dissolution of the Soviet Union even the West eminent authority on Soviet sport, Jim Riordan (1999), rather prematurely declared that 'Communist sports policy in Eastern Europe is dead' (p. 48). The reality was very different and the chief concern of the post-communist sport policy in Russia and elsewhere in Eastern Europe was 'don't throw the baby out with the bathwater' (Girginov, 1998). This chapter examines the elite youth sport policy in Russia by paying particular attention to its evolution, ontological premises, structure and management. It is divided into six sections: the first section provides a background to the emergence of elite youth sport policy; the second section analyses the role of the government in shaping policies in the field; this section is followed by a discussion about the selectiveness of elite sport policy; the fourth and fifth sections focus on the talent identification and development and the competition structure of youth elite sport respectively; and finally the future of elite youth sport is discussed.

Background

The proverbial 'baby' was the body of knowledge that was created over a century as well as the ontological assumptions and worldviews underpinning the sport policy in Russia, which are generally ignored by commentators. For the first time in history, the physiologist Ivan Pavlov linked successfully philosophical views about education in Russia, as an essential adjunct to mental development, to a general theory of physiology. Pavlov's research provided a sound foundation for the whole Soviet system of holistic physical education and training. It was captured by the term 'physical culture', which was associated with philosophers and writers such as Nikolai Dobrolubov,

Nikolai Chernyshevski and Anton Chekhov, a founder of the Russian Gymnastics Society (Riordan, 1980).

The concept of physical culture sees sport as part of a wider civil movement, which promotes a particular view of human progress. It is underpinned by an ontological assumption which places the harmonious and versatile development of the person at its heart, and covers not only the various forms of physical activity and competition, but moral and spiritual education, personal and social hygiene, and actively seeks a balance between the body and mind.

It follows that the social mission of physical culture could be achieved through a centralized and coordinated approach that could only be ensured by the state. The Russian state gradually took the lead and, from the early 1920s, began setting up agencies responsible for physical education and sport. Thus, the development of sport-specific knowledge was inevitably supervised, sanctioned and often commissioned by the state. In this way, sport organizations and research institutions were transformed into repositories of specialized and standardized knowledge on sport. These developments led to the legitimization of physical culture as a structured environment and a system of learning. This system included a host of standards, norms and codes of behaviour, and was supported by regular large-scale surveys (Girginov, 2004). It was also responsible for the high correlation between Olympians and their professional development after retiring from competitive sport. Milshtein (2001) explicated that 80 per cent of Olympic athletes continued employment as coaches, 13 per cent as physical education teachers, 6 per cent as managers, 4 per cent as performance directors and 2 per cent in sports science. Extending top athletes' career in sport has ensured that a great deal of explicit and implicit knowledge is preserved within the system.

The coupling of education with physiology at the beginning of the twentieth century was accompanied by a growing scientific interest in giftedness of children. Dorfman (2000) documented the evolution and uniqueness of the Russian school of thought where sport was also identified as a legitimate area for the development of physically gifted children. As Pautova (2009) argued, modern social perceptions in Russia reflect the importance of talent where 45 per cent of parents associate sport with giftedness, ranking it second after music (55 per cent). The search for talented children in sport was institutionalized with the opening of the first sport schools in 1935 and 1936 in Moscow and Leningrad (today's St. Petersburg) respectively, thus establishing talent identification as a specific policy sector. By 1971, there were 3,813 sports schools in the USSR, with approximately 1.3 million children training. The state commitment to developing gifted children in all fields of endeavour has been reaffirmed recently in a bespoke programme 'Gifted children', which received some US$3.3[1] million for the period 2007–10.

Inevitably, however, after the dissolution of the Soviet Union in 1991, a good deal of system knowledge and structures were 'thrown out with the bathwater'. The system of Olympic preparation of Russian athletes, of which elite youth sport development was an essential part, was completely disturbed. Russia ended up with some 50 per cent of the Olympic system of the USSR in terms of number of sport schools, centres, staff and facilities, as dozens of established national sport centres, equipment and staff remained in the 14 former Soviet republics, now newly formed independent states. The situation was exacerbated by the ensuing political, economic and social crisis, which has led to the transfer of responsibility for Olympic preparation from the State Committee of Sport to the Russian Olympic Committee (ROC) and National Sport Federations (NSF) (Platonov, 2010). Particularly damaging for elite youth sport was the outflow of thousands of highly qualified coaches and scientific and technical personnel. For example, currently more than 400 Russian figure skating coaches are working abroad.

Role of government in shaping elite youth sport policy

Russia's long-term sport policy strategy (2009–2020) addresses four principal concerns, including (i) health and welfare of the population (e.g., 60 per cent of pupils and students have health problems and 40 per cent of conscripts do not meet the army's fitness requirements); (ii) structure and organization of youth sport; (iii) heighten global competition in sport and the competitiveness of Russian athletes; and (iv) innovation and technological backwardness of sport (i.e., lack of modern equipment and information system management) (Council of Ministers, 2009). This strategy both builds on and complements the Federal Programme for the Development of Physical Culture and Sport (2006–2015). The current sports policy has been formalized within the Federal Law, a national strategy for sport, and a range of Council of Ministers' decrees and other policies and guidelines, supported by state guarantees for implementation. The national strategy pursues seven comprehensive objectives, one of which is enhancing the global competitiveness of Russian sport through improvements of the system for sport reserve preparation. The sport reserve includes all young people within the formal youth elite sport development system as depicted in Figure 5.1 below. There are also specific objectives concerning the welfare of children and those working in the sport system.

Clearly, the development of elite youth sport policy has been framed as a complex and long-term process, the successful implementation of which is contingent on a range of internal and external factors. This process should be considered as complementary to a wider concern about the future of Russian youth that was reflected in youth policies of the country. Efforts to address the challenges facing Russian youth, as a result of the dissolution of the Soviet Union and globalization, began in the 1990s under president Yeltsin. The first concerted response came in the form of the national programme 'Youth of Russia 2001–2005', which established a set of ambitious objectives, which on the most part were not met due to inadequate funding and clashing implementation priorities. This programme was replaced by the 'Youth of Russia 2006–2010', which was much more streamlined and requested a 25-fold increase in funding compared to its predecessor. The programme identified three priorities, all of which bear close links with sport including 'informing the youth of potential developments in society and drawing them into social practice', 'fostering youth's innovative activity' and 'integrating into society youths who are in difficult living situations'.

The role of the state in both the youth policy and sport programmes for young people was critical, and as Blum (2006) commented, 'under Russian President Vladimir Putin, [there] has been an increasingly large-scale, systematic campaign to address all issues pertaining to youth. As such, youth policy under Putin represents part of a larger attempt to anchor state and society within a stable institutional framework marked by a mixture of delegation and centralization' (p.107). The political and legislative roles of the state in shaping youth policy in general and sport in particular have been complemented by its economic role expressed in the notion of 'national champions'. This idea is attributed to Putin, which he floated in his 1997 MSc dissertation from the University of St. Petersburg on 'Strategic Planning of the Reproduction of the Resource Base'. According to Jokisipilä, (2011, p.8) the idea of 'national champions' meant that 'large corporations in strategic industries crucial to national security should, as well as seeking to make profits, advance the interests of the nation. With close links to and strong support from the state, these companies would then become big enough to compete with privately-owned multinational companies, turning them into custodians of state interests in international trade'. As illustrated below, there have been several good examples to illustrate the workings of 'national champions' in practice. Nonetheless, the state funding for youth elite sport remains critical: compared to 2013, the expenditures for sport schools in 2014 increased by 18.3 per cent, on staff salaries by 24.4 per cent, on participation in competitions by 45 per cent and on maintenance of sport facilities by 15 per cent (RMS, 2014a). The budget of the Ministry of Sport for 2014, 2015 and 2016 has increased year on year and averages some US$1.130 billion/year, some 70 per cent of which go to elite sport.

The tangible result of the implementation of the first stage (2009–15) of the national youth elite sport strategy envisages that 30 per cent of children aged 6–15 will be involved in specialized sport schools including increasing the number of those specializing in winter sports to 380,000. The second stage (2015–20) projects that the percentage of children in sport schools rises to 40 per cent, of which 430,000 will be in winter sports.

Wide versus narrow selection of youth sports promotion

An overview of youth sports development in Russia suggests that more than 50 sports have been promoted through a well-structured system of schools, training and competition. As a result, in 2012, 19 per cent of all children aged 6–15 were involved in specialized sport schools, and in 2015, some 8,500 junior athletes were selected for the different Russian national squads, and further 10,500 athletes were prepared for the national junior squads. It is envisaged that the percentage of children involved in sport schools will reach 36 per cent in 2016 and 40 per cent by 2020, of which 22 per cent are expected to become a 'Merited Master of Sport', meaning they have won European and World titles in their sport.

Development across different sports has not been equal. Owing to Russia's hosting of the 2018 World Cup, football has benefited from a dedicated long-term development programme (2008–2015). In addition to significant improvements of facilities (between 2009–2012 on average 80 new football pitches were built each year), 3,021 sport schools coaches have upgraded their qualification in line with UEFA's standards and there are some 352,000 registered young football players and over 10,000 full-time coaches. The state-owned Aeroflot has become the major commercial partners of football, while Gazprom, another major state-owned company, sponsors virtually all major football tournaments in Russia.

Figure skating is promoted by the Russian Figure Skating Federation, which is a network of some 120 regional and local federations, 1,136 coaches at all levels and about 90,000 registered figure skaters. The 2014 Sochi Winter Olympic and Paralympic Games provided a significant boost for this sport including $US2.5 million in subsidies for sport development to some 200 skating centres around the country. Generally, figure skating has been in good financial shape not least because of the support of its main commercial partner Rostelecom, the largest state-owned communication provider. This has allowed the Federation to better address a number of long-standing management problems concerning raising its overall professionalism and staff qualifications. A great deal of effort was also exerted in improving work on the regional level and in particular with regional governors in addressing the lack of facilities. The impact of the 2014 Sochi Games was most pronounced in six core areas of the organization. First, the Games helped change the image of the organization from one of underperforming in Vancouver 2010 to a very successful sport winning four Olympic medals including two gold. The changing image of the sport was facilitated by a large measure by the extensive Olympic broadcast where figure skating drew the highest audience ratings displacing even ice hockey as a number one TV sport. Second, the Games have reignited public interest in figure skating where the number of participants grew by 400 per cent. Third, new state-of-the-art infrastructure was built in the host city and beyond, which prompted the Federation to turn its attention to enhancing staff qualifications and management practices. Fourth, the combination of new infrastructure and improved organizational structures and processes has stimulated competition between different regional figure skating centres within the country as well as the internal migration of managers and coaches. Fifth, another important consequence of improved facilities was the introduction of new standards of professional qualifications and management practices for all staff – from the ice makers to coaches and venue managers. Finally, organizational expertise gathered during the run-up and throughout the Games has been codified into various know-how forms, and in particular in the field of technical and event management, which have been widely shared with the national figure skating community (Girginov & Peshin, 2015).

Talent identification and development

As the previous sections demonstrated, Russian talent identification and development system should be considered as an inseparable part of the national system for physical culture and sport. The sport training system represents a long-term, continuous and specially organized and managed process, which is underpinned by well-defined methodological and pedagogical principles and practices. There are three levels of management of the system including federal, regional and municipal. The general model for the preparation of the sporting reserves is depicted in Figure 5.1. It includes three main components: (i) regional clusters of four basic delivery units (Olympic Reserve Schools (UOR), Centres for Sport Preparation (CSP), Centres for Olympic Preparation (COP) and Specialized Children-Youth Sport Schools, (SDUS), infrastructure and chief coach in each sport; (ii) Federal Centre for the Preparation of Sporting Reserves (FCPSR), Federal UOR, related infrastructure and chief coach in each sport; and (iii) Centre for Preparation of National Squads. Athletes with prospects for development move from the regional cluster to the federal level and those with talent progress to the national squads.

The FCPSR was established in 2011 and replaced its predecessor 'The State School for Higher Sport Mastery – Centre for Preparation of National Junior, Youth Squads of Russia' created in 1998. It is the main state partner in developing national elite youth sport policy and strategies for its implementation. It also provides coordination between different centres and organizes various federal sport competitions.

As Figure 5.1 shows, the Russian youth elite sport system is based on a wide network of schools including 2,239 specialized sport schools that have been set up in various educational establishments. A further 2,790 sport schools exist within different sport organizations such as sport clubs and societies. However, all specialized sport schools must follow well-defined

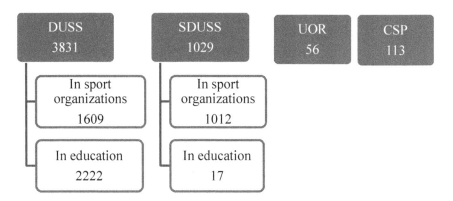

Figure 5.1 Structure of youth elite sport system in Russia DUSS (Children-Junior Sport Schools); SDUSS (Specialized Children-Junior Sport Schools), UOR (School Olympic Reserves), CSP (Centres for Sport Preparation)

methodological requirements regulating their structure, management, educational and sporting processes. These requirements are reviewed on a regular basis by the Ministry of Sport and in their current form are codified in a 135-page-long document (RMS, 2014b). The typical management structure of a DUS (Children-Youth Sport School) includes 33 functional positions ranging from the director to the heads of sciences, education, a psychologist, doctor, nurse and nutritionist, lawyer, porters, and others. This, as well as some other documents, regulates the relationship between DUS and other agencies as well as staff development and remuneration, informational and resource issues, and control procedures. This makes DUS a self-contained system capable of planning and implementing various sports programmes, of participating in competitions and self-managing itself. In this regard, the Russian model of youth elite sport differs from the SPLISS's nine pillars model (De Bosscher et al., 2006), where various factors responsible for success exist independently and are not clearly integrated within a single organizational unit. Table 5.1 shows the main methodological processes and related core activities designed to ensure the smooth functioning of the system for elite youth sport.

The Russian model of talent identification and development includes five interrelated stages, which along with the main structural characteristics of the system are shown in Tables 5.2 and 5.3. There are federal standards for young athletes' preparation for each sport, which clearly determine the minimal age for entering different stages of the sport model, the relationship between general, specific and technical physical training and the tactical-theoretical preparation and participation in competitions.

It is important to note that there are clear criteria for monitoring and evaluation at each stage of the model concerning the progress of individual athletes, coaches and administrators. Recently, a great deal of work has

Table 5.1 Methodological recommendations underpinning the system for youth sport preparation

Main processes	Core activities
Organisation and management	Planning, talent identification and development of individual characteristics/qualities
Delivering training and competition	Physical education, planning and implementing competition and sporting calendar at all levels
Implementing educational programmes	Physical education, developing knowledge and skill base needed to progress in sport, developing healthy way of life
Analysis, correction and improvement of sport training	Developing scientific methodologies for monitoring and evaluation of athletes development and performances
Medical services, recovery, rehabilitation and nutrition	Delivering medical examinations, developing individual rehabilitation and nutritional programmes
Resources, staff, equipment and financial services provision	Planning, budgeting, financing, provision of equipment and staff development programmes

Table 5.2 Russian model of talent identification and development

Stages of sport preparation	Stage duration	Delivery organisation	Optimum group size recommended	Maximum group size allowed	Maximum number of training hours[1]/week
Sporting mastery	Contingent on personal achievements	POP, CSP	1–3	8	32
Improving sporting mastery	Contingent on personal achievements	SDUS, PEO, CSP	4–8	10	24
Training up to 5 years	Further specialization	DUS, SDUS	8–10	12	18
	Early specialization		10–12	14	12
Initial preparation up to 3 years	Over one year	Sport centres, DUS, SS	12–14	20	8
	Up to one year		14–16	25	6
Physical activity and health	No limit	Any licensed provider	15–20	30	6

Source: RMS, (2014b)

Note: [1] This is an academic hour of 45 minutes

Table 5.3 Structural characteristics of the system of Olympic reserve preparation (2014)

Unit Olympic reserve	No	Coaches No	Children No	Total annual Expenditures $US	Cost per child $US
DUS					
6–15 years old	4,835	68,566	3,171,523	1,552,360	479
UOR	56	1,143	12,248	938,590	7,663
COP	171	3,629	36,556	226,057	6,184

Source: Data compiled from (RMS, 2014a)

been extended to improve the data management, scientific and communication services of the system by establishing an all-Russian internet portal 'Sporting Reserves of Russia' (www.sport-rezerv.ru/). Concerted efforts have also been exerted to streamline the work at regional level by creating a cluster model of management of the sporting reserves by more effectively coordinating the strategies of public, voluntary and commercial providers. For example, in addition to their pedagogical and sporting activities, specialized sport school also provide paid services to the general public. The revenue of those services has increased by 43 per cent in 2014 compared to 2013, which indicates that these units have become more than educational establishments and are capable of running commercial operations as well.

The elite youth sport system is complemented by the United Sports Classification System of Russia, which was inherited from the USSR system established in 1935. This system defines the physical education requirements for athletes and includes test standards, principles and conditions that allow athletes to be ranked in all Olympic sports. Since the 1970s those ranks have become very important as they determine not only the standard of individual athletes, but serve also as a benchmark of quality of different schools and their staff. In descending order the rank system includes Merited Master of Sport of Russia (international champion), Master of Sport of Russia (international champion), Master of Sport of Russia (national champion), Candidate for Master of Sport (nationally ranked player), First-Class Sportsman (regional champion), Second Class Sportsman (state champion), Third-Class Sportsman (city champion), First Class Junior Sportsman, Second- Class Junior Sportsman and Third-Class Junior Sportsman. What is more, holders of the top three ranks who work as coaches get a pay rise ranging from 20 to100 per cent from the basic salary.

From a macro point of view, the United Sport Classification System is a systematic development tool used to organize multi-year training of young athletes who enter into schools of physical preparation with the objective of identifying and developing those who had potential through their careers to compete at national and international levels. As the talent development model in Table 5.2 suggests, adopting a multi-year approach to training has enabled these schools to thoroughly develop a general foundation of trainability and general physical preparation. General physical preparation is an essential condition to prime the adaptive response for future specific physical preparation and intensive unidirectional loads. The methodological recommendations provided in Table 5.2 apply to all sports but school directors and coaches are allowed to exercise some discretion in determining individual training programmes depending on an athlete's health, ability and progress.

Competition structure of elite youth sport and coach development

A comprehensive and encompassing competition structure is at the heart of the youth elite sport system. This structure includes five all-Russian year-round competitions called 'Spartakiade' named after the classical Roman figure of Spartacus, the leader of slave rebellion. Spartakides have a long tradition in Russia (or the former Soviet Union) dating back to 1923 when the first edition took place in Moscow. The five Spartakiades for pupils and students are as follows: Spartakiade of School Students; Spartakiade for Young Athletes; Spartakiade of Specialized Sporting Schools, Winter Sparttakiade of Sport Schools and Universiade (for university students). These are very prestigious events and achieving success at any level of competition provides recognition, legitimacy and further support. The main goal of the Spartakiades is to promote sport, to enhance the level of physical preparation of sporting reserves as well as to review the performance of different sport organizations. There are three levels of competition including municipal, federal region and national finals, where the successful teams progress to the next level. For example, the second stage of the third Summer Spartakiade of Specialized Sport Schools in 2014 attracted 10,996 participants from 82 regions, including 8,741 athletes (5,035 boys and 3,706 girls) and 2,255 coaches and administrators. The participation of different organizations was as follows 898 DUS (15%), 2,464 SDUSS (38%), 275 CSP (4%), 482 UOP (8%) and 2,232 others (35%) (RMS, 2014c).

The first Winter Spartakiade of Sport Schools for 10–15 year-olds was held in 2015 and included competitions in 12 sports (biathlon, curling, speed skating, short-trek, ski biathlon, cross-skiing, ski jump, skeleton, snowboard, figure skating, freestyle and ice hockey). Some 1,317 athletes from 178 sport schools representing 48 regions of the country and 373 coaches took part (RMS, 2015).

The year-round competition system has been largely responsible for preparing the sporting reserve that in 2015 includes some 8,248 athletes who were selected by various national squads. Some 17,849 young athletes took part in international sport competitions in 2014 and 7,713 of them have won first place, 5,060, second and 4,767 – third place.

Table 5.4 Coaching staff in Russian elite youth sport (2014)

Organization	Coaches	Full time coaches	Qualification category		Merited Coach of Russia
			Total	Higher and First	
DUS	76,500	44.4 (66%)	26,100 (59%)	21,500	0,910
SDUS	25,600	20.4 (80%)	14,200 (70%)	12,500	1,600
UOR	1,100	0.6 (54%)	4,900 (82%)	4,400	0,140
Total	99,300	68.5 (69%)	42,700 (62%)	36,100	3,300

Source: RMS (2015)

Table 5.5 Functional positions and qualifications of staff working in youth sport organisations

Functional position	Total No	Full time staff	Staff with professional education No/%	
			Total	Staff with sport education
Director	5,117	5,104	5,042 (99%)	3,601 (71%)
Deputy Director	9,810	9,667	9,412 (97%)	4,328 (45%)
Instructor	6,905	6,281	5,981 (95%)	3,778 (60%)
Coach-teacher Total	99,250	68,566	66,146 (96%)	51,756 (75%)
SDUS	25,559	20,350	19,826 (97%)	16,992 (83%)
UOP	1,143	598	594 (99%)	547 (92%)

Source: RMS (2015)

Sport coaching is a recognized profession in Russia and is provided by 25 State Universities specializing in physical culture and sport and 48 Universities with sport faculties through full-time four years courses. In addition to that, the FCPSR trains sport instructors who work at the lower level of the system. Tables 5.4 and 5.5 show the number of qualified coaches working at different organizations dealing with youth elite sport development.

The working conditions of sport coaches are regulated by federal standards, which are reviewed on a regular basis by the Ministry of Sport. There are four coaching qualifications including second, first and higher category and Olympus, which are awarded after a rigorous process overseen by the Ministry of Sport.

Future of elite youth sport

Russia's elite youth sport policy has been shaped by a combination of historical factors and current state interventions. Two policy documents have been particularly influential including the 'Programme for the Development of Physical Culture and Sport in the Russian Federation

2006–2015' (Council of Ministers, 2006) and the 'Strategy for the development of Physical Culture in Sport in Russian Federation until 2020' (Council of Ministers, 2009). The National Programme for Physical Culture and Sport makes a convincing policy case for a national strategy whereas the Strategy spells out in sufficient details the main activities and resources as well as sets the main milestones in the implementation of the Programme.

Further to the four principle concerns that provide a rationale for the state intervention in sport (i.e., health and welfare of the population, structure and organization of youth sport; heighten global competition in sport and the competitiveness of Russian athletes, and innovation and technological backwardness of sport), the Strategy addresses a wider governance issue. It is concerned with the limitations of the existing legal and normative framework regulating the partnership between the public and private sector in providing sport services to the population. As it stands, the framework hampers forming effective partnerships in sport. The state subsidies for specialized sport schools amount only to between 30 and 60 per cent of their overall budget, which has urged them to look for alternative sources of revenue such as commercial sponsorship and provision of services.

The overall aim of the Strategy is to create the political, economic and normative conditions that provide opportunities for people to lead a healthy way of life by offering easy access to sporting infrastructure and services, as well as to increase the competitiveness of Russian sport internationally. The principle outcome of the Strategy is to ensure the long-term sustainable future of physical culture and sport for Russians through innovation in sporting infrastructure, and the provision of financial, human and promotional support. Modernization of the physical education and sport system for all age groups is at the heart of the Strategy.

The 'Programme for the Development of Physical Culture and Sport in the Russian Federation 2006–2015' aims to create the conditions for enhancing people's health through the development of sporting infrastructure, promotion of equal opportunities and accessibility for all, and the inclusion of various target groups in regular physical activities. Both the National Programme and the Strategy provide not only the direction of elite youth sport, but the normative (i.e., methodological principles, targets and criteria for evaluation) framework for the design and delivery of sport programmes and services at the various stages of the youth elite sport system. Despite current challenging economic climate in Russia, the National Programme has attracted a record investment of 106 billion Rubbles ($US 1.7 billion). Reportedly, the stated objective of increasing the percentage of regular sport participants to 25 per cent and for school-aged young people in particular to 32 per cent by 2012 has been achieved (RMS, 2013), but there is a widespread scepticism about the validity of these figures.

Increasingly, the social and economic effectiveness of the Programme has been tied to health and economic outcomes and evaluation criteria. The 'number of working days lost due to any reason' and the 'expenditures on physical culture and sport per capita' have now been established as objective indicators for the effectiveness of the sport system. The Programme is expected to make a significant contribution to reducing state expenditures on medical care and compensations paid due to days taken in sickness (absenteeism). It envisages that by the end of 2015 the average number of days due to temporary absenteeism from work will be reduced by 15 per cent, while the overall economic effect of the Programme is projected to make 13 billion Rubbles (US$210m) of savings to the economy. The main policy rationale behind the Programme concerned with the health of the population and the perceived contribution of sport to work productivity bears similarities with sport participation policies across the world (Nicholson, Hoye and Houlihan, 2011). The expected wider contributions of sport should be seen as an integral part of the process of talent identification and a necessary precondition for enhancing the role of elite youth sport in furthering the competitiveness of Russian sport globally. Hong To, Smolianov and Semotiuk (2013) noted the success of Russia at the 2010 Youth Olympic Games where she entered 96 athletes who won 43 medals of which 18 gold, and saw this as a sign of more successful performances in the future.

The relationship between the Programme's overall objectives and elite youth sport in particular is evidenced by the specific national targets, which envisage increasing: (i) the number of school children and university students taking part in sport from 35% to 60% by 2015 and to 80% by 2020; (ii) the number of people practicing sport within sport organizations (e.g., clubs, centres) from 22% to 35% by 2015 and to 50% by 2020; (iii) the frequency of regular participation from 6 to 8/h week by 2015 with at least 2–3 times/ week, and to 12 h/week in 3–4 times/week depending on the age group; (iv) the number of professional paid physical culture and sport staff from 295,600 to 320,000 by 2015 and to 360,000 by 2020; and (v) the capacity of sport facilities to allow simultaneous participation of people from 22.7% to 30% by 2015 and to 48% by 2020 (Council of Ministers, 2006).

One of the three key objectives of the Ministry of Sport for 2015 was to improve the system for preparation of sporting reserves and Russia's performance at the 2016 Olympic Games in Rio de Janeiro. To that end, it is projected to grow the number of school children and university students playing sport by 3%, from 57% in 2014 to 60% in 2015. Increased youth sport participation has been closely linked to improvements in two critical areas of the system including increasing the average salary of the specialists in educational establishments working with sporting reserves and expanding the units where education and training takes place. For example, sport specialists will get a pay rise in relation to the average salary of the region by 80 per cent in 2014 and 85 per cent in 2015. A further 40 new sections will also be opened in existing DUS, SDUS and COP by the end of 2015, and the share of educational and other institutions providing services to the sporting reserves, as prescribed by the federal standards, will increase by 20 per cent to 70 per cent. These structural developments, together with other measures, will lead to increasing the number of key new positions in institutions dealing with sporting reserves by 1,312, thus bringing the total staff working in this area to 45,274.

The main challenge for the Programme and related elite youth sport model remains its implementation because it rather uncritically assumes a causal relationship between improved conditions for participation and linear growth of the number of young people regularly playing sport and excelling in it. Underplayed have been a range of social and economic factors such as changing lifestyles and value systems, structural and economic inequalities and demographic changes which impact on children and young people's involvement in sport. These changes and the decline in elite athletes' performances have been particularly pronounced in sports where Russian has been traditionally a world leading power in sports such as gymnastics, weightlifting, wrestling and athletics.

A related challenge to the future of elite youth sport is the cumbersome governance structure of sport in Russia. It represents a mix of state-dominated central institutions, supported by a network of rather weak voluntary sport federations and clubs and an emerging private sector with an interest not only in sport as entertainment or personal services, but also as a social provision as well (Lapina, 2005). At present, there are eight state executive bodies with exclusive responsibilities for elite youth sport including the RMS, the Department for Physical Culture and Sport, the State Committee for Physical Culture and Sport, the Sport Committee, the Bureau for Physical Culture and Sport, the Agency for Physical Culture and Sport, the Sport Agency and the Agency for Sport and Physical Culture. The multiplicity of stakeholders creates difficulties in coordinating their work as well as intra-institutional competition, which could be detrimental to the success of national strategy.

The leadership of elite youth sport policy lies with the Ministry of Sport, but the operational management has been tasked to a separate state agency – a Programme Directorate, which is contracted by the Government to deliver the programme. It could be argued that the typical mode of governance within the three tier structure of youth elite sport has been framework regulation. Trieb, Bähr and Falkner (2007) describe framework regulation as a policy instrument that relies on binding law but offers participants more leeway in implementation. The methodological recommendations of the Ministry of Sport clearly allow regions and municipalities to determine their own specific objectives that will be reflective of local contexts.

A further issue concerns the capacity of key structural units responsible for elite youth sport development to deliver effective services. The sport clubs network in Russia is underdeveloped and understaffed, with an average number of seven staff per club. From a policy intervention point of view the school system is comprehensive, compulsory and well legislated for. Conversely, legitimate concerns exist about the quality of education and specialist training provided by some educational institutions which undermines the main premise of the Russian elite youth sport delivery system.

The main priorities of the Ministry of Sport for the 2016–18 period revolve around implementing innovative architectural designs for enhancing the infrastructure for optimal participation in sport; upgrading the network of regional sport training centres for sporting reserves in different sports in different climate zones including building at least two regional centres in rowing and tennis in the Olympic city of Sochi.

The Russian elite youth sport model is a comprehensive and complex educational and management system that has remained anchored in sound pedagogical and methodological principles established over 100 years ago. At its heart is the harmonious development of the person and their ability to excel in sport. Russia's hosting of several mega sport events such as the 2014 Winter Olympics and the 2018 World Cup in football has provided a further boost to elite youth sport. Since 1991, the model has undergone significant transformations that have allowed it a greater degree of autonomy from the state, while enabling it at the same time to become more fully integrated in the changing political and economic conditions in the country.

Note

1 The US$ equivalent of all figures in this chapter is based on an exchange rate of 1US$=62 Rubbles as of the end of October 2015.

References

Blum, D. (2006). Current Trends in Russian Youth Policy, *PONARS Policy Memo*, No. 384

Council of Ministers, (2006). ПРАВИТЕЛЬСТВО РОССИЙСКОЙ ФЕДЕРАЦИИ. ПОСТАНОВЛЕНИЕ от 11 января 2006 г. N 7 О ФЕДЕРАЛЬНОЙ ЦЕЛЕВОЙ ПРОГРАММЕ "РАЗВИТИЕ ФИЗИЧЕСКОЙ КУЛЬТУРЫ И СПОРТА В РОССИЙСКОЙ ФЕДЕРАЦИИ НА 2006–2015 ГОДЫ". (Federal Programme – Development of Physical Culture and Sport in Russia). CM:Moscow.

Council of Ministers, (2009). Правительства Российской Федерации (2009).(от 7 августа 2009 г. № 1101-р). С Т Р А Т Е Г И Я развития физической культуры и спорта в Российской Федерации на период до 2020 года. (Strategy for the Development of Physical Culture and Sport in Russia until 2020): CM: Moscow.

De Bosscher, V., De Knop, P., Van Bottenburg, M. & Shibli, S. (2006). A Conceptual Framework for Analysing Sports policy factors Leading to International Sporting Success, *European Sport Management Quarterly*, 6(2), 185–215.

Dorfman, L. (2000). Research on gifted children and adolescents in Russia: A chronicle of theoretical and empirical development, *Roeper Review*, 22(2), 123–131.

Girginov, V. (1998). Capitalist Philosophy and Communist Practice: The Transformation of Eastern European Sport and the International Olympic Committee, *Culture, Sport, Society*, 1(1), 118–149.

Girginov, V. (2004). Nomen, In Girginov, V. and M. Collins (Eds), *Sport in Eastern European Society: Past and Present*, London: Taylor & Francis (*The International Journal of the History of Sport*, 21(5), 690–709.

Girginov, V., & Peshin, N. (2015). UK and Russian National Governing Bodies of Sport Leveraging of the London 2012 and Sochi 2014 Olympics for Building Organisational Capacities. *Report*. Lausanne: IOC.

Hong To, W., Smolianov, P., & Semotiuk, D. (2013). Comparative High Performance Sports Models. In P. Sotiriadou & V. De Bosscher. *Managing High Performance Sport* (pp.65–86). London: Routledge.

Jokisipilä, M. (2011). World Champions Bred by National Champions: the Role of State-Owned Corporate Giants in Russian Sports. *Russian Analytical Digest*, 95(6) April.

Lapina, J. (Ed.). (2005). The Social Policy of Businesses in Russian Regions: Moscow (Лапина Н.Ю.. Отв.ред. (2005). СОЦИАЛЬНАЯ ПОЛИТИКА БИЗНЕСА В РОССИЙСКИХ РЕГИОНАХ. Сб. науч. тр. / Центр науч.-информ. исслед. глобал. и регион. пробл. Отд. глобал. пробл.; МОСКВА, (Сер. "Федерализм, региональное управление и местное самоуправление").

Milshtein, O. (2001). Olimpioniki (Olympionics). Moscow: Terra-Sport.

Nicholson, M., Hoye, R., & Houlihan, B. (Eds). (2011). *Participation in Sport: International Sport Policy Perspective*. London: Routledge.

Pautova, A. (2009). Одареность в Росии: феноменов сквозь прицел социологических опросов (Giftedness in Russia: a phenomenon through the prism of sociological enquiry). Психологическая наука и образование, 4, 50–60.

Platonov, N. (2010). *High Performance Sport and Preparation of National Team for the Olympic Games*. Moscow: Soviet Sport (In Russian).

Riordan, J. (1999). The Impact of Communism on Sport', in J. Riordan and A. Kruger (eds), *The International Politics of Sport in the Twentieth Century*. London: Routledge.

Riordan, J. (1980). *Sport in Soviet Society: Development of Sport and Physical Education in Russia and the USSR*. London: Cambridge University Press.

RMS. (2013). *Annual Sport Report* (in Russian). Moscow: RMS.

RMS. (2014a). *Information about the System of Preparation of Sporting Reserves in 2014* (in Russian). RMS: Moscow.

RMS. (2014b). *Methodological Recommendations for the Organisation of Sport Training in Russia* (In Russian). RMS: Moscow.

RMS. (2014c). *Report on the 3rd All Russian Spartakiade* (in Russian). RMS: Moscow.

RMS. (2015). *Report on the 1st All Russian School Winter Spartakiade* (in Russian). RMS: Moscow.

Trieb, O., Bähr, H. and Falkner, G. (2007). Modes of governance: towards a conceptual clarification. *Journal of European Public Policy*, 14(1): 1–20.

Chapter 6

Norway

Elsa Kristiansen

Introduction

In 1933, Dano-Norwegian author Axel Sandemose wrote *A Fugitive Crosses His Tracks* where he introduced the "Law of Jante" (Janteloven). The first rule of this literary construct is "you're not to think you are anything special" and, in short, the ten rules reflect dominant social attitudes which may limit the opportunities for individual success in the Scandinavian countries. The mentality *don't think that you are any better than us* is combined in Norway with an egalitarian nature and social democratic ideals.[1] In 2009, the President of the Norwegian Olympic and Paralympic Committee and Confederation of Sports (NIF) tried to challenge this dominant culture when she publicly stated that the best athletes may become victims of the Law of Jante in Norway (A. Andersen, 2009). According to her, you are at risk of being bullied if you stand out as exceptional and talented, and this creates a challenge for coaches, managers and naturally parents in addition to athletes. Successful athletes also address this concept on occasions, such as Gunn Rita Dahle Flesjaa, a successful female mountain biker, who contrasted the Norwegian talent development system with that found in the United States where "they use the best as role models. Being [the] best in Norway could be an obstacle to talent development, as the best is often unnoticed rather than emphasized" (quoted in A. Andersen, 2009, 9).

In addition to this cultural sentiment, at the political level, talent development is structured according to the regulations for children's sport established by NIF (Kristiansen, 2014; Skirstad, Waddington, & Safvenbom, 2012). To have regulations that prohibit sport-specific specialization to protect young athletes is not unique to Norway as they are common in the Nordic countries (S. S. Andersen, Bjørndal, & Rognlan, 2015). NIF has required and expects that all the national federations implement and show commitment to child protection measures (NIF, 2015a). The rules specify when a child may compete locally (age six), when lists of results, tables and rankings may be published and when a young person can compete regionally (age 11), and nationally and internationally (age 13). Hence, sport federations cannot formalize a talent identification and development strategy before the age of 13 (S. S. Andersen et al., 2015). Coaches coming to Norway in order to train our elite athletes are often critical of the Norwegian system. One such critic was ski jumping head coach Aleksander Stöckl, from Austria, who argued that the Norwegian equality model might result in really talented stars never getting the appropriate training, as they keep doing the same as everyone else (Sundt, 2013). With this as context, this chapter will explore the Norwegian situation with a focus on figure skating (early peak performance sport), football (commercial team sport) and cross-country skiing (major national sports with impressive Olympic record).[2]

The national sport system for talent development in Norway

NIF serves as an umbrella organization for elite sport and sport for all. Of the country's five million residents, there are two million members in NIF. There are 54 national sport federations responsible for specific sports in the country and linked to the international federations, 19 District Sport Associations (one for each county) and 11,800 sports clubs (NIF, 2014). NIF use 13 per cent of the total budget from the National Lottery to support sport clubs for children (6–12 years) and adolescents (13–19 years) to increase sport activity, participation and volunteerism. In 2015, the Local Activity Funds were NOK 295,2 million (NIF, 2015c). In short, the government builds and ensures public access to sport facilities, while it is the sport organizations that are responsible for the different talent development initiatives (Ronglan, 2014).

Besides the focus on mass sport, Norway is also a successful Olympic country due to the prominence of winter sports. The Olympic Top Sport Program [hereafter *Olympiatoppen*] has overall responsibility for the development of elite athletes in the country and is generally considered to be an effective talent development agency since its establishment in 1989 (S. S. Andersen, 2009; Augestad, Bergsgard, & Hansen, 2006; Goksøyr & Hanstad, 2012). "The Norwegian model," the collective expertise and shared insight from a wide range of sports through cooperation between Olympiatoppen and the different individual sport federations, has produced consistently good results in the Olympic Games (top 8–10), and it is argued this may give Norwegian coaches and athletes a competitive advantage regarding medals (Goksøyr & Hanstad, 2012). If you are among the top 8–12 in the world in your sport, you might be the recipient of an Olympiatoppen financial scholarship (A, B and U)[3] for established and/or talented performers. In addition to funding, Olympiatoppen also provides medical support to all national teams, and operates the well-equipped national training center. The primary criterion for the allocation of Olympiatoppen's resources is *ranking*, not age, and Olympiatoppen has no specific programs aimed at young people. This situation is due to the fact Olympiatoppen has neither the capacity nor the money to focus on the younger athletes (Kristiansen & Houlihan, 2015).

For the younger athletes, the system is based on a combination of the individual federations, local community-based multi-sports clubs, and a high number of volunteer coaches (Ronglan, 2014), in addition to an increasing number of sport schools (Kristiansen & Houlihan, 2015). As the federations are in charge of both mass sport and elite sport, the youth elite athletes tend to be less well funded – as they fall between elite and mass sport. From the above, it is not surprising that talent development tends to take place among the local and semi-professional clubs in Norway, which reflects the intention of NIF to keep young athletes at home as long as possible. This indicates a model that increasingly relies on strengthening the established achievement communities which rely on systematic exchange of information and expertise at the regional level and local competence and facilitation (NIF, 2015b). The main income for the clubs (run by parents and volunteers) are membership fees and activities, with the public sector providing a third or a quarter of total club income (Ibsen & Seippel, 2010). The importance of local clubs to elite development is further increased by NIF's decision to delegate responsibility for coach education and talent development to the different federations, which then depend on a solid club system in order to fulfill its obligations. For example, in handball, there are no systematic differences between elite and non-elite clubs and all athletes train and compete within the same overall organizational framework (Bjørndal, Rognlan, & Andersen, 2015). These arrangements reflect the chief characteristics of the sport movement of autonomy and self-regulation (Bergsgard & Norberg, 2010). According to Bjørndal and colleagues (2015), the Norwegian system can best be described as heterarchial (rather than hierarchical), due to the complex network of autonomous actors (e.g. the clubs, the sport schools and the initiatives provided by the sport organization) that interact based on their own aims and objectives.

Youth sport policy in Norway

Sport policy is formulated and administered by the Department of Sports Policy within the Ministry of Culture in Norway (Bergsgard, 2007) and by NIF. In order to create a more effective focus on the youth, a youth campaign called the "youth promotion" (*Ungdomsløftet* in Norwegian), designed to increase the promotion and recruitment of more young athletes, leaders and coaches, started in 2011 as a ten-year plan (NIF, 2013). The campaign has a broad focus and is intended to help Olympiatoppen and the national sport federations ensure that the future elite athletes receive a comprehensive follow-up and that as many as possible stay in sport. In addition, NIF has adopted the concept of *regional* elite teams, which seems to work well for some sports and regions. A recent report on the current Norwegian elite sport policy also pointed out that the hosting of the 2016 Youth Olympic Games (YOG) in Lillehammer is a "milestone for NIF's work with Youth Promotion in Norwegian sports. The Commission believes this event gives Norwegian sports a unique opportunity to work purposefully to develop tomorrow's young athletes, coaches, leaders and volunteers" (Tvedt et al., 2013, p. 112).

In addition to being responsible for their own development system and allocation of resources (Kristiansen & Houlihan, 2015), the national sport federations are supposed to "stimulate training and competition environments for young people with special abilities and athletic ambitions" (NIF, 2015b, p. 24). Therefore, the federations are also the ones that set the criteria for the selection of athletes to send to international youth competitions such as YOG (e.g., Kristiansen & Parent, 2014) and the European Youth Olympic Festival (EYOF) (Kristiansen, 2016). Federations' youth policy will determine the approach to this responsibility (this will be elaborated upon later under cross-country skiing). As a result, it might be argued that sport schools (which are a main actor in talent development for the 16–19 age group) together with the (best) clubs are the core units of the sports movement (S. S. Andersen et al., 2015; Bjørndal et al., 2015; Kristiansen & Houlihan, 2015). With these comments in mind, we will now turn to the three sports.

Three sports

As examples of elite youth sport in Norway, figure skating (early peak performance sport), football (commercial team sport) and cross-country skiing (major national sport) will be analysed. Table 6.1 provides a summary of the main characteristics of the three sports.

Figure skating

Of the three chosen sports, figure skating is the smallest one with approximately 300 participants (in 15 clubs) in Norway among the 8,000 members in the Norwegian Skating Association (NSF) (NSF, 2015b). The other sports in the NSF are speed skating, short track speed skating on ice and more recently inline and roller-skating. While Norway has always done well in speed skating with Olympic medalists in every decade, the country has had few international medal winners in figure skating. A notable exception is Sonja Henie (1912–1969), who, in the 1920s–30s, won three Olympic gold medals and 10 world championships – besides pursuing a film star career in Hollywood.

In order to make it as a figure skater – you need to start early (4–6 years old). The earlier you start organized figure skating the better; however, parents may perceive this as problematic due to elite sport for children

Table 6.1 Numbers and support system for figure skating, football and cross-country skiing

	Figure Skating	Football	Cross-country skiing
Members in the national federation	7,658 in Norwegian Skating Federation, 300 figure skaters	366,716 members in Norwegian Football Federation	179, 447 in Norwegian Ski Association
Clubs in Norway	15	1,776	1,020
Sport Schools	No offer for this sport	No exact number, but there are many schools (private, public also secondary schools) offering football	113 private, semi-private and state schools
Support from federation	Minimal for youth athletes, support when representing Norway, Sonja-Henie project	National teams from age group 15–19 for both genders	The first opportunity to be elected for national team is when youth reach 19 years old
Number of athletes in national teams	4 elite athletes and 6 development athletes	3 senior and 13 age group national teams	23 athletes in development teams
National Head Coach	None	Each team has its own coaching group	Extensive entourage for the different national team groups
Support from Olympiatoppen	Minimal, to qualify for Olympics be among 5 in the world. No individual scholarships*	None. No individual or team scholarships*	24 scholarships athletes (12 A, 7 B and 5 U scholarships)*

Sources: NSF, 2015; (NFF, 2014; NIF, 2013; NSF, 2015b; Skiforbundet, 2015) and interviews with representatives from the respective federations.

*Numbers from the 2015/2016 Season (Olympiatoppen, 2015b)

usually being considered inappropriate and a source of social stigma in Norway. In addition, limited access to an ice rink makes it hard to succeed – consequently, parents may have to use their own resources in order to pay for the necessary training hours. Given the social, financial and organizational constraints, it is not surprising Norway had only one qualified participant for the 2014 Sochi Olympic Winter Games, 50 years after the last one.

The story about Norway's 2014 Olympic contestant, Anne Line Gjersem, may serve as a good example of support and management of young figure skaters in Norway. As an identical twin, Anne Line and her sister have always trained and competed together. In 2006, the NSF together with Olympiatoppen started up the "Sonja Henie-project" (NTB, 2014), both (at that time) 12-year-old Anne Line and her sister Camilla were included. The Federation's goal for the project, which used the expertise and resources at Olympiatoppen and organized training camps for five to six athletes yearly, was one qualified Olympic participant. In order to achieve this goal, the athletes were given the opportunity for basic skills training three times a week at Olympiatoppen, plus weekly dancing classes (Gjersem, 2013). After three years of intensive training, Anne Line's results boosted the 2008–2009 season by winning medals for example at the 2009 EYOF. Due to lack of sports schools supporting figure skaters, Anne Line chose to move to Sweden for more intense training and competition. While the federation and Olympiatoppen have helped with resources and competence – the parents have paid for this commitment to figure skating. For ten years, the parents paid over NOK 200,000 yearly for Anne Line and twin sister Camilla to dance on skates, and according to the dad "It's worth it all" (Bugge, 2014).

As an early peak sport, figure skaters are very young compared to other sports, and generally, figure skaters who have not been successful at the national level by the time they reach their late teens will not be successful internationally (Cummins, 2007). For example, Gjersem practices between 800 and 1,000 hours yearly, the same as cross-country skiers who are ten years her senior. Besides encouraging more training at an earlier age, the NSF also has clearer goals of what they expect of the young athletes participating at international competitions. At the 2016 YOG at Lillehammer, the Federation's first officially stated goal was to have one athlete among the top 10 and, for the junior World Championship, to have a participant among the top 20 (NSF, 2011). In many ways, this clear goal contradicts what Olympiatoppen says about a competition like YOG – that it is a "learning process" (Kristiansen, 2016). Hence, in an updated document of the NSF's vision for the same competitions, the top 10 goal for YOG is replaced by "to have a participant in YOG," while the top 20 is kept for the junior World Championship (NSF, 2013a). The NSF adapts their policies, at least in the official documents.

In interviews, a need was identified for some sort of "general manager who could posit knowledge and expertise without any connections to the national team athletes" [International coach]. The coaches are a mixture of Norwegians and foreigners – from countries where figure skating has a more prominent status. For some of the foreign coaches, working within the Norwegian context is frustrating. As one of them outlined in an interview:

> They bring us to Norway because there is a lack of expertise here, but they do not adapt the acquired knowledge. The implementation phase fails, and ... as they do not implement what we suggest. [International coach]

Foreign coaches found the child protection restrictions on international competitions and training to reach the top, particularly challenging. The coaches' frustration and the limited success in elite development in figure skating may be due to the egalitarian mentality, which might explain why the clubs are reluctant to start early with ranking and differentiations among young athletes. The coexistence between elite sport and mass sport remains challenging in Norway – especially for early peak sports. It is argued that if Norway wants another Sonja Henie, it should accept that children aged 12–13 will need to train 25 hours a week (ABC News, 2007). Early specializing is problematic in figure skating, and it appears that committed parents are a necessity though not always a sufficient requirement for figure skating success.

Football

Football is the most popular sport in the world with approximately 265 million players (FIFA, 2007), and is also popular in Norway with 365,000 licensed players (Nygaard, 2012). Despite its popularity in terms of number of participants and sponsorship income, Norway is not a world or European leading nation in men's Football. In the August 2015 FIFA rankings, the Norwegian men's team was ranked 67 (an all-time low), though in October of the same year (and due to two wins), the national men's team rose in the ranking to 34 (FIFA, 2015b). The women's team is more successful (and medal winning) and was ranked number 10 (FIFA, 2015a) and has qualified for all recent major tournaments.

The Premier League for men in Norway is *Tippeligaen*; the equivalent for women is *Toppeserien*. In addition, there are a number of lower division football leagues and football for children and youths, which the 18 regions administer (Haavik, 2012b). Regional leagues for female players in Norway have existed since the 1970s, though the creation of a First Division in 1984 made the league system more structured. Besides the administration of the league, the regions maintain the link to the clubs and oversee coach education and player development. As can be seen, there is a decentralized pattern of talent development in football. In addition, and in contrast, to figure skating and cross-country skiing, football offers the opportunity and support for youth national team practice and competitions for the following age groups: for boys (15, 16, 17, 18, 19 under 21, and under 23), and for girls (15, 16, 17, 18, 19, 20 and under 23). While the importance of being selected is questioned due to lack of consistency over a period of time (Sæther, 2015), the literature also emphasizes that to be (s)elected early in your teens is far from decisive in the development towards becoming a successful senior player (Barreiros, Cote, & Fonseca, 2014).

The Norwegian Football Association (NFF) prioritizes coaching education for those dealing with the young players (NFF, 2012). While the children's regulations (Skirstad et al., 2012) are agreed upon in relation to age for different levels of competition, they are vague in relation to training and development. NFF's vision is "football excitement, opportunities and challenges for all!" (Haavik, 2009, 2). When Rosenberg (a major club for several decades) created a team for boys aged 15, media headlines were generated (Rake, 2007). The professional players are the ones who dominate and shape the debate in the press, and they do not understand why Norway cannot expect more from children 12 years old and up. In this debate a retired professional player, Riseth, has reminded us that "not everything needs to be fun... and we might expect discipline from the age of 10" (Rake, 2007, 10). Again, the mentality to protect children by always having fun is debated by the proponents of elite sport and early specialization.

NFF's "player development" must also be seen in relation to grassroots sport – a constant tension in Norwegian talent development due to funding. Grassroots football and elite football appear equally important to NFF, and supporting local clubs is seen as fundamental to their policy for grassroots football (NFF, 2012). That there exists a synergy between the two has recently been challenged as illusionary (Collins et al., 2012), and it has been argued that the development of elite sport frequently occurs at the expense of grassroots sport (Girginov & Collins, 2004). Girginov and Collins further proposed that lifelong sport participation and elite sport should not be two different policy areas. In light of their argument, the comprehensive cooperation agreement (Telenor Xtra -2012-2015) between the Federation and the Telenor Group (Norwegian multinational telecommunications company) is an interesting achievement. For NOK 50–60 millions, the Telenor Group agreed to sponsor the national female team, and co-sponsor the men's team, to be the main sponsor for the age groups teams (16–19) and to introduce a new after-school activity program for children and youth (Haavik, 2012a). In 2015, 102 clubs benefitted from this agreement, where qualified coaches in this nationwide program train young children – which means that the goal of including 100 clubs was reached (Sæteren, 2015). According to NFF, if children start with organized and high *quality* training at a younger age, there is a belief that Norway's international position (FIFA ranking and success in making play-offs for the men's team) will be improved. Besides the funding described above, parents spend their own resources (time and money) on supporting their children. The recent success of Martin Ødegaard with Real Madrid (signed on as a 16 year old in 2015 after only 23 games in the Norwegian Premier League), fuelled the debate concerning organized training for younger children. Martin has had a very untypical and public rise to fame, as he is a result of early-organized training supervised by his father, who also played professionally for the same Norwegian team years ago. He made Martin commit to additional drills training from a young age:

> He has trained an incredible amount of hours. Secondly, we have trained what I call the correct way. We never train without a football. We have spent an enormous amount of time working on his touch, getting away from pressure…When Martin was 8–9, we started doing drills where he worked on his vision.
>
> (C More, 2015)

The closeness to his father (who also landed a coaching contract with Real Madrid at the same time), and his coaching philosophy (you have to train a lot; you have to train well; and you have train the correct way) (C More, 2015), has exceeded what is "normal" in Norway. The *Ødegaard effect*, has been to create a new ethos based on the acknowledgment that Norway has the skilled footballers and the facilities to make it among the best, but there must simply be an acceptance of the need for training to start at a younger age. Other parents realize that to start young for "talented children" may be the solution. For example, the "summer school" with the Dutch team Ajax, at a cost of 350 euros for a week (Dalen, 2015), has become an alternative for Norwegian parents who can afford it.

Cross-country skiing

Cross-country skiing is of Scandinavian origin, and skiing battalions have been used in the army since the seventeenth century. The sport is often considered the national sport (Hansen, 2014), and to keep it as such is one of the main objectives for the Federation (Skiforbundet, 2015). Of the different sports within the Norwegian Ski Federation (NSF, in Norwegian *Norges skiforbund*), cross-country skiing has the highest number of registered clubs (1020), followed by alpine skiing (200), ski jumping (190), Telemark skiing (75), Nordic combined (68) and freestyle (50) – with some clubs having several of the ski disciplines (Skiforbundet, 2015). The Federation has 1,150 clubs organized in 16 districts (NIF, 2013). In addition to supporting the clubs, the Federation is also concerned with updating venues, trails and facilities, to enhance participation for all and to promote interest in a healthy outdoor life (Skiforbundet, 2015).

Cross-country skiing has a budget almost on the same level as Olympiatoppen (Ronglan, 2014) – due to contracts signed after the 2010 Olympic Winter Games (Hansen, 2014). Ninety percent of NSA's income is from commercial partners, and the budget for 2015 was 80 million NOK. Of this amount, 60 million NOK was allocated to cover the expenses for the national team and 45 million for the regional teams (Vesteng, 2014). For the 2015–2016 season, 47 athletes were part of the different national teams (NSF, 2015a). The junior team aged 18–19 consists of the best juniors, and they follow the competition schedule for their age group. These teams serve as facilitator for young athletes to move up from juniors into the seniors rank, meaning you are among the top tier in the world. Of the senior athletes, 25 athletes receive personal funding from Olympiatoppen (see Table 6.1).

While cross-country skiing has the finances to undertake and support a thorough talent development system, the resources are mostly spent on the senior elite athletes. Instead of supporting the young athletes directly, the ski federation tries to reach as many young athletes as possible and indirectly support them by being responsible for coach education and facilities for training, and supporting clubs/schools so they can develop the talents until they reach the age of 18–19. They also support five sports schools (public and private):

> There are 113 offers of sports schools for the age group 16-19 on the market… Local clubs and schools are the ones responsible for the talent development, for example – there are 350 boys age 16, we have to delegate talent development downwards… After an assessment of the situation in 1987, we decided to support five sports schools. The five schools have a geographical spread of Troms, Agder, Buskerud, Trøndelag and Hedmark… Every year, we host a meeting with these schools, and they get a small amount to cover the costs for the various meetings we want them to attend. They have also helped out in the work of writing the development plan (*Utviklingstrappa*).
>
> [NSF Representative]

In order to get a coherent policy, the Federation has produced a development plan (*Utviklingstrappa i langrenn*) (NSF, 2013b), which was a result of an initiative from Olympiatoppen to define a common language between the different sports in order to assure performance development. Based on the experiences of Norway's most successful coaches and athletes, the development plan describes the steps for athletes aged 13 and up. If they follow these steps, and approach challenges with the knowledge that has fostered some of the world's best cross-country skiers, it is assumed that improvement in elite performance will follow. Timing for the steps are vital, and it is also emphasized that the development steps in training content and quantity must be seen in relation to other activities, and that maybe other activities such as education should have a reduced emphasis in order to allow for a maximal recovery.

As 18–19 years old is considered to be the key age in the development process for the Federation, it is reluctant to select participants for youth competitions such as EYOF and YOG. When discussing the increasing numbers of youth competitions, the Federation was more concerned about keeping to their development plan than meeting the age requirements of a particular event: "we do not enforce the age requirements, we follow our development plans," "we think Olympiatoppen makes more out of this competitions than Junior Worlds which are of a higher standard in our sport," and also "to only qualify two boys and two girls for YOG makes no sense to us, it does not matter who we pick" [NSF Representative]. As such, they do not state that they are negative to the increasing number of youth competitions, but they do not see them as a significant contributions to athlete development. The focus is to make all athletes adhere to the development plan and, if they qualify for a youth competition, it is seen as a good training/learning experience, but it does not mean that they are the future Olympians nor that they "get any special treatment if they succeed."

Final thoughts on the Norwegian Model

Overall, a number of factors in Norway influence athletes' talent development: resources and competences in local clubs; and the position of local coaches in national networks. The differences in support from the clubs were obvious between the three compared sports. Figure skating as a minor, early peak sport with a lack of funding is a tough choice due to the small number of clubs. Not only do the parents have to pay extra for their children to train on ice and for competent coaches, but they also have to encourage their children to adhere to strict training routines from an early age. With less funding, the conflict between elite sport and mass sport becomes very apparent in the local clubs. For the clubs, it might be challenging to reconcile the ambitions of parents and young athletes with NIF's rules regarding children's participation in elite sport. The tensions may encourage clubs to create their own interpretation of the children's regulations about venue capacity, groups and coaching attention. While Olympiatoppen has a more marginal role with the wealthier federations, figure skating welcomed and embraced the Sonja Henie project as much needed technical and financial support to help young athletes to reach goals such as Olympic participation. In contrast, for cross-country skiing and football, this tension is less evident due to the number of clubs at different professional levels available for athletes and parents to select. The two sports with extensive budgets and numbers of participants have chosen different paths to talent development. They can use a decentralized system through the geographical spread of clubs (Ronglan,

2014), in contrast to figure skating that relies on centralized talent development, where the talents might need to move for enhanced quality of training and coaching expertise (S. S. Andersen, 2012). The commercial sport example, football, struggles at the senior men's level to qualify for the major championships (such as European Championship, the World Cup and the Olympic Games), and the number of Norwegian players playing abroad has decreased. Several projects targeting mass sport and young elite athletes have been launched, and the results of these initiatives will be interesting to review in a few years (see for example Sæther, 2015). Apart from the national projects, local competence and having the right people around you continue to be important in the development phase (as illustrated by Martin Ødegaard). For example, a coach will naturally promote "his athletes" if he has a role in the national network. While the coach matters, the athletes must still possess the inner drive for training – and dare to be "unNorwegian" and stand out when it comes to commitment.

As an endurance sport, cross-country skiing does not have to stress an early start to the same degree as football or figure skating. The Federation has delegated talent development to the clubs, the 19 District Sport Associations, sports schools and larger teams in the different regions of the country. This seems to be a well-funded solution for recruitment and with the constant impressive results, it will not be changed any time soon. In many ways, Norway is in an unique position in cross-country skiing (Hansen, 2014), in terms of current success and access to resources (financial and technical) that few other countries can match in this niche sport. For example, the smallest local community may have competent persons to provide coaching in the local club, though the sports schools tend to be a major actor in the years leading up to a national debut. In addition, cross-country is a "family endeavor" where parents are often involved in the entourage, for example in taking charge of ski waxing. Parents do often provide substantial financial support to ensure that their child has the "necessary" number of pairs of skis.

The coexistence between elite sport and mass sport remains challenging in Norway – especially for sports with an early peak. In fact, it might seem as though the resources required for young talents of today to succeed in Norway, as in many other countries, are heavily skewed in favor of those from upper income backgrounds (Kristiansen & Houlihan, 2015; Smith, Haycock, & Hulme, 2013). As the young athletes have to choose to commit to a sport (often when selecting a school), resourceful parents (economic and sports wise) within the sport who know what is required for success are vital (Kristiansen & Houlihan, 2015). Due to the constant specialization of youth sport, it might be argued that resourceful parents will be even more important in the future – especially for federations with a less structured talent development system and low levels of formal professionalization (Ronglan, 2014).

Notes

1 In a recent magazine article, the concept *talent* and the use of it is argued, by Professor Hylland Eriksen, to have become more accepted the past years (Ellefsen, 2015). He further argues that the Norwegian society today is a "post-Law of Jante-society."

2 When reviewing and investigating the Norwegian situation for the three chosen sports, stakeholders (NSO managers, coaches, athletes) with information about talent development were interviewed between February and June 2015 (N=8). In addition to interviews with key informants, sources of data also included document analysis (policies, strategies and evaluation reports at the organizational and operational level and newspaper articles). While information about football and cross-country skiing was easily accessible, more interviews were conducted among stakeholders familiar with figure skating (n=4).

3 The scholarships from Olympiatoppen can be divided into A, B and U stipends (Olympiatoppen, 2015a). All three types grant access to the facilities and resources at Olympiatoppen. In order to obtain the A scholarship (NOK 120.000), you need to be among the top three in the world, while the B scholarship (NOK 70.000) requires good results (usually a final) in the same competition. The U scholarship (NOK 60.000) is for young athletes under the age of 24 who show good results and the potential to reach the top.

References

ABC news. (2007, January 16). Jenter med OL i blikket [Girls aiming for the Olympic]. *ABC News*. Retrieved from www.abcnyheter.no/nyheter/sport/2007/01/16/30092/jenter-med-ol-i-blikket

Andersen, A. (2009, May 6). Paule vil Janteloven til livs [Paule speak against the Law of Jante]. *Aftenbladet*. Retrieved from www.aftenbladet.no/sport/Paule-vil-janteloven-til-livs-2037832.html

Andersen, S. S. (2009). Big success through small, intelligent failures? Experience-based knowledge development in top sports. *Tidsskrift for Samfunnsforskning*, 4, 427–461.

Andersen, S. S. (2012). Olypiatoppen in the Norwegian sports cluster. In S. S. Andersen & L. T. Ronglan (Eds.), *Nordic elite sport: same ambitions – different tracks* (pp. 237–256). Oslo: Norwegian University Press.

Andersen, S. S., Bjørndal, C. T., & Rognlan, L. T. (2015). The ecology of talent development in the Nordic elite sport model. In S. S. Andersen, B. Houlihan, & L. T. Rognlan (Eds.), *Managing elite sport systems: Research and practice* (pp. 49–66). New York: Routledge.

Augestad, P., Bergsgard, N. A., & Hansen, A. Ø. (2006). The Institutionalization of an Elite Sport Organization in Norway: The Case of "Olympiatoppen." *Sociology of Sport Journal*, 23, 293–313.

Barreiros, A., Cote, J., & Fonseca, A. M. (2014). From early to adult sport success: Analysing athletes' progression in national squads. *European Journal of Sport Science*, 14, S178–S182.

Bergsgard, N. A. (2007). *Sport policy – a comparative analysis of stability and change*. Oxford, UK: Butterworth-Heinemann.

Bergsgard, N. A., & Norberg, J. R. (2010). Sports policy and politics – the Scandinavian way. *Sport in Society*, *13*(4), 567–582.

Bjørndal, C. T., Rognlan, L. T., & Andersen, S. S. (2015). Talent development as an ecology of games: A case study of Norwegian handball. *Sport, Education and Society*.

Bugge, M. (2014, February 20). Foreldrene har betalt 2 millioner for tvillingenes satsing [The parents have paid 2 million NOK for the twins sport]. Retrieved July 22, 2015, from www.adressa.no/100Sport/mesterskap/article421435.snd

C More. (2015, January 19). Martin Ødegaard – How they trained him [Video file]. *Tippeligaen*. Retrieved from www.youtube.com/watch?v=NDF6GExwR0U

Collins, D., Bailey, R., Ford, P. A., MacNamara, A., Toms, M., & Pearce, G. (2012). Three Worlds: new directions in participant development in sport and physical activity. *Sport, Education and Society*, *17*(2), 225–243.

Cummins, L. D. (2007). Figure skating: A different kind of youth sport. *Journal of Clinical Sport Psychology*, *1*(4).

Dalen, B. (2015, June 25). På fotballskole hos Ajax [Ajax football academy]. *KristiansandAvis*. Retrieved from www.kristiansandavis.no/?id=1332

Ellefsen, K. (2015, September 17). Talentjakt har blitt stuerent [The search for talents are more accpeted]. *Amagasinet*. Retrieved from www.aftenposten.no/amagasinet/Talentjakt-har-blitt-stuerent-8166174.html

FIFA. (2007). FIFA Big Count 2006. FIFA Communication Divisions. Retrieved from www.fifa.com/mm/document/fifafacts/bcoffsurv/bigcount.summaryreport _7022.pdf

FIFA. (2015a, September 25). The FIFA women's ranking. Retrieved from www.fifa. com/fifa-world-ranking/ranking-table/women/index.html

FIFA. (2015b, October 1). The FIFA men's ranking. FIFA. Retrieved from www.fifa. com/fifa-world-ranking/ranking-table/men/index.html

Girginov, V., & Collins, D. (Eds.). (2004). Sport in Eastern Europe. *International Journal of the History of Sport*, *21*(5), 34–47, Special issue.

Gjersem, C. (2013, September 29). Hun klarte det! [She made it!]. Retrieved from https://camillagjersem.wordpress.com/2013/09/29/hun-klarte-det/

Goksøyr, M., & Hanstad, D. V. (2012). Elite sport development in Norway – a radical transformation. In S. S. Andersen & L. T. Ronglan (Eds.), *Elite sports in Nordic countries. Same ambitions – different tracks* (pp. 27–42). Oslo: University Press.

Haavik, Y. (2009, June 25). NFFs spillerutviklingsmodell [The development model]. Norwegian Football Association (NFF). Retrieved from www.fotball.no/ Landslag_og_toppfotball/spillerutvikling/NFFs-spillerutviklingsmodell/

Haavik, Y. (2012a, February 9). Telenor Xtra – Fotball SFO i 30 breddeklubber i 2012 [Telenor Xtra Football after school offer for grassrot football in 2012]. NFF. Retrieved from www.fotball.no/nff/NFF-nyheter/2012/Telenor-Xtra-- Fotball-SFO-i-30-breddeklubber-i-2012/

Haavik, Y. (2012b, May 23). Facts and history about Norwegian football. Retrieved August 6, 2015, from www.fotball.no/toppmeny/english/Facts-and-history- about-Norwegian-Football/

Hansen, P. Ø. (2014). *Making the best even better. Fine-tuning development and learning to achieve international success in cross-country skiing*. Norwegian School of Sport Sciences.

Ibsen, B., & Seippel, Ø. (2010). Voluntary organized sport in Denmark and Norway. *Sport in Society*, *13*(4), 593–608.

Kristiansen, E. (2014). Regulations of children's sport in Norway. In P. M. Pedersen & L. Thibault (Eds.), *Contemporary Sport Management* (5th edn). Human Kinetics.

Kristiansen, E. (2016). Walking the line: How young athletes balance academic studies and sport in international competition. *Sport in Society*. http://doi.org/10 .1080/17430437.2015.1124563

Kristiansen, E., & Houlihan, B. (2015). Developing young athletes: The role of the private sport schools in the Norwegian sport system. *International Review for the Sociology of Sport*, 1–23. http://doi.org/10.1177/1012690215607082

Kristiansen, E., & Parent, M. M. (2014). Athletes, their families and team officials: Sources of support and stressors. In D. V. Hanstad, M. M. Parent, & B. Houlihan (Eds.), *The Youth Olympic Games* (pp. 106–121). Oxon: Routledge.

NFF. (2012). Handlingsplan 2012-2015 [Action plan]. Norwegian Football Association (NFF). Retrieved from www.fotball.no/Documents/PDF/2012/NFF/ Handlingsplan2012-2015_WEB_enkel.pdf

NFF. (2014). NFF's årsrapport [The annual report from NFF 2014]. Retrieved from www.e-pages.dk/sportmgratis/66/

NIF. (2013). *Årsrapport 2013 [Annual report 2013]*. Oslo, Norway: Norwegian Olympic, Paralympic Committee and Confederation of Sports. Retrieved from www.idrett.no/omnif/idrettsstyret/Documents/NIF%20Årsrapport%20 2013_LR.pdf

NIF. (2014). *Annual Report 2013 "Årsrapport 2013"*. Oslo, Norway: Norwegian Olympic and Paralympic Committee and Confederation of Sports.

NIF. (2015a). Barneidrett [Children's sport]. NIF. Retrieved from www. idrettsforbundet.no/tema/barneidrett/

NIF. (2015b). Den norske toppidrettsmodellen 2022 [The Norwegian Top Sport Model 2022]. Norges Idrettsforbund. Retrieved from www.idrettsforbundet.no/ globalassets/2nyheter---idrett.no/kalle/den-norske-toppidrettsmodellen-2022_ oppfolging.pdf

NIF. (2015c). Støtteordninger [financial support]. Retrieved from www. idrettsforbundet.no/klubbguiden/stotteordninger/

NSF. (2011, May 27). NSFs sportslig satsing kunsløp 2011/2012 [NSF vision for figure skating 2011/2012]. Norges Skøyteforbund [Norwegian Skating Associationion]. Retrieved from http://n-s-f.no/filarkiv/admin/2011/tinget_2011/ sportslig-satsing_k.pdf

NSF. (2013a). Norges Skøyeforbund: Strategi for perioden 2013-2015 [Norwegian Skating Association: The strategy for 2013-2015]. Norges Skøyteforbund [Norwegian Skating Association]. Retrieved from www.skoyteforbundet.no/ omforbundet/Documents/Strategiplan_2013-2015_2.pdf

NSF. (2013b). *Utviklingstrappa i langrenn [Development steps in cross-country skiing]*. Oslo, Norway: Norwegian Ski Association.

NSF. (2015a). 23 utøvere på rekrutt- og juniorlandslaget [23 athøetes on the recruit and junior team]. Retrieved July 28, 2015, from www.skiforbundet.no/langrenn/ nyhetsarkiv/rekrutt-og-junior/

NSF. (2015b). Kuntsløp [Figure Skating]. Norwegian Skating Association (NSF). Retrieved from www.norwayskating.org/kunstlop/kunstlop_om.htm

NTB. (2014, January 20). Første norske kunstløper i OL på 50 år [The first Norwegian contestant in 50 years]. *Dagsavisen*. Retrieved from www.dagsavisen. no/sport/f%C3%B8rste-norske-kunstl%C3%B8per-i-ol-p%C3%A5-50-%C3% A5r-1.279116

Nygaard, R. (2012, October 29). Om KVINNEfotball av en kvinne [About female fottball by a woman]. *Glomdalen*. Retrieved from www.glomdalen.no/pepper/ article6314226.ece

Olympiatoppen. (2015a, May 11). Olympiatoppens utøverstipend – Individuelle utøvere [Olympiatoppen's individual stipend system]. olympiatoppen. Retrieved from www.olympiatoppen.no/om_olympiatoppen/stoetteordninger/individuelt_ utoeverstipend/page5457.html

Olympiatoppen. (2015b, June). Individual stipend (winter sport) 2015/2016. Olympiatoppen. Retrieved from www.olympiatoppen.no/forutovere/for_stipendut %C3%B8vere/stipendtildelinger/media45374.media

Rake, J. (2007, September 7). Tettey kritisk til norsk talentutvikling [Tettey is critical to Norwegian talent development]. *VG*. Retrieved from www.vg.no/sport/fotball/ rosenborg/tettey-kritisk-til-norsk-talentutvikling/a/162074/

Ronglan, L. T. (2014). Elite sport in Scandinavian welfare states: legitimacy under pressure? *International Journal of Sport Policy and Politics*, 1–19.

Sæteren, T. B. (2015, July 30). Telenor Xtra: – Et fint kick off for oss [Telenor Xtra: – A nice kick off for us]. NFF. Retrieved from www.fotball.no/Barn_og_ungdom/ Telenorxtra/2015/Telenor-Xtra---Et-fint-kick-off-for-oss/

Sæther, S. A. (2015). Selecting players for youth national teams – a question of birth month and reselection? *Science and Sport*. http://doi.org/10.1016/j. scispo.2015.04.005

Skiforbundet. (2015). Verdigrunnlag og hovedmål [Values and aims]. Retrieved July 14, 2015, from www.skiforbundet.no/norges-skiforbund/verdigrunnlag-og-hovedmal/

Skirstad, B., Waddington, I., & Safvenbom, R. (2012). Issues and problems in the organization of children's sport: A case study of Norway. *European Physical Education Review*, 18(3), 309–321.

Smith, A., Haycock, D., & Hulme, N. (2013). The class of London 2012: Some sociological reflections on the social backgrounds of Team GB athletes. *Sociological Research Online*, 18(3), 15.

Sundt, J. A. (2013, July 25). Delt om topping i barneidretten [Divided about topping in children sport]. Retrieved from http://www.gd.no/sport/article6775695.ece

Tvedt, T., Røste, E., Smith, M., Høgmo, P. M., Haugen, K., & Rognlan, L. T. (2013). Den norske toppidrettsmodelen-norsk toppidrett fram mot 2022 [The Norwegian top sport model – Norwegian sport towards 2022]. The Norwegian Olympic and Paralympic Committee and Confederation of Sports (NIF). Retrieved from www.idrett.no/nyheter/Documents/Toppidrettsrapporten_2022. pdf

Vesteng, C. (2014, August 29). Langrenn øker budsjettet til 80 mill [Cross-country skiing increases the budget to 80 millions]. *VG*. Retrieved from www. vg.no/a/23284606

Chapter 7

France

Denis Musso

The current system is the outcome of a long process initiated in 1960. The State played an increasingly central role in the organization and development of sport in France from the 1960s until 2007. Since 2007, for budgetary reasons, the State adapted its regulatory function and is targeting its actions more selectively. In a context of public policy review and heightened international sport competition, there is an increased search for effectiveness and efficiency, which leads to the introduction of new processes and changes to stakeholders' roles.

Until the Second World War, the sport system was run largely autonomously by non-profit bodies created on private initiative. The State began to intervene from 1940 in the specific historic context of Nazi Germany occupation. The Sport Charter (*Charte des sports*), in fact the first law on sport, organized a sport system completely dominated by the Government through the change in status of the National Committee of Sport, which became a quasi-governmental body. Even if a liberalization of sport took place in 1945 following the end of war, the State's role was heavily reinforced, including a legal monopoly to organize sport competitions and to select athletes for international competitions. This legal fiction was supplemented by a governmental competence to delegate these roles to the federations, supporting them, provided they strictly respected State rules and control.

Main milestones in the development of the elite sport system

1960: Following very poor results at the Rome Olympics the State decided to take direct charge of Olympic preparations and set up a sport technician corps employed by the State and placed within sport federations to manage both elite sport policy and *sport for all* policy.

1975: The first overall law on sport was adopted which organized the sport landscape and summarized the relationships between the

State, the sport federations, the local authorities and the economic sector. Sport development was defined as a public service mission, and sport federations were identified as implementers of governmental sport policy. The law set up the National Fund for Elite Sportspersons, and the concept of an Elite Sportsperson became a legal qualification defined by each federation.

1979:   The National Fund for Sport development (FNDS) drawn from lottery revenues was created to supplement the Ministry of Sport's budget. Resources were increased through the imposition of a tax on sport TV rights revenues in 2000. In 2006, the FNDS became the National Centre for Sport Development (CNDS).

1982:   The law decentralizing the State resulted in a new distribution of competences between the State and sub-national levels (region, department, communes). However, as the sport domain was not mentioned, sport development remained a shared competence. The State retained responsibility for ensuring the legislation was respected and also retained leadership over elite sport policy and on the definition and award of professional sport diplomas.

1984:   A new general law on the organization and development of sport further extended State intervention and recognized sport development as a matter of public interest. Federations and sport associations were strongly associated with the State's public service mission in relation to sport. The law also established a new body to run elite sport, the National Commission of High Level Sport to coordinate all stakeholders under the leadership of the State, in co-operation with the NOC. The objectives of the National Commission were to designate the elite sportspersons and the elite sports, and to define the selection criteria to attend the Olympic Games.

2001:   The Parliament adopted the 'Loi organique relative aux lois de finance' (Organic Law on Finance Laws; LOLF) a new way to manage the annual State budget. In 2012, the Parliament reinforced rationalization, adopting new programming processes and new governance arrangements for public finances. The budget is allocated to missions, programs and actions (i.e., to objectives rather than to departments). The mission 'Sport, Youth and Association' includes two main priorities: to encourage citizens to participate in a wide variety of sports and for France to rank among the most successful nations in high-level sport. In 2015, the Priority Actions Program (PAP) included five main goals, including to: consolidate the ranking of France among the great sporting nations and improve the employment of elite sportspersons; strengthen respect for ethics in sport and preserve the health of athletes; and tailor sport training and better connect training and education with employment.

In 2013, 43 per cent of French people practiced regularly or with some regularity a physical or sport activity. Globally, the sport system is based on sport associations or clubs; there were 167,086 clubs affiliated to a federation. The number of people licensed reached 15,901,900, of which 5,916,900 were women,[1] more than 24 per cent of the total population. The sport spending amounted to €36.5 billion, of which 45 per cent was from households, 46 per cent from public bodies and 9 per cent from private sector. This represents 1.74 per cent of the gross domestic product (GDP).[2]

The welfare of children in sport

The protection and welfare of young athletes outside the family is regulated and controlled by the State. There are three main sources of rules, the most global of which is the general legislation on the protection of minors. The legislation requires that minors hosted outside the parental home during school hours and outside school time be protected against the risks to their health and to their physical or moral safety. This applies especially during sports camps accommodating children. The camp's organizer has to inform the State representative in the department. Rules control the people, who are allowed to coach children, and also the educational, health and accommodation conditions.

The regulations applicable to sport are the second source, but do not include specific rules for the protection of young people. However, the State aims to guarantee security for all who practice sport. This goal is primarily achieved by State control over qualifications and the requirement that coaches possess a diploma before taking paid employment as a coach. Safety rules are also in force for sports equipment and sports facilities. In addition, a medical certificate is compulsory for delivery of sports licenses, and France has a strong anti-doping policy.

In the field of high performance sport, elite sport policy is strongly based on the athlete's dual career. The aim is to allow athletes to combine high level sport excellence with school, university and professional employment success. There are few specific rules and measures concerning young athletes.

To be included on the list of top athletes, the minimum age is 12 years old and a specific medical examination is compulsory. The Code of Education requires that schools allow the practice of high performance sport and adapt the educational requirements. A ministerial instruction reinforces the requirement to adapt teaching methods and the school schedule, and also to ensure a closer relationship between the school and those in charge of high-level sport training. Monitoring and evaluation are carried out at local, regional and national levels. The policy actors in charge of elite sportspersons are involved in the national network of high level sport in order to facilitate effective communication and coordination.

Analysis of public policy in relation to elite youth sport

Elite sport policy is led by the Ministry of Sport and implemented especially through its centres: the 'Institut national du sport, de l'expertise et de la performance' (INSEP) and 16 'Centres de ressources, d'expertise et de performances sportives' (CREPS). High performance sport is recognized in various laws and regulations, as well as in the Charter of High Performance Sport that mentions the exemplar role of top athletes. The National Commission of High Performance Sport (CNSHN) is the institutional consultative body responsible for all major guidelines for high-level sport. It is chaired by the Ministry of Sport and includes representatives of the State, the NOC, high-level athletes, coaches, referees or high-level sport judges and local authorities. The CNSHN:

- Defines the guidelines of national policy for high performance sport;
- Recognizes the high-level nature of sports disciplines;
- For each discipline, determines the criteria for defining high-level athletes, high-level coaches, referees and judges, young talents and training partner; and
- Delivers an opinion on the number of athletes eligible for inclusion on the list of high-level athletes, the number of high-level coaches, the number of arbitrators and judges of high-level athletes, and the number of athletes who are likely to be included on the young promising sportspersons' lists and on the list of training partners.

High-level sport is based on four established criteria:

- Recognition of the elite sport disciplines: in addition to the Olympic and Paralympic disciplines, other disciplines are recognized as high-level sport disciplines. In the 2013-2016 period, 124 disciplines were recognized as high-level.
- Competitions of reference: These are the official events on the calendar of international sports federations, which lead to the establishment of world reference rankings, namely the (summer and winter) Olympic and Paralympic Games, World Championships and European Championships.
- The list of top athletes: in 2014, 6581 athletes were designated as high-level sportspersons, 64% male and 36% female: 769 as 'elite athlete', 2343 as 'senior athletes', and 3316 as 'youth athletes'. In January 2015, 60% of elite athletes were in educational or professional training situation, 35% in employment situation and 3% were unemployed.
- The routes to sporting excellence ('Parcours d'excellence sportive', PES): The aim is to take into account the needs of athletes from the

moment they are identified as having 'high sport potential' until the completion of their international career and integration into a non-sport career, even if this occurs after the end of their sporting career. These routes to excellence are specific to each federation, which is responsible for establishing processes and support structures to enable sportspersons to reach the highest international levels. There are two main national structures, 'Pôle France Senior et Pôle France Jeunes' (Centres for Sport Excellence and Centres for Sport Excellence-Youth and 'Pôle espoir' (Centres for young promising sportspersons). These centres gather athletes selected by the DTN (National Technical Director) of each federation to be trained sportively and academically. They must be particularly effective in the following areas: sports training, including effective and skilled sports coaches; sports facilities and equipment provision; school, university or professional post-sport career training; and athlete's individual health monitoring.

The routes to sporting excellence have existed since 2009, and they are the most recent addition to the sport performance strategy. Their establishment follows earlier initiatives such as 'Sections sports classes' from 1974 to 1984, 'Permanent Centre for Sport Training and Educational Training' from 1984 to 1995 and 'Elite Sports Access Pathways' from 1995 to 2008. The routes to sporting excellence are built sport by sport from a network of 'structures' that offer the best sports conditions. They are more flexible, more selective (i.e., support fewer athletes) and more demanding. It is the National Commission for High Performance Sport that validates each PES for each Olympiad.

Since the 1960s the sport movement has received specific technical support through the intervention of sport public officials paid by the State. There were 1,680 such officials working in high performance sport in 2015 across 77 federations. In each federation, a DTN is responsible for the design and implementation of the route to sporting excellence. He or she manages all the technical sport advisors, and they are responsible for talent identification and development of elite athletes, the selection of national teams, and the training of coaches. They contribute directly to the State's implementation of sport policy and guarantee consistency between federations and those sports projects prioritized by the Ministry of Sport. This holds for both senior and young athletes.

Since the 1960s the State established an increasingly comprehensive and streamlined system of high performance sport. The system aims to ensure the protection of young athletes. The system is based on legal texts, adherence to ministerial policy, the active presence of public technical staff placed alongside the federations and a series of control, monitoring and coordination mechanisms. However, much responsibility still rests with the young athlete's entourage (parents, coaches, etc.) to guarantee the quality of the conditions and support for young athletes. This responsibility has increased, especially since the introduction of the new policy organized around the routes to sporting excellence, which are more decentralized and individualized.

Faced with increased sporting competition between nations and a proliferation of competitions, the challenge, which is likely to intensify, will be to ensure a flow of talented young athletes who are developed in an optimal fashion. The context of a steady reduction of government expenditure over the medium term, at least, and of the territorial reorganization of the country as well as a new governance system for high-level sport, with greater involvement of the regions and of industry, is proving to be a challenge and a source of tension between the various actors and the State.

Prominence of elite youth sport

The three sports chosen are football, gymnastics and judo. Football is a sport with a strong professional sector and almost two million male and 70,000 female license holders. The second selected sport is gymnastics as an 'early peak performance sport', and the third is judo, a prominent Olympic sport in France. All these sports are part of the French system of high-level sport and, consequently, will have some common characteristics.

The first common characteristic is the intensity of training. Typical for elite athletes would be a weekly training commitment of between 16 and 35 hours, two daily sessions or even exceptionally, three sessions per day five to seven days per week with six days becoming the standard and an annual calendar of activities dissociated from the school calendar, covering 35 to 48 weeks. Particularly during the pre-Olympic years, the intensity of training leaves little room for non-sport activities.

The second pillar is the philosophy of the dual-career, interpreted as the search for the best sports performance while respecting the human being. France won 34 medals at the 2012 London Olympic Games when there were around 6,500 classified as 'High level athlete' of which 3,300 were in the 'Youth' category (with a minimum age of 12 and range similar to the federal level). This highlights the need to give young athletes the same chances of educational success and employability as other young people because of the shortness and uncertainty of a sporting career.

The French policy, which encapsulates the second pillar, was adopted by the European Union as a recommendation in 2012. The French model of sports performance has shown that achieving a balance between sporting and educational ambitions becomes realistic when there is determination and consistency. However, some tensions could surface between the Ministry of Sport and the Ministry of Education. Experience has shown that recommendations and weak rules are not always sufficient to facilitate responsible behaviour by all the stakeholders surrounding young sports-persons. Today, it is probably necessary to also define concrete ethics charters to underline and reinforce the European Union's recommendations.

The reality of the dual-career, especially for high school students, as being strongly rooted in the policy of the French government for decades, however, is facing several problems. Its implementation always proves to be delicate, as each young athlete's circumstances are unique. Second, achieving a life balance is always the result of competing forces between sports and other interests and commitments. Consequently, it is important to bear in mind that, despite the protective framework of regulation, each situation remains fragile.

The problematic trend is the reduction in the availability of time for young athletes to successfully pursue an academic study programme. This issue is related to the increased amount of sport-related time spent on training, competition travel, medical care and compensating rest and recovery activities, such as cryotherapy or hypoxia rooms.

Facing bi- or tri-daily sports training, a viable model of organization is moving towards unity of place providing services for all the needs of young athletes. This efficient solution is achieved to a considerable extent in the sports centres of the Ministry of Sport, even if daily trips for specialist services are sometimes required.

The French vision of the dual-career is too often associated exclusively with the INSEP model, which host 27 'pôles France' (centres of excellence) and benefits from advanced sport structures, training, medical, care, accommodation, as well as teaching staff, researchers, and health care personnel, social assistance and psychologists. However, INSEP remains the exception.

In these settings, the guarantor of the interests of the young athlete remains the sport technical adviser, who is a State appointee exercising either 'pôle' coordinator or national coach functions inside a federation. The time pressure on the sportsperson requires the whole system to become more effective and efficient and to include individualized support, often involving distance learning, throughout the athlete's educational career to university. This system of 321 'poles espoirs', 41 'pôles France Jeune', 113 'pôles France' based on the Ministry of Sport's centres, remains the dominant model; but, there are also 53 'others centres' based on clubs, private companies and families. Consequently, they do not have a very favourable situation.

Process of talent identification, development and other elements

Unlike other countries that undertake talent identification through the systematic assessment of age groups, mostly in schools either by physical tests or by different forms of educational games, in France, talent identification takes place from among young people, who are already members of sports clubs. Whatever the sport, talent identification is based on the sport pyramid, first at clubs then at regional and national levels. Once selected, young athletes will be closely tracked and participate in more courses and be part of departmental, regional and national squads in their age category. Those considered the most talented or the most promising will be grouped in a 'Centres for Sport Excellence-Youth' and be designated as a 'Youth high-level sportspersons', or be grouped in lower-level Centres for Young promising sportspersons.

Gymnastics

The French Gymnastics Federation (FFG) has over 300,000 licensed gymnasts distributed across more than 1,500 clubs and seven different disciplines. The sport does not have a professional sector. The disciplines of gymnastics are considered early maturing and they are considered to require a very large training volume because careers are often short, thereby requiring the intense involvement of all stakeholders. The youth training system has remained very stable due to the culture of the Gymnastics Federation based on a traditional or classical pyramid structure of talent development. The identification of talent begins at the departmental and regional levels, which are based on clubs organized by age categories and disciplines. The top of the pyramid is composed of 22 'Pôles espoirs' and eight 'Pôles France'. Again, the young gymnasts' training is entrusted to the DTN, who leads 77 technical staff placed near the FFG by the Ministry of Sport. In the last evaluation conducted by PES 2009/2012, the structure-oriented strategy, bringing together the best young gymnasts was viewed with dissatisfaction. The rational pathway has produced perverse effects reflected in unsatisfactory results and a destabilization of gymnasts' development due to a rapidly changing training environment because the pyramidal organization of the high level sport structures, that is, frequent moves from club to 'Pôle Espoir', 'Pôle France' and INSEP every two years. This also affects the motivation of coaches because of the turnover of athletes stemming from the annual (re) qualification requirements. The PES 2014/2017 reverses the traditional logic by becoming gymnast-centred rather than club structure-centred and considered as a part of a shared collective project between staff members towards the 2020 and 2024 Olympic and Paralympic Games.

The current Olympic preparation plan focuses on 'responsiveness' and includes several fundamental axes: support for gymnasts, including some financial security for their pathway; supervision of training with the creation of a 'charter of good behaviour'; and innovative methods of preparation and identification of training clubs. In addition, it appears that only ten of 30 high performance 'pôles' are hosted in the Ministry of Sport centres, less than the average rate in France. This is the result of history and reflects the strong regional influence within gymnastics.

The training of young athletes is a particularly sensitive issue in the early peak sports and those requiring high training volumes such as gymnastics. The first FFG category 'future' begins at 9–10 years old, knowing that 12 years old is the legal minimum age to be ranked on high performance sport lists. In the FFG specifications, athletes from the age of 11 are expected to train for 18–25 hours a week in one or two sessions per day for the 'pôles espoirs', and from the age of 12, to train for 20–30 hours a week for 45–48 weeks a year as a minimum, for 'pôle France' athletes.

The desired change of mind-set is to move from the 'culture of excuses' to the 'winning culture'. Finally, two-thirds of 'pôles' are not located in the Ministry of Sport centres. All these elements combine to make gymnastics a risk area concerning the training of young athletes.

Football

The ethos of training young footballers, both male and female, is defined and implemented by the DTN placed within the French Football Federation (FFF). For the period 2013–2017, the ethos is based on the following principles: preparing the talented player to integrate within the top level of their sport; promoting the design of the dual-career pathway; avoiding early specialization; sharing a national, optimized programme of talent identification and development.

Elite men's football is organized as a professional sport, which plays a key role in the training of young players mostly within the 'training centres' of professional clubs. However, since 1999, the State has been concerned to ensure the protection of young players by extending to professional sports training centres the requirements common in the structures of other high performance sports. For women, the situation is different because, except for some clubs integrated in male professional clubs, all structures are amateur. For female footballers, the development pathway of high performance sport is through the 'pôles espoirs' and 'pôles France'. The DTN for football has the responsibility to define a development plan for the training centres of professional clubs and the 'pôles' of high performance football that takes account of the mix of professional and amateur levels of the sport.

A training centre is a structure set up by an association or sport organization allowing young athletes over 14 years to benefit from sports training in order to access a professional sport career, but which also accommodates academic progress at school, vocational or university level. The training centres are accredited for a period of four years by the Ministry of Sport, after consulting the National Commission for High Performance Sport, based on a proposal from the federation. They are controlled by the

State and must respect guidelines proposed by the federation which define the: minimum and maximum age for each age group; minimum and maximum number of young athletes; number and qualifications of persons responsible for sports; medical and social support of young athletes; school, university or vocational education, and assistance provided; agreements between the training centre and schools, universities and vocational structures; facilities that should be available; nature and terms of medical care; weekly duration of training or competition; recovery periods and rest; and accommodation conditions, food and work.

Players aged at least 15 years at an approved training centre must sign a training agreement with the professional club. Their new status is defined by the 'Charter of professional football', which is a collective agreement governing football.

The youth talent identification system for U13 is based on the detection at the local level, and then selection at regional level. For U14 an inter-regional training session is added, and for U15, one inter-regional tournament and two national training sessions are part of the process.

Male footballers. Sports studies classes, where males aged 12–18 years can study at designated colleges and high schools which are numerous across all regions (e.g., Brittany has 81 colleges and 7 secondary schools). Some colleges and schools are designated for elite footballers, who are in the last two years of college or are in U14 and U15 regional squads. There are 19 such colleges all integrated into a certified training centre of professional club. The arrangement is called half-board in the school and training centre. For example, in Paris Saint-Germain's training centre schooling is provided by the 'apprentice training centre', which brings together not only footballers from Paris Saint-Germain, but also athletes from handball, judo and basketball. Young people benefit from apprentice status from 16 years of age, which allows them to practice their sport while preparing their post-competition future.

FFF class centres are divided into two categories with a maximum of 50 young players in the first category and 30 in the second. The categories are differentiated by a range of staff (technical, medical etc.) and performance criteria (number of players becoming professional, number of players who made professional-team matches, number of national selected players, school achievement).

Women footballers. Even if women's football is growing in both popularity and quality at the elite level, it remains far behind the men's game in terms of talent identification and development support. The training of young female players is significantly different. Until 15 years old, girls can be associated with boys in sport studies-classes and Centres for Young promising sportspersons ('pôle espoir'). From 16 years of age, talented girls are gathered in six 'pôles espoirs' and one 'pôle France' located in INSEP since 2013. However, some women's sections, which are integrated with male professional clubs, have begun to establish local training structures.

Professional football is very attractive for both young males and females and some abuses were found and reported. Since 1999, the requirement for State approval of the practices associated with youth football development has improved the professionalization of actors and structures of professional clubs and the overall development of sport preparation. Quality requirements are now in place for school and vocational training, medical care and free time/entertainment. As a result, male football is integrated into the standard sport policy based on the dual-career strategy and is overseen and reinforced by the DTN.

Still, there remains a small number of licensed, but poor quality clubs and examples of poor coaching, especially in those clubs catering to women's football, which provide little added value to the majority of players.

Judo

According to the PES 2013–2017, the French Judo Federation (FFJ) brings together over 600,000 licensed athletes, of which 27 per cent are women. In 2012, one third of the licensed athletes were less than 9 years old, one third between 9 and 14 years old, and the last third over 15 years old. There were 5,708 clubs, 4,800 coaches with a State diploma and 163 sport technical managers from the Ministry of Sport and from FFJ. At the 2012 London Olympic Games, the French judo squad ranked second, with two gold medals and five bronze. Ten of the 14 judokas attending the Olympic Games passed through the high performance pôles. The attention and support that the federation gives to dual career is reflected in the 89 per cent success rate of 339 judokas enrolled in the 'baccalauréat' final high school examination. The medical monitoring rate for top athletes is also high at 85 per cent, with the figures for young promising sportspersons even higher at 95 per cent.

In late 2012, 905 judokas were in the elite sport pathways. 146 were in 'Pôle France Senior' with 79 at INSEP and 67 at the Institute of Judo; 241 judokas were located in the other 4 'pôle France' and 518 young judokas spread over 27 'pôles espoirs'. Based on the official ranking of top athletes, 118 were in Elite and Senior categories, 249 in the Youth category. In addition, there were 25 'sparring partners' and 600 young judokas in the 'Espoirs' list. The 'Espoirs' are 12 years old at least, and recognized as possessing high level sports skills, as certified by the DTN but not meeting all the requirements for inclusion on the list of top athletes.

The report published in 2013 revealed that for FFJ, a recurring problem was the need to better coordinate all the sports structures in the interests of consistency, knowing that 20 per cent of judokas live for a year in a higher level training centre.

The high-level 2013–2020 project targets three priorities: rank France among the world's top two nations in the Olympic Games and World Championships; second, to develop champions who find a place in society (schooling, academic, professional); and third, to ensure that a Judoka reaches his/her highest technical and sporting level which will enable him/her to take other roles in French Judo, as teacher, referee, steward, official etc., once their sporting career ends. This last objective is a return on investment and is part of an original and interesting learning organization concept.

As with every sport, FFJ target international competitions of significance; however, the Judo PES 2013–2017 gives more direction than Football or Gymnastics about education and social integration, indicating a strong commitment to these aspects. Thus the educational support includes: timetables arrangements; back-up training and tutoring; educational support; permission for absence due to sport commitments; e-learning courses; presence of a coach on school boards; and involvement of a representative of the pole in relations with school. At the university level, strong support is also provided according to the FFJ specifications for each level of the 'pôle'.

The FFJ has a contract with each athlete registered with the 'pôle France Senior', which defines the mutual rights and obligations and explains the eligibility criteria for access to financial support ('aide personnalisée'). The current strategy is designed to better tailor each judoka's route and develop exchanges between judokas from different sporting structures as they progress to the regional level. The FFJ organizes the national level training, drawing judokas from each regional judo league that has progression routes from the poles.

Development of youth coaches

In France, for several decades, paid coaching has required a certificate issued or recognized by the State. For about ten years, the vocational field of sport has been structured according to a national collective agreement. The State, through the Ministry of Sport, employs 1,600 technical managers, who are highly qualified and specialists in one sport and are recruited through open competition. These technicians perform the functions of the DTN, national coaches or regional technical advisers. Under the authority of the Ministry of Sport, they are allocated to, and work within, the sports federations. Their mission is mostly focused on the implementation of high-level sports policy and is defined by a tripartite agreement at the national or regional level between the Ministry of Sport, the Federation and the DTN. This unified organization ensures the control of the State over the high performance sport system and ensures a good level of achievement regarding the protection of young athletes, especially in centres belonging to the

Ministry of Sport. The situation may be more fragile in some professional sports training centres as well as in 'pôles' hosted by private organizations and in 'associated structures'.

Vocational and Educational Training (VET) of technical staff is strongly encouraged and personalized. The Ministry of Sport has given INSEP the mission to offer training corresponding to the identified needs and to provide guidance for coaches to achieve excellence. Traditional training activities are complemented by much more personalized training actions. Each federation has its own initial and continuous training programme that is generally designed by the Federal Training Institute to enable each federation not only to develop its training offer, but also to protect its resources by taking advantage of publicly funded training.

Gymnastics

Training of managers and coaches is delivered by the FFG Training Institute and, every year, different courses are offered for various levels of federal coaches. These courses are, in whole or in part, recognized as equivalent to the corresponding State diploma. Specific modules for young children exist, but the training is devoted specifically to each of the seven disciplines of gymnastics. It is within these discipline-focused courses that specific modules concerning the training of young people are found. National coaches and technical officials, as is the case for all Olympic federations' staff, are encouraged by the Ministry of Sport to participate in training sessions included in a national offer.

Football

The FFF offers an annual 15-hour gathering (two days) of all technical staff for women's football. Also, the FFF and the Football Training Institute deliver an annual continuing education program to all the technical staff and coaches, with the following themes: technical management of young people, training centre management, centres training and sport sections, 'pôles espoirs' and national centre.

Judo

Continuing training for judo coaches is undertaken in the classic way, but training is also available at the 'pôles', including INSEP, which are open to all coaches who can attend training courses and exchange ideas with the coaches at the 'pôle.' All coaches can attend a large range of training sessions. FFJ implements a 'College of coaches' based on regular exchange of experiences on training and shared reflections focused on theme days.

Financial, education and organizational issues

Evaluation of the system

A consistent policy and a strong commitment to the development of athletes' dual career are part of the landscape of high performance sport; however, the reality reveals great heterogeneity. For football, in the 'Route of sporting excellence' prepared by the DTN, presented every four years by the federation and approved by the National Commission for High Performance Sport, only the sports results are mentioned. In general, and including gymnastics, there is no assessment of school, university or career progress and achievements. Although the formal absence is not a reflection of reality, it is indicative of the concerns of the hierarchy in the sport.

For Judo, in contrast to gymnastics, the evaluation criteria are precisely defined and cover every athlete and all 'pôles'. For example, in the PES 2013–2017, evaluation of judokas in a 'pôle' is defined as: 'Every judoka has to be evaluated in the three areas of the "triple project"'. An intermediate assessment is carried out in February and a review at the end of season in June. These two assessments will also be an opportunity to verify that the judoka submits well to the regulatory medical monitoring. In sports, evaluations of criteria relate to sports results, involvement in training and progress. In the area of educational training, the criteria are the results of the class council, passing exams, moving to the next grade and behaviour in the training institution. In the third area of the 'triple project', judoka will be evaluated on their technical achievements, kata [technique], and arbitration grade' (see Parcours d'excellence sportive 2013-2017, fédération française judo jujitsu).

Funding

The 'Routes of Sporting Excellence (PES)' include very little about how the dual-career should be financed and particularly the expectations regarding the contribution by families, which can, in practice, range from a few hundred euros to several thousand euros per year. For example, for young skiers, the annual cost of pursuing their sporting ambitions can be as much as €30,000 per year. In some PES, the proportion of the cost of accommodation and catering for the athlete supported by the federation ranges from 100% to 0%. The French Swimming Federation funds 80% of the total cost of training at 'Pôle France' in INSEP and 50% for 'pôle Espoir'. At INSEP in 2015, athletes received a monthly allowance of €1,082. However, the cost of training at the Pôle is not often evaluated precisely. For a region near Paris, supporting a sportsperson was costed at €15,000 per year in 2011. High performance athletes can get public funding in the form of 'personalized support' distributed by the Ministry of Sport through each sporting federation, although this support is mainly allocated to 'Senior' and 'Elite' athletes not the young. Other funding may come from local authorities (municipalities, departments and regions). Athletes may also receive private funding from their clubs and sponsors. This access to financial support is very unequal, as it is the best known athletes who attract the most of financial support.

Future impact of the increasing focus is elite youth sports

High performance sport in France's policy is structured, well established, rooted in the political and cultural landscape and driven and controlled by the State, the NOCs and the federations. This system has generally proved its effectiveness while respecting the integrity and the ambitions of young athletes. However, in a global context of increasing competition and a reduction in the number of young people willing to make the necessary commitment to reach the elite level a bigger effort has to be made to take care of the athletes. The situation is complicated because there is a great heterogeneity among disciplines with differences in contexts and in the developmental path of each sportsperson in the individual disciplines. An observation made a long time ago by INSEP showed that even in a same 'Pôle', each athlete has his/her own personal sporting trajectory in training, development and competition.

The problem of athlete dropout and the need to protect the interests of young talents is recognized by the Ministry of Sport, which has made efforts, in consultation with elite athletes, to create a structure that supports and nurtures their development. The educational facilities are more numerous and include job time arrangements, mentoring, distance learning, remedial support and tutoring, 'catch-up' classes in case of prolonged absences, and tutoring support for athletes living abroad for a long period. The aim is to create a tailored path for each sportsperson.

There are, however, blind spots in the system. The data on the 'employment rate for top athletes' is a challenge even if it is based on a small panel of sportspersons. In 2015, the Priority Actions Program (PAP) aimed for a high rate (88 per cent in 2017) of employment of high-level sportspersons, two years after the end of registration on the list of top athletes. It is also unsatisfactory that there is an apparent weakness in many PES federations regarding individual assessment of learning outcomes and employability. A report of the General Inspectorate of the Ministry of Sport (Monnereau, 2013) recommended in late 2013 that the search for excellence in sports training linked more clearly to the preparation for life post elite sport could reinvigorate the high performance policy path: 'Access to a fulfilling profession in positions of responsibility today sets the standard for the success of the dual career, one that meets the needs of athletes and families. The main risk remains the temptation to focus on the sporting objectives, overshadowing other aspects of youth training.' This risk is especially relevant to those young talented sportspersons who do not have the qualification of 'high-level sport athlete' and who therefore do not have official institutional educational arrangements to support their dual career.

Finally, it is rare that athletes are asked to give their views on, and evaluation of, the system even if they are at the elite level. Sometimes they remain or are left as 'spectators' to their own career development (Aquilina, 2015, p.35). One of the ways to improve the situation could be to foster athlete organizations helping and assisting especially young athletes' The dual career is still seen by many sports federations as a constraint, a palliative, a salve for the conscience, when it is increasingly clear that the dual career is not an obstacle but a precondition for sporting success and the successful development of the individual.

Notes

1 http://ec.europa.eu/public_opinion/archives/ebs/ebs_412_fact_fr_en.pdf
2 www.sports.gouv.fr/IMG/pdf/chiffres-cles_du_sport_2015.pdf

References

Aquilina, D., (2015). Dual-career Management: Challenges and risks in elite sporting careers. In S. Landa (Ed.). *Sport Education and Training in Europe, A dual career for a dual life* (pp. 31–38). Sport and Citizenship Think Tank. Angers, France: Agence Com1ne. http://sportetcitoyennete.com/PDF/publication_double_projet.pdf?PHPSESSID=hd4ht8ci08tmdm9bjj4jk3jik4

Bouchetal Pellegri, F., Leseur, V. & Debois, N. (2006). *Carrière sportive. Projet de vie* (p.51). Paris : éditions Insep, coll. Entraînement.

Cour des comptes. (2013). *Sport pour tous et sport de haut niveau: pour une réorientation de l'action de l'Etat.* Paris: La documentation française.

Javerlhiac, S., Leyondre, F. & Bodin, D. (2011). Sportifs de haut niveau et double projet : entre bonnes intentions et faisabilité. *International Journal of Violence and School, 12,* 26–58.

Karaquillo, J.P. (2015). Statut des sportifs. Report to Secrétaire d'Etat aux sports. Retrieved from www.sports.gouv.fr/Karaquillo/Karaquillo_Rapport.pdf

Landa, S. (Ed.) (2015). *Sport, Education and Training in Europe. A dual career for a dual life.* Sport and Citizenship Think Tank. Angers, France: Agence Com1ne. http://sportetcitoyennete.com/PDF/publication_double_projet.pdf?PHPSESSID=hd4ht8ci08tmdm9bjj4jk3jik4

Monnereau, R. (2013). *Évaluation de la mise en œuvre du double projet des sportifs de haut niveau et des sportifs des centres de formation des clubs professionnels.* Report 2013-M-30 Inspection générale de la jeunesse et des sports to Ministère des sports, de la jeunesse, de l'éducation populaire et de la vie associative.

Part II

The Americas

Chapter 8

Canada

Milena M. Parent, David Patterson and Paul Jurbala[1]

Introduction

In this chapter, we present an overview of the Canadian sport system, to provide context to our ensuing discussion, as well as an overview of public policy associated with elite youth sport in Canada. We then discuss the impacts and influences of the elite youth sport system and public policy on three sports: figure skating, ice hockey and soccer/football. Finally, we provide a critical analysis of elite youth sport in Canada and conclude with two avenues for the future of the elite youth sport in Canada.

The Canadian sport system and public policy associated with elite youth sport

The Canadian sport system mirrors Canada's system of government. As such, we first briefly describe Canada as a Federation, before exploring the Canadian sport system and how Canada views elite youth sport.

Canada as a Federation

In the interest of brevity, two keys elements should be considered when studying Canada as a country. On the one hand, Canada is a decentralized federal democracy with ten provinces and three territories. This means that state powers and responsibilities, such as those for sport or education or immigration, are divided between the national (here, immigration) and provincial/territorial (here, sport and education) governments. The laws and structures associated with the children/youth (e.g., child protection and education) are provincial/territorial responsibilities, resulting in variations across jurisdictions, which have autonomy in this respect. Moreover, municipalities exist at the will of the provincial/territorial governments; as such, municipalities are an inter-provincial responsibility, not a federal responsibility. If the federal government wanted to speak to municipalities, it would need to go through the provinces to do so.

Given the multiple jurisdictions, a high degree of coordination is required, which is usually undertaken by the federal government. On the other hand, along with this highly decentralized structure, Canada's demographic factors must be considered, namely its large geography (second largest country in the world behind Russia) with six time zones, and a small population of just over 35 million people, most of whom reside near its southern border and are not evenly distributed between provinces and territories, ranging from 36,900 in Nunavut to 13,792,100 in Ontario (Statistics Canada 2015). Thus, any policy or decision requiring "equal representation" by province/territory can become a thorny issue. Notwithstanding, over 80 percent of Canada's population is urbanized, meaning access to programming is facilitated; however, for the 20 percent or so living in Canada's widespread rural areas, the situation becomes much more difficult. In the context of sport, especially single-sport development, the pressure to relocate to access quality sport programs can become quite significant. Time and financial costs grow to be substantial. And, this does not even factor in the meteorological aspect.

Combined, these factors result in agreements being put in place over a longer term and pieced together from a variety of sources. Delegation of responsibilities is rarely black-and-white. For example, if there were a United Nations agreement on youth sport needing to be ratified by "Canada," a federal-provincial/territorial (FPT) consultation process would need to be launched. For sport, these FPT consultations often result in agreements in principle. However, a couple of agreements, namely the National Recreation Framework, from a sectoral point of view, and the Social Union Framework Agreement that entrenched the approach to shared jurisdictionality, are in place to lay out the federal government's role in sport, mainly in national programming, including national teams and international representation, and pan-Canadian frameworks for the delivery of sport.

Sport in Canada

The Canadian Sport System is governed by the Physical Activity and Sport Act (Government of Canada, 2003), which has objectives for both sport and physical activity. All physical activity responsibilities are delegated to the Minister responsible for Public Health, whereas all sport responsibilities are delegated to the Minister responsible for Canadian Heritage. Within Canadian Heritage, we also find a Minister for Sport who oversees Sport Canada. Sport Canada acts as a leader and funder, a catalyst for sport delivery by the sector. It does not, however, regulate professional sport; this is the purview of each professional league (e.g., National Hockey League or NHL for professional ice hockey). Canadian Heritage/Sport Canada focuses on system building. This differs from Public Health, which focuses on project-based, community-innovative building projects, sparking local activity through public–private partnerships. Thus, joined-up government is not emphasized in the Canadian federal government.

Overall, coordination between governments is provided through the FPT Sport Committee (FPTSC), which has been in place for over 40 years and includes representation from a selection of provinces and territories, plus Sport Canada. Much of its effectiveness has been credited to the Canada Games, which have forced jurisdictions to work together. Other than the Canada Games, the FPTSC was an important part of the development of the Canadian Sport Policy 2012 (CSP 2012, see below for more information), and it identifies joint priorities for collaborative action over a given five-year period and based on the CSP 2012.

Under the FPTSC, there is the Sport, Physical Activity and Recreation Committee (SPARC), which focuses on topics related to sport, physical activity and recreation, and is composed of representation from all provinces and territories, plus at least two federal departments. Together, the FPTSC and SPARC set the framework for the Canadian sport system and coordinate their respective jurisdiction's activities regarding major sport system components, such as Long-Term Athlete Development (LTAD, technically-sound sport), ethics, safety, and participation diversity. For more on sport policy in Canada, see Thibault and Harvey (2013).

Two key elements in the system: CSP 2012 and LTAD

Led by governments and developed with significant public engagement, the CSP 2012 is the overarching, guiding document for the Canadian sport system. It lays out five policy goals for the Canadian sport system, namely (Sport Canada, 2012, p. 3, emphasis in original):

- **INTRODUCTION TO SPORT:** Canadians have the fundamental skills, knowledge and attitudes to participate in organized and unorganized sport.
- **RECREATIONAL SPORT:** Canadians have the opportunity to participate in sport for fun, health, social interaction and relaxation.
- **COMPETITIVE SPORT:** Canadians have the opportunity to systematically improve and measure their performance against others in competition in a safe and ethical manner.
- **HIGH PERFORMANCE SPORT:** Canadians are systematically achieving world-class results at the highest levels of international competition through fair and ethical means.
- **SPORT FOR DEVELOPMENT:** Sport is used as a tool for social and economic development, and the promotion of positive values at home and abroad.

The CSP 2012's policy values include: fun, excellence, safety, commitment, personal development, inclusion and accessibility, respect, fair play, and ethical behavior (Sport Canada, 2012). In turn, its core policy principles include: sport policies and programming that are values-based, inclusive, technically sound, collaborative, intentional, effective, and sustainable (Sport Canada, 2012). The policy also provides a logic model for its progression over its ten-year lifespan, and is currently monitored by the Policy Implementation and Monitoring Work Group, a first for the Canadian sport system.

Next, LTAD has been adopted by Sport Canada as a national framework for sport development. Advanced by Canadian Sport for Life (CS4L), LTAD is "a multi-stage training, competition, and recovery pathway that guides an individual's experience in sport and physical activity from infancy through all phases of adulthood" (CS4L, 2014, p. 12). Goals for participants include improved competence, personal satisfaction, retention in sport, and increased success in competition (Balyi et al., 2005). Since 2005, mandated by Sport Canada, all 58 Canadian national sport organizations (NSOs) have developed sport-specific LTAD models, and LTAD principles are entrenched as "technically sound sport" in the Canadian Sport Policy 2012–2022. In an effort to align sport delivery, CS4L branched out to engage school-based sport, municipal recreation, and public health sectors as well as a number of other organizations; goals proposed by CS4L include full integration into Canadian sport, recreation, education and health organizations at municipal, provincial/territorial and national levels (Norris, 2010).

The rapid penetration of LTAD is due in large part to support by Sport Canada and the Provincial/Territorial (P/T) governments and their influence upon government-funded NSOs and provincial/territorial sport organizations (PTSOs). Between 2008 and 2014, Sport Canada invested over $8 million[2] into LTAD development and implementation (Dowling, 2014). However, NSOs and PTSOs together constitute less than 25 percent of Canadian sport and recreation organizations (Misener & Doherty, 2009), so LTAD integration across the entire sport system depends on the ability of community sport organizations (CSOs) to understand, adopt and implement a relatively complex set of principles and practices. In practice, integration of LTAD into programming implies coach education, adapted training programs and competitions, modifications to sport venues and equipment, redeployment of volunteer staff, and reorganization of participants and teams.

The adoption of LTAD in Canada and a number of other nations has prompted research on its implementation and effectiveness. While LTAD has been criticized as lacking scientific validation (Collins & Bailey, 2013), LTAD and similar stage-based sport development models have been adopted in several nations including the UK and Australia (Gulbin et al., 2013). Research on LTAD implementation in Canada suggests that CSOs and coaches may follow LTAD principles in idiosyncratic ways due to the complexity of the model, lack of resources, lack of understanding or support from the parents of young athletes, and failure of the NSO to modify its competitive formats to match LTAD principles (Banack, Bloom, & Falcão, 2012; Beaudoin, Callary, & Trudeau, 2015; Frankish, 2011; Jurbala, 2015, in preparation). The social effects of standardized systems are also disputable: Lang (2010) sees LTAD as a normative model used to enforce conformity and discipline, which deprives coaches of fulfilling interaction with athletes. While adopted as a pan-Canadian initiative to improve the quality of sport program delivery and participant experience, the possibility of misinterpreting or selectively applying LTAD for other ends is always present.

The Canadian sport system

Canada's sport system mirrors the decentralized federal structure, with NSOs linking to PTSOs, which in turn link to local clubs and leagues (CSOs). Sport Canada funds 55 sports with an overall annual funding budget of CAD$200 million, though there are many more that exist. While Sport Canada acts as a leader of sorts, there is no one body responsible for technical direction in the Canadian sport system, as there are in many other countries such as Norway (e.g., Norwegian Olympic and Paralympic Committee and Confederation of Sports); instead, there are multiple (multi-sport) non-governmental franchise holders that do so (e.g. Canadian Olympic Committee, Canadian Paralympic Committee, Commonwealth Games Canada, and Canada Games Council). Although this approach allows a potential reduction of hierarchical, bureaucratic processes, it does result in some duplication of efforts and resources.

Sport Canada's funding is complemented by these other organizations, which provide specific programs and services. In fact, Sport Canada provides funding to a number of these multi-sport service organizations (MSOs) (e.g., Coaching Association of Canada, Own The Podium (OTP), and the Canadian Sport Centers/Institutes) given their particular roles in the sport system or in order to address particular systemic challenges, often in conjunction with certain provinces. The thought behind shifting some funding decisions to MSOs such as OTP was to remove, at least in theory, the political influence on elite sport funding decisions, as well as the recognition by Sport Canada that they may not actually possess the full expertise in-house to make these decisions. As a consequence, about $64 million out of Sport Canada's $200 million is allocated to sports based on OTP recommendations.

Similarly to the broader Canadian context, sport delivery in Canada is network-based, combining public, non-profit and for-profit organizations, clubs and leagues, as well as individual contractors. This is also the case for Olympic Games delivery in Canada (Parent, 2015). Some jurisdictions, such as the province of British Columbia, use the Centers and Institutes to have integrated (medical) support teams and a quality training environment for

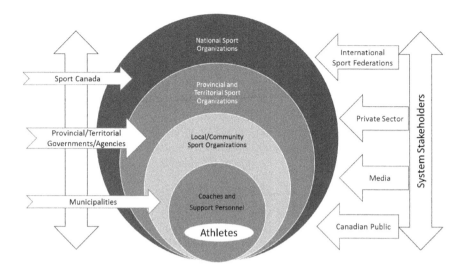

Figure 8.1 The Canadian sport system – a multi-level, multi-jurisdictional, federated system

Adapted from information provided by Sport Canada, Department of Canadian Heritage

athletes, so they become tangible focal points demonstrating the interconnected nature of the Canadian sport system regarding the coming together of facilities and service providers. Due to its federated nature, the sport network overalps within itself as well as with complementary sectors and delivery organizations that provide programming with a sport component, such as schools, municipalities, recreation assocations, businesses and/or franchises. In effect, the Canadian sport system is a hierarchical, multi-level, and multi-jurisdictional network. Thus, proper coordination is a critical factor in the system's effectiveness and efficiency. Figure 8.1 illustrates the key components of the Canadian sport system.

The elite youth sport context

Elite youth sport is an area of shared jurisdictions, mainly at the provincial/territorial level, and responsibilities, as it touches different ministries, such as Canadian Heritage, Public Health and Education. Elite youth sport is not explicitly defined or used as a framework for programming in any national policy document in Canada; however, elite youth sport can be seen to co-exist in the Train-to-Train and early Train-to-Compete LTAD stages, providing some noteworthy challenges to systematic athlete and sport development due to its emphasis on competition and early specialization, as well as consequences on increasing sport costs and decreasing access. Sport Canada, among other national-level organizations, therefore must look at how sport participation and excellence are complementary ideals versus competing objectives, understanding that a greater number of trained and skilled athletes at every level of the LTAD system will result in more positive outcomes for both international sport competition results and a generally healthier Canadian population.

The process of talent identification has long been lamented as an area in need of improvement (e.g., Balyi et al., 2005). The identification of talented youth who may be able to compete in the high performance realm is often haphazard and reliant on chance meetings between talent identifiers and young athletes. The difficulty of talent identification in the Canadian context is exacerbated by two key factors: the structural and organizational diversity of the components of the Canadian system, and the sheer geographic size of the country. There are over 17,000 CSOs in Canada (Mulholland, 2008) covering many sports, some multi-sport clubs and not including agencies such as Canadian Olympic and Paralympic Sport Institutes and educational institutions. The diversity on an organizational level means that there are rarely the kind of bottlenecks built into the system that would allow talent to be "funneled" towards the structures, facilities and coaches that are looking for it. Of note, as is outlined further below, educational systems largely do not provide this bottleneck and even when they do so, do not do so in a consistent manner. Secondly, in sports where the pinnacle of competition is the national team program (as opposed to more diffuse professional leagues), the size of Canada becomes a real barrier. With a nation spread over some six time zones and nearly 10 million square kilometers, the task of just seeing youth level athletes to identify talent levels is Herculean. While some sports have adopted "talent combines" and other talent identification schemes, the structures and size of Canada conspire to make this process both inherently and extremely difficult.

To attempt to overcome some difficulties, in 2014, OTP launched a funding program delivered through NSOs and Canadian Sport Centers to support the development of "next generation" athletes. These athletes are identified as having podium potential, and estimated to be six to eight years from Olympic participation. Such athletes are in the late Train to Train stage of LTAD, aged 14–18 in many sports. This reflects a trend toward earlier identification of athletes for high performance development at or just after the pubertal growth spurt. The success of this "Next Gen" program has yet to be determined, however.

Next, as education and sport are provincial jurisdictions, sport development practices vary from one province/territory to another. This is also the case with sport schools. For instance, the province of Quebec has a well-developed sport-school system where the school schedule and teaching format is moulded around the student's athletic calendar; thus, exams can be taken while off-site or delayed until the student returns home, without any penalty. In contrast, Alberta, British Columbia and Ontario also have sport schools, such as the National Sport School in Calgary (Alberta), which are linked to charter schools, with some having an athletic performance focus, but others using sport as basis for theme learning or as part of holistic learning experience to develop the whole person (see Balderson, 2015; Way, Repp & Brennan, 2010 for more information).

The development of youth coaches/coaching practices designed for young athletes is a strength of the Canadian system. The National Coaching Certification Program (NCCP) was instituted in 1974 as a comprehensive training and development program for sport coaches, and is in use by all Canadian NSOs and PTSOs. Managed by the Coaching Association of Canada (CAC), the NCCP was reorganized in the early twenty-first century from its original delivery model to a new competency-based framework, which certifies coaches based on demonstration of sport-specific abilities in the context of the stage of athlete development (e.g., initiation, development, high performance). There were over 1.8 million sport coaches in Canada in 2005 (Misener & Danylchuk, 2009), and the NCCP trained over 46,000 coaches in 2015 (CAC, n.d.). Coach certification is required by NSOs, PTSOs and CSOs for participation in many leagues and events. Notably, certification to an advanced level is required for coaches at the Canada Games, the national Games for high performance provincial/territorial-level athletes (Canada Games, n.d.). Recognized as a world leader for the coaching profession, the NCCP is an important mechanism for establishing consistent standards and behaviors among coaches, including for ethical conduct. At the time of writing this chapter, the NCCP development track for high performance coaches is in revision, but is expected to feature personal development plans and in-service training for national team coaches and technical leaders.

Beyond coaching, competition structure, including competition formats, rules, eligibility and scheduling, is an important sport system driver. The cost of travel to and participation in competitions and tournaments is a significant participant expense, particularly as parents and siblings often accompany youth competitors. Competitions are frequently used for athlete selection and scouting, so participation in such events is essential for athletes on a high performance track. The LTAD framework suggests that as coaches base training programs around competition structures and rules, a process of competition review and restructuring is essential to aligning competition with sport development objectives, and Sport Canada has supported the cost of such reviews for a number of NSOs. However, this has not resulted in a decrease in the number and scale of competitions. Sport Canada's contribution to the hosting of international events in Canada includes a base amount of $19 million to cover responsibilities in the *Federal Policy on Hosting International Sport Events*; however, major sports events, such as the 2010 Olympic Winter Games, 2015 Pan and Para-Pan American Games and FIFA Women's World Cup Canada 2015 require significant funding above and beyond the $19 million, for which policy and additional funding approvals are sought on an exceptional, case-by-case basis. The belief that participation in high-level competitions is critical to athlete success also results in pressure on NSOs to name teams for, and provide support to, events such as junior world championships, youth Games, and other international events.

We find pressures from the sports and franchise holders (e.g., International Olympic Committee, Commonwealth Games Federation) to participate in elite youth sport competitions. Thus, each NSO is tasked with identifying the appropriate events for sport development progression towards senior events, where competition for results is the focus. However, beyond being an excuse for an international trip, the quality of the event is not always high; thus, NSOs often use a self-funding model for athletes to participate in these events, be they Youth Olympic Games (15–18 years old), Universiades (17–28 years old), or any other similar event. As such, athletes within higher socio-economic status families are more likely to be the ones to go to these events, thereby skewing the population and putting into question the existence of and participation in such events. Thus, in Canada at least, elite youth sport seems to be a phenomenon to manage as opposed to a goal to achieve.

Overall, we find a growing sophistication in sports, with programs becoming increasingly structured, time intensive, and expensive. Despite introduction of the LTAD framework with its emphasis on early multilateral development and later specialization, pressures to specialize early, popular ideas regarding talent identification and the "need" to start early to attain sport success, the increasing number of international elite youth events positioned as integral to sport development, and the prevalence of sponsorships, cash and other in-kind prizes for young competitors, reflect a general trend toward elitism in youth sport. Collectively, these decisions, pressures, and popular ideas affect not only the young athletes but also their entire family. Interestingly, there does not seem to be evidence, in Canada at least, of young athletes who enjoy success as a young athlete also experiencing success later in their athletic careers. This would suggest that young athletes are not well served by the current system.

Elite youth sport examples

We now provide an outline of the practice of elite youth sport using three sports as exemplars, notably: figure skating as an example of an early peak performance sport; ice hockey as an example of a commercial team sport; and soccer/football as an example of a prominent Olympic sport in the country. Sport participation for the 15–19 year old group has decreased significantly between 1992 and 2010, dropping from 77 percent to 54 percent (Canadian Heritage, 2013; O'Reilly, et al., 2015; Policy Research

Group, 2010). However, 62 percent of sport participants aged 15–19 participated in competitions and tournaments, which represents a slight increase from 2005 (59 percent) (Canadian Heritage, 2013).

Figure skating – the early peak performance sport

Figure skating is a popular sport in Canada, and Canadians have a tradition of being among the strongest nations in the world on the national and international stages. The elite youth development of figure skating athletes, as a partially early peak performance sport (early peak in women's singles, later peaks in pairs and dance), figure skating has a flexible program that identifies and develops athletes based largely on geographical footprints.

Skate Canada, the governing body for the sport in Canada, is divided into geographically bound "sections." These sections, largely aligned with provincial boundaries, provide the competition environments at the early stages of youth development with the training environment situated at the local club level. Unlike many other Canadian sports (see ice hockey and soccer below), professional coaching is generally required at the CSO level, starting with the introduction to the sport.

Skate Canada, along with its constituent (provincial) sections, has created regional training centers that provide a concentrated training and competition environment for elite youth development skaters. These centers are coordinated by both the NSO and by some section members. This has created a mix of training options for elite youth competitors, which is appropriate given the wide variance in ages of specialization in the sport.

Competitively, figure skating offers national championship-level competition at several tiers of competition. Unlike other Canadian sports (such as ice hockey and soccer below), qualification for these tiers is not based on the age of the competitor but more on their skill level. A minimum skill level in each discipline is outcome-based, with scored specialty elements (such as jumps or spins) being the standard, rather than basic skating skills (such as edging or stroking) that comprise the scored element. The objectivity of the measures, and the impact on judging, results in a tiering scheme that is both more objective and more applied in competition than in practice (or try-outs) compared to team sports. Other sports profiled in this chapter do not have minimum skill levels objectively defined; instead, they rely on the subjective judgment of coaches who select teams for various levels of competition.

Ice hockey – the commercial team sport

Ice hockey is the official winter sport of Canada and is the most popular sport in the country based on revenues, television engagement and, anecdotally, measured by cultural import. However, by participation numbers, it falls behind soccer (see below).

Canadian elite youth development in ice hockey is driven largely by CSO-level competition at community, semi-professional and professional levels. Of note, in ice hockey (and in some other sports such as athletics, basketball and softball), the border with the United States is very permeable, in both directions, to athletes. Finally, elite youth development in ice hockey is meaningfully different by gender, with ample competitive and training opportunities for men and significantly limited opportunity for women.

 CSO-level youth development for ice hockey is anchored in the voluntary sport club model. Even in larger cities, it is common for volunteers to operate youth sport structures and to provide coaching, even at the elite development level. From the ages of five through to 18, athletes are predominantly in the CSO system.

For men and boys, there is a semi-professional option for ice hockey players at the youth development level. Junior hockey is offered in several tiers. Major Junior hockey is the top tier with competition that is overtly designed to prepare players for the National Hockey League (NHL) and higher levels of elite competition. Canadian Major Junior Hockey is organized into the Canadian Hockey League, which is further comprised of three member leagues, the Western Hockey League, the Ontario Hockey League and the Quebec Major Junior Hockey League. In smaller Canadian cities, Major Junior Hockey can be the "big ticket in town," drawing the community together to support its team, much like one would see in cities with NHL teams. Major Junior Hockey is usually viewed as semi-professional, with the players receiving a small stipend for playing as well as scholarships that offer educational support upon completion of the junior playing career. At this level of competition, players are drafted onto teams (as young as age 15) and can be traded from one team to another, very much emulating the model of North American professional sport.

It must be noted that in ice hockey, youth elite development continues into the major professional level of competition. The minimum age for competition in the NHL is only 18 years of age. This means that athletes are at times playing in major professional ranks while still eligible to play at the U20 level internationally. This also means that athletes are expected to continue their development as youth athletes even while competing at the senior elite level and with considerably more compensation.

For women, the options are more limited during the elite youth phase. Women competing in ice hockey are likely to start out in the same club system as men, often playing with men, but their elite youth development is geared towards intercollegiate competition in the youth phase. Women's ice hockey in Canadian Interuniversity Sport is a key developmental avenue towards national and Olympic team participation, with the National Collegiate Athletic Association also providing a key avenue. For women, there is no analogous competition to Junior hockey, where they may receive compensation. In fact, the only professional league for women, the National

Women's Hockey League only launched in 2015, with a competing elite league, the Canadian Women's Hockey League having a longer history, but one checkered with financial and structural challenges.

Soccer/football – the prominent Olympic sport in the country

While ice hockey has traditionally been considered Canada's winter sport, soccer (or football to non-North Americans) has surpassed hockey as the leading participation sport for youth in the past two decades. In 2010, soccer was the number one youth sport in Canada with 42 percent of youth participants, followed by swimming (24 percent) and ice hockey (22 percent) (Canadian Heritage, 2013), although Soccer Canada has reported declines in youth registration 2010-2014 (Soccer Canada, n.d.). As the sport grew, Canada hosted FIFA Women's, U20 and U17 World Cups, and currently has three Major League Soccer franchises (Montreal, Toronto, Vancouver), but despite the popularity of the game, Canada has ranked on average ninth (women) and seventy-seventh (men) since FIFA created its world rankings. Thus, the rapid expansion of interest and participation in Canadian soccer has brought both riches and unprecedented pressures to the sport. The bronze medal won by the Canadian women's team at the 2012 London Olympic Games, the nation's first in a team sport, was supported by nearly $14 million in OTP funding in the decade spanning the 2008 Beijing through 2016 Rio Olympic Games (Own The Podium, n.d.), while the lesser-performing men's side receives no OTP funding. This has intensified demands that Canada climb into the ranks of leading soccer nations through intensive player development programs for both sexes.

Soccer Canada and its P/T affiliates have responded with a number of initiatives to improve high performance development, particularly through restructuring and creation of new leagues that create pathways to high performance soccer. For younger age groups, new high performance leagues for identified U13–U17 youth players, including British Columbia Soccer's Premier League and Ontario Player Development League (OPDL), lead to provincial and national team selection. Clubs chosen for these leagues must demonstrate compliance with LTAD and other technical standards and pay high fees which are passed on to players: in the inaugural year of OPDL, clubs expected to charge $4,500 per player, but inter-club competition resulted in an unsustainable average fee of $3,200 (Jurbala, 2015). The provincial and national associations also operate programs to hothouse selected young players, such as Soccer Canada's Women's "Excel" program for U13-U17. This has led to intense competition for selection among young players, and a corresponding growth in the number of private soccer academies catering to youth development. These academies themselves compete for legitimacy: the Soccer Academy Alliance Canada, representing over 20 academies, recently negotiated an accreditation agreement with the Ontario Soccer Association.

Competition between young players for selection to elite clubs and development programs, together with competition between organizations for legitimacy and access to players, can be construed as inevitable developments in "the global sporting arms race" (DeBosscher et al., 2009), evidence of the rampant commercialization of youth sport (Coakley, 2010), or both. The rapid rise of soccer as the youth sport of choice in Canada has resulted in a proliferation of clubs, private academies, and high performance development programs and with this, ever more expensive programs for identified, "elite" youth. The resulting competition between soccer providers is mirrored, and arguably stimulated, by competing institutional logics in Canadian sport including the LTAD "quality sport" vs. OTP "excellence" programs funded through Sport Canada, and a broader communitarian vs. individualist conflict felt at the community club level (Jurbala, 2015).

Discussion and conclusions

Based on the above, we see the Canadian sport system and the aspects associated more closely with elite youth sport have some strengths but also weaknesses. Regarding strengths, the Canadian sport system demonstrates diversity and innovation in:

- the quality of its programs;
- individuals' high level of knowledge and expertise;
- being a world leader in a number of aspects of sport system development such as coach certification, anti-doping efforts, the integration of para-sports, demonstrating diversity in the system, the development of newer winter Olympic sports, and being trailblazers in women in sport; and
- the implementation of a system-wide LTAD framework.

Regarding its weaknesses, the Canadian sport system faces difficulties in terms of having:

- an entrenched, federated system with overlapping, sometimes redundant, hierarchical, multi-level and multi-jurisdictional aspects, which makes it difficult to regroup and coordinate this diverse system;
- programs that are not well adapted to the diverse Canadian population and which tend to de-select rather than encourage continued participation;
- programs which inadequately develop skills and attributes needed for progression and/or lifelong involvement; and
- a geographical spread which hinders coordination among sport system stakeholders.

These issues can therefore affect the growth of elite youth sport in the future. Clearly, elite youth sport is a challenge for the Canadian LTAD approach; however, it provides NSOs with additional opportunities to pick the appropriate events that can become vehicles (as opposed to ends in themselves) for progression through the particular sport's development process.

There are also a number of policy challenges to consider for the Canadian sport system and the place of elite youth sport within it. First, there is a decreasing athlete pool entering youth sport due to sedentary behavior, a lack of unstructured play to develop diverse skills, decreasing availability of quality physical education, and logistical/economic challenges to develop diverse movement and sport skills. These factors contribute to athletes being poorly prepared to engage in elite sport and more likely prone to injury. The entrenched practices of early de-selection combined with proper skill development concentrated at later stages serve to further skew the athlete pool. Second, elite youth sport is often limited to those with economic means; thus, structuring programs specifically for elite youth sport further stratifies by social and economic factors. Third, a poor understanding and the popular conceptualization of talent identification and development can lead to inadequate and counter-indicated programming. The assumptions that state-of-the art equipment or facilities are required at all sport development stages, that starting to specialize early is better, as well as the over-emphasis on competition and competition results at early stages, are not proven evidence-based practices. Fourth, although certain jurisdictions are using Centers and Institutes as tangible coordination mechanisms, there are private performance centers being created; while this can increase the potential for access to a sport and opportunity to practice that sport, it conversely increases the complexity of coordinating the system and the costs (as it skews the sport's practice towards those within higher socio-economic status). Fifth, despite sustained investments in the sport system by various jurisdictions, many sport organizations continue to struggle with planning processes, technical oversight and long-term development. Embedding LTAD within sports' sport development processes has proved challenging given the entrenched, established ways of operating, as well as the little collaboration found between sports and between sport organizations. This has potentially negative implications for multi-sport activities and talent transfer between sports and also results in inadequate systems to ensure safety (harassment- and abuse-free sport experiences) and diverse engagement in the sport system.

In conclusion, there are a number of intertwined socio-cultural and political dimensions that make elite youth sport particularly challenging in the Canadian context. To avoid ending on such a negative note, we offer two avenues for potential solutions: 1) a paradigm shift by moving towards a more community-based, multi-sport approach, to engage communities and families in sport instead of focusing only on the youth and moving the youth faster through the system; and 2) a legislative approach to help "protect" youth. Though likely not to the extent found in Norway, given the multi-jurisdictional nature of the youth file in Canada, some form of legislative protection could help mitigate negative consequences of too early specialization (e.g., injury or dropping out of sport).

Notes

1 The authors would like to thank Sport Canada for their invaluable assistance.
2 All amounts in Canadian dollars.

References

Balderson, D. (2015). Sport academies: A growing phenomenon in Canadian schools. *Physical & Health Education Journal, 80*(4), 27–29.

Balyi, I., Cardinal, C., Higgs, C., Norris, S., & Way, R. (2005). *Long-term athlete development – Canadian Sport for life.* Retrieved March 10, 2009, from www.ltad.ca/Groups/LTAD%20Downloads/English/LTAD_Resource_Paper.pdf

Banack, H. R., Bloom, G. A., & Falcão, W. R. (2012). Promoting long term athlete development in cross country skiing through competency-based coach education: A qualitative study. *International Journal of Sports Science and Coaching, 7*(2), 301–316.

Beaudoin, C., Callary, B., & Trudeau, F. (2015). Coaches' adoption and implementation of sport Canada's long-term athlete development model. *SAGE Open, 5*(3). doi:10.1177/2158244015595269

Canada Games. (n.d.). *Sport Selection.* Retrieved November 5, 2015 from www.canadagames.ca/content/ Sports/sport-selection.asp

Canadian Heritage. (2013). *Sport Participation 2010.* Ottawa, Canada: Her Majesty the Queen in Right of Canada.

Canadian Sport for Life. (2014). *Long-Term Athlete Development.* Vancouver: Canadian Sport Centre Pacific.

Coaching Association of Canada. Annual Report 2015. Retrieved November 5, 2015 from: www.coach.ca/files/2014_15_ANNUAL_REPORT_FINAL_ENG.pdf

Coakley, J. (2010). The "Logic" of Specialization: Using Children for Adult Purposes. *Journal of Physical Education Recreation and Dance, 81*(8), 16–25.

Collins, D., & Bailey, R. (2013). 'Scienciness' and the allure of second-hand strategy in talent identification and development. *International Journal of Sport Policy and Politics, 5*(2), 183–191. doi:10.1080/19406940.2012.656682

DeBosscher, V., DeKnop, P., Van Bottenburg, M., Shibli, S., & Bingham, J. (2009). Explaining international sporting success: An international comparison of elite sport systems and policies in six countries. **Sport Management Review 12**(3): 113–136. DOI: 10.1016/j.smr.2009.01.001

Dowling, M. S. (2014). *Under new governance? Examining the role of Canadian sport for life in sport policy and governance.* PhD thesis. Edmonton, Alberta: University of Alberta.

Frankish, M. T. (2011). *Better understanding the adoption of the long-term athlete development model: Case analyses of cross-country ski coaches.* Masters thesis. Ottawa, Ontario: University of Ottawa.

Government of Canada (2003). Physical Activity and Sport Act, c. 2 C.F.R.

Gulbin, J. P., Croser, M. J., Morley, E. J., & Weissensteiner, J. R. (2013). An integrated framework for the optimisation of sport and athlete development: A practitioner approach. *Journal of Sports Sciences, 31*(12), 1319–1331. doi:10.10 80/02640414.2013.781661

Jurbala, P. (2015). *Birth of a league, death of community sport? A multi-level contextual analysis.* In preparation.

Lang, M. (2010). Surveillance and conformity in competitive youth swimming. *Sport, Education and Society, 15*(1), 19-37. doi:10.1080/13573320903461152

Misener, K., & Danylchuk. (2009). Coaches' Perceptions of Canada's National Coaching Certification Program (NCCP): Awareness and Value. *International Journal of Sport Science and Coaching,* 4(2), 233 DOI: http://dx.doi.org/10.1260/174795409788549580

Misener, K., & Doherty, A. (2009). A case study of organizational capacity in nonprofit community sport. *Journal of Sport Management, 23*(4), 457–482.

Mulholland, E. (2008). *What sport can do: The true sport report.* Issue Brief. Ottawa, Canada: True Sport.

Norris, S.R. (2010). Long-term athlete development Canada: attempting system change and multi-agency cooperation. *Current Sports Medicine Reports, 9*(6), 379–382.

O'Reilly, N., Berger, I. E., Hernandez, T., Parent, M. M., & Séguin, B. (2015). Urban sportscapes: An environmental deterministic perspective on the management of youth sport participation. *Sport Management Review, 18*(2), 291–307. doi: http://dx.doi.org/10.1016/j.smr.2014.07.003

Own The Podium. n.d. *Funding.* Retrieved from http://ownthepodium.org/Funding.aspx

Parent, M. M. (2015). The Governance of the Olympic Games in Canada. Sport in Society, in press, doi: 10.1080/17430437.2015.1108652

Policy Research Group. (2010). *Environmental Scan 2010: Trends and Issues in Canada and in Sport.* Ottawa, Canada: Author.

Soccer Canada. n.d. *Annual Report 2014.* Retrieved November 5, 2015 from: www.canadasoccer.com/files/CanadaSoccer_AnnualReport2014_EN_web.pdf

Sport Canada. (2012). *Canadian Sport Policy 2012.* Ottawa, Canada: Author Retrieved November 2, 2015 from http://sirc.ca/csp2012.

Statistics Canada. (2015, September 29). Population by year, by province and territory Retrieved October 5, 2015, from www.statcan.gc.ca/tables-tableaux/sum-som/l01/cst01/demo02a-eng.htm

Thibault, L., & Harvey, J. (Eds.). (2013). *Sport Policy in Canada.* Ottawa: University of Ottawa Press.

Way, R., Repp, C., & Brennan, T. (2010, July). Sport schools in Canada: The future is here. Retrieved January 15, 2016 from http://canadiansportforlife.ca/sites/default/files/resources/Sport%20Schools%20in%20Canada.pdf

Chapter 9

United States of America

B. Christine Green and Matthew B. Greenberg

The US sport system is complex, chaotic, and competitive. In short, it reflects the broader cultural and political milieu in which it is embedded (Sparvero, Chalip, & Green, 2008). There is almost no government involvement in youth sport at the federal level. This does not reflect the importance of sport in the United States. Rather, it is consistent with the federalist system of government in which the federal government is granted its powers through the US Constitution and its amendments; all powers not explicitly granted to the federal government by the Constitution devolve to the individual states. Sport is not mentioned in the US Constitution. In fact, no federal agency is charged with overseeing sport in the United States, and there is no Minister of Sport or Cabinet-level sport appointment in the US system. Instead, US athletes are developed through a cacophony of public, private and not-for profit sport organizations.

Recruitment into youth sport traditionally occurred through public parks and recreation programs provided at low cost by municipal government, through schools, or through nonprofit sport clubs or multi-sport organizations such as the Young Men's Christian Association (YMCA), the Boys and Girls Clubs of America (BGCA), Jewish Community Centers (JCCs), the American Legion, local youth sport associations, and numerous other sport providers. Over the past 20–30 years, there has been a strong shift away from recreational leagues and teams toward elite pay-to-play clubs. Many of these clubs field elite travel teams for athletes from the age of seven. Travel teams are more likely than recreational teams to have professional coaches, and to require young athletes to specialize in one sport and to play that sport year round. The emphasis on elite youth sport begins early in childhood. American culture has long valued individual achievement. Youth sport has become parents' go-to venue for pushing their children to achieve. This has created a market for specialized sports training, coaching, and events targeting young athletes. The aggregate expenditures for equipment, fees, and uniforms to participate in youth sports have been estimated to exceed US$5 billion annually (UFonline, 2015). In addition, the aggregate annual expenditure for travel to youth sport contests is estimated at a further US$7 billion (Cook,

2014). Indeed, the cost to participate in youth sport has risen precipitously in recent decades, and continues to rise. A recent study by Turbo Tax (Turbotaxjen, 2013) estimated that parents spend an average of $671 per year on their child's recreational participation. Elite youth sport participation costs many thousands of dollars more, with parents easily spending 10 to 20 percent of their income on their child's sport (Sullivan, 2015).

Elite youth sport development is far from systematic. Pathways to excellence vary considerably, with a wide array of organizations across sectors competing for athletes, coaches, support services, and personnel. This competition has resulted in a near ubiquitous use of the label 'elite' to describe youth sport programs. As in most countries, US National Governing Bodies (NGBs) articulate a pathway to excellence in their sports. However, those pathways fail to acknowledge the range of alternatives within the pathways, some being complements and some being impediments to elite youth development.

Elite youth school sport

School sport offers one such pathway for elite youth athletes *in some sports* (e.g., basketball, football, baseball). Middle schools, junior high schools, and high schools provide elite sport opportunities to youth athletes. School districts and sport programs within the schools are governed at the local and state levels. Schools will sponsor a Varsity, Junior Varsity, and sometimes a Freshman team across a selected range of sports. For the 2014–2015 school year, basketball was the most widely offered high school sport for both boys and girls with 18,072 and 17,653 schools fielding teams for boys and girls, respectively (National Federation of State High School Associations, 2016). Outdoor track and field teams were fielded by 16,358 (boys) and 16,309 (girls) high schools. Baseball, cross-country running, and (gridiron) football round out the top five high school sports for males. For females, the top five is rounded out by volleyball, fast-pitch softball, and cross-country running. It is interesting to note that although soccer is offered by fewer high schools, the number of soccer players in high schools is in the top five for both girls and boys.

Public schools are funded by tax dollars. Consequently, they are expected to provide opportunities to young athletes from all socioeconomic levels. In theory, this is the case. In practice, it is often not the case for three reasons. First, since American public schools are locally funded, the funds available to support school-based sport vary substantially among school districts. The more affluent a community, the more funds are available for sport, so the greater the range and quality of sport opportunities (Walters, 2001). Second, as local school systems face budgetary pressures, athletes are being asked to pay to play (Bucy, 2013). Although these amounts are relatively small, some families cannot afford for their children to participate. Third, school sport is insufficient (and sometimes unnecessary) for elite development. It is increasingly difficult to be selected for a high school team unless one has entered the sport at an early age, specialized in that sport, and been selected to play on an elite travel team. So what at first glance seems to be a merit-based system, is decidedly skewed toward families with greater means to support their children's early sport experiences. It is rare for an athlete to make a high school team without having played for a club team in the years leading to the high school years.

Historically, high school sports served as the feeder system for college and university sport. Most sports represented in colleges[1] and universities are also offered in high schools. It is fair to say that, for some families, elite youth sport participation is seen as an investment with a university scholarship the potential payoff (Farrey, 2009). High school participation alone is rarely enough to land a college scholarship. College sport recruitment is fraught with regulations, ostensibly to protect elite athletes from having their lives disrupted by the recruitment process. University coaches are limited in the times of the year they can contact youth athletes, the places at which they may speak to youth athletes, the age at which athletes may be contacted, and the medium by which they may contact athletes, to name just a few limitations. Universities are not allowed to host try-outs for athletes prior to their arrival on campus as a registered student (National Collegiate Athletic Association, 2015). Talent identification, then, is limited. An elite young athlete must be noticed by a university coach to have any chance of playing at that level. High school seasons often overlap with college seasons, making it difficult for college coaches to visit high schools to identify and evaluate talented players. Not surprisingly, a plethora of alternative opportunities has emerged to provide athletes with ways to showcase their talents in front of coaches and recruiters.

In some ways, and for some sports (e.g., gymnastics, tennis, skiing), high school teams and competitions no longer represent the top echelon of performance, and may not always attract the best athletes. It is important to remember that school sport policies, like other educational policies, are determined by state educational authorities and local school boards. Some school districts have adopted policies that are antithetic to the development of elite youth sport. For example, many school districts restrict the number of hours of practice, some make it illegal to train on the weekend, and still others rule players ineligible if they play on a team outside of the school. In theory, these rules are adopted to protect youth from prioritizing sport over their education. In practice, these policies restrict players from the type of training that may be necessary to attain elite status. This is not true for all sports, nor do all school systems adopt such policies. The point is that there are no consistent national policies for elite youth sport development, nor are the rules consistent from state to state or school district to school district. Alternative providers have stepped in to provide elite sport opportunities for school-age athletes – providers who are not subjected to the restrictions imposed by the schools.

Elite youth club sport

Youth sport clubs in the United States do not conform to a single organizational structure or purpose. In fact, youth sport clubs can be found across all three economic sectors (public, private for-profit, and private not-for-profit), although elite clubs tend to be either not-for-profit or for-profit organizations. Public sector teams are rarely elite as their mission typically mandates inclusion over elite selection. Clubs are affiliated with a wide array of leagues and governing bodies. Local community clubs are ubiquitous. These are most often not-for-profit clubs offering a number of sports depending on the season and local interests. These clubs can serve a large number of participants and typically offer in-house recreational opportunities for all participants, select teams by age group, and a menu of personal player development opportunities (e.g., additional skill training sessions, physical training sessions, camps and clinics). Volunteer coaches (often parents) are the norm at the recreational level and for many of the select teams. Single sport clubs often include an academy level as a bridge between recreational and select teams. Clubs with more elite aspirations will hire professional coaches for their select teams, and in some cases for their academy teams. Costs are significant. The more elite the program, the higher the expectation that an athlete will specialize in a single sport, and compete year round.

National organizations for elite clubs

Clubs can affiliate with any number of national organizations for competition, insurance, and other benefits. Most National Governing Bodies (NGBs) have a competitive structure and event sanctioning for elite youth sport clubs. For example, USA Volleyball sanctions age-group competition teams with 12 national qualifying tournaments and a national championship in seven age divisions for girls. National championships in youth volleyball are also hosted by the Amateur Athletic Union (AAU), which hosts national championships in more than 25 sports (Amateur Athletic Union of the United States, 2016). National organizations in other sports (e.g., soccer, basketball) also offer event-based national championships for age-group teams, and are now providing an elite, national league structure for youth teams. The US Youth Soccer National League competition, for example, is for the nation's top 16 teams in the Under-14, Under-15, Under-16, Under-17 and Under-18 boys and girls age groups. The National League claims to offer elite youth players, "additional exposure to collegiate, professional and U.S. National Team coaches and the highest level of competition in the country. Teams earn their spot in the National League via success in the US Youth Soccer

Regional Leagues and the US Youth Soccer National Championship Series" (US Youth Soccer, 2012). Corporations are also in the game. Nike EYBL (Elite Youth Basketball League) and GEYBL (Girls' Elite Youth Basketball League) showcase elite players in four regional leagues. As with the majority of elite youth sport clubs, leagues, and events, Nike EYBL offers, 'unprecedented exposure' (Nike EYBL, 2016) to its participants.

National governing body pathways for elite youth development

The clearest and most integrated pathways for truly elite youth sport are those provided under the auspices of each sport's National Governing Body. These pathways vary from sport to sport in response to the overall competitive environment for providers of the sport. Training programs, camps, and youth and junior national team experiences are common programs for elite development through NGBs. Yet few athletes develop exclusively through NGB pathways. Nearly all begin in recreational leagues and settings, participate in school sport, club sport, or (when available) both school and club. However, many Olympic sports are not offered through the schools. In that case, NGB-affiliated clubs hold a key position in the development pathway with try-outs for elite development opportunities or selection occurring at national championship events. Unlike the vast majority of "elite" youth sport offerings, the training programs, camps and national team opportunities are the province of a small group of select athletes (cf. Green, 2005).

Systemic themes

Four themes resonate across US elite youth sport settings. One is the importance of exposure for talent identification. The quest for exposure drives athletes and parents to select clubs with travel teams and professional coaches. It motivates clubs to increase the range and frequency of travel to competitions, and is used to legitimize membership fees that can top $10,000 (Kelley & Carchia, 2013).

The second theme is only visible when one considers the plethora of pathways available to elite young athletes: competition. As youth sport provision has moved from a social good to a primary business opportunity, the competition for athletes, coaches, and sponsors has become intense. Competitive success is the currency that builds coaches' careers, clubs' reputations, and recognition for sponsors. This, in turn, brings in better athletes and increases the potential fees participants (or their parents) are willing to pay. With much at stake, the contingencies on coaches, club and school administrators result in pressure to recruit younger and younger athletes, to keep top athletes locked into a single sport and club, and to place the competitive success of the team over the development of individual athletes. On a positive note, the competition among youth sport organizations has resulted in a wide variety of youth sport offerings, both at the elite level as well as the recreational level. Programs work to differentiate themselves from one another in ways that can create playing opportunities that cater to a wide range of needs and interests, whether this is in the type of sport offered, the ways in which the sport is provided, or the non-sport elements of participation.

The third theme is one of privilege versus socioeconomic disadvantage. School sports are arguably the most accessible for youth of all socioeconomic backgrounds. They are largely taxpayer funded, and do not require parental support (e.g., as coaches, referees, or administrators). Yet, school sport opportunities are limited. In the best conditions, schools may field three teams in a sport. More likely, there is a varsity and sometimes a junior varsity team. That means that only a select few athletes can make the team. Athletes who have played for years in clubs with professional coaching and travel opportunities (including associated high levels of competition) have an advantage over players from low-cost recreational programs. Thus, there is an inherent bias in the selection procedures. Given the expectation that coaches' teams will win immediately and consistently, there is scant attention to young athletes' long-term potential.

The fourth theme is investment. For many youth athletes and their parents, the holy grail of sport participation is the college scholarship. Some parents will invest well over the cost of a college education on their children's sport participation. Ironically, those families most well-positioned to afford a college education for their child are also the ones best able to support their child's athletic career. In fact, the average female athlete on a college scholarship comes from an upper middle class background (Cheslock, 2008). While it is unlikely that families do not recognize other benefits of elite youth sport, this single benefit drives an inordinate number of decisions for elite youth participants. And yet, the range of sports offered at the university level is quite restricted. Many Olympic sports are not represented in the schools at all, and others are only marginally represented. More importantly, the odds of attaining a college scholarship are quite small, and most scholarships do not cover the full cost of attendance (Scholarshipstats. com, 2015). Still, the investment theme is an overpowering narrative throughout elite youth sport in the United States – one that is vastly out of proportion to the reality of elite youth sport, but that is consistent with the high value placed on achievement in American society.

Policies affecting elite youth sport

The United States has few policies that affect sport, and even fewer that impact youth athletes. For the most part, policies affecting elite youth sport participants are those of governing bodies rather than of government.

The President's Council on Fitness, Sports and Nutrition (PCFSN) was established by executive order in 1959 to advise the President on matters of physical activity, health, and nutrition of all Americans, with particular emphasis on youth (President's Council on Fitness, Sports, and Nutrition, n.d.). However, the initiatives of the PCFSN are focused on healthy lifestyles, and have little to do with the development of elite youth athletes.

The federal government is tangentially involved in Olympic sport in the United States. The Amateur Sports Act of 1978 charged the United States Olympic Committee (USOC) with the authority to govern Olympic sport and promote amateur sport in the US. Yet, there is no accompanying budget appropriation attached to the Act, nor are there any provisions for federal oversight of the USOC. The Amateur Sports Act was revised slightly in 1998 to reflect changes in Olympic policies around amateurism, and to expand the USOC's role in Paralympic sport. Although the Amateur Sports Act explicitly requires the USOC (and the NGBs) to develop grassroots participation as well as competitive excellence, the USOC has chosen to ignore provisions having to do with grassroots sport development. Instead, it states that its purpose is 'to generate resources in support of its mission, which is to help American athletes achieve sustained competitive excellence' (United States Olympic Committee, 2016a, p. 1). As there is no enforcement mechanism in the Amateur Sports Act, there is no consequence for abrogating its grassroots sport development provisions. Consequently, the USOC is focused solely on short-term elite sport development.

The Office for Civil Rights (OCR) enforces Title IX of the Education Amendments of 1972 (P.L. 92-318). Title IX is federal legislation that prohibits discrimination based on sex in education programs that receive federal money. It covers any education program that receives federal aid, including interscholastic and intercollegiate sport settings. Under Title IX, schools receiving federal public funding are required to comply with one of three criteria: (a) the percentages of male and female athletes must be substantially proportional to the percentages of male and female athletes enrolled; (b) the school must have a history and continuing practice of expanding athletic opportunities for the underrepresented sex; or (c) the institution must fully and effectively accommodate the interests and abilities of the underrepresented sex. The immediate effect of the Act was to increase the quantity and diversity of sport opportunities for women (Carpenter & Acosta, 2005). However, as budget issues arose, schools seeking to comply with the regulation sometimes made the choice to cut men's programs to achieve compliance (Sparvero, Chalip, & Green, 2008). Men's Olympic sports such as wrestling, tennis, and gymnastics were forced to rethink their pathways for elite success as school-based opportunities dwindled.

Elite youth sport pathways

Early peak sport: gymnastics

USA Gymnastics (USAG) is the National Governing Body for gymnastics. The main development pathway in gymnastics is through USAG. Gymnastics is offered in some high schools (122 offer men's gymnastics; 1,550 offer women's gymnastics) and universities, but girls in these programs are no longer on the elite pathway. Although tumbling and gymnastics programs are a staple of public recreation programs and many nonprofit organizations, the pathway to elite gymnastics begins in a gymnastics club affiliated with USA Gymnastics' Junior Olympic program. The goal of the Junior Olympic (JO) system is to create elite level athletes. The women's JO program is made up of ten levels (1–10) based on mastery of the required routines at each level (usagym.com). Levels 1–6 are the compulsory levels in which every athlete competes in the same routine. As the athlete advances in level, the routines become more difficult. To increase the degree of difficulty, new techniques are added. The age groups where competition begins in each state differs, with some states holding competitions for level 3 and below while others begin at levels 4 and 5. State championships are predominantly held at levels 5 and 6, with age restrictions taking effect at level 4 (6 years old) and level 5 (7 years old) (usagym.org). As an athlete reaches level 7, there is a shift between compulsories and optional. USAG mandates certain skills while limiting others that are deemed too difficult. Beyond the core requirements, athletes are free to have their own choreography and work with the coach to create the routine best suited for them. Level 8 also comes with skill restrictions, but once a gymnast makes it to levels 9 and 10 the restrictions are removed. New scoring mechanisms are added in levels 9 and 10, and they apply to the top level of participation which is called 'Elite'.

The elite level for girls is divided into two categories: junior (11–15yrs) and senior (16+). The athletes who make it to the elite level have the opportunity to be selected for the national team and represent the US in events, both foreign and domestic (USA Gymnastics, 2016). The lifestyle of an elite female gymnast is relatively short and intense. It is an early peak sport with most female gymnasts reaching the top level prior to age 16. The intensity of training required to participate in elite gymnastics results in a fairly small pool of potential athletes. Families are often forced to move or to send their daughter to live away from home to train with an elite coach. Many athletes are home schooled and relegated to strict training and nutritional plans. Coaches dictate training and competition schedules, and parents often are relegated to planning travel and supporting training at expensive gyms and tournaments. The athletes are under an immense amount of pressure in relation to their age and maturity levels, and the need to succeed quickly can result in burn out or drop out (Ryan, 1996).

The Elite Program for boys has two competitive level components – a Junior Division and a Senior Division. An athlete must be 12 to 18 years of age to compete as a Junior Elite and must be at least 16 years of age to participate internationally as a Senior Elite. Like the women's Junior Olympic program, the men's JO program consists of 10 levels of increasing difficulty. The first three levels are part of the Basic Skills Achievement Program; the rest are part of the Age Group Competition Program. The JO program leads into the three level Junior National Team Program. Male elite gymnasts are typically older than their female counterparts. Consequently, unlike women's programs, university teams can be part of the elite development pathway for men. In fact, it is common for some of the US men's senior national team to train with a university team.

Commercial sport: basketball

Basketball is arguably the most popular and prominent participative sport in the United States. Across the United States, basketball is played on many levels, from pick-up games in the driveway to competitive league play in school gymnasia. More high schools field basketball teams than field any other sport. This is true for both boys and girls. Yet high schools are no longer the sole province of elite teams and players. For elite youth basketball in the United States, there is no institution more prominent than the Amateur Athletic Union (AAU). The AAU has helped to grow the sport of basketball throughout the country, and is a breeding ground for elite youth players to participate and test their skills.

Aspiring elite players often participate on a select AAU team in the high school offseason. As the AAU produced talent that went on to successful college and pro careers, parents and coaches took notice. Corporations also took notice and began to enter the fold, sponsoring teams with equipment and money. Companies like Nike and Reebok sponsor and host camps and clinics across the country where they bring in top players from all over the country to showcase their skills in front of scouts and experts. In 2010, Nike started EYBL, a national elite league for select players. Adidas and Under Armour soon followed with their own leagues. McDonald's has long sponsored McDonald's All American teams who then compete in an East versus West game, which is also sponsored by McDonald's. These leagues and events are breeding grounds for elite youth athletes and also serve as showcases for college coaches to see the up-and-coming stars of tomorrow.

As more money is pumped into elite youth basketball, players are specializing early and competing year round. Evaluation and scouting services have been created to analyze and rank players as young as fourth grade (~10 years old). These services assist coaches to build relationships and alliances with potential college and professional stars from an early age, and provide players with exposure that can result in a college scholarship. All of this occurs outside the direct purview of USA Basketball, the National Governing Body for the sport. USA Basketball invites top players to its trials to select athletes for its U16, U17, U18 and U19 national teams to compete in international competitions, such as the Youth Olympic Games, World University Games, Pan-American Games, and other junior championship events. The training camps associated with preparation for these events is the only exposure the top US players get to international rules and competition.

National sport: swimming

Swimming provides an instructive contrast to basketball and gymnastics. Unlike basketball, swimming makes scant use of the AAU, but does rely extensively on its National Governing Body (USA Swimming) for development. Unlike gymnastics, it is widely represented in school sport programs. So, by the time they reach high school, swimmers typically split their year between the high school season (fall or winter, depending on locale) and the club season (summer plus whatever is not covered in local schools). Wherever there is a school-based competitive swimming program, swimmers must balance the demands of school and club. In order to prevent athlete burnout, rules typically forbid swimmers from training at both club and school simultaneously. Thus, schools and clubs must coordinate their programs so that swimmers have a natural transition between the two. Since the sport is included in many college programs, scholarships are available for male and female swimmers, which is an incentive for many young swimmers. Although Title IX has extended that opportunity to female swimmers, it has reduced the number of opportunities for male swimmers, as over 70 universities have discontinued their men's swimming programs in order to meet Title IX equity guidelines (Ryther, 2007).

Swimmers typically begin as children by transitioning from learn-to-swim into a competitive program. Many competitive swimming clubs operate only in the summer, while others are year round. While summer club programs tend to be relatively low-pressure with high-reward, year round programs tend to be high-pressure with low-reward. Competitive swimming excellence is produced almost exclusively through the year round club programs (in cooperation with school seasons where required). The difference in the pressure-to-reward ratio between summer-only and year round programs makes it challenging for swimmers to transition from a summer club to a year round club. The result is that the vast majority of summer club swimmers do not transition into year round swimming, and remain only recreational competitors, which limits the pool of potential elites.

USA Swimming works to enable clubs to incentivize development by comparison to personal bests rather than results in competition. For each stroke and distance, time standards are set from B through to AAAA. Swimmers are recognized for reaching a new time standard, and competitions for year round club swimmers are often graded such that particular time standards must be met to enter and compete. Time standards to qualify for state, regional, and national championships are also set. Thus the standard of competition is kept relatively even at each swimming meet, and swimmers are encouraged to compete against their previous best as much as they do with each other.

USA Swimming's development system for its elite youth includes Zone Select Camps for elite swimmers between the ages of 12 and 14; National Select Camp for 14 to 16 year olds; National Junior Team for the top six boys and top six girls in each Olympic event. In addition, USA Swimming supports junior and senior teams to international competitions. Qualification for these development opportunities is based on times at qualifying events.

Talent identification and development

As the three examples suggest, talent identification and development of elite youth athletes varies significantly from sport to sport. Timed or objectively measured sports such as swimming, track and field, and weightlifting can identify high performing athletes by their times, distances, or weight lifted. However, early identification based on performance fails to account for long-term potential in the sport (Green, 2005). Talent identification in less objectively measured sports is even more difficult, and is often confounded by relative age effects (Andronikos et al., 2016). Each of the NGBs of the sports described above has a system for talent identification that begins at early ages and seeks to bring high performing youth into the development system where their performance can be nurtured and monitored. These systems often fail to account for the many development systems that are outside NGB pathways.

As we saw earlier in the chapter, school-based development is often driven by the incentive of university participation, preferably via scholarship. Clubs, AAU teams, stand-alone events such as all-star games and camps often benefit from the obsession with 'being seen' by college coaches. Thus, in many sports, talent identification is often in the hands of college coaches. The development of individual athletes can be lost in the necessity for coaches to win immediately. Winning, after all, brings with it prestige, attention, and (for coaches and clubs dependent on fees) marketing appeal that attracts participants. Famous athletes and coaches have criticized AAU basketball for a failure to develop players' skills. As reported in the *Wall Street Journal* (Clark, 2009):

> "It's a bad system for developing players," says Orlando Magic coach Stan Van Gundy. "They aren't learning to handle the ball, they aren't learning to make plays against pressure. The emphasis with our high-school players is to get exposure and play as many games as you can

and show everybody how great you are. If I can win the 11-and-12 year old league and tell all my friends about it that is a whole lot more important than if my kids actually get any better or learn anything about the game."

In short, the focus on exposure in much of the US elite youth sport system works against the development of strong skills by shifting to a heavy tournament playing schedule at the expense of training. In team sports, early specialization in a playing position may create winning teams, but leaves players with limited skills. A rapidly growing ten-year old who is tall for his age may be a dominant center, and might be labeled "talented." However, by specializing in that position, he may never fully develop dribbling skills. Later, as an average height 17 year old, he may be less competitive at the center position and may not have the skills to play guard. This is not for a lack of "talent," but rather a failure of the development system.

To be fair, many American NGBs are now adopting the American Development Model (ADM), an athlete development system patterned after the long-term athlete development recommendations recommended by Balyi and his colleagues (2013). Created by the United States Olympic Committee, in partnership with the NGBs, the ADM "utilizes long-term athlete development concepts to promote sustained physical activity, participation in sport, and Olympic and Paralympic success" (United States Olympic Committee, 2016b). Alas, the ADM is dependent on coordination among levels and providers of sport. That works if development occurs within a single system, like under the auspices of the NGB. It does not work for athletes with more convoluted development pathways, as occurs in most American sports. The ADM also mandates physical literacy training and sport sampling for children and pre-adolescents. That is not readily implemented in a system where coach and club revenues depend on sport-specific foci and early specialization, as has become common in American youth sport.

At first glance, the lack of clear, consistent pathways for the development of elite athletes in the US seems insurmountable. Yet, elite young athletes are often able to overcome the shortcomings of the chaotic development system. In fact, the chaos is seen as normal, and even has some benefits over more centralized, coordinated development systems. These benefits fit well within the overall culture of the US with its avowedly capitalist economy, belief in individualism and thirst for achievement. The high cultural value placed on sport, with a renewed parental interest in supporting potential achievement of one's children and a reluctance to allow young people unsupervised free play has led to the creation of a large and varied industry for the development of youth athletes in the US. The number of clubs has risen as coaches have embraced a business model that allows them to earn a living as a youth sport coach and/or administrator. With the increase in clubs has come the need to differentiate club services to create a competitive advantage in the marketplace. As clubs differentiate their services, training methods, and philosophies, athletes are better able to find a program that fits their needs. This has the added benefit of aiding retention.

An emphasis on elite performance and aspirations to reach 'the next level' has spawned businesses that provide private, one-on-one coaching, physical training (e.g., strength, agility, flexibility), nutrition, videography, matching services to match athletes with coaches, and leadership academies to develop the intangibles that can lead to further elite opportunities. As long as there are resources to invest and people wanting to invest them to improve sport performance, there will be services to meet the demand. There are even boarding schools for youth as young as five years old, such as IMG Academy whose purpose is "enabling and inspiring athletes to rise up to their full potential" (IMG Academy, 2016). Unlike public schools that consider sport an extracurricular activity, private academies place no restrictions on training times, and instead fully integrate sport training, physical training, nutrition programs, education, and life skills. It is important to note that coaching is central to nearly all of these ancillary services.

Coach development

Coach development, like athlete development, is inconsistent across types and levels of sport provision in the United States. NGBs typically have their own coaching accreditation programs. Schools often do not require any type of coaching certification, but will require first aid and CPR. Although it varies by district, many schools prefer that coaches are full-time teachers in the school district. Consequently, coach pay is often nominal, and full time-coaching positions in high schools are rare. College coaches may hold coaching certifications, or may not, depending on the sport. Other organizations suggest, offer, or require coaches to undertake basic introductory training for coaching youth, but do not require sport-specific coach training. Many of the independent coaches offering skills training have no official qualifications other than experience. No specific degree or certification has been established as the standard needed to coach; however, there are degrees and certificates available at the bachelor's and master's degree levels. Youth sport coaches are, however, typically required to pass background checks to assure that they have no history of criminal behavior or child abuse.

Basic youth sport coach training is offered through a variety of nonprofit organizations such as the Positive Coaching Alliance, the National Alliance for Youth Sports (NAYS), and others. These programs largely target community sport coaches, including parent coaches, and do not provide the level of training to coach elite youth athletes. Elite coach training, then, remains the province of the NGBs. Some individual sports (e.g., athletics, swimming) also have a coaching association that provides coach education and coaching resources to members.

The future of elite youth sport in the United States

Although it is common to refer to "the American sport system," the phrase is actually a misnomer. There is no such thing. Rather, there are multiple systems working in parallel, which sometimes coordinate and sometimes do not. Government has no oversight or governance role except at local levels, where governments provide sport through public recreation, and in the educational system when some sports are provided for a few students for parts of the year. With the arguable exception of public recreation, the parallel systems are predominantly focused on filtering to find and serve elite youth athletes whom it is hoped might eventually become elite performers in national and international competitions.

The apparent chaos in the system is a product of fundamental American ideologies that distrust government intervention in social and economic life. For the most part, the system operates under free market principles. This is the source of American exceptionalism in sport. It is fair to wonder whether the successes enjoyed by American professional and Olympic athletes are a result of the comparatively free market for youth sport provision or are in spite of it.

As we have seen, there are multiple pathways and multiple programs for young people. Each sport is free to develop itself in its own way, and entrepreneurs within sports are free to formulate and deliver distinctive programs. The result is a system that perennially seeks to develop excellence among young competitors, and to do so as completely and rapidly as possible. In sports for which scholarships or lucrative professional contracts beckon, there are particular incentives for young athletes to do whatever is necessary to excel and be noticed.

On the other hand, the system clearly disadvantages late bloomers. Coming to a sport late in childhood or in adolescence is disadvantageous, at least initially. Similarly, a late growth spurt or late pubescence may also be disadvantageous in the context of sport programs that demand early competitive success. Further, the early specialization demanded in American youth sport programs, especially those claiming to be elite, is contrary to principles of long-term athlete development. So, perhaps the relatively laissez-faire approach to American youth sport programming encumbers significant disadvantages.

In short, the seemingly chaotic nature of American youth sport delivery might have the advantage of being conducive to innovation and excellence. There are multiple ways and means to create and find excellent athletes. Yet, that same innovation and focus on excellence is focused on short-term successes. Many potential athletes are driven out of elite sport long before their ultimate potential can be assessed, and programs emphasize short-term rather than long-term athlete development. The challenge is to determine how to balance the American insistence on free market approaches to sport development with the requirements of a long-term perspective when developing young athletes. As we have seen, there are entrenched economic and social interests which rely on early selection and specialization.

Interestingly, the market for youth sport programs in the US may be undergoing an initial stage of change. In 2013, a national campaign to reform youth sport in order to make it more inclusive and more consistent with principles of long-term athlete development was initiated under the title "Project Play." The movement garnered support from sport leaders throughout the country, and released its manifesto at the beginning of 2015 (Aspen Institute, 2015). There has been a parallel effort in one American state (Chalip & Hutchinson, 2016), which several others are planning to emulate. Whether these efforts will succeed in altering the landscape of American youth sport remains to be seen.

Note

1   In the United States, the term, "college" refers to an institution of higher education beyond high school (Year 12). The distinction between a college and a university is one of size and scope of offerings.

References

Amateur Athletic Union of the United States. (2016). *Sports*. Retrieved April 10, 2016 from: www.aausports.org

Andronikos, G., Elumaro, A. I., Westbury, T., & Martindale, R. J. J. (2016). Relative age effect: Implications for effective practice. *Journal of Sports Sciences, 34*, 1124–1131.

Aspen Institute. (2015). *Sport for all, play for life: A playbook to get every kid in the game*. Washington, DC: Author.

Balyi, I., Way, R., & Higgs, C. (2013). *Long-term athlete development*. Champaign, IL: Human Kinetics.

Bucy, M. (2013). The costs of the pay-to-play model in high school athletics. *University of Maryland Law Journal of Race, Religion, Gender & Class, 13*(2), 278–302.

Carpenter, L. J., & Acosta, R. V. (2005). *Title IX*. Champaign, IL: Human Kinetics.

Chalip, L., & Hutchinson, R. (in press). Reinventing youth sport: Formative findings from a state-level action research project. *Sport in Society: Cultures, Commerce, Media, Politics*. DOI: 10.1080/17430437.2015.1124562

Cheslock, J. (2008). *Who's playing college sports? Money, race and gender*. East Meadow, NY: Women's Sports Foundation.

Clark, K. (2009, July 13). American kids flunk basketball 101. *The Wall Street Journal*. Retrieved April 10, 2016 from: www.wsj.com/articles/SB10001424052 9702046219045742482822882869744

Cook, B. (2014, November 8). *Private developer's struggles a lesson in why youth sports complexes built with public money.* Retrieved April 10, 2016 from: www.forbes.com/sites/bobcook/2014/11/08/private-developers-struggles-a-lesson-in-why-youth-sports-complexes-built-with-public-money/#72c2bf341c87

Farrey, T. (2009). *Game on: How the pressure to win at all costs endangers youth sports, and what parents can do about it.* New York: Ballentine.

Green, B.C. (2005). Building sport programs to optimize athlete recruitment, retention, & transition: Toward a normative theory of sport development. *Journal of Sport Management, 19,* 233–253.

IMG Academy. (2016). *Our purpose.* Retrieved April 10, 2016 from: www.imgacademy.com/about/our-purpose

Kelley, B., & Carchia, C. (2013, July 11). "Hey data data – swing!". *ESPN Magazine.* Retrieved April 10, 2016 from: http://espn.go.com/espn/story/_/id/9469252/hidden-demographics-youth-sports-espon-magazine

National Collegiate Athletic Association. (2015). *2015-2016 NCAA Division I Manual.* Indianapolis, IN: NCAA.

National Federation of State High School Associations. (2016). *2014-15 high school athletics participation survey.* Retrieved April 10, 2016 from: www.nfhs.org/ParticipationStatistics/PDF/2014-15_Participation_Survey_Results.pdf

Nike EYBL. (2016). *About.* Retrieved April 10, 2016 from: www.nikeeyb.com/about/

President's Council on Fitness, Sports, and Nutrition. (n.d.). *About PCFSN.* Retrieved on April 10, 2016 from: www.fitness.gov/about-pcfsn/

Ryan, J. (1996). *Little girls in pretty boxes.* New York: Doubleday.

Ryther, M. (2007). Swimming upstream: Men's Olympic swimming sinks while Title IX swims. *Marquette Sports Law Review, 17*(2), 679–707.

Scholarshipstats.com. (2015). *Odds of a high school athlete playing college sports.* Retrieved April 10, 2016 from: www.scholarshipstats.com/varsityodds.html

Sparvero, E., Chalip, L., & Green, B.C. (2008). Laissez faire sport development: Building elite athletes in the United States. In B. Houlihan & M. Green (Eds.), *Comparative Elite Sport Development* (pp. 242–270). Oxford, UK: Butterworth-Heinemann.

Sullivan, P. (2015, January 16). *The rising costs of youth sports, in money and emotion.* The New York Times, retrieved from: www.nytimes.com/2015/01/17/your-money/rising-costs-of-youth-sports.html?_r=1

Turbotaxjen. (2013). *High cost of youth sports* [Online image]. Retrieved April 10, 2016 from http://blog.turbotax.intuit.com/income-and-investments/high-cost-of-youth-sports-infographic-14689/

UFonline. (2015, March 14). *The economy of youth sports* [infographic]. Retrieved April 10, 2016 from: ufonline.ufl.edu/inforgraphics/youth-sports/

United States Olympic Committee. (2016a). *Inside the USOC.* Retrieved April 10, 2016 from: www.teamusa.org/about-th-usoc/inside-the-usoc

United States Olympic Committee. (2016b). *ADM American development model.* Retrieved April 10, 2016 from: www.teamusa.org/About-the-USOC/Athlete-Development/American-Development-Model

USA Gymnastics. (2016). *Women's elite/pre-elite/TOPs program overview.* Retrieved April 10, 2016 from: https://usagym.org/pages/women/pages/overview_elite.html

US Youth Soccer. (2012). *Homepage.* Retrieved April 10, 2016 from: http://championships.usyouthsoccer.org

Walters, P. B. (2001). Educational access and the state: Historical continuities and discontinuities in racial inequality in American education. *Sociology of Education,* 74(4), 35–49.

Chapter 10

Brazil

*Fernando Marinho Mezzadri, Marcelo Moraes e Silva
and Fernando Renato Cavichioli*

Introduction

In the academic literature on public sport policy, the issues involving young
athletes and the systems that have been developed to promote their
development are receiving increasing attention (Green & Oakley, 2001;
Digel, 2002; Houlihan, 2002; De Bosscher, et al., 2010; Vaeyens et al.,
2009). In Brazil, despite this issue being broached early and discussed since
the 1970s (Da Costa, 1971) and debate having been intensified in the
following decades (Böhme, 1994; 1995; 2007; Gaya & Silva, 2002; Massa
et al., 2010; Massa et al., 2014), the thematic relation with public policies
and the notion of a system is still in its infancy (Mazzei et al., 2012; Meira,
Bastos, & Böhme, 2012). Therefore, these elements make the issues of this
chapter a timely contribution to a series of important discussions about the
relationship between youth and sport within government and sports
organizations.

Böhme (2007) points out that at the 1997, 1998, 2001, 2003 and 2005
scientific congresses of the Centres of Excellence in Sport (Rede CENESP),[1]
the theme of the young sport talents[2] was the subject of academic discussions.
Stimulated in part by these discussions, the project "Esporte Brasil" (Sport
Brazil) was created in 2001. This project aimed to develop reference
standards for physical fitness and physical growth of school children (Gaya
& Silva, 2002). From this initial phase the project entitled "Talento
Esportivo" (Sport Talent) was developed in 2004, which is currently known
as "Brasil Potência Esportiva: Detecção de Atletas Esportivos" (Brazil Sport
Power: Detection of Sports Athletes). All actions were the responsibility of
the centre, linked to the Federal University of Rio Grande do Sul (UFRGS)
(Ministry of Sport, 2015).

Despite important measures organized by the Brazilian government
around this network of universities, the federal government did not
contribute to the formulation of public policies for the development of
young athletes, with the measures taken becoming only isolated actions
that did not benefit high performance sport of the country. According to

Böhme (2007), to effectively improve high performance sport, it is necessary to create more effective means of training, education and sport practice. In her opinion, the main measures required to be taken are the following: a) the elaboration of training guidelines in the long term; b) the implementation of policies for different sporting activities; c) the modification of the competitive model, in order to avoid premature elimination of young athletes; d) the restructuring of the organizational model; e) and training and professional retraining. Note that all the points made by the author are also aspects related to the notion of a sport system (Houlihan, 2002; Green & Oakley, 2001; Digel, 2002). As Godoy (2013) points out, Brazilian sport does not have an institutionalized system and the issues discussed by Böhme (2007) remain elusive, hampering athletes' development towards higher performance levels.

Only at the turn of the twenty-first century did the winds of change begin to blow in Brazilian sport. At this time, several events came together to provide new possibilities for the development of sport in Brazil. The main events included the following: a) the creation, in 2003, of a Ministry of Sport (Starepravo, 2011; Mezzadri et al., 2014); b) the organization of national conferences and the systematization of a national sport policy (Godoy, 2013); c) a discussion about the implementation of a "National Sport System" (Godoy, 2013); and d) the choice of Brazil to host major sporting events (Figuerôa et al., 2014).

With these developments, a series of public policies were initiated by the Ministry of Sport (Starepravo, 2011; Mezzadri et al., 2014). In terms of training of young sport talents the key development was the creation in 2011 of a "National Training Network," which aimed to coordinate all athletes of the country, from the base to the highest levels of performance (Brasil, 2011a). However, this government project is still in its infancy, and is missing several elements needed for it to become a reality in Brazilian sport. The present chapter seeks to unravel how this network is being constituted, especially in relation to the training and development of young athletes.

To understand this public policy, it is necessary to illustrate the institutional setting in which it was created. With the election of Luiz Inácio "Lula" da Silva to the Presidency in 2003, sport became part of the political agenda and continued to be in the Government of his successor President Dilma Rousseff,[3] according to Starepravo (2011) and Mezzadri et al. (2014). In this context the government organized three national conferences (Brasil, 2004; 2006; 2010) and published a "National Sport Policy" (Brasil, 2005), and a series of documents that indicated the need for the creation of a National Sport System (Godoy, 2013). It was from this system that the creation of a "National Training Network" was conceived, gaining greater impetus after Rio de Janeiro was chosen as host of the 2016 Olympic Games. For these reasons, the Brazilian government, in order to meet the demands made by the new political agenda, implemented the National Training

Network. This chapter explores how this network is being constituted, unraveling the main aspects that compose it.

The role of the conferences and the "National Sport Policy": elements for the creation of the "National Training Network"

According to Starepravo (2011), the first of the national conferences was entitled: "Esporte, Lazer e desenvolvimento humano" (Sport, Leisure and Human Development). It was established by a Presidential Decree in January 21, 2004 and was envisaged as a space for discussion, formulation and deliberation of public sport policies in Brazil. This first conference involved around 80,000 people, 873 municipalities, 26 States and the Federal District. Godoy (2013) points out that the arguments that legitimized the efforts around this event emphasized social inclusion, and the final document resulting from the discussions ensured greater transparency and popular participation in the process of sport management, in addition to having supported the development of the "National Sport Policy" and the indication of the need to create a "National Sport System."

In the section of the document concerning performance sport it is possible to see the intention to encourage the establishment of a secure base for performance sport in Brazil. All issues raised are intended to coordinate performance sport in a "National Sport System," based on a large network to be implemented nationwide. The policy document sought to emphasize, at least in discursive terms, the training of young Brazilian athletes aiming to "detect and develop potential sport talents and improve the performance of high performance athletes and para-athletes" (Brasil, 2004, p. 14).

This first conference became the basis for the systematization of the "National Sport Policy" (Brasil, 2005). Starepravo (2011) points out that the previous version of the sports policy had been drafted in the 1970s, under the military dictatorship, and had as the main objective the massification of sport, the strengthening of the ideology of a national representation and the development of physical fitness in the population in general. In this sense, the new policy formulated in 2005 started the process of sport democratization and universalization, citizenship development and the encouragement of sport in its different manifestations. The policy included the objectives to:

- Democratize and universalize access to sports and leisure, with a view to improving the quality of life of the Brazilian population.
- Promote the construction and strengthening of citizenship by ensuring access to sport practices and to their underpinning scientific-technological knowledge.
- Decentralize the management of public policies for sport and leisure.

- Promote the practice of educational and participatory sport for the entire population, in addition to strengthening the cultural sports identity from the policies and integrated actions with other policy areas.
- Encourage the development of potential sport talents and improve the performance of high performance athletes and para-athletes, promoting the democratization of high performance sport. (Brasil, 2005, p. 32)

As can be seen, the notion of democratization appears throughout the entire document, showing that sports practices, in their various manifestations, should be offered to the population as a whole. In relation to the high performance strand, the need to invest in young talent is emphasized, as it was in the text of the first conference, because youth are responsible for feeding an effective performance system in Brazilian sport.

To effectively articulate these goals, the new policy indicated the need for the organization of a "National Sport System." Among the goals established for the creation of this system, the most remarkable referred to the definition of the roles of the institutions and agents that make up the Brazilian sports scene. This model, initially proposed in the documents prepared by the Brazilian government, approaches that Green and Oakley (2001) describe, highlights that sports talents should receive all necessary support for their complete training. To conclude this issue, Houlihan (2002) indicates that for a sport system to be effective it needs to have a distribution of responsibilities between the central and the sub-national levels of government. In the case of Brazil, which is a Federal State, this would occur through a clear division of roles between the federal government, the state, and municipal administrations.[4]

Such issues become very important in performance sport. After all, the role of the state in the development of young sports talents is complex and carries a degree of responsibility consistent with their level of importance within the federalist system. The federal government cannot by itself meet the demand for performance sports, requiring the support of other institutions and agents that compose the sport arena. In this sense, the construction of a "National Sport System" could be the binding element in the process of training athletes at their different levels.

> A public policy lacks rationality, because there are few ways to solve a situation in which social needs and organized demands increase, as in the case of sport. Rationality and control can multiply the effects of public policy and, for that, it is essential that there is coordination between the spheres of Government – Union, States and Municipalities –, the powers – Legislative and Executive –, sports entities and society so that all work around common goals. Only then will duplication of efforts be avoided and actions will be coordinated, expanding the focus on performance.
>
> (Brasil, 2005, p. 30)

Duplication of effort should be avoided at all costs, since overlapping of actions weakens any attempt to organize a "National Sport System." In this sense, cooperation is necessary throughout the process to actually transform sport into a State policy in Brazil:

> (...) It is imperative to deepen institutional links in order to establish a network of intervention. To do so, it is first necessary to develop collaborative and cooperative actions between the Ministry of Sport and the other ministries, between the Union, the States and municipalities, and between governmental and non-governmental entities and the private sector. The approach of these institutions could bear fruit in the consolidation of partnerships allowing the realization of the initiatives, avoiding the fragmentation of resources and facilitating the continuity of the programs. Concentrating efforts and optimizing the use of resources is the first step towards the achievement of the intended goals.
>
> (Brasil, 2005, p. 30)

As shown in the passage above, the "National Sport Policy" indicates the need to concentrate efforts and optimize resources to develop sport in the country within a systematic logic. In the specific case of performance sport, the document indicates the need to insert the young sports talents into a system that actually develops the performance and enables them to strive to greater heights in competitive sport.

Starepravo (2011) notes that in the second National Sports Conference, held in May 2006, a discussion and evaluative reflection of the implementation of the "National Sport Policy" was sought. Again the observance of sport as a social right was emphasized, as well as the need for the creation of a "National Sport System," because its absence generated the various sport problems that the country had, such as: the huge number of Brazilians excluded from sports; the lack of material and structural conditions for the population to access sport; and the limited number of high performance athletes (Brasil, 2006).

As already emphasized in the first conference on "National Sport Policy" the definition of tasks becomes crucial, since it is necessary to delimit the role of each institution in the Brazilian sports area, according to the final document of this conference, "to carry out basic, high performance and leisure sport projects in partnership with the three levels of Government" (Brasil, 2006, p.55). This attribution of tasks is fundamental, because it allows a reduction in the degree of overlapping of the actions taken by federal entities:

> Those who participate in the system have direct and indirect relationships with sport in all its dimensions (...). Each participant has a particular

responsibility in the system, depending on the nature of this participation and the type of relationship they have with sport.

(Brasil, 2006, p.14)

With regard to the development of young athletes, the document virtually reproduces what had already been agreed at the previous conference and in the new sport policy. That is, only with the establishment of a national system would high performance sport reach a higher level:

Expansion and revision of the policy of creation of centers of excellence, being organized by the Universities and implemented via resources of public-private partnerships (PPPs) that meet the several Olympic and Paralympic, high performance non-Olympic and non-Paralympic sports, as well as leisure activities, with the necessary infrastructure and guidance of qualified professionals, considering the technical and sport management aspects required to develop talents in sports in base categories, being possibly implemented in the regions, States and municipalities.

(Brasil, 2006, p.14)

It should be noted that the emphasis in the document was on the decentralization of federal power. The federal government started to demand greater participation of the states and municipalities in the process of Brazilian sport development.

In June 2010, the Ministry of Sport promoted the organization of the "Third National Sport Conference." The event proposed to prepare and plan Brazilian sport for the following ten years. The theme was: "Ten-year sport and recreation Plan: 10 points in 10 years to project Brazil to the top 10." According to Godoy (2013), in this Conference, the theme of the previous event, which was about the creation of the "National Sport System," was abandoned. For the authors, this change of course was mainly due to the hosting of sporting mega-events in Brazil. As such, public policy was realigned, placing greater emphasis on high performance sport.

As stated in the theme of the conference, the aim of the event was to draw up a 10-year plan to project Brazil to be among the 10 greatest sporting powers. Despite a more peripheral profile, the creation of the "National Sport System" remained present in the discussions. The difference is that it started to be discussed almost exclusively from the perspective of performance sport, because the system needed to be established to carry out the training of base athletes and especially to regionalize Brazilian sport, which remained very centralized in the major cities in Southern and Southeastern Brazil (Brasil, 2010). To address this issue, the text of the third conference points to the need for the creation of a public institution for the management of performance sport in the country:

Goal 1: To implement and manage the National Training Network, stimulating the use of the network of facilities provided with the use of sport/social clubs infrastructure, S system, military facilities among others, performing Municipal, State and Federal public selecting processes for sport and para-sport coaches and experts, with specialized physical education teachers.

Goal 2: To implement the National Training Network in the 5 Brazilian regions by 2014, involving all structures (Federal, State, Municipal, private) covering all States and the Federal District, with the creation of new training centres, integrated with research, sports technology and evaluation centres to provide multidisciplinary support to athletes.

(Brasil, 2010, p.2)

Note that this "National Training Network" is an attempt to map all the institutions and agents involved in the Brazilian sports arena. It will be a highly intricate network in order to be responsible for following young athletes until their arrival at the highest competitive levels.

"National Training Network": approaching a systemic logic

Created by Federal Law 12,395 in March 2011, the "National Training Network" is one of the main legacy projects of the Rio 2016 Games. It aims to create a holistic infrastructure in Brazilian sport, linking the existing and/ or under construction sports facilities throughout Brazil. The network would be composed of national, regional and local high performance training centers. It will be coordinated by the Ministry of Sport, in partnership with the Brazilian Olympic Committee (BOC) and the Brazilian Paralympic Committee (BPC),[5] federations, states and municipalities. It will cover structures of several sports, including multisport complexes, offering space for detection, education and training of athletes and teams, focusing on several different sports (Ministry of Sport, 2015).

In its proposal, the "National Training Network" would be the structure carrying through young talents from their first steps in sport until a potential arrival at the major international competitions. The structure is clear in the two articles of the law that established the network:

Art. 16. The National Training Network is created under the Ministry of sport, composed of national, regional or local high performance training centres, coordinated for the training of the Olympic and Paralympic programs, from the base to elite sport.

Art. 17. The National Training Network will encourage regional and local development of talents and young athletes, in coordination with the Brazilian Olympic Committee and the Brazilian Paralympic Committee, in addition to regional and local centres, in the form and conditions defined in an Act of the State Minister of Sport.

(Brasil, 2011a, p.2)

The proposal for the "National Training Network" also acknowledges that the network will provide for the enhancement and exchange of coaches, referees, managers and other sport professionals. The work will be based on the application of Sports Science to the training of athletes. This is a project for the development of performance sports, from the base up to the highest levels of competition. The organization chart is displayed in Figure 10.1.

As can be seen in the Figure 10.1, young people arrive in the network through sports initiation programs offered at school and in more general programs providing sports for the population. The main programs of the federal government in this area are the "Second Half," "Sport and Leisure in the City Program (PELC)" and "Athletes at school."[6] When a young person begins to stand out in any type of sport held in these more general programs, they can join one of the local training centers, going through regional and national centers to reach the Olympic Training Centre.

Figure 10.1 National Training Network

Source: Ministry of Sport (2015).

However, when doing research for this chapter we could not find information on how each sport will make this referral, leaving the functionality of the process very unclear. This framework is due to the fact that Brazil, as pointed out by Mazzei et al. (2012) does not provide a system for identifying and developing young athletes. This assessment was confirmed by Mazzei et al. (2015, p. 101) in a subsequent paper which concluded that: "There are no policies aimed at developing talents in Brazil ... the development of athletes in Brazil occurs through isolated initiatives without organisation. ... In most cases the rise of sport talent in the Brazilian reality occurs with 'luck' and is not the product of consistent and planned programs." Even when talent detection and selection programs are designed they often lack effective implementation. According to Mazzei et al. (2014, p. 407), such programs as the "Discovery of Sporting talent Program and the scientific research and innovation in sport (CENESP network) ... are not in operation." This general assessment is confirmed at the level of individual sports where talent identification and development is described as uneven and unsystematic. Filho et al. (2014, p. 549) in a study of talent development in judo and swimming reported that over three-quarters of the coaches that they interviewed concluded that there was "no national talent development system in place for either sport." Such talent identification and development as existed was organized by individual clubs or through talent spotting at inter-club or open competition. "[D]eveloping sports talent in the Brazilian reality [was] through individual [club] projects (judo) and sporadically by the governing body of the sport (swimming)" (2014, p. 549). While the absence of a systematic talent identification and development process is in part the consequence of weak leadership by the national governing bodies it is also partly the consequence of the fact that sport in Brazil is controlled by private entities (BOC, CPB, federations/associations and clubs). Therefore the sport training is done with the minimum of transparency and in accordance with the will of these private groups, hampering much access to information by the public and the federal government.

To implement this network, the federal government signaled for the initial construction of a total of 285 "Sports Initiation Centres," located in 263 municipalities and that would cover 13 Olympic, 6 Paralympic and 1 non-Olympic sports. At first the Olympic sports to be included were the following: athletics, basketball, boxing, handball, judo, wrestling, taekwondo, volleyball, fencing, rhythmic gymnastics, badminton, weightlifting. The Paralympic sports were table tennis, wheelchair fencing, judo, powerlifting, table tennis, sitting volleyball, goalball; and the non-Olympic sport of futsal. This is very limited if we consider that there are 37 Olympic sports, 22 Paralympic sports and a great range of sports that are not part of the framework of the Olympic-Paralympic Games (Ministry of Sport, 2015).

In the documents of the Ministry of Sport, there was no indication of how many regional and national centers were intended to be built. The only information found mentions a few structures installed for sports such as: canoeing; judo; athletics; badminton; diving; cycling[7]; some structures involving a range of sports; and a Centre for Paralympic sport. In the regions, only the Northeast was awarded a facility in the city of Fortaleza, the capital of Ceará state. The Olympic Training Centre would take the structures built for the 2007 Pan American Games and the new facilities being built for Rio 2016, all located in the city of Rio de Janeiro, in the Barra da Tijuca and Deodoro neighborhoods (Ministry of Sport, 2015).

As can be seen, the "National Training Network" is constituted of several "branches," in different spheres, and the emphasis is placed upon the training of young Brazilian athletes.

Sports Initiation Centre: where everything should begin

By devising the "National Training Network" the Federal Government seeks to minimize the long-standing problem of a lack of infrastructure for the development of performance sports in Brazil (Da Costa, 1971). Therefore, the so-called "Sports Initiation Centre" was designed, according to the Ministry of Sport (2015), as an initiative that aimed to build sports facilities with the adoption of official parameters in order to improve the offer of public high-quality sports equipment infrastructure, encouraging sports participation in areas of high social vulnerability, allowing the talent identification and the training of athletes throughout the country and stimulating the development of the base of high performance sport in several different sports.

This project is included in the second phase of the "Growth Acceleration Program (PAC)."[8] Ordinance number 54 of March 21, 2014 approved the Instruction Manual for the Contracting and Implementation of Programs and Actions of the Ministry of Sport. Under these rules, for a municipality to receive a center it has to fulfill some bureaucratic requirements, such as: a) to verify its ability to accommodate the construction; b) to meet the schedule of the selection process; c) to provide supporting documentation proving the control of the land offered for the implementation of the centre; d) to prove the availability of land in conditions of access and suitable features for construction; e) to ensure that the land is in a region of social vulnerability; f) to commit to the management and maintenance of sports equipment; g) and to have a specific body responsible for the development of sport in the area (Secretary, Directory, city and/or equivalent) (Brasil, 2014). The maximum number of proposals to be submitted is defined on the basis of the population of the municipalities, as shown in Table 10.1.

In these proposals, municipalities are eligible to receive one of the three models of existing centres, according to the size of the land available: 2,500 m², 3,500 m² and 7,000 m². The centres will be initiated by the Federal

Table 10.1 Relationship between population and number of municipality's proposals

Municipal population	Proposal limit
Over 2 million	5
From 800,000 to 2 million	4
From 500,000 to 800,000	3
From 300,000 to 500,000	2
Up to 300,000	1

Source: Ministry of Sport (2015).

Government in partnership with the municipal administrations and are currently in the execution phase. The proposals from the municipalities were selected in December 2013 and are in the phase of conducting surveys, setting project foundations and designing implantation plans. The works will start only on December 30, 2016, meaning that this policy is, up to now, more of a political ambition than a reality for Brazilian sport (Ministry of Sport, 2015).

At the present stage, 256 municipalities have been selected, representing all Brazilian States, a low percentage considering that Brazil is composed of 5,570 municipalities, meaning only 4.6 per cent of the municipalities will receive sports facilities. A more detailed analysis can be made using the data set out in Table 10.2.

As seen, only a small proportion of the Brazilian municipalities will be initially included in this governmental action. This fact can hinder the access of youth to sports practices, making it necessary that such a policy is expanded to other Brazilian municipalities. In addition, in the case of municipalities with more than 800,000 inhabitants, a wider study is necessary to understand

Table 10.2 Relationship country region, total population, population (10–19 years), states, municipalities, the number of sports centers, the proportion of people per center, the proportion of people (10–19 years) for center and center average by state.

Region	Total Population	Youth (10–19) Population	States	Muni-cipalities	Sport Centres	Population per Centre	Youth Population per Centre	Centre's per State
Centre-West	14,423,952	2,584,087	4	467	20	721,197	129,204	5.0
Northeast	53,907,144	10,543,892	9	1,794	77	700,092	136,933	8.55
North	16,318,163	3,504,340	7	450	26	627,621	134,782	3.71
Southeast	81,565,983	13,414,602	4	1,668	96	849,645	139,735	24.0
South	27,731,644	4,698,293	3	1,191	37	749,503	126,980	12.3
Total	193,946,886	34,745,214	27	5,570	256	757,605	135,723	9.48

Source: IBGE (2015); Ministry of Sport (2015)

how to serve the different areas of these cities in a homogeneous way, instead of concentrating action only in some regions.

Another analysis that could be made from the data in Table 10.2 is related to the young population within Brazil. Considering that the target population for these spaces would be individuals between 10 and 19 years, a total of 34,745,214 Brazilians, each centre would have to service an average of 135,723 individuals, a high number from which to develop sporting talent. The number becomes even more troubling because of the centralization of facilities in some cities, leaving a significant portion of young people without access to institutionalized sport practice.

Although these problems exist, the establishment of these centers is already indicative of improving distribution of access to sports for young people, because as seen in Table 10.2, all regions of the country will be served. These measures show that this distribution may provide in the future a new geography for sports initiation in Brazil, spreading wider than being restricted to the South and Southeast regions, the most developed in the country, where there is currently the best sporting infrastructure.

Concluding comments

As has been shown in the course of this text, the creation and institutionalization of the Ministry of Sport as a body to directly coordinate and execute public policies played a significant role in sport being represented and integrated into the Brazilian political system for the first time in the history of the country. Since its creation, the Ministry has identified and promoted several actions for the development of sport in Brazil through a complex set of arrangements involving the three levels of government (federal, state and municipal).

After the design of the new ministerial portfolio, three conferences were held with the central objective of formulating guidelines for the preparation of public policies for the sector. In 2005, the National Sport Policy was approved, a result of the deliberations that occurred during the first conference in 2004. This measure seems to have served to institutionally guarantee the legal basis of sport in the political sphere, if not in reality, with the government at least fulfilling its official commitment to comply with the constitutional precept of promoting sport as a social right. Alongside this, Brazil won the right to host a series of sporting mega-events, prompting the federal government to pay greater attention to the development of young athletes in the long term.

Out of this context arises the basis for the creation of a "National Training Network," a policy that aims to better distribute sport across Brazil. This network will focus on developing the young athlete since their sports specialization process until their possible entry into the highest levels of competition. However, as the "National Training Network" is still in the implementation phase, it is now more a political wish than a reality for the nation's sport.

It is important to emphasize that this discussion involves, in addition to spaces managed by the government, a network of private sports institutions with a historically significant contribution to training athletes in Brazil. After all, much of the initiation in the country has traditionally been in social clubs such as the Clube de Regatas Flamengo, Minas Tênis Clube, Esporte Clube Pinheiros and the Sociedade de Ginástica Porto Alegre (SOGIPA). All of them have an important record of supporting performance athletes. However, according to a report carried out by the Brazilian government, through the Court of Auditors, the geographical concentration in the Southern and Southeastern States as well as the cost to join a club ensure that only a small portion of Brazilians have access to sports practices. In addition to this, clubs receive different types of public funding through initiatives such as the Agnelo/Piva Law; State-owned Enterprises, Brazil in High Performance Sport Program and the Incentive to Sport Law (Brasil, 2011b).

In this sense, it is believed that the "National Training Network" could in future be a policy having a great impact on the country. However, it needs to be expanded to a much larger scale than the present condition. If such changes materialize, perhaps Brazilian sport will have, for the first time, conditions to create a universalized "National Sport System," which would meet the needs of the entire Brazilian population, while also contributing to the training of young sports talents to reach excellent heights in major world competitions.

Notes

1 Rede CENESP (CENESP network) was created by the Brazilian Government in 1996, to be a partnership with two universities in Brazil, with the purpose of promoting the development of new sport talents by encouraging sport in schools, clubs and the community. In 2001 the program started providing athletes and coaches with the necessary support in Applied Sports Science. Human resources, equipment and the facilities of fourteen Brazilian universities became available to serve the sports community through the following actions: evaluation of athletes, talent detection, human resource development, research and technology, and the promotion of technical and scientific events (Ministry of Sport, 2015).
2 In the area of high performance sport, the term "sport talent" is used to refer to young people who have potential, a special aptitude, or a great aptitude for sports performance (Böhme, 1994).
3 Luiz Inácio "Lula" da Silva was elected in 2002, taking office in January 2003. He was the first President from the working class in Brazil and represented the Workers Party (PT), a political party espousing a left-wing ideology. He governed Brazil for two terms, from 2003 to 2010. His successor was his former Minister and Chief of Staff Dilma Rousseff, elected in 2010 and assuming the post in January 2011. She was re-elected in 2014.

4 As Franzese (2010) points out, from 1988, Brazil became a peculiar case of a federal nation consisting of three levels of government, with political, administrative and financial autonomy, with the municipalities considered Federative entities alongside the States and the Union. Each has exclusive competencies, being responsible for the formulation and management of various public policies.
5 The BOC and CPB are the national committees affiliated respectively to the International Olympic Committee (IOC) and the International Paralympic Committee (IPC). The two national committees are composed of the national confederations of each mode present in the framework of the Olympic and Paralympic competitions and duly affiliated to their international federations. Due to the territorial dimension of the Brazil national confederations are in turn formed by the respective federations of each sport specific (Meira, et. al., 2012; Godoy, 2013).
6 A more in-depth analysis about the "Second Half" and the "Sport and Leisure Program in the City" can be found in the works of Sousa, Alves, Ribeiro, Teixeira, Fernandes & Venâncio (2010) and Santos, Starepravo and Souza Neto (2015). For the "Athletes at School" program, a more detailed analysis can be found in the article of Reis, Athayde, Nascimento & Mascarenhas (2015).
7 As can be seen in data released by the Ministry of Sport (2015), currently, only a slightly more systematized network has been suggested in Athletics.
8 Created in 2007, in the second term of President Lula (2007–2010), the Growth Acceleration Program (PAC) promoted the resumption of planning and execution of great social, urban, energy and logistics infrastructure works in the country, contributing to accelerated and sustainable development. Initiated as a strategic plan of investments to improve the country's infrastructure, PAC has contributed decisively to increasing job offers and income generation, and increased public and private investment in fundamental works. In its first four years, PAC helped to double Brazilian public investment (from 1.62% of GDP in 2006 to 3.27% in 2010) and it helped Brazil to generate a record volume of jobs – 8.2 million jobs were created during the period. In 2011, in the Government of Dilma Rousseff, PAC entered its second phase, with the same strategic thinking, enhanced by years of experience in the previous phase, more resources and more partnerships with States and municipalities, for the execution of infrastructure works that could improve the quality of life in Brazilian cities (Gonçalves & Paiva, 2014).

References

Böhme, M. T. S. (1994). Talento esportivo I: aspectos teóricos. *Revista Paulista de Educação Física*, 8(2), 90–100.
Böhme, M. T. S. (1995). Talento Esportivo II: Determinação de Talentos Esportivos. *Revista Paulista de Educação Física*, 9(2), 138–146.
Böhme, M. T. S. (2007). O tema talento esportivo nas ciências do esporte. *Revista Brasileira de Ciência e Movimento*, 15(1), 119–126.
Brasil. (2004). *I Conferência Nacional de Esporte* – I CNE, Brasília.
Brasil. (2005). *Política Nacional de Esporte*. Brasília.
Brasil. (2006). *II Conferência Nacional de Esporte* – II CNE, Brasília.

Brasil (2010). *III Conferência Nacional de Esporte* – III CNE, Brasília.

Brasil (2011a). *Lei n° 12.395, de 16 de março de 2011*. Altera as Leis nos 9.615, de 24 de março de 1998, que institui normas gerais sobre desporto, e 10.891, de 9 de julho de 2004, que institui a Bolsa-Atleta; cria os Programas Atleta Pódio e Cidade Esportiva; revoga a Lei n° 6.354, de 2 de setembro de 1976; e dá outras providências. Brasília.

Brasil (2011b) *Tribunal de Contas da União*. Esporte de alto rendimento / Tribunal de Contas (TCU) Brasília: Secretaria de Fiscalização e Avaliação de Programas de Governo.

Brasil (2014). *Portaria n° 54, de 21 de março de 2014*. Aprova o Manual de Instruções para Contratação e Execução dos Programas e Ações do Ministério do Esporte inseridos no Programa de Aceleração do Crescimento – PAC, visando à implantação de infraestrutura esportiva. Brasília.

Da Costa, L. P. (1971). *Diagnóstico de Educação Física/Desportos no Brasil*. Ministério da Educação e Cultura.

De Bosscher, V., Shibli, S., van Bottenburg, M., De Knop, P., & Truyens, J. (2010). Developing a method for comparing the elite sport systems and policies of nations: A mixed research methods approach. *Journal of Sport Management*, 24(5), 567–600.

Digel, H. (2002). Sport Sociology: A comparison of competitive sport systems. *New Studies in Athletics*, 17(1), 37–50.

Figuerôa, K. M., Sevegnani, P., Mezzadri, F. M., & Moraes e Silva, M. (2014). Planejamento, ações e financiamento para o esporte em tempos de megaeventos. *Motrivivência*, 26(42), 55–71.

Filho, F., Meira, T. B., Bastos, F. C., & Böhme, M. T. S. (2014). Judo and swimming talent development in Brazil, *Abstract for presentation at 19th European Association for Sport Management conference*.

Franzese, C. (2010). *Federalismo cooperativo no Brasil:* da Constituição de 1988 aos sistemas de políticas públicas (Doctoral dissertation Fundação Getúlio Vargas).

Gaya, A. P. B., & Silva, G. (2002). Projeto Esporte Brasil–Indicadores de saúde e fatores de prestação esportiva em crianças e jovens. Manual de aplicação de medidas e testes motores. *Revista Perfil*, 6(6), 09–34.

Godoy, L. (2013*).* O *sistema nacional de esporte no Brasil*: revelações e possíveis delineamentos. (Doctoral dissertation, Universidade Federal do Paraná).

Gonçalves, R., & Paiva, A. (2014). Ainda à espera de soluções... *Conjuntura da Construção*, 12(2), 10–11.

Green, M., & Oakley, B. (2001). Elite sport development systems and playing to win: uniformity and diversity in international approaches. *Leisure Studies*, 20(4), 247–267.

Houlihan, B. (2002). *Sport, Policy and Politics: A comparative analysis*. Routledge.

IBGE. *Portal do Instituto Brasileiro de Geografia e Estatística*. Available on: www. ibge.gov.br/ [Accessed September 2015].

Massa, M., Uezu, R., Böhme, M. T. S., Silva, L. R. R., & Knijnik, J. D. (2010). Desempenho esportivo no judô olímpico brasileiro: o talento é precoce? *Revista Brasileira de Ciência e Movimento*, 18(1), 5–10.

Massa, M., Uezu, R., Pacharoni, R., & Böhme, M. T. S. (2014). Iniciação esportiva, tempo de prática e desenvolvimento de judocas olímpicos brasileiros. *Revista Brasileira de Ciências do Esporte*, 36(2), 383–395.

Mazzei, L. C., Bastos, F. C., Ferreira, R. L., & Böhme, M. T. S. (2012). Centros de Treinamento Esportivo para o Esporte de Alto Rendimento no Brasil: um estudo preliminar. *Revista Mineira de Educação Física, Ed. Esp.(1)*, 1575–1584.

Mazzei, L. C., Bastos, F. C., Böhme, M. T. S., & Meira, T. B. (2014). Rio 2016: Sport policies, *Abstract for presentation at 19th European Association for Sport Management conference*.

Mazzei, L. C., Meira, T. B., Bastos, F. C., Böhme, M. T. S., & De Bosscher, V. (2015). High performance sport in Brazil: Structures and policies comparison with the international context, *Gestion y Politica Publica*, Volumen Thematico, 83–111.

Meira, T. B. Bastos, F. C., & Böhme, M. T. S. (2012). Análise da estrutura organizacional do esporte de rendimento no Brasil: um estudo preliminar. *Revista Brasileira de Educação Física e Esporte*, 26(2), 251–62.

Mezzadri, F. M., Moraes e Silva, M., Figuêroa, K. M., & Starepravo, F. A. (2014). Sport Policies in Brazil. *International Journal of Sport Policy and Politics*, (ahead-of-print), 1–12.

Ministério do Esporte. (2015). Portal do Ministério do Esporte do Brasil. Available on: www.esporte.gov.br/ [Accessed September 2015].

Reis, N. S., Athayde, P. F. A., do Nascimento, E. L., & Mascarenhas, F. (2015). Programa de formação esportiva na escola–Atleta na Escola: fundamentos lógicos e circunstâncias históricas. *Motrivivência*, 26(44), 190–206.

Santos, E. S., Starepravo, F. A., & Neto, M. S. S. (2015). Programa "Segundo Tempo" e o vazio assistencial na região Nordeste. *Movimento*, 21(3), 759–771.

Sousa, E. S. D., Alves, V. D. F. N., Ribeiro, C. A., Teixeira, D. M. D., Fernandes, D. M., & Venâncio, M. A. D. (2010). *Sistema de monitoramento & avaliação dos programas Esporte e Lazer da Cidade e Segundo Tempo do Ministério do Esporte*. Belo Horizonte, O Lutador.

Starepravo, F. A. (2011). *Políticas públicas de esporte e lazer no Brasil*: aproximações, intersecções, rupturas e distanciamentos entre os subcampos político/burocrático e científico/acadêmico. (Doctoral dissertation, Universidade Federal do Paraná).

Vaeyens, R., Güllich, A., Warr, C. R., & Philippaerts, R. (2009). Talent identification and promotion programmes of Olympic athletes. *Journal of Sports Sciences*, 27(13), 1367–1380.

Part III

Africa

Chapter 11

South Africa

Cora Burnett

Introduction

This chapter addresses elite sport policy, public delivery systems, and management of elite youth sport in South Africa. It also positions and reflects on government agencies and other key stakeholders delivering elite sport development for young athletes against the background of challenging socio-economic realities. National policy frameworks and legislation guide the alignment of stakeholders and delivery systems for elite youth sport and athlete development.

The South African sport system and policies provide the blueprint for elite youth athlete and coach development. Increased exposure competitions, like the Youth Olympic Games (YOG), translate into early professional orientations for young athletes. The challenges faced by athletes and coaches (micro-system) and sport federations (meso-level) affect the delivery system, and reach beyond systemic and policy issues. It questions practices that may negatively influence an athlete's holistic development and welfare. The individual athlete and coach become dehumanised, like spokes in a wheel, since they are positioned on a path of elite sport performance with an entrenched ideology of winning and excellence.

Conceptual framework

The conceptual framework draws on multidisciplinary paradigms, including the stakeholder theory where key stakeholder cohorts are identified in terms of organisational focus (Freeman, 1984). Clarkson's (1995) classification reveals primary and secondary agents with further layering of the power-legitimacy-urgency framework (Mitchell, Agle & Wood, 1997).

National governments are main stake-owners and held accountable by the broader public through the public media, for youth sport development. In the case of South Africa, governmental departments involved in youth sport development mainly include Sport and Recreation South Africa (SRSA) as Ministry and the Department of Basic Education under whose jurisdiction competitive school sport is implemented country wide. Other key stakeholders include the National Olympic Committees (NOCs) which in South Africa is represented by an umbrella body, the South African Sports Confederation and Olympic Committee (SACOC) to which all national sport federations are affiliated. The national sport federations are considered as the main brokers and custodians of elite athlete development, including talent identification of young athletes. The national sport federations may directly collaborate with their international counterparts for assistance, but in the case of Olympic Sports, SASCOC would be the intermediary body to ensure that young sporting talent is identified, nurtured and developed. This body would liaise with the International Olympic Committee (IOC) or International Federations and often utilise Olympic Solidarity Funding for athlete preparation or coaches training through exchange programmes or capacity building initiatives. The collaboration of International Sport Federations and national sport federations with the government sector, are key in hosting international competitions. The latter is viewed as crucial for the depth of youth sport development as it affords relatively more athletes to participate in such events (if they should qualify), as well as creating an awareness of the sport (and sport participation) in the country.

Hosting the 2022 Commonwealth Games in Durban, within the province of KwaZulu-Natal is thus considered of major importance for the country and for elite sport development, following the successful hosting of the 2010 FIFA World Cup. Whereas the Commonwealth Games or World Championships contain significant value for talent identification and showcasing the country as a 'sporting nation', regional competitions bear more political significance for African countries sharing a common Pan-African reality. For instance, the Association of African National Olympic Committees of Africa (ANOCA) and Region V responsible for identifying host countries for the All Africa Games and ANOCA Youth Games, has a high level of political significance. Such competitions are also considered as stepping stones for the region's emerging young athletes on their way to become national and international stars.

The scaffolding of events – from the provincial to the national, and from the regional to the Commonwealth Games, World Cups and Olympic Games, correlate with policies and systems of long-term athlete development at different levels of engagement. Well-structured athlete development frameworks and sport academic systems, positioned by SASCOC and with national sport federations taking the lead, ensured that a cohesive system is implemented from grassroots (e.g. schools and junior sport clubs) to provincial, national and international levels. These sport bodies are also engaged in implementing a long-term participant development framework with the option of exit levels and deviations from a narrowly defined development pyramid. This comprehensive system also includes clear levels and identified (international and national) federations' requirements relating to coach development where relationships between elite sport policy systems follow global practices.

In terms of the development of elite young athletes, micro-level considerations include positioning young athletes as being from a certain generation (e.g. X, Z and Y) (Shilbury, Sotiriadou & Green, 2008), and thus the socialisation process and athletic identity formation are inevitably influenced by culture and an 'ideology of excellence' (Green & Houlihan, 2004: 388). Another layer of significance entails the nature and status of individual sports with traditionally male sports such as rugby, football and cricket enjoying national and commercial priority (Sotiriadou & Shilbury, 2009).

Effective and responsible coaching thus facilitates positive youth development (PYD) (Camiré, Trudel & Forneris, 2014). It addresses the 'winning versus development' dichotomy, and questions the proposed linear athlete-focused pathway inherent in LTAD programmes and policy-driven systems (David, 2005). This also brings teacher-coaches into the fold, broadens the spectrum of creating an enabling environment, and focuses on schools in the breeder-feeder system of elite sport (Penney & Houlihan, 2003). Such approaches add to an already crowded policy space in search of systems integration (Houlihan, 2000, p. 171).

Policy-level systems delivery and stakeholder positioning seem to be highly institutionalised, yet are eroded by multiple influences. Such influences include the cost factor (Houlihan & Zheng, 2013), competing national developmental needs (Bailey & Talbot, 2015; Burnett, 2015b), educational priorities (Van Deventer, 2007), and an international success benchmark – all impacting in different ways on young aspiring athletes and the degree of institutionalisation of elite youth sport (Houlihan & Zheng, 2013). It is against this background that the current South African sports system is discussed.

South African sports system

Current South African sports systems are not shaped for optimal delivery on health, quality of life, or elite sport development. They are constructed to address the lingering legacy of Apartheid (1948–1994) where legislation chartered a path of disenfranchisement of the majority of the population (Maralack, 2014). The language of redress in the Mandela era (1994–1999) initially focused on nation-building and reconciliation, followed by the establishment of a democratic sport system and policy changes that set a course of social transformation (Pillay & Bass, 2008). The complexity of multiple systems in delivering on Mandela's inspirational vision of the transformative power of sport placed the focus on creating an equitable sport dispensation.

The first central policy focusing on *Getting the nation to play*, encapsulated by the White Paper on Sport and Recreation for the Republic of South Africa (SRSA, 2013), guided the implementation of mass sport participation programmes, such as a community-based programme (*Siyadlala*, since 2004) and the School Sport Mass Participation Programme implemented in 2006, at previously disadvantaged schools to be absorbed by a national school sport initiative. This initiative stems from the development of the 2005 Framework for Collateral Co-ordination and Management of School Sport in Public Ordinary Schools (Act No 13 of 2005), and the Memorandum of Understanding between SRSA and the Department of Basic Education (DBE) (SRSA, 2011). The traditional sport development triangle requires a comprehensive and integrated system where the delivery of competitive and elite athletes are dependent on a well-developed and coordinated system – from the foundation to the highest levels – from grassroots and club level and sport code committees to high performance centres and provincial sport academies.

DBE is responsible for physical education (currently integrated in the subjects Life Orientation and Life Skills with limited hours of active participation), intra- and inter-school, as well as regional and intra-provincial sporting competitions. SRSA, in collaboration with SASCOC and its provincial sport academy system and national sport federations, is structured to facilitate sport and athlete development in a coordinated way (SRSA, 2012a).

Public schools – including ex-Model C schools (categorisation for relatively well-resourced schools mainly attended by the white population during the Apartheid years) – may offer certain priority sports, and use teachers and/or external coaches for their school sport programmes. The number of priority sports differ between different types of schools and may range from only soccer, netball and athletics at the poorer (township or rural) schools, to prioritising other team sports such as rugby, cricket and hockey (ex-Model C schools). Private schools afford their own specialised and diversified programmes (including more specialised sports such as swimming and golf), yet have to channel youth elite sporting competitions through the existing channels to qualify for provincial and national sports colours.

Other key stakeholders delivering on elite sport and athlete development are the 26 public higher education institutions in South Africa. In a national study reporting on their positioning within the sport delivery system, seven key pillars were identified. Most relevant for elite youth sport, are their roles in delivering education and training, providing scientific support, facilitating junior sport development (e.g. sport schools or junior leagues), facilitating sport participation and specialisation, conducting research, offering access to physical resources, and acting as stakeholders in various sport-related domains (Burnett, 2010).

The policy framework for elite youth sport in South Africa

The White Paper for Sport and Recreation (SRSA, 2013) was the first, and still remains the only comprehensive sport and recreation policy framework

(Maralack, 2014). The policy underpins the framework and identifies the different roles and responsibilities of main multi-sectorial stakeholders in sport. It provided the basis of the very first National Sport and Recreation Plan (NSRP) and is the blueprint for a transformed landscape of South African sport (SRSA, 2012a). The NSRP subscribes to the Constitution's democratic principles and awards the Minister of Sport legislative powers to oversee the development and delivery of sport and sporting talent throughout the country. The Ministry of Sport's role and responsibilities for elite youth sport development include the following main and secondary policies and acts:

- the Constitution of the Republic of South Africa, 1996 (Act No. 108 of 1996);
- the SA Schools Act, 1996 (Act No. 84 of 1996);
- the National Sport and Recreation Plan (2012);
- the White Paper on Sport and Recreation (revised in 2011);
- the National Sport and Recreation Act, 1988 (Act No. 110 of 1998) and Amendment Act No 18 of 2007;
- the South African Institute for Drug Free Sport Act of 1997 (Act No. 14 of 1997) and Amendment Act 25 of 2006; and
- School Sport Mass Participation Policy (2011).

The National White Paper on Sport and Recreation identified the following main strategies relating to elite youth sport development, namely: i) school sport; ii) institutional mechanisms (facilities, sport councils, academies, and coaching); iii) mass mobilisation for active participation in sport as the basis for high-performance sport; and iv) governance-related issues in terms of stakeholder collaboration, administrative support, and alignment across and within the nine South African provinces (SRSA, 2013a).

With the vision (2030) of delivering *An Active and Winning Nation*, through nation-wide consultation SRSA identified 31 strategic objectives, with 25 of these objectives focusing on elite sport participation (SRSA, 2012a). It is also against these policy frameworks that the main drivers (SRSA, SACOC, and sport federations) are monitored to implement the Transformation Charter, and their performance is measured by a multi-dimensional score card system (SRSA, 2012b).

The four dimensions propagated in the Transformation Charter set out a course of reframing, restructuring, revitalising, and renewing the sport landscape against the socio-moral and human justice framework, and the high levels of inequality within the South African context. SRSA and its stakeholders are bound by this Charter to focus talent development at youth levels of the previously excluded black majority, stating:

> The South African Government is committed to correct this and to ensure that our national teams are representative of the total South

African population. To have a real and lasting impact on our nation we cannot compete with the exclusion of certain parts of the population.

(SRSA, 2012b, p. 14)

The social transformation of elite sport is currently the main drive with resources allocated to achieve the targets, inclusive of having 'ethnic blacks' and 'girls/women' featuring in elite teams. This is evident in SASOCs selection criteria for the 2014 Nanjing Youth Olympic Games stated under By-Law Rule 40 of the Eligibility Code: 'A minimum of 50% of athletes should be from the previously disadvantaged sector' (SASCOC, 2013).

The challenge of balancing the transformation scoreboard with that of international success is no easy feat. Not only is there internal resistance to prospective (racial) quotas in elite youth sport teams, but winning seems to be an even more elusive outcome for young athletes competing against the world's best. Shortly after the 2014 Nanjing Youth Olympic Games, SASCOC's president Gideon Sam voiced this sentiment as follows:

A handful of Federations in this country lay claim to a well-resourced system of identifying talent, nurturing and putting it on the international platforms to perform. Just think how many high jumpers we have had after Hestrie Cloete and Jacques Freiting? Really nothing to write home about.

There is no glamour nor is there money in development and development acutely meant for the previously disadvantaged athletes. Then we go to the Youth Olympic Games, as recently seen in Nanjing, China and we discover that we are actually all seriously disadvantaged.

(SASCOC, 2014)

Such narratives support the complexity of a system and policy to effectively deliver on a high level of expectations across a spectrum of priority sports that carry special political significance. Past Olympic successes led to the prioritisation of sports codes like athletics, canoeing, cycling, rowing and swimming, while the Sports Ministry (SRSA) selected athletics, basketball, cricket, football, gymnastics, netball, rugby, volleyball and chess as priority codes for competitive school sport at the national level of competition (SRSA, 2015). Codes selected for discussion in this paper include swimming as an early peak sport, rugby as a highly commercialised sport and cycling as an Olympic sport.

Elite youth sports: South African examples

Swimming

Since 1992 South Africa has consistently produced medallists in swimming, with Penny Heyns emerging as the 'Golden Girl' at the 1996 Olympic Games.

Since then world-class male swimmers achieved Olympic success at the subsequent Summer Olympic and Paralympic games. Chad le Clos rose to stardom during the 2010 Youth Olympic Games in Singapore, winning five gold medals. He continued his success at the 2012 London Games by winning gold medals in the 100m and 200m butterfly, and several gold and silver medals in the 2014 Commonwealth Games and 2015 FINA World Cup.

Another rising star is Rita Naude, a 17 year old who won various medals in international competitions. Her story resonates with many others whose competitive careers started at a very young age. She relates her entry into the world of swimming:

> I started swimming lessons at the age of four and started participating in galas from my first years at school... The first South African team I was selected for was the junior team to Nigeria in Grade 7. Since then I've had the privilege of competing internationally in a national team every year – to Zambia, Australia twice, Dubai, Botswana and now, most recently, Zimbabwe.
>
> (Etheridge, 2015b)

She chose not to participate in the 2014 Nanjing Youth Olympic Games as it did not fit into her competition scheduling at that time. She currently trains about eight times per week in the pool and three times a week in the gymnasium before school. Twice a week she trains before school, while the other training sessions are completed after school. For her, an average set range of swimming is between five and six kilometres.

It is apparent that young elite athletes have little time outside their training regimes and have to specialise at a very early age. For her, it began in her early school years. As in the case of Chad le Clos, parental involvement such as providing transport to galas, and offering emotional support and material resources were crucial to follow a swimming career. In this sense parents, as much as other supportive systems, are significant facilitators in their children's sporting lives (Clarkson, 1995).

Rugby

The 1995 and 2007 Rugby World Cup wins for South Africa's national team (the Springboks) contributed to the high level of commercialisation of the sport. From a young age, rugby players are lured by lucrative contracts from schools and universities (sport scholarships), as well as rugby unions (at the provincial level) signing young players. The 14 independent rugby unions in South Africa regularly contract young players to play in various domestic competitions, whereas the South African Rugby Union offers player contracts for the Six Nations Championships, the Rugby World Cup, and test matches.

Under-19 and under-20 domestic competitions, as well as a highly successful university televised competition, feed into the national junior and senior competitions. Players are mainly developed at school level with national-level schoolboy rugby competitions receiving relatively extensive media attention. National ranking lists are regularly published for under-14, under-15, under-16, and first XV school teams. Primary and secondary national school competitions are held, with the Craven Week (known as Coca-Cola Craven Week) being the most prominent (since 1964) event where talent scouts and agents recruit young players for a rugby career. In 2015, two squads of 26 players were chosen at this tournament to play international games against Wales, France, England and Italy (SA Schools, 2015). In this sense, elite youth sport closely mirrors its senior counterpart in socialising young players into a high level of competition.

With a feeder system of incoming young talent and for economic reasons, South African players may opt for an international rugby career. The French Top 14 league offers lucrative contracts. *News 24* (2014) reported on several South African players being contracted by overseas clubs with earnings of more than R600 000 per month. As per media reports during the 2015 Rugby World Cup, Bryan Habana is identified as the highest earning South African player, earning about R1 million monthly. In South Africa, players are contracted at different levels, and the sport at large benefits from three tiers of sponsors, including tournament sponsors.

With Rugby Sevens becoming a Commonwealth and an Olympic sport, the selectors are still recruiting junior talent from the XV's game. South Africa became part of the World Series in 1999, which gave impetus to talent development for this particular sport. National selection and leagues for Rugby Sevens start at the under-16 week, and since 2013 special camps are organised for talented players. From 2016, Rugby Sevens will have its own sponsors and the two entities will be (commercially) separated (Interview Rugby Sevens Coach, 2015).

Because rugby is a high contact sport, there is significant concern regarding injuries sustained by young players. Research reported a relatively high incidence of injuries, being 34.2 per 1,000 player-hours, with 9.5 being considered as 'severe' (Haseler, Cormant & England, 2010). Up to 14 per cent concussions were reported in South African schoolboy rugby, which questions the effect of contact sport on the health of the players (Shuttleworth-Edwards et al., 2008).

Because limited opportunities for girls exist to play rugby, the sport is still widely considered a dominant male (and masculine) institution. Rugby competitions for female teams are marginalised, under-resourced, and seldom feature in the public media.

Cycling

Cycling South Africa (CSA) is tasked by SASCOC to control five different disciplines, which comprise road cycling, track cycling, mountain biking, 'mixing', and paracycling. According to the current President of CSA (interview), cycling is currently the tenth most popular sport in South Africa with a membership of 526,900, of whom 422,000 are junior riders (13–18 years), and 104,900 are adult riders (19 years and older). This profile only accounts for the competitive cyclists registered in a formal club structure. It is estimated that about 22 per cent of cyclists belong to such a structure, of which 4 per cent makes up an elite athlete group (with provincial and national colours).

As in rugby, most of the participants are male, and among the junior cyclists, 67 per cent are boys. Cycling also has a very young participant profile, with 30 per cent of participants falling between the age group of 19 and 24 years. Among the elite group, about 15 juniors excel at provincial level, and are earmarked for international success, with the assistance from provincial sport academics.

CSA's strategic focus is to develop the sport nationwide through the school sport system. According to CSA's Vision 2020, they focus on increasing the grassroots base of participation, especially among the previously disadvantaged communities. To achieve this goal they are dependent on sponsorships, and they recently distributed 26,000 bicycles to about 100 schools. The recipients of these bikes could use them as their main 'transport' to school, and were required to also participate in local cycling competitions (Burnett, 2015a).

Such outreach projects are dependent on sponsorship and volunteer support. Like other sport federations, CSA adheres to the internationally recognised high performance (SPLISS) model described in De Bosscher et al. (2009). This is just one of the federation's grassroots initiatives. CSA is vocal about the safety of their members training on the open roads and promote youngsters taking up cycling in a secure environment.

Young elite riders mostly aspire to compete in the Tour de France, Olympic Games, and World Championships where South African cyclists have had relatively moderate success in the past. Due to early specialisation in a particular cycling discipline, it is a challenge to field competitive riders in the YOG. The YOG feature road racing, mountain biking, and BMX riding, but only two boys and two girls are eligible to compete. Some riders have to double up and participate in a non-specialised event, which increases their risk of injury.

A dual paradigm for development exists – at the one end of the continuum a pool of potential talent is developed and at the other end young elite riders are nurtured and pushed for international success. Success means relatively more resources and priority sport status, which in turn creates an upward mobility status for athletes and the federation (Sotiriadou & Shilbury, 2009).

Systems, practices and competition structures

SASCOC (established in 2004 as a Section 21 Company) is the controlling body for all high performance sport in South Africa, including elite youth sports. The body's main function is to promote and develop high performance sport in the country and to manage the preparation and delivery of Team South Africa at multi-sport international competitions (SASCOC, 2015). For elite sport participation of youth, SASCOC coordinates and monitors elite sport delivery's main national agencies, inclusive of the United School Sports Association of South Africa and University Sport South Africa.

In consultation with national and international experts, SASCOC developed a LTAD framework and a Long Term Participant Development (LTPD) framework (*South African Sport for Life*). The implementation of a LTAD framework draws on the school sport and community club feeder systems. Inter-school and inter-club competitions are well established in South African society and are co-funded by multiple stakeholders such as SRSA, DBE, and local sponsors (e.g. an Afrikaans daily newspaper *Die Beeld*).

Sport federations are the custodians of sport, and they are dedicated to elite youth talent identification and development. For instance, the South African Rugby Union's affiliates structure clubs and events from the under/9 year age group, with well-structured competitions at primary school (under/14) and high school levels (under/15, under/16, under/18 and under/19). National level competitions for rugby include special school competitions such as youth weeks (including Academy Week and Craven Week) and national junior squads to compete in the International Rugby Board (IRB) Junior World Championships.

All federations that work in close collaboration with schools observe a similar trend. In some cases, a special sport school is established, such as the one under the auspices of the University of Pretoria where a special curriculum is followed and young elite athletes train daily under the supervision of coaches and support staff at the university's High Performance Centre. Through their high performance centres, universities collaborate with a myriad of stakeholders to offer scientific support, opportunities for elite participation, and collaborate with provincial sport academies and councils for talent identification and development. Several universities have junior clubs in a variety of sports to ensure that they identify and develop future student-athletes (Burnett, 2010).

Most federations and schools pay special attention to transformation targets in their catchment areas to ensure that their teams are representative of a broad South African demographic profile (Maralack, 2014). Thus, there is a special drive for sport and talent development in collaboration with previously disadvantaged schools and municipalities. The latter stakeholder is mainly responsible for management and infrastructure development of community-based sports facilities, although they also offer sport programmes and events. At a national conference co-hosted by SASCOC and the South African Local Government Association (SALGA) in 2015, strategic directives were formulated to optimally utilise community sport facilities for competitive sports, in addition to providing competitions. Many such facilities are mostly used for soccer teams as the South Africa Football Association (SAFA) has a nation-wide club-system reaching remote corners of the country.

Elite soccer players are 'traded' from a very young age by professional soccer leagues (PSL). It seems that commercial sports such as rugby, cricket, soccer, and to some extent athletics, dominate the sport scene for young athletes. The ideology of excellence becomes paramount in view of possible career advancement and access to external rewards (Sotiriadou & Shilbury, 2009). Offering international competitions in South Africa is also a strategy to develop local interest and talent in view of scarce resources and the expense associated with competing internationally.

Coaching education and practices for young athletes

National sports federations, in collaboration with their governing body (SASCOC), are responsible for formal sport-specific coach training. SASCOC's Coaches Commission oversees the implementation of the national Coaching Framework. National sports federations mostly work through their international body to provide expert coaches. For example, the British coach Frank Dick, ex-coach of various gold medallists, has been contracted to assist in the preparation of South African athletes for Rio 2016 (Etheridge, 2015a). In some cases, coaches also learn from other successful South African coaches who act as mentors in the field, and offer opportunities for aspirant coaches to 'shadow' them.

At a national level, formal training for coaches is offered by Higher Education Institutions' Departments of Sport Science, Human Movement Studies, or related entities (e.g. Sport Bureau or High Performance Centre) (Burnett, 2010). Other registered service providers with the national training institute (Cathsseta) may offer accredited training courses in collaboration with the relevant sports federation to certify the level of qualification.

Universities, sports academies, and private schools are the main employers of elite coaches, whereas many coaches at the grassroots levels are school-based teacher-coaches, parents, or volunteers who take on the coaching responsibility in the absence of professional coaches. In such a role, parental involvement becomes even more significant, and emerges as an 'issue' or discourse when patterns of 'reverse dependency' emerge and young athletes experience increased pressure to excel in sport.

As elite junior athletes move through the ranks, they may be exposed to different coaches at the same time, such as having a local coach, then being allocated a national coach during training camps, and another coach accompanying a national team. Many coaches struggle to find full-time employment because the coaching profession is not well-established outside commercial sports such as rugby, cricket and soccer. Such sports provide a relatively stable professional environment for coaches, and in their professional structures they would have age-group specialist coaches within their coaching fraternity.

Issues in youth sport development and athlete welfare

The absence of quality physical education at public schools and the lack of age- and gender-appropriate coaching, create real barriers in the initial phases of learning general motor skills (around the age of 12 years). Physical education was phased out during the new political dispensation and replaced with Life Orientation, a subject that offers minimal active physical activity at school level (Van Deventer, 2007). Incorrect coaching and emulating professional training regimes, leave athletes with inadequate skill development, which is difficult to rectify at a later stage. At schools, teachers do not always have the required coaching expertise to optimally facilitate physical literacy and sport education during the formative years of 'learning to train'. This results in under- or over-training, with a focus on 'winning' rather than on the process of the holistic development of an athlete. Teacher-coaches are constantly confronted with a role conflict of being an 'educator' or 'coach'. This especially holds true in high performance programmes and in sports in which schools compete fiercely.

Parents are often not equipped to respond to elite young athletes' needs, and may unintentionally add pressure according to their personal ideas of what constitutes 'good parenting' (Coakley, 2015). This is exacerbated when a parent also acts as coach. Highly authoritarian coaches (parent or external coach) often fully control young athletes' lives, perpetuating a relatively high level of dependency. This feeds into the traditional coach-centred and hyper controlled environment with athletes failing to take responsibility for their sporting careers. When a coach misuses his/her authority, this transgression places young athletes at risk. By not considering or recognising different levels of maturation, coaching practices may place young athletes at risk of having to cope with too much pressure, and they often experience unrealistic expectations from multiple agencies and individuals. This situation increases in complexity when different levels of maturation come into play, resulting in neglect of some and lack of stage-progression by others.

Undue pressure from coaches, schools, and parents contribute to high levels of stress and early burnout (Coakley, 2010). Specialisation that occurs too early compromises the young elite athlete's holistic development, and fosters a narrow sporting identity, resulting in psychological trauma when the athlete fails, gets injured, or retires from competitive sport.

The contextual realities of 'social transformation targets' may exclude or discourage young athletes from specialising in a particular sport and translate into 'racial stacking' patterns in sports like rugby and cricket. The injury profile of contact sports like rugby and boxing are well-kept secrets, and account for the cost and suffering of affected individuals (Haseler, Carmont & England, 2010).

Despite international agencies' vision to hold 'youth games' as a platform for elite youth development, such vision may contribute to negative practices of specialising too soon, pressure to perform, and poorly informed career choice for youngsters who often have to sacrifice their childhood for an uncertain career outcome.

Future trends and the impact of selected elite youth sports

In South African sport, the scene is set for early specialisation and talent identification with an increased effort to recruit young athletes from previously disadvantaged populations. The focus on 'winning' will continue to elicit the support from significant others (e.g. parents and teachers) who may push young athletes to excel, despite the personal cost. Commercial sports have the allure of fame and fortune, particularly because the popular media packages it persuasively. Elite youth athletes are often portrayed as heroes by the media, contributing to popular social affirmation of the elite sports ethos.

Mass participation programmes are costly, and less expensive priority sports will increasingly feature in such programmes. This may include indigenous games that may offer competitions but are implemented for achieving political goals. Where programmes provide a safe and caring environment, the joy of participation and positive outcomes may translate into long-term active participation and render optimal health benefits. A broad-based participation profile and self-selected participation in a variety of sports may remain the prerogative of the more affluent individuals, as is the case globally.

References

Bailey, R. & Talbot, M. (Eds.). (2015). *Elite Sport and Sport-for-All: Bridging the Two Cultures?* London: Routledge.

Bleakley, C., Tully, M. & O'Connor, S. (2011). Epidemiology of adolescent rugby injuries: a systematic review. *Journal of Athletic Training, 46*(5), 555.

Bosscher, V. D., Knop, P. D. & van Bottenburg, M. (2009). An analysis of homogeneity and heterogeneity of elite sports systems in six nations. *International Journal of Sports Marketing & Sponsorship*, 10(2), 111–131.

Burnett, C. (2010). *Delivery for the Sport Industry by South African Universities*. Johannesburg: University of Johannesburg.

Burnett, C. (2015a). *Olympic Movement stakeholder collaboration for delivering on sport development in eight African (SADC) countries*. Advanced Olympic Research Grant Programme 2014/2015. Lausanne: International Olympic Committee.

Burnett, C. (2015b). 'Opportunities for "all" versus "gold" for sport and country.' In R. Bailey & M. Talbot (Eds.), *Elite Sport and Sport-for-All: Bridging the Two Cultures?* (pp. 85–99). London: Routledge Taylor & Francis Group.

Camiré, M., Trudel, P. & Forneris, T. (2014). Examining how model youth sport coaches learn to facilitate positive youth development. *Physical Education and Sport Pedagogy*, 19(1), 1–17.

Clarkson, M. E. (1995). A stakeholder framework for analysing and evaluating corporate social performance. *Academy of Management Review*, 20(1), 92–117.

Coakley, J. (2010). The 'logic' of specialisation: Using children for adult purposes. *Journal of Physical Education, Recreation & Dance*, 81(8), 16–25.

Coakley, J. J. (2015). *Sport in Society: Issues and controversies*. 11th Edition. New York: McGraw Hill Education.

David, P. (2005). *Human Rights in Youth Sport: A critical review of children's rights in competitive sport*. London: Routledge.

De Bosscher, V., De Knop, P., Van Bottenburg, M., Shibli, S. & Bingham, J. (2009). Explaining international sporting success: An international comparison of elite sport systems and policies in six countries. *Sport Management Review*, 12(3), 113–136.

Donnelly, P. & Petherick, L. (2004). Workers' playtime? Child labour at the extremes of the sporting spectrum. *Sport in Society*, 7(3), 301–321.

Etheridge, M. (2015a). Frank Dick. Tapping in. *SASCOC. Road to Rio*. April, May, June 2015, pp. 25–26.

Etheridge, M. (2015b). Going great lengths. *SASCOC. Road to Rio*. April, May, June 2015, pp. 35–36.

Freeman, R. E. (1984, 2010). *Strategic Management: A stakeholder approach*. Cambridge University Press.

Green, M. & Collins, S. (2008). Policy, politics and path dependency: Sport development in Australia and Finland. *Sport Management Review*, 11(3), 225–251.

Green, M. & Houlihan, B. (2004). Advocacy coalitions and elite sport policy change in Canada and the United Kingdom. *International Review for the Sociology of Sport*, 39(4), 387–403.

Haseler, C. M., Carmont, M. R. & England, M. (2010). The epidemiology of injuries in English youth community rugby union. *British Journal of Sports Medicine*, 44(15), 1093–1099.

Höglund, K. & Sundberg, R. (2008). Reconciliation through sports? The case of South Africa. *Third World Quarterly*, 29(4), 805–818.

Houlihan, B. (2000). Sporting excellence, schools and sports development: The politics of crowded policy spaces. *European Physical Education Review*, 6(2), 171–193.

Houlihan, B., & Zheng, J. (2013). The Olympics and elite sport policy: where will it all end? *The International Journal of the History of Sport*, 30(4), 338–355.

International Olympic Committee (IOC). (2015). *2020 Olympic Agenda*. www. olympic.org/Olympic-agenda-2020. Accessed 20 September 2015.

Lee, A. J., Garraway, W. M., Hepburn, W. & Laidlaw, R. (2001). Influence of rugby injuries on players' subsequent health and lifestyle: beginning a long term follow up. *British Journal of Sports Medicine*, 35(1), 38–42.

Maralack, D. (2014). Country Report: South Africa. In M. Keim & C. de Coning (Eds.), *Sport and Development Policy in Africa: Results of a Collaborative Study of Selected Country Cases* (pp. 129–151). Stellenbosch: AFRICAN SUN MEDIA.

McVeigh, J. A., Norris, S. A. & Wet, T. D. (2004). The relationship between socio⊠ economic status and physical activity patterns in South African children. *Acta Paediatrica*, 93(7), 982–988.

Mitchell, R. K., Agle, B. R. & Wood, D. J. (1997). Toward a theory of stakeholder identification and salience: Defining the principle of who and what really counts. *Academy of Management Review*, 22(4), 853–886.

News 24 (2015). *Rugby re-defined*. www.rugbyredefined/2014/02/22. Accessed 18 October 2015.

Penney, D. & Houlihan, B. (2003). Higher education institutions and specialist schools: potential partnerships. *Journal of Education for Teaching: International research and pedagogy*, 29(3), 235–248.

Pillay, U. & Bass, O. (2008). Mega-events as a response to poverty reduction. The 2010 FIFA World Cup and its urban development implications. *Urban Forum*, 19, 329–346.

Prinsloo, E. (2007). Implementation of life orientation programmes in the new curriculum in South African schools: perceptions of principals and life orientation teachers. *South African Journal of Education*, 27(1), 155–170.

Richter, L., Norris, S., Pettifor, J., Yach, D. & Cameron, N. (2007). Cohort profile: Mandela's children: the 1990 Birth to Twenty study in South Africa. *International Journal of Epidemiology*, 36(3), 504–511.

SA Schools (2014). *Craven week*. www.rugby 365.com/schools/144-craven week. Accessed 11 October 2015.

SASCOC (South Africa Sports Confederation and Olympic Committee) (2013). *Policy and general eligibility and selection criteria for multi-coded games (2013-2016)*. www.SASCOC/General-Selection-Policy-20131.pdf. Accessed 17 October 2015.

SASCOC (South Africa Sports Confederation and Olympic Committee) (2014). www.sascoc.co.za/2014/09/12/presidents-voice-gideon-sam-52. Assessed 11 October 2015.

SRSA (Sport and Recreation South Africa). Memorandum of Understanding. www. SRSA.gov.za/MediaLib/Downloads/Home. Assessed 14 January 2016.

SRSA (Sport and Recreation South Africa) (2012a). *National Sport and Recreation Plan*. Pretoria: SRSA.

SRSA (Sport and Recreation South Africa) (2012b). *Transformation Charter for South African Sport*. Pretoria: SRSA.

SRSA (Sport and Recreation South Africa) (2013). The White Paper on Sport and Recreation for the Republic of South Africa. Pretoria: SRSA.

SRSA (Sport and Recreation South Africa) (2015). Bennet Bailey – Comparing the talent identification system of SASCOC priority codes to that of current best practices. www.SRSA.gov.za/pebble.asp?relid=1678. Assessed 14 January 2016.

Shilbury, D., Sotiriadou, K. P. & Green, B. C. (2008). Sport development. Systems, policies and pathways: An introduction to the special issue. *Sport Management Review*, *11*(3), 217–223.

Shuttleworth-Edwards, A. B., Noakes, T. D., Radloff, S. E., Whitefield, V. J., Clark, S. B., Roberts, C. O., Essack, F. B., Zoccola, D., Boulind, M. J., Case, S. E., Smith, I. P. & Mitchell, J. L. G. (2008). The comparative incidence of reported concussions presenting for follow-up management in South African Rugby Union. *Clinical Journal of Sport Medicine*, *18*(5), 403–409.

Sotiriadou, K. (2009). The Australian sport system and its stakeholders: development of cooperative relationships. *Sport in Society*, *12*(7), 842–860.

Sotiriadou, K. P. & Shilbury, D. (2009). Australian elite athlete development: An organisational perspective. *Sport Management Review*, *12*(3), 137–148.

Spamer, E. J. (2009). Talent identification and development in youth rugby players: A research review. *South African Journal for Research in Sport, Physical Education and Recreation*, *31*(2), 109–118.

Steenveld, L. & Strelitz, L. (1998). The 1995 Rugby World Cup and the politics of nation-building in South Africa. *Media, Culture & Society*, *20*(4), 609–629.

Van Deventer, K. J. (2007). A paradigm shift in Life Orientation: A review. *South African Journal for Research in Sport, Physical Education and recreation*, *29*(2), 131–146.

Part IV

Asia

Chapter 12

China

Xiaoyan Xing

The 2008 Beijing Olympic Games witnessed the pinnacle of China's elite sport prowess. Of particular note, 62 winners of the 51 gold medals were developed by its sport schools (Liu, 2010). This chapter describes and analyses policy and management of elite youth sport in China.[1] Fieldwork for this study was mainly conducted in Beijing and Zhejiang province, both situated in China's economically advanced regions. Thus, caution is required when using findings of this chapter to interpret the overall development of elite youth sport in China.

The role of government in developing elite youth sport

China's elite sport system, financed and managed by the government, was developed in the 1950s (Hong, 2008). In the 1990s, the former State Physical Culture and Sports Commission (hereafter SPCSC) was restructured as the General Administration of Sport of China (hereafter GASC) as a governmental institution along with over 20 National Sport Management Centres (hereafter NSMCs) as public institutions in response to the nation's reform to a market economy (Li, 2000). Nonetheless, the basic feature of the system, often described as *Ju Guo Ti Zhi*, remained intact (Hong, 2008; Hu, 2015a). The essence of *Ju Guo Ti Zhi* was governmental actions of gathering resources nationwide to accomplish major tasks (Interview #27). *Ju Guo Ti Zhi* was most salient in China's elite sport system and culminated in the country's preparation for and organization of the Beijing 2008 Olympic Games. Yet, it was also used by the Chinese government to facilitate scientific innovation such as launching manned spaceships (Zhong, 2009).

Known as the three-tier training network, China's elite youth athletes typically progress through three stages. National and provincial elite athletes (hereafter first-line or *zhuanye* athletes) form the top of the training network. Different from professional athletes, *zhuanye* athletes in China have trained for the country and can be considered as sporting civil servants (Bao, 2010).

Being a first-line athlete was treated as a career type in public sport institutions in China (National Personnel Department, 2007). A job contract with a full welfare package was signed when the athlete was accepted to the provincial *zhuanye* sport team (GASC, 2007). Among China's 26,381 first-line athletes, 42 per cent were younger than 20 years, and 50 per cent were between 20 and 30 years (GASC Sport Economics Department, 2012). An additional training stipend was provided to around 2,000 of them who trained with the national team, yet their employment was maintained at the province where they signed their job contracts (GASC, 2003a). The lower tiers of the training network accommodated 59,842 students in 212 middle sport schools (hereafter second-line athletes) and 438,240 students in 1,552 amateur sport schools (hereafter third-line athletes) (GASC Sport Economics Department, 2012). While amateur sport schools are typically within the jurisdiction of county and city sport bureaus, middle sport schools typically offer high level training and secondary vocational education to older athletes at city and provincial levels.

In terms of management, GASC's Competition and Training Department was in charge of athlete training and competition; the Youth Sport Department was in charge of sport schools and the development of youth athletes; the Science and Education Department was in charge of athlete education and coaches' professional development; and the Personnel Department was in charge of coaches' and elite athletes' employment as well as athlete service and career support (GASC, n.d.). The 16 NSMCs of Olympic sports, directly affiliated to GASC, assumed the role of the sport's national governing body (NGB) affiliated to the relevant International Federation. The National Training Bureau, also a GASC subsidiary, managed the venues and facilities of the national training centre, provided logistical services to and academic studies for national team athletes (GASC, n.d.). Responsibilities and organizational linkage of China's 32 provincial, 437 municipal, and 2,661 county-level governmental sport organizations resembled those at the national level (GASC Sport Economics Department, 2012). As shown by the dotted lines in Figure 12.1, the relationship between sport organizations of governments at different levels was to offer expert guidance (*yewu zhidao*), not administrative order (*xingzhen minlin*). The most significant influence on a local sport bureau is its local government, not the hierarchically superior sport bureau. However, policy directives were provided by the GASC to align the objectives of the local sport bureaus to achieve elite sport objectives.

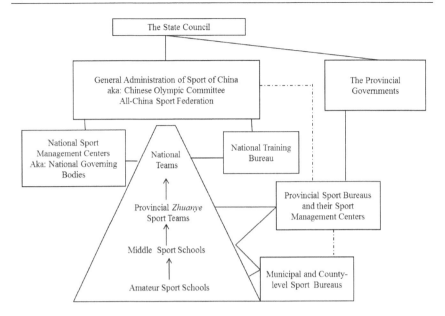

Figure 12.1 The government-run elite sport system in China

Public policies affecting elite youth athletes

The *Compulsory Education Law of the P.R.C.* (promulgated in 1986 and revised in 2006) prescribes that China offers nine-year compulsory education to all school-age children and adolescents (Hu, 2006). The law applies to school-age elite youth athletes in China and serves as a fundamental principle when drafting elite youth sport policy.

The prominence and development path of elite youth sport

Diving was chosen as an early-peak sport and table tennis as a major national sport. Both are among China's top Olympic medal sports. Similar to most Olympic sports in China, these two sports develop elite athletes via the three-tier training network. Football was chosen as a commercial team sport and was used to examine the market-based sport development model since the 1990s and the ways through which it develops elite youth players which are significantly different from the traditional model. This will be addressed in the section on 'Issues and trends'.

As shown in Table 12.1, by the end of 2012, 356 sport schools in China's 29 provinces were involved in youth table tennis player training and, on a much smaller scale, 74 schools in 19 provinces were involved in diving. There were more first-line divers than second-line divers, revealing variations in the athlete development pattern across sports.

Table 12.1 Training networks for table tennis and diving (GASC Youth Sport Department, 2014; GASC Sport Economics Department, 2012)

Sport	Number of Provinces	Number of Sport Schools	Number of First-line Athletes	Number of Second-line Athletes	Number of Third-line Athletes
Table tennis	29	356	803	1,769	31,267
Diving	19	74	488	447	1,828

A typical Chinese table tennis player was introduced to the sport at the age of 6 or 7 years old and entered middle sport school between the ages of 10 and 13 years. The promising players at middle sport school were then selected to the provincial team, signalling the start of a *zhuanye* sport career. At the national level, the national youth table tennis team consisted of approximately 100 players between the ages of 13 and 17 years and the national table tennis team with approximately 100 players aged 17 years or older (Interview #16).

Similarly, the Chinese divers started training at the age of 5 to 6 years old. They were typically introduced to gymnastics as the entry sport. For instance, the diving team of Beijing Muxuyuan Sport School recruits 7 to 8 third-line athletes around the ages of 7 or 8 years each year. These athletes may know nothing about diving and may even not yet have learned to swim but they have typically trained in gymnastics for 1 to 2 years. After a two-year trial period, they may proceed to Beijing *zhuanye* diving team or exit the system (Interview #21). In other words, Chinese divers may start competitive sport training at the age of 5 to 6 years, learn diving skills at the age of 7 to 8 years and become *zhuanye* athletes at the age of 9 to 10 years. They trained around 15 hours per week when learning gymnastics at amateur sport schools; their weekly training load was increased to 25 to 30 hours after entering Muxuyuan Sport School; and the weekly training was further lengthened to around 35 hours after they became *zhuanye* athletes (Interview #21). The ages of divers in the Chinese national team ranged from 13 to 30 years (Interview #19).

Implementing the performance objectives of elite youth sport

China's Olympic Medal Winning Programmes outlined the country's elite sport objectives and strategies (Tang, 2007). One pivotal policy consideration was to align all stakeholders, be it institutional or individual, to maximize Olympic medals. Three key mechanisms were in place to achieve China's 'Olympic Glory', namely, the inclusion of Olympic medals in the National Games, the evaluation and designation of the National High-performance Reserve Talent Base; and using talent outputs as a major criterion when determining coaches' professional ranks. All three have fundamentally shaped how elite youth athletes were developed in China.

Registration, representation and competition

Although the provincial governments played a critical role in developing elite youth athletes in China, they have had their own elite sport agenda aiming at medals at the National Games (Tang, 2007; Zhang, 2012). To solve conflicts of interest experienced in the 1980s, a set of reforms for the National Games was adopted to align provincial and central government interests. Since 1993, National Games in China have been held every four years after the year of the Summer Olympic Games; their sport programmes were aligned with Olympic sport programmes; scores and medal rankings of the provinces were developed; and of utmost importance Olympic medals were included in calculating the rankings (Zhang, 2012). One Olympic gold medal was counted as two National Games gold medals to the winner's registration unit (*zhuce danwei*, typically a province) at given national Games (GASC, 2010). Such a policy served to draw all resources into the elite sport system to train Olympic athletes and set the foundation for *Ju Guo Ti Zhi* in China's elite sport.

An athlete's representation qualification is at the core of this mechanism. To attend the top-level national competitions, a Chinese elite athlete must be registered annually by his/her representation unit (*daibiao danwei*, typically a province) at the GASC. Prior to the first registration, an agreement of representation qualification was signed between the athlete and the registration unit (GASC, 2003b). This agreement was critical in that it awarded the registration unit the ownership of the national and international medals the signed athletes might win in the future. Over 20 years' evolution, a highly elaborated and exhaustive set of rules were developed for athlete registration, athlete exchange and medal score calculation, involving first-time registration, dual-registration, change of registration unit and so on (GASC, 2003b). A similar system was established at local levels (Interview #1 and #4), forming a complex athlete representation and medal conversion network fraught with tensions in relation to power and fame, but ultimately leading to the Olympic medals.

A sport's registration regulations decided who can attend what types of national competitions and at which age. In the case of diving, there is no required minimum registration age. Taking the Beijing diving team as an example, divers were typically registered between the ages of 8 and 10 years old (Interview #21). However, divers having competed at national youth competitions cannot come back to the national age-group competitions which are less competitive. Registration regulation had a profound impact on athlete advancement. The Tsinghua University diving team served as a prominent example in this regard. The team was launched in 1997 as an exemplar for higher educational institutions to develop Olympic-level athletes. A few Olympians came out of the team at its prime time. However, after the GASC revised the dual registration rule in 2001, Tsinghua divers were no longer allowed to register for their provinces for the National Games at the same time as being contracted to train and study at Tsinghua. In order to secure the prospect for athletic career advancement, the top divers all left Tsinghua to join their provincial teams, and the team was consequently no longer able to develop elite divers (F.Yu, 2010).

In table tennis, a player must be at least 11 years to be registered (National Management Centre, 2015). The national youth competitions were held in different places for different age groups from U13 to U17 ('Jingsaijihua', 2015). The promising players who topped these competitions were admitted to the national youth table tennis teams.

For both sports, only elite youth athletes in the three-tier training network were allowed to attend major national competitions. In terms of competition arrangements, the national youth competitions were typically held twice a year, one in winter and one in summer to accommodate school schedules ('Jingsaijihua', 2015). In recent years, sports with a strong participation base such as table tennis and swimming were gradually opened its lower level competitions to entry-level youth athletes outside the training network.

The national high-performance base programme

Sport schools are the main sites for cultivating elite youth athletes in China. The National High-performance Reserve Talent Base Designation Programme (hereafter High-performance Base Programme) was launched in early 2000 by the GASC to motivate sport schools to contribute to the Olympic Medal Winning Programmes and to direct how these schools operate (Song, 2015). The High-performance Base Programme runs every four years. Sport schools with High-performance Base status were provided with additional funding and resources. For the London cycle, 334 sport schools were awarded the 2013–2016 National High-performance Base title (Song, 2015). The evaluation method for the 2017–2020 High-performance Base included 17 indicators in five areas (GASC, 2014b). To qualify for application a sport school must, among other things, have garnered 30 points from major international medals won by its former athletes in the past Olympic cycle. In the conversion matrix, an Olympic gold medal was equal to 30 points and medals of other colours or types worth fewer points. Similar programmes were developed by local sport bureaus and NSMCs to mobilize sport schools to cultivate athletes for Olympic medals.

Determinants of sport coaches' professional ranks

Criteria used to determine coaches' professional rank have profound ramifications for their job performance. The Standards of Sport Coaches' Professional Ranks in China were developed in 1958 and revised four times after that. Today the 1994 version is in force (Wang, Wang & Chen, 2011). Similar to teaching, the coaching profession in China was divided into five ranks with national coaches (equivalent to a full professor) at the top of the hierarchy. Coaches are required to meet conditions in areas of tenure, educational degree, research, foreign language status and talents produced to climb the ranks (National Personnel Department, 1994). For sport school coaches to reach the top, among others, the most challenging and uncertain criterion was that they had to 'produce three national athletes, and win one world gold medal or multiple Asian gold medals within seven years since the coached athletes moved up' (National Personnel Department, 1994). The criterion oriented the coaches to coach for Olympic medals. In fact, medals were not only essential for the coach's professional rank but also directly linked to monetary reward. A detailed method was in place to decide the amount athletes and coaches should receive from the government for winning medals at major international competitions (National Personnel Department, 1996).

The development of elite youth coaches

Like teachers in China's public schools, coaches in China's three-tier training network are full-time public employees. Most of these coaches went through the training network as athletes and obtained bachelor's degrees in athletic training or related sport majors. It is not uncommon that a *zhuanye* athlete stays on to assist coaching after retirement while finishing up his/her higher education. As shown in Table 12.2, table tennis had a larger number of coaches than diving. There were more diving coaches for elite sport teams than those at amateur sport schools, revealing the variation in development patterns across sports (Green, 2005).

Overall, the statistics revealed there were significantly fewer coaches at middle sport schools than coaches of elite sport teams. There were 22,312 coaches in 2012, with 6,177 at *zhuanye* sport teams, 3,704 in middle sport schools, and 12,303 in amateur sport schools.[2] Conversely, there were 26,381 *zhuanye* athletes in comparison to 59,842 students in middle sport schools (GASC Sport Economics Department, 2012). One potential explanation is that some middle sport schools are struggling to recruit enough students to fill the places available for cultivating elite youth athletes (Jin et al., 2010). Consequently, though there was a large number of second-line athletes, only a portion of them were trained to be elite youth athletes. This illustrates the troublesome situation faced by sport schools in China.

Table 12.2 Coaches in table tennis and diving (GASC Sport Economics Department, 2012)

	Table tennis		Diving	
Elite Sport Teams	223	22.5%	102	43.8%
Middle Sport Schools	141	14.2%	41	17.6%
Amateur Sport Schools	626	63.0%	84	36.1%
Total	993	100%	233	100%

It should also be noted that the statistics only included coaches in the three-tier training network and the actual number may be greater. For instance, Beijing Haidian Amateur Sport School was one of the National Table Tennis Talent Reserve Bases. The school had 15 table tennis coaches, only five of whom were on the roster and the other ten were temporary coaches from private tennis clubs, schools and universities (Interview #3). Since there had yet to be mechanisms in place to include part-time coaches or coaches of private sport clubs, the actual numbers of coaches as well as athletes in a given sport in China was in fact unknown. This again reflected the incomplete adaptation of China's elite sport system amid the country's gigantic socioeconomic transformation.

The living conditions of sport school coaches were less than satisfactory. The criteria for coaching career progression were so hard, particularly the weight given to medal outputs, that among the 15,936 Chinese sport school coaches in 2012, only 47 of them held national coach rank, even fewer than China's gold medal winners at Beijing Olympics. One senior coach said that, 'For us to produce a world champion is like to win a lottery' (Interview #5). Similar views were expressed by an amateur sport school principal, 'Using the criteria for P.E. teachers, she (referring to a female coach with nearly twenty-year tenure) should have obtained the senior rank years ago' (Interview #6).

Education and welfare of elite youth athletes

The ways in which elite youth athletes in China were developed have drawn international critics (c.f., Hong, 2010). Hong was right to observe that:

> Under the control of the communist authority, the education of Confucian culture and the influence of the global commercialism the system... continues to produce... sports stars for national pride, ideological superiority, social conformity and economic advance.
>
> (p. 352)

Nevertheless, this was not to say that the Chinese sport authorities were ignoring elite youth athlete education and welfare. In fact, significant policy and managerial endeavours were made to improve the situation from the 1980s although the outcome was far from satisfactory.

Policies on elite youth athlete education and welfare

Purporting to overhaul the entry and exit obstacles afflicting the three-tier training system, *the Guidance on Further Strengthening Athlete Education and Athlete Support* (hereafter Directive 23) was the first athlete education and welfare regulation declared by the State Council in China (State Council, 2010). On the exit end, in addition to the full employment package as a state employee, *zhuanye* athletes were provided with one year transition time after retirement for them to get ready for the next career, and a retirement fee was provided to those who chose to search for jobs themselves (GASC, 2007, 2014a).[3] Notably, a Division for Athlete Service and Support was set up in GASC's Personnel Department in 2010 to provide career development support. A similar organizational structure was developed at provincial level (GASC Personnel Department, 2015).

On the entry side, Directive 23 was intended to improve the quality of education offered to elite youth athletes by bringing academic programmes in sport schools back to the development and supervision plan within the budget of the educational administrative authorities in China. In 2012, a total of 420 sport schools ran their education programmes outside of the education system, the number was reduced to 194 in 2015, and were to be fully eliminated by the end of 2015 (Guo, 2015). For the first time, the National Education Inspectorate launched a special inspection of public sport schools in October 2015 (National Education Inspectorate, 2015). In this connection, the GASC's evaluation of the High-performance Base Programme for the Rio cycle states, 'Sport schools in provinces where serious issues were detected during special athlete education inspections were not allowed to apply for the designation' (GASC, 2014b).

Further, a creative measure was introduced according to which athletes attending national youth competitions were required to complete academic exams as pre-qualification. Seventeen sports adopted the pre-competition academic exam in 2013 and the number increased to 22 in 2014. Similar measures were adopted by the provinces (Guo, 2015).

Education of first-line athletes, particularly those in national teams, was clearly the weakest link in the training network. The Directive 23's policy makers clearly recognized this issue. Section Three of the Directive spelled out measures to 'make use of national teams' demonstration effect in athlete education, and to improve academic study at elite sport teams' (State Council, 2010). In response, specific education programmes for athletes in national teams were developed ('Guojiadui', 2010). A Notice on Relevant Issues on Further Strengthening National Team Athlete Education was promulgated in early 2015 (GASC, 2015a).

Directive 23 in 2010 put the issue of athlete education and welfare in the limelight and made it one of the top priorities for elite sport in China. However, the issue of athlete education in China can be traced back to the 1960s. To facilitate training and competition, education programmes for young athletes in sport schools were established outside the regular educational system, and the trend of focusing on training and minimizing education *(zhongxunlian qinxuexi)* was perpetuated (Yu et al., 2008). Since then, a two-pronged approach to athlete education was used by the Chinese sport authorities to mitigate the problem. The first prong was to establish academic programmes within the elite sport system. The second prong was to create higher education opportunities for elite youth athletes by removing or lowering academic requirements for admission to universities.

In relation to the first prong, in the 1980s, professional sport colleges were established with the sole purpose of providing 'tailored' education to first-line athletes. For instance, the former Zhejiang Professional Sport College was established in 1983, providing education to elite athletes from grade three in elementary school to second year college students (Research group of GASC Science and Education Department, 2002). In 2012, there were 14 professional sport colleges in China (GASC Sport Economics Department, 2012). These institutions, although readily furnishing *zhuanye* athletes with a college degree, were not well recognized due to their poor quality and were often the least preferred by the athletes if they had other educational opportunities. An interviewee from the former Zhejiang Sport School commented, 'Ironically, all the best athletes training at the Zhejiang Sport College chose not to attend university here but to have their higher education elsewhere' (Interview #4).

In addition, vocational programmes in sport were added to middle sport schools capitalizing on China's preferential policy to develop vocational education in the mid-1980s. For instance, the Beijing Shichahai Sport School founded in 1956 started its vocational programmes in 1986. Consequently, the school expanded its mission to cultivate P.E. teachers and sports cadres ('Fazhan Lishi,' n.d.). The vocational programme in sport schools equipped the elite young athletes with the requisite qualification to be P.E. teachers or to work in other related occupations. In retrospect, job prospects for sport school graduates in the 1990s were exceptionally favourable. One interviewee from the GASC Science and Education Department recalled, 'It looks like we successfully solved the problem of elite athlete education and job placement in [the] 1990s' (Interview # 14). Nonetheless, the promulgation of *the Law of Education of PRC* in 1995 lifted the requirement for being a teacher (Jin et al., 2010). Meanwhile, the priority for the country's education policy moved to tertiary education in the late 1990s. With the rapid expansion of university enrolment, it was even difficult for an average university graduate to find a job (Chen, 2008). The job prospects for middle sport school graduates were extremely difficult (Jin et al., 2010).

The second prong was to generate higher education opportunities in regular universities. There were mainly two routes through which a Chinese elite youth athlete could secure a place at a university. *Zhuanye* athletes who had won medals at designated major national and international competitions could apply to enter universities without taking an entrance examination (GASC Science and Education Department, 2014). In 2005, over 660 *zhuanye* athletes were admitted to 64 universities via this programme (GASC Science and Education Department, 2015). The universities ranged from top ones in China such as Tsinghua University and Fudan University, to less known ones. Interestingly, only a few of these athletes chose to major in management, art or even history. Over 90 per cent of them chose to major in athletic training or other sport related majors. To a certain extent, this served as a reflection of their inadequate academic preparation. The second route was to set up academic programmes in regular universities specifically designed for those with a sport specialization. Applicants were required to reach a certain sport performance level. Meanwhile, the academic requirement was much lower compared with that required by China's national college entrance examination. In 2015, there were about 101 universities in China offering such academic programmes in athletic training and traditional ethnic sport, with an enrolment size of around 15,000 (GASC & Ministry of Education, 2015).

These arrangements benefited a large number of elite youth athletes, including the author herself, who would otherwise have lost their higher educational opportunities due to the daunting multi-year labour required to prepare for the national college entrance exam on one hand, and the substantial amount of study time lost to training and competition on the other hand (Zhong et al., 2012). Yet, the way these arrangements were established also meant that an athlete's chance of higher education hinged on athletic performance, not academic performance. To a certain extent, this perpetuated the vicious cycle of putting emphasis on training and neglecting study (Zhong et al., 2012). The same interviewee from the GASC Science and Education Department observed, 'We have been making patches (on athlete education) all the time without solving the problem at the root. Patches are not the more the better' (Interview #14). Comments made by a top GASC administrator went directly to the point, 'Athlete education in China was an unsolvable issue. When the time comes that the Central government and the society no longer want Olympic medals, the issue will be solved by itself' (Interview #26).

Studying and living situations of elite youth athletes

Fieldwork revealed the trend that the higher the level of training, the more severe was the damage to athlete education. In amateur sport schools, athletes typically attended nearby elementary schools and trained after school. There was little compromise in relation to their training. For instance, table tennis players at the Beijing Haidian Amateur Sport School studied at the adjacent elementary school. In addition to training sessions on Saturday mornings and afternoons, they trained from 4pm to 7pm and did homework after training every weekday during the evening self-study sessions organized by the sport school. The principal of the school explained:

> There was little negative impact on these athletes' education. They only train after school. Table tennis players are smart. We admit around 10 kids and send 2 to 3 to the second-line team each year. Many of our athletes were admitted to top middle schools after graduation from elementary school.
>
> (Interview #3)

Fieldwork at a county-level amateur sport school in Zhejiang rendered similar results. The school had even regularly hired experienced teachers to tutor their students' homework during the evening self-study sessions (Field Notes).

The education of elite youth athletes was clearly compromised when they progressed to become a second-line athlete and more so when entering a *zhuanye* sport team (Yu et al., 2008). For instance, the six middle sport schools in Beijing also served as the city's elite sport team training bases. Younger athletes in these schools went to nearby regular elementary schools but only for the morning sessions. One interviewee explained, 'Elementary schools arrange the main subject courses in the morning so they will not miss much' (Interview #21). The athletes started to receive in-house education when they entered grade seven. The second-line athletes attended five morning study sessions each week and first-line athletes only had three sessions (two morning sessions and one evening session) to meet the 12 school-hour requirement set by the GASC (Yu et al., 2008). Within national teams, academic study was irregular (Interview #16, Interview #19).

In term of living conditions, the first- and second-line youth athletes typically trained, studied and lived in their sport schools or *zhuanye* sport teams all year round. To a certain extent, they were babysat by their coaches and school/team administrators/managers. Typically, a highly-detailed daily schedule was developed for them. Team managers and coaches spent large amounts of time overseeing their daily life outside training. It was a standard practice that coaches inspected athletes' dormitories prior to curfew time every day except Saturday night to make sure their athletes went to bed on time. For athletes younger than 12 years old, cell phones were kept by their coaches. Similar to boarding school students, athletes, for instance in the Beijing Table Tennis team, could go home every Saturday and report back to the team on Sunday evening if their family lived nearby. For those whose families lived further away, their parents usually came to visit them during holidays (Interview #18). Considering that the athletes may have been too young to take care of themselves, the Beijing Diving team had the practice of allowing the divers' parents to enter the dormitories from 6:30pm to 8:30pm daily to help with homework, laundry and other things (Field Notes). For national teams, it was common practice that athletes joined their coach's family for major Chinese holidays such as the Spring Festival. In some sense, quasi-blood relationships were developed between coaches and athletes in line with the traditional Chinese form of apprenticeship (He, 2013).

Coaches and team managers played such a crucial role in youth elite athletes' lives that their influence extended well beyond the field of play. One interviewee from the GASC Personnel Department commented:

> If we can effectively mobilize the coaches to push the athletes to learn, the results will be significantly different. In one provincial fencing team, each fencer played good bridge simply because their coach was a bridge fanatic and had them to play bridge once a week. And they learned that way.
>
> (Interview #12)

This observation was supported by findings from the fieldwork. Jane, a member of the Beijing Diving Team, with the help of her coach, successfully secured an athletic scholarship from a US university in 2014. She won one gold medal at the All-American Collegiate Diving Championship, achieved a 3.87 GPA during her first year's study, and returned to train with her team in the summer. Her coach explained:

> Each athlete is different. We make arrangements (for their further education and job placement) according to their personal preferences and characteristics. Jane was a good student all the time and had won the Excellent National Elite Athlete Student Award. I trust her ability and begged the American university coach to save aside a spot for her. We significantly reduced her training load and had her study English intensively for the TOFEL exam. And she made it!
>
> (Interview #21)

Although few in number, there are foundations and non-profit organizations in China providing elite youth athletes with academic and career development services (Chinese Athletes Educational Foundation, n.d.). Jane mentioned that she had benefited greatly from Lining Foundation's English programme, specifically designed for elite youth athletes free of charge (Interview #22).

Issues and trends of elite youth sport in China

Threats to the three-tier training network

In contrast to the US's laissez-faire sport development system (Bowers, Chalip & Green, 2011), the Chinese assembled one of the most effective elite youth sport pipelines to maximize Olympic medals. The pipeline was successful in producing Olympians. However, the predominant emphasis on medal outputs severely undermined its sustainability and legitimacy (Y. Yu, 2010).

Amateur sport schools in China have diminished at an alarming rate from 3,687 in 1990 to 1,552 in 2012 (GASC Sport Economics Department, 1990, 2012). With the improved living conditions, Chinese parents are increasingly unwilling to send their children to sport schools (Xing, 2010). A coach in an amateur sport school mentioned:

> Nowadays, even parents in the countryside were unwilling to send their children to sport schools. It was so difficult for the hard sports (*ku xiangmu*) to recruit. When the parents came for a visit, coaches of our weightlifting team had to stop lifting weights and bring the kids out to run.
>
> (Interview #5)

For popular sports such as swimming, even though recruitment was not difficult, parents only wanted their children to learn the sport, not to be a *zhuanye* athlete. A swimming coach from the same school lamented, 'I had three swimmers selected by the provincial coach in past two years. One was by Shiwen Ye's coach! The parents agreed at the beginning but all changed their minds. I don't know what to do with this' (Interview #26).

Even more dangerous, both Chinese coaches and parents considered attending sport schools as a way out for children who were not good at study: 'It is good for the kid as it (having a sport specialization) offers an additional way out particularly if the kid is not a good student' (Interview #5). Another interviewee from the Beijing swimming team explained:

> We offered 25 admissions but only half came last year. The parents waited to see if their children were also admitted to the swimming team of the top middle schools. For those still coming to us, they simply know that their children would not keep up with the rigorous study in the top middle schools.
>
> (Interview #20)

These quotes reveal that the issue of athlete education in China was not only exacerbated by an overemphasis on medal outputs but also by the social perception that only those who are not good at study or who do not like study shall consider becoming *zhuanye* athletes (Zhong et al., 2012). Directive 23 was clearly intended to change this stereotype. It is anticipated that athlete education and career support will continue to be a key policy area for elite youth sport in China as long as Olympic medals continue to be politically and socially desired.

The increasingly diversified elite youth sport development system

A range of elite youth athlete development routes was observed. Firstly, athletes of newly inducted Olympic sports such as golf and rugby were mainly developed via the private sector while receiving subsidies from public sport organizations. For instance, though housed in the Beijing Shichahai Sport School, none of the golfers in the Beijing team trained there. The golfers merely received subsidies from the school in exchange for their representation of Beijing in national competitions (Field Notes). In addition, the Chinese universities played a limited role in cultivating elite youth athletes in sports such as track and field as in the case of Tsinghua University's track and field team (Gao, Zhao & Wang, 2014). Further, families started to play a role in nurturing athletes in professional and upper-class sports such as snooker, tennis, figure skating and ice hockey. Last but not least, although the three-tier training network remains as the main platform for developing elite youth athletes, since the 1990s substantial policy efforts have been made by the GASC on selected sports such as football and basketball to reform its elite sport system.

The football reform and impacts on elite youth player development

Football was chosen to pioneer reform in 1992 for three reasons. Firstly, China's transition from a planned economy to a market-based economy mandated reform in the sport sphere. Secondly, professional football was a global trend at the time. Finally, the mediocre performance of the Chinese men's football team on the international stage made the potential cost of reform [for the Olympic Medal Winning Programmes] affordable (CFA, n.d.). A number of key milestones marked the football reform which was heightened in 2015 with the promulgation of the *Notice on the Overall Plan on Chinese Football Reform and Development* (hereafter Directive 11).

- In 1994, the Chinese Professional Football League was formally established. Professional football clubs, financed and managed by companies, were gradually established and the former *zhuanye* (men's) football teams were transformed into professional teams. The Chinese Super League (CSL) was launched in 2004.

- Despite the fact that the Chinese men's football team, for the first time in history, qualified for the World Cup Finals in 2002, the years from 2001 to 2009 witnessed a period of turmoil, in Chinese football with a breakout of gambling and faked games, briberies, and corruption. This was ended by judicial interventions with a number of top officials from the Chinese Football Association (CFA) being sentenced in 2012.

- In April 2009, the GASC and Ministry of Education jointly promulgated *the Notice on Implementing National Youth Campus Soccer Activities*. Since then campus football has been promoted in public schools nationwide to build youth participation.

- In March 2015, Directive 11 was issued unprecedentedly by the General Office of the State Council with the ultimate goal of improving the performance of the Chinese men's football team. One of the main measures was to adjust and reorganize the CFA to accord it more autonomy. As a result, the Chinese National Football Management Centre was closed and CFA was officially 'unhooked' from GASC in August 2015 (Hu, 2015b). Similarly, provincial football associations will all be 'unhooked' from local sport bureaus by the end of 2017 (Interview #31).

Since the 1990s, the mechanism of cultivating elite youth football players changed dramatically. Most provincial sport bureaus phased out youth football teams in sport schools. The newly established professional football clubs were either incapable or not motivated to develop elite youth football players. On the other hand, entrepreneur-founded football schools sprung up to capitalize on the business opportunities generated by the professional football league. In the late 1990s, there were over 3,000 football schools and youth football training clubs registered with the CFA and the number dropped to merely 20 in 2007 due to the chaos of the market, corruption and scandals associated with the professional football league (Interview #28).

Youth player training was believed to be the weakest link of Chinese football. Over the years, a mixed channel of player development was instituted. In 2013, there were only 126 teams attending the U19, U17, U15, and U13 national youth football competitions. Sixty-four of these teams were filled by professional football clubs, 45 by provincial sport bureaus, and 17 by schools of various sorts. The numbers of CFA registered players for the U17 and U15 age brackets were respectively 3,107 and 3,891 (CFA, 2014). Similar to sport school students, the youth football players at football schools or youth football training clubs have their training sessions after school study. Yet, they pay to train. The Evergrande–Real Madrid Football School founded in 2012 was invested in and created by the Evergrande group which has also owned a CSL football club since 2010. The school, located in Guangzhou's suburban area, recruits elementary students with football talent nationwide and the students pay 50,000 Chinese *renminbi* (approximately 7,000 euro) each school year for accommodation, meals and so on (Hengda Zuqiu, 2015). Although the tuition fee was believed to be reasonably priced compared with that of an average boarding school, the challenge was that most Chinese parents were not interested in their children becoming professional football players, particularly in developed regions. An interviewee from the Beijing Football Association explained:

> There are only about 20 to 30 youth football training clubs in Beijing. [Except for three or four], most of them focus on participation by offering entry-level football classes. They have not reached the stage of fostering competitive football players. The clubs have [to have enough students] to survive. The top priority of the parents is their children's study, then exercise for health, and then to play football for enjoyment. With Beijing's ever tightened policy on its population size, it is difficult for children without Beijing residence to study and train here. Children outside Beijing are capable of sustaining the hard training. The Beijing kids, though smart, their parents have loftier plans for them than to engage them in a football career.
>
> (Interview # 30)

In addition, professional clubs do not appear to be keen on youth player development. Although all 32 professional football clubs of CSL and League One had second line teams and U17 teams, 69 per cent of CSL professional football clubs did not spend the 4 million Chinese *renminbi* (approximately 554,800 euro) on youth player training stipulated in CFA *Professional League Club Admission Criteria and Examination Methods* (Yan, 2014). Although huge amounts of venture capital flowed to the football market, particularly after Directive 11, the professional football clubs typically prefer paying exorbitant prices to buy players for a quick return than developing youth players as a long-term investment (Zhao, 2016).

From the perspective of the sport authorities, the National Games were again used as a lever to encourage local sport bureaus to invest in elite football player development. An interviewee from CFA commented:

> In those years [when corruption was rampant], [professional football] clubs almost stopped developing youth teams. We [at CFA] were not in the position to run the clubs. ... Campus football is mainly for participation. ... We can only depend on sport bureaus and football associations. Since the 2009 National Games, we set up U18, U20 football competitions. And we also designed U16, U18 football competitions at City Games [now changed to National Youth Games]. A provincial U16 team competed at the City Games was at the right age

to attend the U18 competition of the National Games two years later. Such an arrangement forced the sport bureaus to finance a team for four years. So, the young players would not be dismissed at the age of 16 years or 18 years old.

(Interview # 28)

Clearly, elite youth football development in China was a joint function of the 'invisible hand' of the market and the government. Yet, neither of them, enacted by an array of agents including the GASC, football associations, local governments, sport bureaus, business tycoons, professional football clubs, football schools, youth football training clubs, Ministry of Education (for campus soccer), education bureaus, public schools, had settled on the 'new' football development system amid the reform. Change was ongoing. One trend seems to be professional clubs taking a more active role in youth player development. An interviewee from Shanghai Football Association mentioned, 'the three professional clubs in Shanghai now began to collaborate with elementary schools and youth football training clubs to develop young players' (Interview #31). Response from a senior manager of a CSL club in Beijing corroborated that, 'nowadays, the player prices, including Chinese players are high. Many capitals relentlessly seek players with high performance-price ratio. The clubs began to see youth player development as a revenue source' (Interview # 29).

Changes to the National Games

Some major uncertainties lie ahead of China's elite sport system. On the dark side, the gold-medal-first view dominating China's elite sport since the 1980s has led to doping, cheating, fixed results, bribery and corruption and drawn the GASC criticism nationwide (Meng, 2015). In response to a special inspection organized by China's Central Commission for Discipline Inspection in 2014, as part of the new government's anti-corruption campaign, the GASC vowed to correct the negative features caused by treating gold-medal success as the sole measure of an official's achievement (Wee, 2015). Among other corrections to be implemented, future National Games would only announce competition results but not medal and total score rankings of the provinces that had linked Olympic medals to the National Games (GASC, 2015b). While helpful in stopping corruption, this action also means an end to the mechanism of drawing nationwide resources into elite sport system for Olympic medals (Zhang, 2012). It also means that local governments will be less motivated to invest in elite sport in the future. How that may affect China's elite youth sport system remains to be seen.

In conclusion, China's mature elite youth sport system has been successful in producing top Olympic athletes over the past 30 years. Yet, the complications of going after medals at all costs are increasingly acute and met with social resistance (Y. Yu, 2010). These issues are symptomatic of a rapidly developing nation in the midst of transformation. Being part of that transformation, the elite sport system in China has been pushed to adjust to keep up with nationwide reform and social change. However, in order to continually satisfy the nation's appetite for Olympic medals, it has been concurrently fettered by an outdated model rooted in a planned economy watchfully guarded by those with vested interests (Hu, 2015a; Xing, 2014).

Acknowledgements

This work was supported by Beijing Social Science Fund (# 14SHC031), Beijing Higher Education Institution Young Scholar Development Plan (# CIT&TCD201404170), Sport Philosophy and Social Science Research Fund of General Administration of Sport of China (# 2048SS14079).

Notes

1 Data were obtained via 31 semi-structured interviews and a large number of communications via phone, email, WeChat on mobile device, informal conversation with administrators, officials, coaches, and athletes from the GASC, NSMCs, provincial elite sport teams, local sport organizations, and sport schools during the period of 2014 to early 2016. Relevant policy documents, reports and academic work in Chinese between the years of 1990 to 2015 were obtained for triangulation and cross-validation.

2 Number of coaches from *zhuanye* sport teams, middle sport schools, and amateur sport schools were not summed to the total of 22,312 in *the 2012 Yearbook of Sport Cause Statistics* as a few of them were employed by other organizations. This is also the case for coaches' numbers in table tennis and diving as shown in Table 12.2.

3 Due to Beijing's strict population policy, *zhuanye* athletes without Beijing residence were not eligible to receive the retirement fee. The issue garnered media attention in late 2015. A news story on November 12, 2015 that some Beijing *zhuanye* athletes did not receive their retirement fees can be found at http://news.xinhuanet.com/politics/2015-11/12/c_128421497.htm. It was subsequently solved by the Beijing Sport Bureau in early 2016. Beijing *zhuanye* athletes without the city's resident status who made their retirement since 2004 can reclaim their retirement fee along with relevant monetary compensations (Interview #12). This discrepancy of policy implementation is an indication of the not unusual phenomenon in China that local implementation of national sport policies are constrained by policies promulgated by other national ministries or local policies.

References

Bao, M.X. (2010). *Zhongguo zhiye tiyu pingshu.* *[Commentary on Chinese Professional Sport]*. Beijing, China: People's Sport Press.

Bowers, M., Chalip, L. & Green, B.C. (2011). Beyond the façade: Youth sport development in the United States and the illusion of synergy. In B. Houlihan & M. Green (Eds.), *Routledge Handbook of Sports Development* (pp.173–183). London: Routledge.

CFA. (2014). Zuqiu guihua. [Plan for football]. In GASC Youth Sport Department (Ed.), *Aoyun xiangmu jingji tiyu houbei rencai peiyang zhongchangqi guihua [The middle to long term plans of Olympic sports to cultivate elite sport reserved talents]* (pp.431-443). Beijing, China: People's Sport Press.

CFA. (n.d.). *Guanyu zuqiu gongzuo de diaoyanbaogao. [Research report on football]*. Unpublished work report.

Chen, X.P. (2008). Daxue kuozhao ba nian: Huixiang daxuesheng jiuyenan chengyin fenxi [Eight years after university enrollment expansion: Analyzing why it is difficult for college graduates to obtain emloyments]. *Educator, 2008(15)*, 24–26.

Chinese Athletes Educational Foundation. (n.d.). Fazhanshi. [Development history]. Retrieved from www.chinese-athletes.org/about.php?subid=4

Fazhan lishi [History of development]. (n.d.). Retrieved from www.bjschtx.com/Column_Content.asp?Column_ID=11249

Gao, Y., Zhao, Z.J., & Wang. B.B. (2014, August 22). Tsinghua tianjingdui de gushi. [The story of Tsinghua Track and Field team]. *Qinghua University News*. Retrieved from http://news.tsinghua.edu.cn/publish/news/4205/2014/201408220 91407570162376/201408220 91407570162376_.html

GASC. (2003a). *Guojiadui renshi guanli zanxing banfa. [Temporary method on personnel management of the national teams]*. Retrieved from www.sport.gov.cn/n16/n1092/n16879/n17366/1461323.html

GASC. (2003b). *Quanguo yundongyuan zhuce yu jiaoliu guanli banfa. [Nationwide management method on athlete registration and exchange]*. Retrieved from www.sport.gov.cn/n16/n33193/n33208/n33433/n33688/127349.html

GASC. (2007). *Yundongyuan pinyong zanxing banfa. [Temporary method on athlete hiring]*. Retrieved from www.gov.cn/zwgk/2007-09/18/content_753347.htm

GASC. (2010). *Zhonghua renmin gongheguo dishierjie dongji yundonghui jingsai guize zongze. [General rules of competition regulations for the 12th Winter National Games of P.R.C.]*. Retrieved from www.sport.gov.cn/n16/n33193/n33208/n33433/n33703/1702697.html

GASC. (2014a). *Guanyu jinyibu zuohao tuiyi yundongyuan jiuye anzhi gongzuo youguan wenti de tongzhi. [Notice on issues related to further improving job placement of retired athletes]*. Retrieved from www.sport.gov.cn/n16/n1077/n1467/n4028874/n4028934/5779981.html

GASC. (2014b). *Guojia gaoshuiping tiyu houbei rencai jidi rending banfa. [Method on evaluation of National High-performance Reserve Talent Bases]*. Retrieved from www.sport.gov.cn/n16/n1251450/n1251465/n1252727/n1252812/5899552.html

GASC. (2015a). *Guanyu jinyibu jiaqiang guojiadui yundongyuan wenhuajiaoyu gongzuo youguan shiyi de tongzhi. [Notice on relevant issues to further*

strengthening national team athlete education]. Retrieved from www.
ydyeducation.com/2015/gzdt_0511/16.html

GASC. (2015b). *Guanyu xunshi zhenggai qingkuang de tongbao. [Circular on
correction situation in response to the inspection].* Retrieved from www.ccdi.gov.
cn/xwtt/201501/t20150123_50542.html

GASC. (n.d.). *Guojia tiyu zongju zhuyao zhize. [Main responsibilities of the General
Administration of Sport].* Retrieved from www.sport.gov.cn/n16/n1077/5768068.
html

GASC & Ministry of Education. (2015). *2015 putong gaodeng xuexiao danzhao
guanli banfan. [The 2015 management method on special university admission of
sport specialization programmes].* Retrieved from www.ydyeducation.com/2015/
ggtz_0102/2.html

GASC Personnel Department. (2015). *Yundongyuan baozhang gongzuo shouce.
[Handbook of working on athlete support and service].* Beijing, China: Author.

GASC Science and Education Department. (2014). *Guanyu zuohao 2015 nian
youxiu yundongyuan mianshi jinru gaodeng xuexiao xuexi youguan shiyi de
tongzhi. [2015 Notice on related issues for elite athletes to enter higher education
institution with admission waiver].* Retrieved from www.sport.gov.cn/n16/
n1077/n1467/n1701156/n1701173/6003909.html

GASC Science and Education Department. (2015). *Guanyu 2015 nian youxiu
yundongyuan mianshi ruxue tuijiani mingdan de gongshi. [Public announcement
of the name list of elite athletes who enter university with admission waiver in
2015].* Retrieved from www.sport.gov.cn/n16/n1077/n1467/n1701156/
n1701173/6440543.html

GASC Sport Economics Department. (1990). *Tiyushiye tongji nianjian. [The
yearbook of sport cause statistics].* Beijing, China: Author.

GASC Sport Economics Department. (2012). *Tiyushiye tongji nianjian. [The
yearbook of sport cause statistics].* Beijing, China: Author.

Green, B. C. (2005). Building sport programmes to optimize athlete recruitment,
retention and transition: Toward a normative theory of sport development.
Journal of Sport Management, 19, 233–253.

Guo, J.J. (2015). *Zai 2015 nian quanguo qingshaonian tiyu gongzuo huiyi shang de
jianghua. [Speech on the 2015 National Youth Sport Congress].* Retrieved from
www.sport.gov.cn/n16/n33193/n33208/n1581724/n1581739/6228808.html

Guojiadui yundongyuan suzhijiaoyu fang'an. [National Team Athletes
Comprehensive Education Plan]. (2010, December 17). Retrieved from www.
sport.gov.cn/n16/n1077/n1467/n1701156/n1701206/1750044.html

He, J. (2013). *Hanxuebaoma: Woguo youshi yundongxiangmu yundongdui
'jinqinfanzhi' xianxiang de shehuixue yanjiu [Ferghana horse: The sociological
study of inbreeding phenomenon of dominant sport team in China].* Beijing,
China: Chemical Industry Press.

Hengda zuqiu xuexiao richang zhaosheng jianzhang [Evergrande Football School
Recruitment Brochure]. (2015, October 17). Retrieved from www.evergrandefs.
com/admission!showZSJZContent.htm?menuCode=256&menuLevel=3&url=ad
mission!showZSJZContent.htm

Hong, F. (2008). China. In B. Houlihan & M. Green (Eds.), *Comparative elite sport
development: System, structures and public policy* (pp.26–52). London: Elsevier.

Hong, F. (2010). Innocence lost: Child athletes in China. *Sport in Society: Cultures, Commerce, Media, Politics*, 7, 338–354. doi: 10.1080/1743043042000291677

Hu, J.T. (2006). *Zhonghua renmin gongheguo yiwu jiaoyufa. [The Compulsory Education Law of the P.R.C.]*. Retrieved from www.gov.cn/flfg/2006-06/30/content_323302.htm

Hu, X.Q. (2015a). *An analysis of Chinese Olympic and elite sport policy discourse in the post-Beijing 2008 Olympic Games era.* (Doctoral dissertation, Loughborough University, London, UK). Retrieved from https://dspace.lboro.ac.uk/dspace-jspui/bitstream/2134/17458/3/Thesis-2015-Hu.pdf

Hu, X.Q. (2015b, October). Chinese football and its number one fan. *The APPS Policy Forum*. Retrieved from www.policyforum.net/chinesefootballandits numberonefan/

Jin, X.B., Chi, Y., Yang, J.S., Jiang, G.J., Fang, C., Zhang, J., ... Sun, Q.K. (2010). Woguo zhongdeng tiyu yundong xuexiao banxue moshi yanjiu [Research on operational model of middle sport schools in China]. *Xi'An Tiyu Xueyuan Xuebao*, 27(2), 142–145.

Jingsaijihua—2015 nian quanguoxing danxiang bisai. [Competition schedule: 2015 National Competitions of the NGBs]. (2015). Retrieved from www.sport.gov.cn/n16/n33193/n33208/n33433/n2108404/6355674.html

Li, Y.L. (2000). Jinjitizhi zhuangui shiqi zhongguo jingjitiyu yunxing de yanjiu. [Study on the adjustment of the Chinese elite sport system during economic transformation]. (Doctoral dissertation, Beijing Sport University, Beijing, China). Retrieved from cnki database.

Liu, P. (2010, November 17). *Zai guanche luoshi 'guanyu jinyibu jiaqiang yundongyuan wenhua jiaoyu he yundongyuan baozhang gongzuo de zhidaoyijian'zuotanhui shang de jianghua. [Speech on the meeting discussing the implementation of the Guidance on Further Strethening Athlete Education and Welfare]*. Retrieved from www.sport.gov.cn/n16/n1077/n1467/n1701156/n1701221/1750122.html

Meng, D.C. (2015). *Biele jinpai zhishang: cong guojatiyu zongju xunshi zhenggai tongbao kan tiyu zhengjiguan. [Bye-bye to the gold medal dominant view: Examining the medal view from the GASC's inspection correction circular]*. Retrieved from www.ccdi.gov.cn/yw/201502/t20150202_50861.html

National Education Inspectorate. (2015). *Guanyu kaizhan gongban tiyu yundong xuexiao yundongyuan wenhuajiaoyu gognzuo zhuanxiang dudao de tongzhi. [Notice on implementing athlete education special inspection in public sport schools]*. Retrieved from hwww.zjedu.gov.cn/news/144446880299061338.html

National Management Centre for Table Tennis and Badminton of GASC. (2015). *Guanyu kaizhan 2015 nian quanguo pingpangqiu yundongyuan jiaolianyuan zhuce gongzuo de tongzhi. [Notice on 2015 national registrations of table tennis players and coaches]*. Retrieved from http://tabletennis.sport.org.cn/home/xhgg/2014-12-08/457002.html

National Personnel Department. (1994). *Tiyu jiaolianyuan zhiwu dengji biaozhun. [Criteria on sport coaches' professional ranks]*. Retrieved from www.sport.gov.cn/n16/n33193/n33208/n33478/n33988/127222.html

National Personnel Department. (1996). *Yundongyuan jiaolianyuan jiangli shishi banfa. [Implementation method on rewarding athletes and coaches]*. Retrieved from www.sport.gov.cn/n16/n1092/n16864/326395.html

National Personnel Department. (2007). *Guanyu tiyu shiyedanwei gangweishezhi guanli de zhidaoyijian. [Guidance on employment categories in sport public institutions]*. Retrieved from www.sport.gov.cn/n16/n41308/n41323/n41345/n41486/n44382/n44502/172242.html

Research group of GASC Science and Education Department. (2001). *Woguo youxiu yundongyuan wenhua jiaoyu gongzuo diaocha baogao. [Investigation report on the situation of elite athlete education in China]*. Unpublished work report.

Song, L.W. (2015). *Guojia gaoshuiping tiyu houbei rencai jidi rending gongzuo de xianzhuang diaocha yu duice yanjiu. [Investigation on the evaluation of National High-performance Reserve Talent Bases]*. (Master's thesis. Capital University of P.E. & Sports, Beijing, China). Retrieved from cnki databse.

State Council. (2010). *Guanyu jinyibu jiaqiang yundongyuan wenhuajiaoyu he yundongyuan baozhanggongzuo de zhidaoyijian. [Guidance on further strengthening athlete education and athlete support]*. Retrieved from www.sport.gov.cn/n16/n1077/n1467/n1701156/n1701206/1809596.html

Tang, Y. (2007). Dui woguo aoyun zhengguang jihua de duowei shenshi. [A multi-dimensional analysis of Chinese Olympic Gold Medal Winning Programme]. *Wuhan Tiyu Xueyuan Xuebao, 41(2)*, 16-21. doi:10.15930/j.cnki.wtxb.2007.02.005

Wang, J.L., Wang, J., & Chen, K.Q. (2011). Woguo jiaolianyuan jishu dengji zhidu de fazhan yange. [A historical review of regulations on coaches' technical levels in China]. *Tiyu Wenhua Daokan, 2011*(4), 16–19.

Wee, S. (2015). *China's anti-graft unit tells sports to play fair, drop gold medal fever*. Retrieved from www.reuters.com/article/2015/01/27/us-china-sports-corruption-idUSKBN0L007420150127#sUMs81LMuPK6RIXG.99

Xing, X. (2010). Youth Olympic sport development in China. In Parks, J., Quarterman, J., & Thibault, L. (Eds). *Contemporary Sport Management* (4th edn) (p.282). Champaign, IL: Human Kinetics.

Xing, X. (2014, July). *Sport policy directions and changes in China: A forward looking*. Paper presented at the 2014 Conference of the International Sport Sociology Association, Beijing, China.

Yan, Q. (2014, November 11). Zhongguo zuqiu qingxun diaocha. [Investigation on youth training of the Chinese football]. *Netease Sport*. Retrieved from http://sports.163.com/14/1111/14/AAPE7VND00051C89.html

Yu, F. (2010). *Zhenshi rensheng: Wo de tiaoshui wangshi. [Real life, My diving story]*. Beijing, China: China City Press.

Yu, Y.H. (2010). Juguotiyu tizhi de 'renshouxing' weiji. [The legitimacy crisis of China's Juguotiyu sports system]. *Tiyu Yu Kexue, 31*(1), 1–4.

Yu, Z.G., Liu, W., Kang, S.P., Xie, Y.G., Zhang, X. & W, L.J. (2008). Woguo youxiu yundongyuan wenhua jiaoyu xianzhuang diaocha baogao. [Investigation on culture education conditions of elite athletes in China]. *Tiyu Kexue, 28*(7), 26–36.

Zhang, J.H. (2012). Quanyunhui zhidu 60 nian yanbian (1949-2009): Jiyu lishi zhidu zhuyi de fenxi. [The 60 years evolution of the National Games institution (1949-2009): Based on the analysis of historical institutionalism]. *Zhongguo Tiyu Keji, 48*(2), 10–19.

Zhao, Y. (2016, February 17). Ma Dexing: Zhongguo Qingxun hai weishang Zhegngui. [Ma Dexing: Youth training in China not on the right way]. *China TV*

Sports. Retrieved from http://sports.sina.cn/share.d.html?from=qudao&wm=304
9_0016&docID=fxpmpqt1368448&luicode=10000359&wb2sina=1&c=iphone
&ua=iPhone6%2C2__weibo__5.7.0__iphone__os8.4.1

Zhong, B.S., Zhang, L.Q., Hao, X.C., Xing, X.X., Yin, J., Pan, Y.X. ... Xu, D.P.
(2012). *Guoji jingji tiyu tixi he qingshaonian yundongyuan wenhua jiaoyu.
[International elite sport system and academic education of elite youth athletes].*
Beijing, China: Beijing Sport University Press.

Zhong, S.H. (2009). Lun keji Ju Guo Ti Zhi. [A discussion on Ju Guo Ti Zhi in
science and technology]. *Kexuexue Yanjiu, 27*(12), 1785–1792. doi: 10.16192/j.
cnki.1003-2053.2009.12.020

Chapter 13

India

Packianathan Chelladurai and Usha Sujit Nair

India is the second most populous country in the world after China with more than 1.295 billion people as of 2014 (World Bank, n.d.). According to the CIA (2015) World Factbook, the Indian population consists of people of Indo-Aryan origin (72 per cent), Dravidian origin (25 per cent), and Mongloid and others (3 per cent). While nearly 79.8 per cent of the population follow Hinduism, 14.2 per cent follow Islam, 2.3 per cent follow Christianity, 1.7 per cent adhere to Sikhism, and 2 per cent follow other religions (CIA, 2015). There are 23 officially recognized languages belonging to the Indo-Aryan branch spoken by 75 per cent of the population and the Dravidian branch spoken by the reminder of the population (New World Encyclopaedia, 2015).

The total worth of the Indian economy in 2014 stood at 2.183 trillion dollars at current prices placing it at the seventh rank in the world and at 8.027 trillion dollars corrected for purchasing power parity making it the third largest economy in the world (Knoema, 2015). However, when this wealth is shared by the total population, the per capita wealth amounts to only about 1,688 dollars placing India at the 140th rank in the world.

The age distribution of the population is of special interest to this book focused on youth. The CIA (2015) notes that 28.09 per cent of the Indian population (n = 1.252 billion) are between the ages of 0–14 years and 18.06 per cent are between 15–24 years. That is, 46.15 per cent of the Indian people (or approximately 577 million; males ≈ 306 million; females ≈ 271 million) are under the age of 25 which means that there is no dearth of human capital which can be put in pursuit of excellence in sports.

On the economic side, one estimate puts India's middle class to grow to 583 million people by 2025 (Mustafi, 2013). One of the reasons advanced for India's poor performance in sport was that the Indian masses did not have the wherewithal to participate in sport. Now that the middle class is burgeoning, that excuse would not hold water anymore. In sum, India has the resources in terms of (a) young people under the age of 25 years and (b) monetary resources as reflected in the growing middle class to engage in pursuit of excellence and excel in sports. All that is needed is a national mindset that values excellence in sports.

Sports in modern India

In modern times, India is not known for its performances in international sport competitions apart from the fact that it had won six consecutive Olympic gold medals in field hockey from the years 1928 to 1956, and again in 1964 and 1980. Since then, Indian hockey has struggled to regain its former glory.

While India's performance in the 2014 Commonwealth Games held in Glasgow (15 Gold, 30 Silver and 10 Bronze for a total of 64 medals) and in the 2014 Asian Games held in Incheon (11 Gold, 10 Silver, and 36 Bronze, for a total of 57 medals) compares favourably with its performances in the previous editions of these two Games, India's performance at the 2012 London Olympic Games surprised the nation. Although the haul of medals was meagre (2 Gold, 4 Silver, and 6 Bronze medals), it was the best ever performance of India at the Olympics. In fact, the previous record was only three medals.

Presently, Sports Authority of India (SAI), a unit of the Government of India has embarked on enhancing the performance potential of Indian athletes through its various schemes. As can be expected from a government programme, the policies and programs of the SAI tend to treat all sports and all regions of the country uniformly. As such, the unique needs of specific sports and the athletes thereof are not attended to. Unfortunately, the National Sports Federations (NSFs) which represent the respective international federations do not appear to be proactive in promoting excellence in their respective sports. It is not clear if their efforts are stifled by the dominance of SAI and its policies. However, India is faring well on the international scene in two sports, namely cricket and badminton. They are showcased in the following paragraphs.

Cricket

Cricket has become India's national game and has done extremely well in international competitions. Cricket is so popular in India that fans would consider it their religion and the cricket heroes their gods. The game is played in every nook and corner of the country – the streets, the rice and wheat fields, parks, parking lots, etc. So, it is not surprising that India produces some of the best-known international stars in cricket. The board of Control for Cricket in India (BCCI) should a take a large share of the credit for the emergence of cricket as the national sport of India. From its early days, it has garnered the support of the media, the government officials, the politicians, and business and industry which, in turn, facilitated the growth of cricket in India. It organizes the very popular national tournaments such as the Ranji Trophy, Irani Trophy, Duleep Trophy, Deodhar Trophy, and Challenger Trophy. These tournaments feature the best talents from the various states and regions of India. In addition, each of the 29 state-level cricket associations conduct high level tournaments among the districts in the respective states. These tournaments are well covered by both the broadcast and print media which helps sustain the status of cricket in the Indian national psych.

Currently, the International Cricket Council ranks India fifth in Test Championship, second in One Day International (ODI) Championship, and sixth in Twenty20 Championship. India had done better than this in the previous years. Currently, India can boast of having the world's showcase tournament for Twenty20 cricket, a shorter format of cricket consisting of only 20 overs. It is the Indian Premier League, the world's richest cricket tournament, whose brand value was estimated to be over US$ 3.2 billion in 2014 (American Appraisal, 2014).

Badminton

India is faring very well in Badminton also. The World Badminton Federation places India's K. Srikanth in the fifth rank in men's singles and Setiawan and Ahsan are ranked number two in Men's doubles. On the women's side, Saina Nehwal, till recently number one women's player in singles, now holds the second rank. The rise of the high performance standards in Indian badminton can be attributed to the hard work by a select few badminton academies headed by former badminton stars such as Prakash Padukone and Pullele Gopichand. The growing popularity of badminton in India has attracted Malaysian state badminton players such as Yogendran and Yeoh Kay Bin to open a badminton academy in the southern city of Chennai (Sports 247, 2016).

In addition, the Badminton Association of India has also provided the groundwork for the badminton talent to rise to the top. It organizes various tournaments to cater to the needs of veterans, seniors, juniors, sub juniors. More importantly, these tournaments are carried out in different regions of the country. Individual players of both genders and various age groups are ranked on the basis of their performances in some of these tournaments.

A popular move undertaken by the Badminton Association of India is the initiation of a professional league comprised of six teams located in six of the largest cities in India. The prize-money offered in the tournament is $1 million. What is equally significant, is that the association has launched the Shuttle India program wherein school boys and girls from the six franchise cities get to compete against each other alongside the professional competitions. These moves will certainly spur the growth of badminton excellence in India.

Gymnastics

Gymnastics has a short history in India. Yet, Ashish Kumar won the Bronze medal in the 2010 Commonwealth Games held in India, the first ever medal in Gymnastics for India in an international competition. On the women's side, Dipa Karamarkar won a bronze medal in the 2014 Commonwealth Games held in Scotland, and a bronze medal in the 2015 Artistic Gymnastics Asian Championships. Given the lack of popularity of gymnastics in India and that the Gymnastics Federation of India has been characterized as inefficient (Luthra, 2014), the achievements of Kumar and Karamarkar are praiseworthy. The successes of these two individuals would spur the young boys and girls of India to pursue excellence in the sport.

The sport system in India

India is one of the countries where the central government has considerable influence in the sport sector. Such influence and control is exercised by the Ministry of Youth Affairs and Sports and its specialized unit, the Sports Authority of India.

Policy of the Ministry

The National Youth Policy 2014 of the Ministry of Youth Affairs and Sports aims to promote, among other things, a strong and healthy generation equipped to take on future challenges (Ministry of Youth Affairs and Sports, 2014). Under this broad aim, the Ministry lists two priority areas: (a) Health and Healthy Lifestyle, and (b) Sports. As for the priority area of sports, the Ministry is set to increase access to sports facilities and training, promote sports culture among youth, and support and develop talented sports persons. With a view to encouraging mass participation in sport, the Ministry provides access to sports facilities and coaching in both urban and rural areas through programs like Rajiv Gandhi Khel Abhiyan (Abhiyan means mission or campaign), National Playing Fields Association of India, and the Scheme for creation of urban infrastructure at various levels.

The National Youth Policy of 2014 also envisages promoting the sports culture among the youth of the country. It is noted in the policy that 'A sports culture needs to be promoted among youth. The youth must be enabled to consider sports not just as recreational activity but also as potential career option. This would require a greater focus on sports activities as a part of the curriculum at school and college levels' (National Youth Policy 2014, p. 49). The policy also envisages leveraging state governments, educational boards, and the National Cadet Corps for further integration of sports into their formal education system. Another aim of the

National Youth Policy is to support the development of talented sportspersons which would require a seamless channel for talent identification, coaching, participation in competitions, incentives and performance successes.

Policy of SAI

The SAI, in turn, lists on its website (www.sportsauthorityofindia.nic.in/index.asp?lang=1) the following as its aims and objectives:

- To promote and broad-base sports in the country.
- To implement schemes/programmes for achieving excellence in sports in different disciplines at international level in order to establish India as a major sporting power.
- To maintain and utilize on behalf of the Government, stadia which were constructed/renovated for the IXth Asian Games held in 1982 and the Commonwealth Games in 2010.
- To act as an interface between the Ministry of Youth Affairs & Sports and other agencies concerned with the promotion/development of sports in the country, i.e., State Govt., U.T. Administration, IOA, National Sports Federations (NSFs), Sports Control Boards, Industrial Houses, etc.
- To establish, run, manage and administer the institutions to produce high calibre coaches, sports scientists and physical education teachers.
- To plan, construct, acquire, develop, take over, manage, maintain and utilize sports infrastructure and facilities in the country.
- To initiate, undertake, sponsor, stimulate and encourage research projects related to various sports sciences for upgradation of sports, sportspersons and coaches.
- Other incidental issues concerning promotion, development and excellence in sports.

Training Centres of SAI. In order to achieve the above aims and objectives, the SAI has set up 12 SAI Regional Centres and Educational Institutes, 56 SAI Training Centres, 19 Special Area Games Centres, and 11 Centres of Excellence.

Academic wings of SAI. The SAI also administers two academic wings to produce highly qualified coaches and physical educators. The planners had diligently differentiated the two processes of training coaches for the pursuit of excellence in sports and training physical educators for the promotion of participation in sports. The Netaji Subhas National Institute of Sports (NSNIS) focuses largely on training coaches, sport psychologists, and experts in sports medicine. The NSNIS is affiliated with recognized universities to offer graduate degrees, post graduate diplomas, and certificates in sports coaching, sports medicine, sports massage, and ground management.

The Lakshmibai National College of Physical Education is affiliated with the University of Kerala and offers master of physical education (MPE), post graduate diploma in health and fitness management (PGDHFM), and master of philosophy (MPhil) degrees. Formerly, the SAI also managed the larger Lakshmibai College of Physical Education in Gwalior. In 2000, this unit was renamed Lakshmibai National Institute of Physical Education (LNIPE) and is deemed to be a university. It now operates independent of the SAI but under the jurisdiction of the Ministry of Youth Affairs and Sports.

Schemes of the Ministry of Youth Affairs and Sports

Human resources development in sports

The Department of Sports within the Ministry of Youth Affairs and Sport established in 2013 a special scheme named Scheme of Human Resources Development in Sports which (a) awards fellowships for advanced graduate studies in sports related disciplines, (b) encourages participation in seminars, workshops, and conferences, (c) assists match officials (referees and umpires), coaches, and other support personnel to enhance their expertise, (d) provides grants for research projects, and (e) assists financially the publication of high-quality material relevant to sports.

Come and Play Scheme

Instituted in 2011, this scheme is part of the legacy plan which specifies that the sports stadia and other facilities be used not only for pursuit of excellence but also for recreational purposes by the masses. When it was first launched in Delhi, it is reported that a maximum of 12,000 people used the facilities per day (The Times of India, 2011). The current level of participation in all SAI facilities across India is not known. This scheme also aims at encouraging promising youngsters (between the ages of 8 and 17) to use the facilities under the jurisdiction of SAI and its branches. These youngsters are placed in age groups of 8–10 years, 10–12 years, and 12–17 years and assigned SAI coaches who train them. Competitions are arranged among teams within each age group. Better performers in these competitions are encouraged to train and compete for inclusion in the higher level training schemes.

Community Connect

Launched in 2014, the Community Connect Scheme is designed to encourage citizens to participate in activities carried out in the infrastructure under the jurisdiction of the SAI. This facilitates the maximum utilization of the stadia and at the same time promotes a healthy lifestyle among the populace. In addition, the scheme has created academies for football, cycling, swimming, and shooting for developing talent. Prominent sports persons, private enterprises, and relevant sports federations help in running these academies. There is also a proposal to establish a national sports museum.

Scheme for international competitions

In addition to the above ongoing schemes, Ministry of Youth Affairs and Sports had also undertaken special schemes to enhance the performance of Indian athletes in international competitions – Scheme for Preparation of Indian Athletes for Commonwealth Games 2010 and 'Operation Excellence for London Olympics-2012'. The major efforts in these schemes involved comprehensive and intensive training within India and abroad, and participation in international sports competitions. The total amount spent on preparation for the Commonwealth Games was Rs. 678 crores (approximately 1,040 million US dollars at the exchange rate of 65 rupees per dollar) and for OPEX 2012 was Rs.142.47 crore (just over 219 million US dollars). Efforts made by the Ministry and SAI under OPEX 2012 Project yielded remarkable results for the country which secured six medals (2 Silver and 4 Bronze) in the London 2012 Olympic Games. This is by far the highest medal haul ever for India in Olympic Games. In the 2014 Commonwealth Games, India secured 15 gold medals, 30 silver medals, and 19 bronze medals for total of 64 medals. This was also the best ever performance of India in the Commonwealth Games.

Recognition of outstanding sportspersons

The best Indian sportspersons in each sport is given the Arjuna Award named after one of the heroes of the epic Maha Baratha. The Best Indian coach in each sport is presented with the Dronacharya Award named after the great mentor in Maha Baratha. The Rajiv Gandhi Khel Ratna Award honours the best performance by a sportsperson or sports team in a year across all sports. Incidentally, Rajiv Ghandhi was the assassinated prime minister of India.

Schemes of Sports Authority of India

The website of the SAI lists its schemes under the headings SAI Sports Promotional Schemes. They are described below.

National Sports Talent Contest (NSTC) Scheme

Instituted in 1985, the National Sports Talent Contest Scheme is aimed at scouting sports talent in the 8–14 years age group and developing them into medal prospects. Students who had done well in district, state, and national level competitions are accepted into the scheme. Selected students are paid a token amount of 4,150 rupees per year to cover the sports kit, insurance, and competition expenses and an annual stipend of 3,000 rupees.

Coaches trained at the SAI's National Institute of Sports are assigned to selected schools that have good sports infrastructure and have done well in sports competitions. These coaches, in turn, are expected to enable promising youngsters to pursue excellence in sports. Athletics (track and field), basketball, football, gymnastics, hockey, kabaddi and kho-kho (indigenous sports), swimming, table tennis, volleyball, and wrestling are the sports selected for training. In addition, the scheme also trains athletes in indigenous games and wrestling. The distinct feature of this programme is that the promising youngsters are trained in their own schools. So far, the scheme includes 14 schools for international sports and 10 schools for indigenous sports and wrestling, which train 805 boys and 255 girls for a total of 1,060 athletes.

Army Boys Sports Company Scheme

The SAI and the Indian Army collaborate to exploit the Army's extensive sports infrastructure and the 'disciplined environment' to train 8 to 16 year old boys who had done well in state and national level competitions in archery, athletics, basketball, boxing, diving, fencing, football, gymnastics, hockey, rowing, shooting, weightlifting, and wrestling. The scheme provides for the boarding, lodging, equipment, competition, insurance, and medical expenses. More than 1,000 boys are under training in 18 army Centres. An added benefit for the trainees is that they will be absorbed into the army after they attain 17 ½ years of age.

SAI Training Centres

This is a collaborative scheme between the SAI and state governments wherein a state government provides the infrastructure for the training of 12 to 18 years old and the SAI provides boarding and lodging, scientific training, and equipment to the trainees. The trainees are those who have excelled in the sports in the NSTC Scheme described earlier. Currently, there are 56 STC Centres across the country where 5,394 trainees (3,807 boys and 1,587 girls) are being trained. It is unfortunate that females are underrepresented in this regimen.

Special Area Games Scheme

In order to reach the would-be sportspersons in accessible tribal, rural, and coastal areas, the SAI has instituted a scheme named Special Area Games

Scheme (SAG). The aim of the scheme is to spot the talent in 12–18 years age bracket and train them to be excellent in sports. As is the case with other programmes, the expenses in terms of boarding and lodging, competition, education, insurance and other sundries are covered by the SAI. At the time of this writing, there were 1,676 trainees (boys = 961 and girls = 715) in 19 SAG Centres.

As an extension of the programmes designed to cater to promising athletes between 12 and 18 years of age, the Centres of Excellence are located in the regional centres of SAI. Those who have excelled in the schemes explained earlier are recruited into these Centres of Excellence and all of their expenses are covered by the SAI. At the moment, there are 15 Centres of Excellence grooming 556 athletes (288 boys and 268 girls).

Target Olympic Podium

The Target Olympic Podium was launched by the Ministry of Youth Affairs and Sports under the National Sports Development Fund for identifying and developing sports talent to compete in the 2016 and 2020 Olympic Games. Forty athletes from different disciplines such as athletics, badminton, boxing, sailing, shooting and wrestling have been identified and are being trained. As of 1 November 2015, 13 athletes in track and field competitions, both the men's and women's field hockey teams, eight shooters, and one wrestler have qualified for the 2016 Olympics in Rio.

Vision 2020

The SAI's ambitious plan labelled Vision 2020 has set the goal of winning 25–30 medals in the 2020 Olympic Games (The Times of India, 2013). The plan is expected to cost Rs. 984 crores (or approximately USD151 million). The process begins with identifying approximately 2,500 talented individuals in all disciplines identified by the International Olympic Committee and grooming that talent in national coaching camps, and exposing them to international competitions. The cost includes a stipend of Rs. 3,000 per month per individual, and the offer of an incentive of Rs. 300,000 ($ 4,615) for individuals who qualify for the 2020 Olympic Games and Rs. 150,000 ($ 2,300) for team members who qualify for the same event.

Government support for NSFs

As in many other countries, the Government of India also supports NSFs financially and facilitates the national teams participate in international competitions. The funding process begins with the SAI determining (a) the eligibility of NSFs for recognition, (b) the quantum assistance to NSFs, (c) the conditions for government support, and (d) assistance to NSFs for long-term development. The SAI also facilitates the identification, training and coaching of athletes by providing support including infrastructure, equipment and such other assistance as envisaged in the long-term development plans. An amount of Rs.185 crore (approximately 30 million dollars) is set aside for support of NSFs (http://yas.nic.in/sites/default/files/Outcome%20Budget%202014-15.pdf).

The Ministry of Youth Affairs and Sports recognizes and affirms the idea that the NSFs are fully responsible for the overall direction and management of the governance of their respective sport. They are expected to follow the principles laid down by the International Olympic Committee and the Indian Olympic Association as well as those of the international federation governing a given sport. However, following the *Golden Rule* where the one who has the gold makes the rules, the government tends to control the affairs of the NSFs to a greater extent than in other Western countries. Such control is exercised by the Ministry of Youth Affairs and Sports and the SAI.

Role of the private sector

The role of the private sector takes three different forms – private sports academies, corporate social initiatives and professional sports franchises.

Private academies

A growing trend is for former athletes taking on an entrepreneurial role and starting sports academies in various sports such as cricket (e.g., Sehwag Cricket Academy), tennis (e.g., Britannia Amritraj Academy, Bhupathy Tennis Academy), badminton (e.g., Gopichand Badminton Academy, Prakash Pudukone Academy), football (Baichung Bhutia Football School). These academies serve as platforms for former athletes to transmit their experience and knowledge of a given sport to aspiring youth who desire to excel in that sport.

These academies have produced some outstanding athletes. For example, Tintu Luka who won the gold medal in women's 800 meters in the 2015 Asian Athletics Championships is from the Usha School of Athletics. The tennis stars Leander Paes and Rohit Rajpal are from the Britannia Amritraj Academy, and currently World No. 2 badminton star Saina Nehwal hails from the Gopichand Badminton Academy. While these academies play such an important role in developing talent, many of them are not profitable enterprises and thus they cannot be sustained over a period of time. It is necessary to study the successful academies, the factors that make them successful, and then replicate those success factors in other academies.

Corporate social initiatives

Another emerging and encouraging feature of the Indian sports scene is the involvement of industrial and business enterprises in the promotion of sports as one of their corporate social responsibility initiatives. For instance, the corporate giant TATA organizes nationwide talent search, selects promising talented athletes and trains them in TATA's own sports academies such as the TATA Archery Academy, TATA Athletics Academy and TATA Football Academy (Srivatsava et al., 2012). TATA also sponsors other sports academies like the Prakash Pudukone Badminton Academy. These efforts have resulted in contributing 60 per cent of the national football team players, in winning medals in archery and badminton at the Commonwealth and Asian Games. Other corporate social initiatives promoting sports include the Mittal Champions Trust funded and managed by the Mittal industrial enterprise and which has produced medals in shooting and wrestling at the 2012 London Olympic Games; and Jindal Steel Works Foundation's squash academy and Birla's Guru Hanuman Akhara, both of which can boast of producing several international players in squash. It is unfortunate that the Mittal Champions Trust has since closed down (Indian Express, 2014).

Professional sport franchises

One indelible mark of a sport culture within a country is the existence of successful professional sport leagues. In addition to the most successful Indian Premier League in cricket with eight franchises, there are the Hockey India League with six teams, the Pro Kabaddi League with eight teams, the Indian Super League in football with eight teams, the Indian Wrestling League with eight teams, the Indian Badminton League with six teams, the Indian Golf League with eight teams, the Indian Volley League with six teams, and the proposed Indian Athletics League with eight to ten teams. It is hoped that these young leagues will expand in future years to include more teams to represent all regions of the country. While the growth of professional sport franchises will be contingent on the development of a sporting culture in the country, we can also expect these growing professional sport leagues will contribute to the inculcation of a sporting culture.

Development of youth coaches

The National Skill Development Corporation established to facilitate the development and upgrading of the skills of the growing Indian workforce studied the availability of qualified coaches and the demands for such coaches (National Skill Development Corporation, 2012). It found a great deficiency in skill levels of available coaches and a gap in the number of coaches available and the needed number of coaches. Coaches do not get the right training at the outset, and there is no continuing education opportunities for them. According to the report, the estimated demand for sports and fitness coaches for India in 2012–13 was 134,188 while the demand for support personnel in terms of track and field experts, nutritionists, psychologists and sports medicine experts was 196,131. The report also forecasts that the demand of sports coaches, nutritionists, physios, masseurs would increase to approximately 49 billion hours or 0.8 million persons by the year 2022.

Role of the government in training trainers/coaches

Both the Ministry of Youth Affairs and Sports and the SAI have instituted some schemes to train coaches. They are described below.

Rajiv Gandhi Khel Abhiyan (RGKA)

The Ministry of Youth Affairs and Sports has its Rajiv Gandhi Khel Abhiyan (RGKA) named after the assassinated Prime Minister Rajiv Gandhi. The hindi word *khel* means sports and *abhiyan* means mission or campaign. Its objectives are:

- to provide universal access to sports in rural areas and promote a sports culture among both boys and girls;
- to harness available and potential sporting talent among rural youth through a well-designed competition structure from the block level;
- to put in place an effective mechanism to identify and nurture sporting talent in rural areas;
- to make focused efforts to give adequate training and exposure under existing schemes of the Ministry of Youth Affairs & Sports (MYAS) and SAI, to promising sportspersons coming out of this process;
- to promote both indigenous and modern games; and
- to create seamless integration between the competition structure right from the panchayat (village) level through to the national level in order to facilitate exponential growth in the number of high-performing sportspersons (Press Information Bureau, 2015).

The scheme undertakes to (a) train and hire kridashrees (i.e., community coaches) who serve as sports trainers in rural communities and (b) recognize officials at the state level who would train the community leaders. So far 2,126 officials have been trained at the state level. They are expected to train 20,000 Kridashrees a year till the target figure of 200,000 is reached.

SAI's National Coaching Scheme

This scheme deploys SAI trained coaches to serve in its own operational schemes described earlier. In addition, SAI lends the services of its coaches to state governments for conducting degree/diploma courses in various sports disciplines and for coaching/training at the schools run by the central government and at various other universities. The total number of coaches sanctioned for this scheme is around 1,524 coaches (http://yas.nic.in/en/yas1/writereaddata/linkimages/9907827142.pdf).

Government sports institutes

The government subsidized sports institutes at the Netaji Subhas Bose National Institute of Sports, Lakshmibai National College of Physical Education (LNCPE) Thiruvananthapuram, along with SAI's Southern Centre in Bangalore and SAI's Eastern Centre in Kolkata, and the Lakshmibai National Institute of Physical Education in Gwalior which offer courses in coaching and allied areas for about 2,000 students in masters and doctoral level degrees. It is also proposed by the Ministry of Youth Affairs and Sports to establish the National Institute of Sports Science and Medicine in line with similar facilities in advanced countries to support the development of high performance sports.

Physical education colleges

There are several colleges of physical education in almost every state that offer degree/diploma courses in coaching and the students with these degrees are absorbed in the school system of various states. Based on the number of students enrolled in the coaching courses, we can estimate that about 5,000 coaches may be certified every year. However, this figure falls very short of the annual demand of approximately 37,000 coaches (ww.nsdcindia.org/sites/default/files/files/sports.pdf). Another issue in this regard is that women constitute less than 16 per cent of the coaching ranks.

State sports authorities

The policies and programs of the central government are more or less replicated in the 29 states of the Indian Union. For example, the state of Tamilnadu has its own *Sports Development Authority of Tamil Nadu* (SDAT) which aims to promote sports and physical fitness throughout the state with a special emphasis on talent identification and development, competition culture, sports infrastructure, and appropriate coaching methods (http://sdat.tn.gov.in/). SDAT provides monetary support to the state-level sport organizations, organizes and/or supports residential and non-residential coaching camps in various sports, has set up a talent spotting scheme, offers cash incentives to high level performers in sports, and runs its own centres of excellence and sports hostels. In addition, SDAT has established specialized academies for sprint and jumps, cricket, volleyball, diving, field hockey, table tennis, swimming, squash rackets, etc. SDAT also organizes and/or supports competitions in various sports at the district and state levels. Finally, the state body carries out the programmes assigned to it by the SAI. A unique way several states support sportspersons is to set aside a certain number of seats for admission into high demand educational programs such as engineering, agriculture, medicine, etc. This preferential admission to higher educational institutions has proved to be a great incentive for youngsters to pursue excellence in sports.

Discussion

The considerable involvement of the central government in promoting sports in general, and excellence in sport in particular is laudable. However, we can advance several reasons why this top-down approach be reversed such that efforts in this regard would emanate from the state governments and the excellence produced at the state level can move up to the national level. First, the Indian constitution states that sport comes under the purview of state governments in their respective states (Seventh Schedule). Second, the sporting talent at the youth level are in educational institutions which are completely under the jurisdiction of the state governments. To avoid the frictions between the coaching endeavours of different programmes of the SAI and the educational efforts of local schools, it is advisable to root the coaching efforts through the state-level educational ministries and/or through the state level sport authorities. Finally, when the state governments get involved in promoting and channelling excellence in sports, there is room for interstate rivalry to emerge. Such rivalries are highly conducive for a greater focus by the state governments on pursuit of excellence in sports. Even more importantly, the interstate rivalry will kindle the enthusiastic support of the citizens of a state to support morally and otherwise the state-level endeavours. Such rivalries between proximate and similar teams may contribute to higher levels of motivation, effort, and performance of team members (Kilduff, Elfenbein & Staw, 2010). Such rivalries would also have a profound effect on the coaches, managers, sponsors and fans.

It was noted earlier that some of the private sports academies that have been successful in producing champions, were not profitable enterprises. The SAI may step in to help these academies flourish by providing financial assistance. Even more importantly, the SAI may forge a public–private partnership between itself, the sector of private academies, and educational institutions to leverage the diverse expertise among government, academic, and private enterprises to address the coaching needs of the nation. The emerging sports related public-private partnerships in the Western nations may serve as models for such a move in India.

Another glaring deficiency in the Indian sporting scene is the dearth of women in the coaching ranks. It is noted that only 16 per cent of the coaches are women (www.nsdcindia.org/sites/default/files/files/sports.pdf). Given that women's sports are achieving parity with men's sports in terms of number of competitions and the number of medals awarded to men and women, India should encourage and support women's sports which would, in turn, necessitate the training and hiring of more women coaches.

Several of the acquaintances of the authors have noted that the physical stature of Indians does not augur well for their performances in international sport. It is true that Indians are among the shortest populations in the world. The average height of Indian men is said to be 5 feet 5 inches or 165 cm, and that of Indian women to be 5 feet or 152cm (Krishnan, n.d.). However, there are three conditions that counter this argument. First, in the normal curve of the distribution of heights, 2 per cent of the Indian population would fall at the high end of the height distribution. That would mean 25 million Indians (2 per cent of 1.25 billion) could be really tall. Compare this to the less than the three million population of Lithuania which is a powerhouse in basketball. The point is that India can find tall and talented athletes for sports where height matters. In fact, the Dallas Mavericks of the National Basketball Association has drafted this year the Indian-born Satnam Singh Bhamara to play for the team (Kotloff, n.d.). He is 7 foot 2 inches tall and 19 years old. His entry into the NBA should encourage other tall Indians to pursue excellence in basketball. The other condition is that in some sports (e.g., gymnastics) height is not a contributing factor for success. Finally, some sports do have classifications (e.g., weightlifting, boxing) based on weight which means that a small stature may indeed be a contributing factor for success in lower weight classes.

In conclusion, the future of Indian sports and its performance in international competitions look very bright. The role of governments at the federal and state levels in promoting sport and sport performance as told in this chapter will have an impact on talent identification and development. Further, with the growth of the middle class and the increasing disposable income, sport consumption is projected to grow from USD 1 billion in 2005 to USD 6 billion in 2025 (Mukherjee et al., 2010). With such a huge jump in disposable income, Indians are likely to expect excellence in sport and, more importantly, be willing to pay for it. In sum, one can expect the foregoing factors impel sport and physical activity to flourish at both participatory and elite levels, and the emergence of world-class athletes.

References

American Appraisal (2014). Clearing the fence with brand value. Retrieved from www.american-appraisal.co.in/AA-Files/Images_IN/AAIIPL.pdf

CIA (2015). CIA World Factbook. Retrieved from www.cia.gov/library/publications/the-world-factbook/geos/in.html

Indian Express (March 12, 2014). Laxmi Mittal trust which funded India's star athletes shuts down. Retrieved from http://indianexpress.com/article/india/india-others/mittal-trust-which-funded-indias-star-athletes-shuts-down/

Kilduff, G.J., Elfenbein, H.A. & Staw, B.M. (2010). The psychology of rivalry: A relationally dependent analysis of competition. *Academy of Management Journal*, 53(5), 943–969.

Knoema (2015). World GDP ranking 2015. Retrieved http://knoema.com/nwnfkne/world-gdp-ranking-2015-data-and-charts

Kotloff, B. (n.d.). The biggest leap yet: Satnam Singh becomes the first Indian player drafted into the NBA.www.nba.com/india/news/the_biggest_leap_yet_for_india_2015_06_26.html

Krishnan, M. (n.d.). What is the average height of Indiana man and woman? (www.quora.com/What-is-the-average-height-of-Indian-man-and-woman

Luthra, C.S. (2014). Indian gymnasts' CWG participation in doubt over selection issues. dna, 10 July 2014. Retrieved from www.dnaindia.com/sport/report-indian-gymnasts-cwg-participation-in-doubt-over-selection-issues-2000982

Ministry of Youth Affairs and Sports (2014). National Youth Policy-2014. Retrieved from http://yas.nic.in/sites/default/files/National-Youth-Policy-Document%20.pdf

Mukherjee, A., Goswami, R., Goyal, T.M. & Satija, D. (2010). Sports retailing in India: Opportunities, constraints and way forward. Working Paper

Mustafi, S.M. (2013). India's middle class: Growth engine or loose wheel? *The New York Times*. 13 May 2013. Retrieved from http://india.blogs.nytimes.com/2013/05/13/indias-middle-class-growth-engine-or-loose-wheel/?_r=0 http://data.worldbank.org/country/india

National Skill Development Corporation (2012). Skill gap study for sports. Retrieved from www.nsdcindia.org/sites/default/files/files/sports.pdf

New World Encyclopaedia (2015). Languages of India. Retrieved from www.newworldencyclopedia.org/entry/Languages_of_India.

National Youth Policy-2014. Ministry of Youth Affairs & Sports, Government of India. New Delhi.

Press Information Bureau. (2015). Objectives of PYKKA Scheme. Retrieved from http://pib.nic.in/newsite/PrintRelease.aspx?relid=123456

Sports 247. (2016). Malaysian shuttlers opens badminton academy in India and China. Retrieved from http://data.worldbank.org/indicator/SP.POP.TOTL

Srivastava, K.S., Negi, G., Mishra, V., & Pandey, S. (2012). Corporate social responsibility: A case study of TATA group. *IOSR Journal of Business and Management*, 3(5), 17–27.

The Times of India (2011, Oct 9). Maken launches 'cone and play' scheme across India. Retrieved from http://timesofindia.indiatimes.com/sports/more-sports/others/Maken-launches-come-and-play-scheme-across-India/articleshow/10290790.cms

The Times of India (2013). SAI expedites efforts to make 'Vision 2020' a reality. (19 May 2013). Retrieved from http://timesofindia.indiatimes.com/sports/more-sports/others/SAI-expedites-efforts-to-make-Vision-2020-a-reality/articleshow/20134525.cms

World Bank (n.d.). Population, total. Retrieved from http://data.worldbank.org/indicator/SP.POP.TOTL

Chapter 14

South Korea

Eunah Hong

The national elite youth sports system in South Korea

The policies in elite youth sport were developed and implemented by the authoritarian governments of the 1960s and for many subsequent decades in South Korea (hereafter Korea), the focus was firmly on winning medals in sports mega-events such as the Olympics and Asian Games. It was taken for granted that athletes should conform to excessive training as instructed by their coaches, concentrate on training regimes and participate in competitions and be absent from school in order for them to achieve a meaningful outcome.

The issue of athletes' welfare did not emerge on the public agenda until the twenty-first century, when a series of incidents occurred in Korean elite youth sport. First, in 2000, the Korean Swimming Association (KSA) stripped a young swimmer, Jang Hee Jin, of her national athlete status because she had asked the KSA if she could not stay in a Tae Neung Village (a training camp for national athletes in Seoul) but commute from home so that she could attend classes at her school. The request was treated with silent contempt by the KSA and the management of the Tae Neung Village. Jang made a decision to travel to the US where she could pursue her swimming as well as her academic career. Second, in 2003, a blaze tragedy at the bunker house of Chun-An primary school boys' football team led to the abolition of training camps in primary and middle schools across the nation. Third, in 2005, a group of short track national athletes were unwilling to put up with the inhumane treatment and violence of their coaches and left the training camp.

These incidents not only captured the attention of the public but also triggered the launch of the Civil Network for Justice in Sport (CNETJS), the first non-governmental organization in the field of sport. The CNETJS worked to promote a healthier athletic lifestyle and culture, to put a stop to athletic abuse, and to counsel and sanction appropriately (Civil Network for Justice of Sports, 2015, www.sportscm.org/about_us.htm). Consistent pressure from NGOs, media and academia on the government to implement policies that could change the lives of student athletes bore fruit with, for example, the introduction of the 'Guarantee Policy of Study Rights' and the inauguration of the 'Weekend Football League for Primary, Middle and High school', of which more details will be provided later on.

It is hard to pinpoint a sole organization in charge of elite youth sport in Korea. The Ministry of Culture, Sport, and Tourism (MCST), the Ministry of Education (MOE), the Korea Sports Council (KSC), the Korea Foundation for the Next Generation Sports Talent (NEST) and the Korea Sports Promotion Foundation (KSPO) are all involved in the Korean elite youth sports policy.

Discussing the organizations in order, the MCST sports section, as of August 2015, is divided into six teams: Sports Policy; Sports Promotion; Sports Industry; International Sports; Disability Sports; and Pyeong Chang Olympic Support. The Sports Policy Team work on a number of tasks related to youth elite sport including supporting athletes and teams in sport schools, developing student athletes and supporting national youth sport competitions (Ministry of Culture, Sport and Tourism, 2015).

The MOE is another important organization in Korean youth sport. The '2015 School Sport Main Tasks Plan' published by the MOE includes several policies which concern the rights of student-athletes and their education. The Plan included policies: to eradicate camp training and limit the number of participants in national competitions; establish an obligation to enable regular attendance at classes; to seek measures to improve academic achievement of young athletes; to reinforce the protection of human rights of young athletes; to train coaches to work with school teams; and to establish systems to improve the transparency of the training of school sports teams (Ministry of Education, 2015).

The KSC, established in 1920, has continued to support school sports teams financially with the MCST, aiming to fund 75 teams with ₩2 million per team in 2013. The objectives of the KSC are the promotion of the sports movement, the promotion of school sports and sport for all, and the enhancement of national prestige through developing talented athletes, which indicates the KSC's strong commitment to school sport (MCST, 2013).

Transformed from a non-profit organization in 2007 to a public organization in 2010, NEST is important to mention when it comes to youth sports policies. NEST has four key areas to oversee: identifying and nurturing sports talents; career development of next generation sports talents; strengthening job competencies; and the promotion of advanced educational culture. Of particular importance in relation to youth sport is NEST's role in the identification and nurturing of sports talents. NEST started with a budget of ₩500 million, which had increased to ₩11.9 billion by 2013 through various projects (MCST, 2013). More information about NEST is provided below.

The KSPO was created on April 20, 1989, as a public foundation, to commemorate the 1988 Seoul Olympics. The KSPO's main tasks are to support businesses with respect to sports promotion, sports related scientific research, and wholesome youth development, in order to maximize the efficient management of the National Sports Promotion funds (NSPF) (KSPO, 2015). The NSPF was inaugurated with ₩352 billion, a combination of a surplus of ₩311 billion from the 1988 Olympic Games and ₩41 billion from the National Sports Promotion Foundation. To support the wide range of projects and programmes with which it is involved the KSPO(2015) sought to acquire funds from various channels including: tax on the entrance fee for golf club membership; and revenue from the sports lotto (lottery), cycle racing and motorboat racing.

Talent identification and development of coaches in Korean youth elite sport

Considering the development of elite sport, the role of Sports Middle/High Schools (SMHS) cannot be neglected. The Ministry of Sport took the initiative to build specialist sport middle and high schools in 1971 (Hong, 2010; Lee, 2003). The first sports school established in Seoul in 1971 was successful and this prompted other cities to create six middle schools and fifteen high schools (Hong, 2010; Lee, 2003). Moreover, in 1972, the School Talent Scheme, the system to award special rights to enter schools for student athletes who display extraordinary ability in order to identify and develop young people with talent, was launched (Ministry of Education, Science, and Technology, 2009). It is noteworthy that the SMHS has run sports like athletics and gymnastics, individual sports with a few school teams and weightlifting and wrestling which were not perceived as popular sports by the public (Hong, 2010; Kim, 2004).

The current structure for talent identification and training for Korean elite sport is as shown in Figure 14.1. 'Superior athletes' are defined as those who set the record or receive prizes in national competitions or are dispatched to international competitions (except friendly ones) and those who are approved by the Minister of Culture, Sport and Tourism (Lee, 2010). The strategy to support the national team was established in 1965 and a more systematic strategy was developed in 1993 when demand to win medals in the Olympics began to increase (Lee, 1992). While the KSC is in charge of all four projects from *Kumnamoo to* National Athletes, NEST is responsible for the 'Sports Talent' programme.

'Sports Talent': NEST

NEST started a 'Sports Talent' project in July, 2009. Lee and Park (2014) identified four major sources which underpinned the initiation of the 'Sports

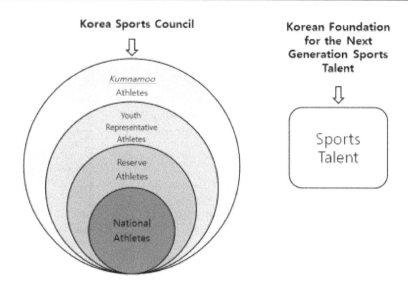

Korea Sports Council

⇩

Kumnamoo
Athletes

Youth
Representative
Athletes

Reserve
Athletes

National
Athletes

**Korean Foundation
for the Next
Generation Sports
Talent**

⇩

Sports
Talent

Figure 14.1 Development system for superior athletes and its links

Source: Adapted from Lee (2010: 15). A study of the development strategy of connections for a superior athletes' nurturing system

Talent' scheme, based on the works of Shin (2009), Yang (2011), and Choi (2011). First, the project reflected the individuals' demand of those who wanted to achieve their potential in various areas, including sport. Second, it has always been the government's aim to elevate Korean sports' global competitiveness. Third, it was a countermeasure to the phenomenon of a reduced number of young athletes because of low birth rate and the reluctance of parents to devote their time or their children's lives to sport from an early age. Fourth, the necessity for scientific and efficient identification of sports talents was seen in a new light. Sixteen centers were designated across Korea and young talents in athletics, swimming and gymnastics could receive quality coaching and mentoring at these venues. Six hundred and ninety students from the second to sixth grade at primary school, who showed potential to become elite athletes, were chosen. As Lee (2010) clarified, 'Sport Talents' imposes a limit in terms of eligibility, in other words, students who do not have any experience as an elite athlete, that is, those who have never registered in National Governing Bodies (NGB) can apply and be selected. This feature distinguishes 'Sports Talent' from '*Kumnamu* Athletes' which is composed of registered elite athletes.

The selection process consists of application, the KOSTASS assessment, expert observation and interviews. KOSTASS is an identification system invented by the Korea Institute of Sports Science in 2007. KOSTASS is comprised of 16 tests: The details of KOSTASS are illustrated in Table 14.1.

Table 14.1 KOSTASS fitness measurement

Component	Measurement factor	Test	Unit
Growth and Maturity	Length	Height, sitting height	cm
	Weight	Body weight	kg
	Circumference	Girth of chest	cm
	Body composition	Fat percentage	%
	Level of maturity	Bone age examination	~years old
Fitness	Upper limb endurance	Push-up, chin up(boys)	Number of times/ minute
		Hanging on the chin-up bar(girls)	second
	Upper limb power	Basketball throw	cm
	Core endurance	Sit ups	Number of times/ minute
	Lower limb muscular endurance	Half squat jumps	Number of times/ minute
	Lower limb power	Standing long jumps	cm
	Cardiovascular endurance	Shutter runs	Number of times
Sport ability	Speed	50m sprint	Second
	Agility	Side steps	Number of times/ 20 seconds
	Flexibility	Bend upper body from sitting position	cm

Source: Ewha Education Center for Gifted Young Athletes, 2015

The Ewha Women's University is one of the 16 centers designated by NEST. According to Korean Foundation for the Next Generation Sports Talent (2015), selected youngsters will participate in the programme once or twice a week, not exceeding 200 hours in a year. Students in the lower grades will learn basic skills, and experience diverse programmes that arouse their interest in sports. Students in the higher grades will focus on improving individual performance and participating in competitions. It is noteworthy that students can experience various education programmes and activities including character building, career paths in sport, first aid, role play, sports nutrition, sports psychology, the principles of exercise, production of sports books, team building emphasizing creativity (Ewha Education Center for Gifted Young Athletes, 2015).

Between 2010 and 2014, a total of 3,345 students graduated from the programme and the details are shown in Table 14.2. It is expected that some of these students will become elite athletes in a few years' time and will contribute to the development of elite sport in Korea. More information on 'Sports Talent' students on proceeding to a school of a higher grade is shown in Table 14.3.

Table 14.2 Development system for superior athletes in Korea (2010–2014)

Year	2010	2011	2012	2013	2014
Number of students	608	707	751	752	752
Number of centers	11	13	16	17	17

Source: www.nest.or.kr/nest/subHomePage/scienceHome/leftMenu/aboutSH/bu_1.do

Table 14.3 Number of students who entered sport middle schools (SM) or ordinary schools through sports talents schemes (OS)

Year	Number of students	Percentage
2010	8 out of 65 (8 SM)	12.3%
2011	11 out of 81 (8 SM, 3 OS)	13.6%
2012	30 out of 132 (14 SM, 16 OS)	23%
2013	24 out of 131 (14 SM, 10 OS)	18%
2014	43 out of 237 (26 SM, 17 OS)	18%

Source: www.nest.or.kr/nest/subHomePage/scienceHome/leftMenu/aboutSH/bu_1.do

'Kumnamoo *Athletes*'

'*Kumnamoo* Athletes' identification projects began in 1993 for the purpose of supporting reserve athletes (Lee, 1992). The literal translation of '*Kumnamoo*' is a 'dream tree', a metaphor for young children who show special talents in a specific field, for example, sport. First, students from primary schools are targets of '*Kumnamoo* Athletes'. In 2002, the programme recruited students for three sports only (athletics, swimming, and gymnastics) which were considered to be the foundation of any sport. Skating and ski disciplines were added in 2003 for the Winter Olympics. In 2013, 693 young people were chosen as '*Kumnamoo* Athletes' from 18 sports (MCST, 2013).

There are four stages in the process of selecting '*Kumnamoo* Athletes', as shown in the extract below from the MCST' Sports White Paper (2013, 253–265): Recommendation – Temporary Selection – Measurement and Evaluation – Final Selection. First, coaches in school sports teams and sport governing bodies recommend talented children to regional sports associations. Through the assessment at the association level, a pool of athletes is proposed to the NGB of each sport. Second, NGBs select three times the number of athletes to be actually recruited. The Korea Institute of Sports Science (KISS) measures athletes' physical traits, fitness and sports performance ability, and conducts psychological examinations and calculates all the points given to each athlete depending on their age, sport and so on. The NGB's Committee for '*Kumnamoo* Athletes' makes a final decision after reviewing all the results provided by KISS.

'*Kumnamoo* Athletes' are privileged to participate in a training camp for 30 days in the summer and winter vacation periods. The government covers all the fees incurred at the camp, makes nine monthly payments of ₩500,000 to one coach per sport, and pays for the accident insurance. '*Kumnamoo* athletes' coaches travel across Korea to where '*Kumnamoo* athletes' are based and reviews individual athletes' training progress and discusses their difficulties if there are any. It is also the job of coaches to analyse the athletes' sports performance and physical shape and keep all the necessary records which are published regularly.

'Youth Representative Athletes'

'Youth Representative Athletes (YRA)' was initiated as a way to revitalize non-popular sports such as athletics, swimming and gymnastics and developed as a link between '*Kumnamoo* athletes' and 'Reserve Athletes'. YRA are drawn from 26 sports excluding professional sports and selected to include those that need substantial support in terms of training and competition. These sports must have records of medals in the international competitions or show a high level of potential to acquire medals in the future. Generally speaking, athletes between 14 and 19 years old can be considered and prize-winning records, individual records and potential are all examined by experts. YRA train for 20 days during vacations at either a summer or a winter training camp as a one-off occasion. In 2013, 854 YRA and 149 coaches participated in this scheme. Over two weeks, 300 people from 20 sports trained abroad including in European countries. It is also notable that 26 coaches in 26 sports and 10 physiotherapists were appointed full time. A total of ₩2.858 million was invested into YRA in 2013 according to the Sports White Paper by MCTS (2013).

'Reserve Athletes'

'Reserve Athletes' (RAs) are split into 24 summer sports and 4 winter sports. 1,300 RAs and 153 coaches were selected in 2013. First, schools' RAs receive substantial funding for sports equipment and entry fees for competitions. Second, intensive technical training is provided in vacations and evaluation is undertaken for individual performances. Third, some of the superior RAs will be given the opportunity to go abroad and train as preparation for the Olympics and Asian Games. Full-time coaches will be in charge of technical training. According to the MCTS (2013), ₩7,320 million was given in total for the RA project. Of particular note is that ₩1,921 was spent on 34 coaches in 26 sports to cover salaries, insurance and severance pay. The budget for the RA project comes from the KSPO (Korea Sport Promotion Foundation). Among a number of projects, the KSPO (2015) concentrated on the development of athletes and coaches and supporting school sports teams which are directly connected to elite youth sport. As of September 2015, the KSPO has provided ₩13.1 billion for the RA project (training costs for RAs and salaries for full-time coaches).

Lee (2010) pointed out that the system for providing athletes below national athlete level began to take shape from 1965 but not much progress was seen due to the lack of budget and a specific plan. With the 1988 Seoul Olympics as a source of momentum, an initiative to identify and develop reserve players was promoted and this contributed to gaining fourth position in the Olympic Games. According to Oh (2013), talent identification and training of those athletes was under the leadership of the KSC, however, it has become a role of the NGBs from 1983, in other words, the NGBs have taken responsibility for selecting talented athletes (Oh, 2013).

Commercial team sport: football

Despite the historic success of men's football in the 2002 FIFA Korea/Japan World Cup at which Korea reached the semi-final, there seemed to be some urgency that the KFA should seriously consider setting up a youth system to produce a more reliable flow of quality footballers. The immediate task of the KFA was to send several players overseas to locations such as France, Brazil, England and Germany with full funding. This project continued for a few years before it was stopped in 2009. It has been reported that there were several reasons for the project being discontinued. For instance, there was considered to be a risk that the project might be undermining the motivation of the young players to return home to play for the top professional K-league clubs in in Korea because of their experience of playing in foreign leagues.

In relation to the youth development system, the KFA did not employ full-time staff for different age groups until 1999. Coaches combined daily coaching jobs with coaching the teams for the KFA, and they were called up whenever tournaments were scheduled. This system called into question the transparency of players' selection and put pressure onto the coaches. In 2000, for the first time in the KFA, full-time coaches were employed and they were able to begin to concentrate fully on the team management of the age group they were assigned to. In 2013, under the leadership of the new president Chung Mong Gyu, the Korea FA (KFA) dispatched groups of experts to Germany and France to observe and learn from successful examples.

Based on their report reflecting the best practices and ideas gathered in European contexts and modified to Korean methods, the KFA (2015) announced an inspiring plan called the 'KFA Golden Age' (KGA). With the vision of 'creativity based on the basics and challenge', the targets of this programme were boys and girls between 11 and 16 years old, which is the period that the KFA considered was when children can learn football techniques at the fastest speed. The KFA employees 15 full-time youth coaches and 90 quality coaches across the country, recommended by regional FAs which are in charge of the KGA. When it comes to the selection process of players, on-the-spot observation of KFA coaches, as well as recommendations from team coaches, needs to be conducted in order to maximize the transparency and diversity of chosen players. The KGA provides opportunities for a wide range of young people, 1,750 in 21 regional centers, 600 in five metropolitan city centers and 325 in the KFA Talents center. This is a significant increase compared to the previous system in which only 280 players were given the chance to experience the coaching programme organized by the KFA. The function of each center is described in Table 14.4.

The KFA runs its own coaching education programmes and grants qualifications. According to the Regulation of Coaching Education (Korea Football Association, 2014), ten categories are defined, the details of which are shown in Table 14.5. It should be noted that AFC stands for Asian Football Confederation and the club team is composed of non-elite students. Generally speaking, school team means youth elite sports teams.

In order to qualify as an AFC D coach, the applicant should be 19 or older and complete 40 hours of education over five days. Two theory tests, including the rules of the game, and one practical test are conducted. As

Table 14.4 Function of each center

	Regional center (21)		Metropolitan city center (5)		KFA Talents center	
Supervision	City, Province FA		KFA+16 City, Province FA		KFA	
Frequency	Twice a month (each age group, 12 times/year)		Twice a year (each age group)		Twice a year (each age group)	
Number of participants	U14~15 U13 U12	25 each (boys: 20 Girls: 5)	U15 U14 U13 U12	30 each	U16 U15 U14 U13 U12	40, 5 days 60, 4 days 125 (boys: 100, girls: 25) 3 days
Responsibility	KFA full-time coaches and regional coaches		KFA full-time coaches and regional coaches		KFA full-time coaches	
Duration	9 months (March–November)					

Source: www.kfa.or.kr/kfa/program_goldenage.asp

Table 14.5 Categorization and number of football coaches (as of January 2015)

	Category	Teams allowed to coach	No. coaches
1	AFC D	U8 youth team, youth team in the club(non-elite) teams or school sport club teams(non-elite)	951
2	AFC C	Primary school team and U12 club teams	2,941
3	AFC B	Middle, high school team and U18 club team	1,224
4	AFC A	Every team in Korea, national team in any age group	811
5	AFC P	Every team in Korea, national team in any age group	70
6	AFC GK Level I	Primary school team(U12) and U12 club team	67
7	AFC GK Level II	Middle, high school team and U18 club team	193
8	AFC GK Level III	Every team in Korea, national team in any age group	66

Source: KFA(2014). Regulation of Coaching Education, p.2 and extracted from www.kfa.or.kr/info/judment.asp

AFC D is the lowest football coach level, it seems that the KFA encourages people with an interest to take up the course without imposing strict conditions. To be certified as an AFC C coach, either you have to have acquired an AFC D qualification more than six months previously, played football in a KFA-registered team for seven years or played professionally for five years including at high school and hold all the relevant documentation. The duration of the course is 85 hours over two weeks and three theory examinations and three practical tests are compulsory. The last level as a youth football coach, AFC B, is more intensive than the other courses. The number of theory and practical tests is the same as AFC C; however, one dissertation (research presentation) is also required. The course runs over three weeks for a total of 107 hours and the top 20 per cent of the participants can be proposed to join an AFC A course by an instructor. Teams that the coaches are able to instruct are illustrated in Table 14.5. In addition, it is necessary for qualified coaches to participate in the refresher courses held every four years, except for the highest AFC P which is every two years.

Commercial individual sport: women's golf

With regard to golf in Korea, the player whose name must be mentioned is Seri Pak, who inspired the whole nation by winning the 1998 US Open. Her famous bare-footed shot from the hazard of deep water moved Koreans who were having a difficult time in the midst of IMF crisis. The majority of female golfers we see these days are 'Seri Kids' who were inspired and motivated by Pak's performances and took up the game. As a result, Amy Yang's victory at the 2015 Honda LPGA (Ladies Professional Golf

Association) in Thailand marked eight consecutive wins for players with Korean heritage. It also meant that 12 out of the last 14 LPGA competitions were won by one of nine Korean residents, Lydia Ko (Korean-New Zealander) and Christina Kim (Korean-American) (LPGA, 2015). Statistics from the Korea Junior Golf Association (KJGA) provide further evidence of the growth in the number of young female golfers. The number of girls playing golf in middle and high schools has increased dramatically from 136 in 2000 to 311 in 2015 and from 162 in 2000 to 382 in 2015 respectively. This is a significant contrast to the number of boys playing golf in middle and high schools. The number of middle school boys remained the same, at 335, in 2015 as it was in 2000. As for high school boys, the number dropped from 678 in 2000 to 608 in 2015 (KJGA, 2015).

There has always been a high level of curiosity as to why Korean ladies are so good at LPGA. *The Economist* (2012) pointed out a few reasons: the cultural reason in terms of competitiveness and pursuit of perfection by constant repetition, the environment, the passion of Korean fathers to push their daughters harder than anywhere else in the world, and a lack of space which leads players to play balls at driving ranges instead of on a proper course. This all sounds reasonable; however, it is not sufficient to explain the different level of success between men and women's golf, though, and more studies are needed to find out the reasons behind the success of Korean women's golf.

As Lim (2014) said, it is worth pointing out that the stand-by national player system contributed to the improvement of Korean golfers' performance. The Korea Golf Association (KGA) requires thorough and detailed regulations. According to the KGA's regulations published in 2015, there are two kinds of stand-by national player's categories. One is stand-by national players excluding primary school students, the other is junior stand-by national players determined from fifth- to sixth-grade primary school students. The total of 27 female players (the same number as men) consists of 8 national athletes, 16 stand-by national players and 3 junior stand-by national players. Different marks are allocated depending on the level of national and international competitions and the criteria to select stand-by national players is also illustrated well.

In accordance with training coaches of elite youth sport, NEST focuses on strengthening the competencies of coaches. Specifically, the task targets coaches in (elementary, middle and high schools and university) school sports teams across levels and sports. The curriculum constitutes understanding how school sports teams function including management skills, training for coaches' qualities and ethics, coaches' professional training such as sports science, training design and evaluation processes. A total of 4,092 coaches have participated in the programme between 2011 and 2014. The programme aims to provide knowledge and skills based on sports science so that coaches can be equipped with up-to-date information and teaching methods (Korean Foundation for the Next Generation Sports Talent, 2015).

Prominent Olympic Sport: archery

Archery is one of the prominent Olympic sports in Korea and 33 medals have been won since the 1984 Los Angeles Games (19 gold, 9 silver, and 5 bronze). This opened the door for Korean coaches to travel to other parts of the world to share their knowledge and experience, and as a result, 15 Korean coaches accompanied athletes from 12 countries at the 2012 London Olympic Games (Oh, 2013).

The well-known phrase to express a high level of Korean archery is 'To pass National Athletes' and the selection process is more difficult than winning a medal in the Olympics'. Of particular note is the systematic and transparent procedure of finalizing the list of national archers which prevents any controversy. With regards to archery, in September 2013, the Korea Archery Federation (KAF) selected Under 15 youth national players as a part of the Korean Archery Grassroots Expansion and Mid/Long term Development Plan. Four groups were categorized by ability and named with some revision based on the four stages suggested by the KSC.

First, was the National Youth Representative (NYP) group: 10 boys and 10 girls who achieved a certain result in national competitions were chosen. Their training was based on the teams to which each student belongs. During vacation periods, all players were invited to a training camp and given the opportunity to be coached by elite coaches.

The second group, the Young Adult Representatives (YAR), were those the KAF selected from among the Under 16 talents who were selected based on a careful application of the KSC's guidelines and were supported to develop as National Reserve Athletes in the near future.

The third group was the National Reserve Athletes (NRA). The KAF hosts 'National Athletes Trials' and ranks athletes with those ranked one to eight designated as 'National Athletes'. Except for those eight top players, one company team, one university team and two high school teams are named as national reserve athletes and they are eligible to join training specifically for the NRA with the permission of the team they play for.

National Athletes is the final group. The KAF hosts seven 'National Athletes Trials' annually and chooses the top eight as national athletes as mentioned above. They are composed of two teams, ranked 1–4 (Team A) and ranked 5–8 (Team B). Team A stays in a camp for training all year around and participates in various international competitions and the Olympic Games. Team B trains in their own team and joins Team A during the winter training camp only (Korean Archery Grassroots, 2013; Oh, 2013). The effectiveness of this system was illustrated in the recent Youth World Archery Championships. In 2013, the 'Recurve' women junior's gold, silver and bronze medals were all won by Koreans and the 'Recurve' Women Cadet's gold and bronze medals were also won by Korean girls. Two years later, a number of Korean youths won medals: a bronze medal for individual men, gold and silver for individual women, gold for the men's and women's group and gold for the mixed.

The competition structure and issues associated with the growth of elite youth sport

When discussing Korean elite youth sport, two national competitions with a long tradition cannot be missed. One is the National Sports Festival (NSF) which began in 1920 as the National Chosun Baseball Competition. The NSF has become established as the gateway to becoming a star athlete and has played a leading role in discovering gifted talents and advancing sports performances (Park, 2012). The competition is held in different cities and towns every year for the purpose of balanced development across Korea in terms of sport. In the 96th Festival in Kang-Won Province from October 16 to 22, 2015, 22,000 athletes from high schools, universities and general adult teams, plus 8,000 officials participated in 47 sports. The MCTS and KSPO provided assistance. In addition to a number of awards, a decoration by the President or Minister of the MCTS is given to the athletes who set a Korean record or achieve an improved outcome. For non-recording sports, athletes who displayed extraordinary performances in the Festival can be considered.

The other competition is the National Junior Sports Festival (NJSF), which was separated from the NSF in 1972. As the MCST (2013) stated, some significant changes can be found in the history of the NJSF. Overall the scoring system was abolished (1980–1981) and reintroduced (1982) and the Festival was stopped in 1989 as a number of concerns and complaints were raised such as over-competition among cities/provinces, athletes' excessive training, and school absenteeism. The period of the NJSF was moved to August in 2010 to guarantee student-athletes' academic rights, however, the Festival was moved back to its previous May dates, due to concerns for athletes' safety in the hot and humid summer. The KSC hosted the NJSF in 2015 on Jeju Island from 30 May to 2 June in conjunction with the MCTS, MOE and KSPO. A total of 12,312 athletes of ages ranging from 10 to 15 years old and 4,911 officials participated in the Festival. The names of the coaches (including teachers) who showed excellence have been proposed for decoration by the Ministry of MCTS or Ministry of Education. In 2015, the KSPO (2015) provided funding totalling ₩8.6 billion for the NSF and ₩9.8 billion for the NJSF.

Now we will focus on the culture of Korean youth elite sport. As the words 'driving excellence in sport' demonstrate, Korean student-athletes have often not had the opportunity to pursue their academic work. The desire to change the elite sports system was expressed but was not taken seriously as it was argued that the student athletes needed to concentrate on their training to gain outstanding results at all costs. One of the urgent issues for the elite sports system to be changed was the competition structure. Most of the NGBs planned a number of competitions across a year regardless of when it was term time. It was taken for granted that student athletes were not able to attend any classes at all or participate in morning classes only if permitted because of competitions held during the semester. A study by Kwak, Kim and Joo (2011) shows that only 1.6 per cent of student athletes attend classes and that no system to compensate for those absences has been put in place. It was not a surprise at all to see those who were forced to be absent for a certain period of time were left behind by general students. An agreement was reached that the government must act sooner rather than later in order to foster an environment in which elite athletes can be assured of their academic rights which will equip them with the same basic knowledge, skills and socializing abilities as ordinary citizens.

Long and enduring discussions on this issue were reignited at the announcement of the 'Normalization Policy of School Sport Teams' by the Ministry of Culture, Sport and Tourism and the Ministry of Education and Human Resources. Having seen the legislation of 'School Sport Promotion Law' in 2013, Yu (2005) pointed out that blame should not be directed onto students but is the result of compromise among schools, coaches, and parents who are willing to agree to the current system as long as the students acquire certain results. 'Minimum Academic Ability Standard' began to be applied to student athletes in 2011 for primary fourth to sixth grade and gradually expanded up to the final year in high school. In principle, the grades for the five subjects (Korean, English, Math, Social Studies and Science) and the three subjects (Korean, English, and Social Studies) for primary/middle schools and high schools are reference points respectively. Compared to the average marks of the relevant year students, the percentage of primary, middle and high school marks required are 50 per cent, 40 per cent, and 30 per cent respectively. If student-athletes fail to meet the requirements, they must attend a special programme prepared by a school or education office in the cities or provinces (Ministry of Education, 2015).

In 2009, the Korea Football Association (KFA) emerged as the leader in changing the competition structure in cooperation with the Ministry of Education, Science & Technology, the Ministry of Culture, Sport and Tourism, Chosun Ilbo (one of the main three newspapers) and a special sponsor Daekyo, an educational company launching a completely new format of 'elementary, middle, and high school leagues'. The core difference was that all the games had to be held on weekends, public holidays and after school during the week instead of holding national tournaments during the semester. With the slogan of 'Play, Study, Enjoy!' student-athletes registered in the KFA and trained and competed after school so that they could acquire knowledge and virtues as well as physical fitness. As of September 2015, 774 teams in 86 regions have completed in 5,776 matches. This means that each team will have at least 18 matches in a season and more if they progress to the grand final which provides more chances for players to participate in a game (KFA, 2015). In the past, it was not difficult to observe that the losing team left the competition immediately due to the nature of the 'tournament' (knock-out) and it was deemed unhelpful for the development of athletes in a macro perspective.

In the 'Sport Vision 2018' published by the MCTS in 2013, the government's commitment to identifying and developing young future athletes was revealed. The number of 'sport talents', 'Kumnamoo Athletes' and 'Youth Representative Athletes' is projected to grow from 2,550 to 4,200. Also, strengthening athletes' and coaches' welfare policies and the improvement of human rights is one of the main elements of the 'Sport Vision 2018'. In 2014, the MCST announced a '4 Sport Evils Hot Line' following a comprehensive audit of sport governing bodies. The 4 Sport Evils refers to biased refereeing; (sexual) violence; corrupt admission (for example, an ex-athlete's parents hand over a bribe to a coach, or a coach at a high school offers a bribe to a university coach for entrance to the university); and the privatization of organizations. (The phenomenon that a sport governing body is run by an intimate group of people resulting in a number of problems including poor financial management and a lack of a monitoring system regarding the whole operation of the organization.) The 'Committee for Eradicating 4 Sport Evils' was formed under the leadership of the 2nd Minister of the MCTS and constituted athletes, coaches and referees who are currently in the field of sports, experts in the '4 Sport Evils', and police and civil group representatives. Of particular note, it was pointed out that there was a lack of clarity regarding the punishment of perpetrators of (sexual) violence incidents in sports. The MCTS (2015) planned to order a whole revision of 'Regulations of Athletes Committee in KSC' as well as the compulsory duty of inviting external professionals in forming an Athletes Committee.

The established youth development system for singling out gifted archers is expected to attract young people as long as Korean archery keeps generating results in sport mega-events like the Olympic Games. The fact that the number of Korean coaches, who are contributing to the development of archery abroad, is growing with the consequence that the gap between strong nations in archery is tending to get narrower has made the KAF discontented with the past achievements. Rigorous and persistent efforts should be executed in order to sustain the transparency of the selection process at any level so that young athletes with great potential stay in sport and strive for excellence. In football, the success of Korean players in Europe's top leagues such as a former Manchester United player Park Ji Sung and Son Heung Min, who transferred from Leverkuzen to Tottenham Hotspur in 2015 inspires the young generation to a great extent. Having launched the 'KFA Golden Age' programme, KFA expects to witness more Koreans in the European leagues. Unlike archery, the way to assess someone's ability as a footballer is not straightforward. To identify the special talents of individual athletes requires a high level of expertise, coaching experience, understanding of sports science and so forth. Reflecting on the feedback from diverse stakeholders and panels of experts in relation to the 'KFA Golden Age' project, the KFA is committed to improving the situation every year. 'Super-heated' parents, who strongly believe their children will become the next Park Ji Sung or Son Heung Min, need advice from parents who have already gone through this process. Golf seems to have a similar feature to football as the number of athletes to leave Korea grows. It is good news to see the increase in girls who are eager to become professional golfers and are motivated by the performances of Korean golfers obtaining the LPGA trophies in recent years.

To summarize the Korean elite youth sports policy, we should focus on the agreement embodied in the 'Guarantee Policy of Study Rights', as the first step in relation to policies about student-athletes' welfare. Appropriate enforcement of this 'unfamiliar policy', at least for Koreans, will change the perception of parents and students that they had to sacrifice other aspects of normal life once they choose to become elite athletes. At the same time, this will encourage student-athletes to find interests other than sport and prepare for the future in case they get injured or face situations that lead them to abandon their athletic career (Won and Hong, 2015). With the implementation of competition structure depending on the nature of the sport, protection of young athletes from exploitation and any type of violence and the open culture for them to inform of any mistreatment by coaches and others are critical in fostering a pleasant and positive environment for Korean youth elite sport. This will upgrade the status of Korea from one of the most successful nations to one of the most developed sports nations with the combination of excellent sports performances and a healthy youth development system.

References

Choi, E. C. (2011). Identifying Sport Talents in Each Region, Development status and Future Direction. *Sport Science*, Winter, 11–18.

Civil Network for Justice of Sports (2015). Retrieved from www.sportscm.org/about_us.htm

Economist (2010). Retrieved from www.economist.com/blogs/gametheory/2012/01/korean-golfers

Ewha Education Center for Gifted Young Athletes (2015). Internal Documents.

Hong, E. (2010). An analysis of the sport policy process in the Republic of Korea: the cases of elite sport development and sport for all. (Thesis PhD), Loughborough University.

Jeong, H. J. (2009). Upper Cut: one hit towards sacred and inviolable Korean Sports. Seoul: Miji Books.

Kim, S. Y. (2004). A study on the Sports Policies of Korean Regimes. (Unpublished PhD Thesis, Chosun University).

Korea Football Association (2014). Regulation of Coaching Education.

Korea Football Association (2015). Retrieved from www.kfa.or.kr/kfa/program_goldenage.asp

Korea Football Association (2015). Retrieved from www.kfa.or.kr/info/judment.asp

Korea Football Association (2015). Retrieved from www.kfa.or.kr/league/league_school.asp

Korea Junior Golf Association(2015). Retrieved from http://www.kjga.or.kr/n_Public/s45.asp

Korea Sports Promotion Foundation (2015). Retrieved from http://english.kspo.or.kr/?menuno=348

Korea Sports Promotion Foundation (2015). Retrieved from www.kspo.or.kr/?menuno=646

Korea Sports Promotion Foundation (2015). Retrieved from www.kspo.or.kr/?menuno=206

Korea Sports Promotion Foundation (2015). Retrieved from http://english.kspo.or.kr/?menuno=348

Korean Foundation for the Next Generation Sports Talent(2015). Retrieved from www.nest.or.kr/nest/subHomePage/scienceHome/leftMenu/aboutSH/bu_1.do

Kwak, E. C, Kim, Y. K., & Joo, B. H. (2011). A Study on Student-Athletes' Learning Environments in Secondary Schools and Systematic Alternatives. *Korean Journal of Sport Pedagogy*, 18(1), 1–16.

Ladies Professional Golf Association (2015). Retrieved from www.lpga.com/news/stats-and-stuff-south-korean-golfers-on-a-victory-streak

Lee, H. R. (2003). A study on Korea sport history, 1st edn, Kookhak Jaryowon, Seoul, Korea.

Lee, M. C. (1992). Development Strategy of Excellence Athletes. Korea Institute of Sport Science.

Lee, Y. S. (2010). A study on the link between systems of youth development. Korea Institute of Sport Science. Research Report, 10-01.

Lee, G. I. & Park, J. Y. (2014). The task of sport gifted children education to review with educational perspective. *The Korean Journal of Sports Science*. 23(5), 1031–1050.

Lim, J. T. (2014). Korean women professional golf players' entry process and success factors in the LPGA Tour. (Thesis PhD), Kyungpook National University.

Ministry of Culture, Sport and Tourism (2013). Sports White Paper. Seoul.

Ministry of Culture, Sport and Tourism (2015). Retrieved from www.mcst.go.kr/web/s_about/organ/main/mainOrgan.jsp

Ministry of Culture, Sport and Tourism (2015). Retrieved from www.mcst.go.kr/web/s_notice/press/pressView.jsp?pSeq=13310

Ministry of Culture, Sport and Tourism (2015). Retrieved from www.mcst.go.kr/web/s_about/organ/main/mainOrgan.jsp

Ministry of Education (2015). Ministry of Education/Ministry of Culture, Sports and Tourism. '2015 School Sport Main Tasks Plan'.

Ministry of Education, Science and Technology (2009), internal document.

NEST (Korea Foundation for the Next Generation Sports Talent). Retrieved from www.nest.or.kr/nest/subHomePage/guideHome/leftMenu/aboutGH/bu_1.do

Oh, K. M. (2013). Comparison of the Archery rearing programs for elite student athletes between South Korea and Australia. (Thesis PhD). Korea University.

Park, J. K. (2012). Management Plans of Integration of 'National Sports Festival' and 'National Sport for All Festival' for Development of Community Sport. *Journal of Korean Society of Sport Policy*, *10*(4), 177–187.

Shin, S. Y. (2009). Current Status and Tasks of Sport Talent Athletes Project. *Sport Science*. Winter, 9–15.

Sports Industry Research Center in Seoul National University (2011). *A Report on the analysis of 2011 High School Weekend Baseball League and Improvement Plan*. Seoul.

Won, H. J. and Hong, E. (2015). The development of sport policy and management in South Korea. *International Journal of Sport Policy and Politics*, *7*(1), 141–152.

Yang, G. S. (2011). Case Studies on identification and Nurturing of Sport Athletes. *Sport Science*. Summer, 64–69.

Yu, T. H. (2005). The problem and the prospect of Korea school athletic sport. *Korean Journal of Sport Pedagogy*, *12*(2), 91–108.

Part V

Oceania

Chapter 15

Australia

Russell Hoye

Elite youth sport policy in Australia has never really enjoyed prominence as a discrete set of coherent policy objectives or investments from Federal governments of either side of politics since the late 1970s when the Australian Federal government first started articulating specific policy objectives for sport. Sport policies focused on Australian youth over the last four decades have emphasised growing participation rates under the guise of delivering health benefits and more latterly combating the obesity epidemic among young Australians (Hoye & Nicholson, 2011). A further, more overt, policy driver for growing participation rates has been increasing the talent pool from which might emerge the next crop of talented athletes, football players, netballers and other sportspeople to compete in Australia's multitude of national sport leagues as well as represent the country in Commonwealth and Olympic Games and World Championship events (Hoye & Nicholson, 2009; Nicholson & Hoye, 2011).

The National Junior Sport Policy (NJSP; ASC, 1994) and the subsequent Junior Sport Framework (JSF; ASC, 2014) are the two policy documents that have been developed to shape youth sport policy, including elite youth sport policy, in Australia. The specific policy initiatives that have focused on supporting elite youth sport and the environment in which it is provided have included member protection policies to ensure sport organisations deliver a safe, fun, quality and inclusive environment for participants, a national talent identification programme and attempts to shape the athlete pathways and academy programmes focused on supporting promising elite youth athletes.

This chapter describes the role of government in developing policies to protect the welfare of children involved in sport, identifies the elements of public policy related to elite youth sport development, and highlights a number of sports as examples of how government policy flows through to practice. It also explores the talent identification pathways in place in the Australian sport system, how sports have structured coach development or pathways to support elite youth athletes, and concludes with an analysis of a number of specific issues associated with the achievement of elite youth sport outcomes for governments, sport organisations and individuals.

National sport system and elite youth sport policy

The Australian sport system is based on the many tens of thousands of non-profit clubs and associations run by volunteers that deliver sport participation opportunities and events, provide development programs for coaches and officials, identify and develop talented athletes, train volunteers to run clubs and events, promote their 'product' in a very competitive market and work with governments at local, state and national levels to run facilities, events and programmes. As Hoye and Nicholson (2011) explained, the majority of sport clubs and associations in Australia are governed through a complex federated model, with national sport organisations (NSOs) funded by the Australian government to deliver what have been long-standing public policy objectives focused on enhancing elite performances and increasing participation in sport. These NSOs work with affiliated state sport organisations (SSOs) to deliver sport development programmes in each of the eight states and territories of Australia, which in turn also receive varying degrees of funding support from their respective state or territory government. Within each state or territory, local or regional clubs and associations work at the 'coalface' of sport; coaching teams, recruiting and managing volunteers, developing the skills and abilities of athletes and administering competitions and events. These clubs and associations generally work with local governments, the major providers of stadia and other facilities used by sport organisations and participants.

Federal government policy is determined by the federal Minister for Sport. The policy delivery arm of government is the Australian Sports Commission (ASC), the national sport agency that works directly through more than 120 NSOs by funding their activities, with an emphasis, as argued by Green (2007) and still evident today, of supporting elite sport rather than mass participation. The ASC, via funding and service agreements, and through annual reviews that monitor performance and allocate funding on the basis of each NSO's achievements, ensures that NSO planning and activities are aligned with the ASC's strategic objectives and government policy aims.

The decade since the election of the Rudd Labour government in late 2007 saw arguably the most change to how federal governments have supported sport in Australia. Six months into their term, the Rudd government released a discussion paper titled 'Australian Sport: Emerging Challenges, New Directions', which argued that new directions were needed to how government supported elite sport and the connections between sport participation and the health of Australians. The discussion paper posited that 'in recent times, junior and community sport has been approached with a focus, almost exclusively, on increasing the pool from which our elite athletes can be drawn' and that 'whereas early federal sports policy had a clear focus on community physical activity and "Life. Be In It" style programs, this has declined over time to become virtually non-existent' (Commonwealth of Australia 2008, p.

5). The sport portfolio was moved to the Health department, underscoring an intent that sport would be used as part of a suite of approaches to preventative health programs of government (Nicholson & Hoye, 2011). However, despite these changes, Australian sport policy remained largely unchanged, in large part because the Rudd government commissioned an investigation of the Australian sport system and Australian sport policy in August 2008. The 'Independent Sport Panel', chaired by David Crawford, was charged with making recommendations on the specific structures, programmes and reform required to ensure the continuing robustness of the Australian sport system. The panel's terms of reference focused on five key areas:

- Ensure Australia's continued elite sporting success.
- Better place sport and physical activity as a key component of the Government's preventative health agenda.
- Strengthen pathways from junior sport to grassroots community sport right through to elite and professional sport.
- Maintain Australia's cutting edge approach to sports science, research and technology.
- Identify opportunities to increase and diversify the funding base for sport through corporate sponsorship, media and any recommended reforms, such as enhancing the effectiveness of the Australian Sports Foundation.

As Nicholson and Hoye (2011) summarise, the Panel's report, titled 'The Future of Sport in Australia' was presented to the government in October 2009 and contained several recommendations with significant implications for the Australian sport system. First, the Panel recommended that the government should develop a national sports policy framework, to include measurable objectives and priorities for public funding within the key areas of high performance sport and sport participation, strategies to deliver the objectives, and a clear articulation of the roles and responsibilities of the various levels of government in delivering the strategies. Second, the Panel recommended that the Australian Sports Commission should provide leadership, but should not be involved in service delivery. As such, it recommended that the Australian Institute of Sport be separated from the Commission. Third, the Panel recommended that the various State and Territory Institutes of Sport be merged with the Australian Institute of Sport to form a single entity funded by the federal government. Finally, the Panel recommended that a national curriculum for sport and physical education be considered. The report generated considerable debate, particularly around the issue of the funding balance between high performance and participation sport, with advocates for high performance sport such as the Australian Olympic Committee, critical of any suggestion that funding to high performance sport be decreased.

In May 2010 the Rudd government released 'Australian Sport: The Pathway to Success', which it claimed was its new sport policy as well as its response to the report of the Independent Sport Panel. The government did establish a National Sport and Active Recreation Policy Framework, but did not split the Australian Sports Commission and the Australian Institute of Sport. The government also did not support merging the state and federal Institutes of Sport into a single entity or fully support arguments for increasing sport and physical education in the school curriculum. The rest of the Rudd and subsequent Gillard Labour governments were bereft of substantial policy development affecting elite youth sport until the release of Winning Edge in 2012, a policy that refocused the ASC and AIS on high performance sport.

Winning Edge 2012–2022 (Australian Sports Commission, 2012) was launched with great fanfare in 2012 and continues to be the cornerstone of Australia's sport policy. Its tag line of 'Our game plan for moving from world class to world's best' highlights the focus of federal government policy. The policy aims are to deliver:

- consistent and sustainable success for Australian athletes and teams on the world stage;
- greater levels of accountability for performance results;
- improved governance structures and contemporary reporting and monitoring of performance; and
- engaging, uniting, inspiring and motivating all Australians.

This current policy continues the rhetoric that 'high performance success is not only good for our athletes and our sense of national pride, it also contributes to other important Government objectives in areas such as participation, economic development, health and education' (ASC, 2012, p. 3). The specific sections of the current policy directly relevant to elite youth are focused on unearthing and nurturing talent and include three strategic foci:

1   Conduct annual 'Sports Draft' and 'Second Chance' programmes for Olympic, Paralympic and Commonwealth Games sports.
2   Develop niche-sport talent initiatives (for example, combat sports, target sports, acrobatic sports).
3   Explore opportunities for women in high performance sport, dedicated national sporting organisation (NSO) pathway managers, and talent enrichment team for pre-elite athletes.

I will return to explore these three initiatives later in this chapter in the section on talent identification and an exploration of how elite youth sport development is managed in three different sports.

The release of the 'Play. Sport. Australia' policy in March 2015 (Australian Sports Commission, 2015) was couched as the ASC's 'participation game plan' for getting more Australians playing organised sport in reaction to falling rates of regular participation in organised sport, particularly for children as they enter later teenage years, declining rates of participation in all forms of physical activity by children and young people, declining competence among school-aged children for basic motor skills, and increasing rates of obesity among Australian children. The aims of this participation focused policy are to 'to better understand what is happening in sport, help drive demand for lifelong participation in sport and support the network that supplies sport — our sporting organisations' (ASC, 2015, p. 12). In relation to the first aim, of being more informed of what is happening in the sport market, the ASC has invested in a new national participation survey, an increasingly important exercise given the cessation of sport participation data collection by the Australian Bureau of Statistics after 2012 and the end of the Exercise, Recreation and Sport Survey in 2010, the two previous sources of sport participation data used by the ASC, other government agencies, researchers and the sport industry. The ASC also aims to continue its periodic attempts at bespoke research such as its market segmentation and future of Australian sport projects. The Clearinghouse for Sport information portal for the sport sector will continue to be supported by the ASC as its primary means of distributing information to the sector.

The second focus of the participation policy is to actively deliver programmes to increase rates of participation in organised sport and to work with the NSOs to enhance programme offerings. The direct intervention programme from the ASC is the Sporting Schools programme focused on children aged 5 to 12 and youth aged 13 to 17 through funding access programmes for before, during and after school sport activity. The ASC will also fund NSOs directly to develop new innovative programmes that will be rolled out through their respective association and club systems and agree on participation targets. The final element of the ASC's attempts to directly influence participation rates will be targeted support for selected NSOs to align their plans with other sport sector partners such as State Departments of Sport and Recreation and other providers.

The final focus of the participation policy is to improve the capability and capacity of the Australian sports system through supporting NSOs to improve their governance, product development and commercial sustainability, workforce development to have more educated and trained people working in the sport system, enhancing coaching and officiating development, improving information on national facility requirements, digital leadership to ensure sports can communicate and interact with their participants, supporting efforts for NSOs to deliver safe and inclusive environments and to improve the quality of people serving on NSO boards (ASC, 2015).

The final element of federal government policy relevant to elite youth sport is the Junior Sport Framework (ASC, 2014) noted in the introduction to this chapter. The JSF is a collection of guidelines, templates and resources designed for adaptation and adoption by NSOs to shape the delivery of sport for children aged 7 to 12 and youth aged 13 to 17. The JSF is deliberately designed to be flexible and recognises that 'Every sport's participation and athlete development structure will be slightly different, but take into consideration a number of core principles upon which junior sport policies and program development are based' (ASC, 2014, no page). These principles are listed as:

1   Recognition that motivation for participation is based upon 'enjoyment'; which may include many things; such as having fun, acquiring skills, and experiencing positive self-concept and interaction with others;
2   Flexibility in program design to account for the variability in the rate of maturation among children. Program design may also consider whether gender inclusion (i.e. boys and girls competing together) is desirable and age appropriate;
3   Recognition of the physical and psychological developmental stages and capabilities that exist during childhood. Programs must respond to the capabilities and age appropriate needs of children. The emergence of 'modified' sports programs is a direct response to these needs;
4   Inclusion principles that allow a variety of sport and physical activity opportunities to take place in a safe environment. Child protection in a sporting environment is an overall consideration; and
5   Development of 'pathways' so that sporting experiences and learnt skills become part of a long-term or lifetime continuum. (ASC, 2014, no page)

The flexibility inherent in the JSF is to enable sports to develop their own junior sport policies that address athlete wellbeing, development, and long-term participation. In this way, an NSO can combine general policies on safety and child protection with specific policies germane to the nature of the sport training and competition structures such as limiting children's exposure to too many competitions, excessive travel, pressures, or injury risks or address childhood maturation considerations (ASC, 2014, no page).

The ASC has been instrumental in shaping policy for harm minimisation and the protection of children through the development of a member protection policy template and associated resource kit delivered via a website Play by the Rules (www.PlaybytheRules.net.au). The Play by the Rules website was first developed by the South Australian Department for Sport and Recreation in 2001 as an interactive education and information website on discrimination, harassment and child protection in sport and is now a unique collaboration between the Australian Sports Commission, Australian Human Rights Commission, all state and territory departments of sport and recreation, all state and territory anti-discrimination and human rights agencies, the Office of the Children's Guardian and the Australian and New Zealand Sports Law Association (ANZSLA).

(Play by the Rules, 2016, no page)

The website provides information, resources, tools and free online training to increase the capacity and capability of administrators, coaches, officials, players and spectators to assist them in preventing and dealing with discrimination, harassment, child safety and integrity issues in sport (Play by the Rules, 2016).

Talent identification and elite youth sport exemplars

As noted in the previous section, talent identification for elite youth is undertaken by NSOs and supported by the network of national and state institutes for sport in line with the Winning Edge policy and takes three forms. First, the Australian Institute of Sport works with NSOs to conduct an annual 'Sports Draft' for Olympic, Paralympic and Commonwealth Games sports. The AIS Sports Draft (AIS, 2016) is designed to provide athletes with a fast-tracked development opportunity to transfer into an Olympic or Commonwealth Games sport. In 2015, the AIS focused on four sports: rugby 7s for women, combat sports (judo, boxing and taekwondo), cycling (sprint track, lead riders), and paddling (kayak sprint and canoe sprint). The sports draft process is highly individualised with athletes expressing their interest online, selected to attend state-based selection trials, and then athletes are matched to attend familiarization sessions at a local club before being invited to a selection camp, where they are subjected to a range of physical, skill-based and psychological challenges, and provided free training and evaluation by coaches and sport scientists. Athletes that are then selected (drafted) are invited to train with a national coach in their home city and commit to a daily training program, be subject to regular monitoring and evaluation from head coaches or AIS specialists, and attend training camps. If the athletes progress to meet certain selection criteria, they then may become eligible for national selection in their new sport.

The AIS and ASC also offer talent transfer opportunities for professional athletes who are delisted, suffer a sport-specific career-ending injury or are wanting to extend their careers to be transferred to Summer and Winter Olympic sports for competition in 2016, 2018 and 2020, and for athletes to transition from sports that have similar skills (for example, gymnastics, diving and aerial skiing) (ASC, 2012). While most athletes who take up these talent transfer opportunities will not be junior athletes, these opportunities are still available for aspiring elite youth athletes.

Aside from these specific talent identification schemes designed to bolster Australia's medal hopes in specific Olympic, Paralympic and Commonwealth Games sports, the AIS has shaped the development of elite youth athletes within a new sport pathway framework of Foundation, Talent, Elite and Mastery (FTEM). This framework is designed to assist NSOs evaluate and design their respective sport pathway and development programmes to identify the specific roles that parents, teachers, clubs, coaches, institutes and academies and NSOs should play in nurturing talent and delivering sport participation opportunities. In order to see how this framework is applied in practice, the elite youth development pathway is reviewed for three different sports; gymnastics (an early peak performance sport), Australian Rules football (a commercial team sport) and hockey (a major Olympic sport).

Gymnastics Australia

Gymnastics Australia manages a sophisticated talent development programme across the four disciplines of gymnastics that offer a pathway to Olympic and Commonwealth Games selection: Men's Artistic, Women's Artistic, Rhythmic Gymnastics and Trampoline Gymnastics. They also support national squads and teams in aerobics and acrobatic gymnastics. The following material has been sourced directly from the Gymnastics Australia website (www.gymnastics.org.au).

Gymnastics Australia works in partnership with the Australian Institute of Sport, State Institutes and Academies of Sport, State Associations and High Performance gymnastics programmes to create a system capable of delivering international sporting success. Talented young individuals who have been identified as having the potential to perform at the international level are directed towards High Performance programmes which have the capability to provide the specialised training, resources and support required. The Pathways team provide leadership and guidance for the gymnastics implementation of the Australian athlete development framework, the FTEM model, developed by the Australian Institute of Sport. Applying this model to each unique gymsport provides Gymnastics Australia a clear understanding of both the number and quality of athletes required at each level of the pathway to sustain the success of GA's National teams in the future. Pathways programmes include the Team Future high performance development programme, and the Spin to Win talent identification and transfer programme.

Team Future is the GA branding of its high performance development program across all Olympic Gymsports. Team Future activities encompass a holistic development programme for young gymnasts ranging in age from

10 to 18. Activities are delivered within two main camps per year for each gymsport. National and senior coaches act as 'Master Coaches' to mentor developing junior coaches. The programme not only includes technical instruction but includes athlete and coach leadership education and development in the areas of physical development and assessment, psychology, nutrition and physiology. Other areas include contemporary upskilling in areas such as senior athlete mentoring, media skills, public speaking, drug and social media awareness. Developing athlete and coach competencies will enhance the daily training environment, which is essential to long-term development. Team Future unites all developing gymnasts around the country who are successfully competing at an appropriate level and whose programmes are embracing the Individual Development Element Assessment List (IDEAL) Skills Assessment programme. This assessment is the testing of gymnasts' progress in developing the comprehensive array of skills that will be the foundation of future high performance success. IDEAL skills provide a road map of the 'Ideal' skill progressions and development for young gymnasts. Ensuring IDEAL skills is supported by coaches delivers a level of accountability and is the underpinning process to Individual Athlete Plans (suitable for athletes progressing to Junior and Senior National teams). The benefits of this approach are articulated by GA to be:

- The programme provides direction, additional to the competitive programme.
- The programme encourages mastery and retention of basic movement patterns in conjunction with advanced skill learning.
- Clearly outlines a sequential method of skill learning which will eliminate 'holes' in the gymnast's future programme.
- Provides a strong base for which the most complicated and difficult skills can be learnt in the future.
- Athletes and coaches can clearly see how each gymnast's skills are tracking; athletes can see how they are improving.

A custom designed database named the Virtual Assessment Tool (VAT) that enables handheld skill capture and web based assessment/reporting has been built to enable assessment and tracking of each athlete along the gymsport skill curriculum which involves approximately 600 athletes at any time. Talented athletes are identified and added to the pathways database up to four Olympic cycles in advance. This assessment process underpins the development of talent identified athletes and ensures that their coaches remain informed about the progress they are making.

The final element of the Gymnastics Australia elite youth development investment has been supported by the Federal Government's AIS Competitive Innovation Fund. 'Spin to Win' is a collaborative project led by GA in partnership with Diving Australia, Ski & Snowboard Australia and the

Olympic Winter Institute of Australia. It is a sophisticated Talent Identification and Transfer programme which results in having high-quality acrobatic talent training in the most suitable High Performance Sport Development Pathway. 'Spin to Win' aims to build a successful and sustainable national system of talent identification, development and transfer to maximise podium performances at world championships and Olympic Games in each sport in the future given they all have one thing in common – an acrobatic skill base developed through early involvement in gymnastics.

Hockey Australia

The elite youth talent identification and player development pathway for field hockey in Australia has also been developed in conjunction with the AIS FTEM framework. The following material has been sourced directly from the Hockey Australia website (www.hockey.org.au).

Hockey Australia, in conjunction with the Australian Institute of Sport (AIS), has developed a player pathway to capture the different forms of participation and address the current shortfalls in applied research and practice specific to athlete development. The FTEM framework integrates three key outcomes of sport participation: active lifestyle, sport participation and sport excellence. It provides a practical method to assist all hockey stakeholders to construct a more functional athlete and sport development system. The FTEM framework can be used as a practical planning and review tool for a broad range of sporting stakeholders including parents, teachers, clubs, coaches, sports science and sports medicine personnel and the elite level hockey programmes. This enhanced understanding of the hockey pathway will help us to improve the experiences of more people, at more levels of the pathway, more often. A feature of this approach is the creation of age-based development squads outside of the national senior men's and women's programmes.

The Jillaroos, Australia's junior women's programme, and the Burras, Australia's junior men's programmes represent the peak of age-group hockey and exists to provide junior athletes appropriate development opportunities as they progress through the player pathway. The Jillaroos and Burras represent Australia at the Junior World Cup, the pinnacle of international junior hockey, every four years. These programmes operate a flexible selection model; in the year before and year of a Junior World Cup they contain athletes aged 21 and under. In the two years following a Junior World Cup the programme includes athletes up to the age of 23. Athletes from these programmes also represent Australia at the Youth Olympic Games and the Australian Youth Olympic Festival under the direction of the Australian Olympic Committee. These programmes provide a critical pathway for athletes to transition into the development and senior programmes.

Through the National Futures programme and National Training Centre network Hockey Australia facilitates a targeted development programme for 16–18 year olds providing camps and competition against countries such as New Zealand, Japan, India, South Africa and visiting university and school teams from Asia. At under-16 level, Hockey Australia also has a memorandum of understanding with School Sport Australia (SSA) which allows them to interface with the annual schoolgirls and schoolboys carnivals and to support international tours that All-Australian U16 teams embark on annually. This program is critical to the early development of athletes that may be 4–7 years away from representing Australia at senior level.

Australian Rules football

In contrast to the Gymnastics Australia and Hockey Australia talent identification and pathways that are designed in line with the AIS FTEM framework, the Australian Football League, as the governing body for Australian rules football, has developed a talent identification and player development pathway to support a national league that requires 80–100 new players per year. As the most commercially successful sports league in Australia it receives very little government funding and therefore operates somewhat independently of federal government policy for elite youth sport. The following material has been sourced directly from the Australian Football League website (www.afl.com.au) and is provided to illustrate the variety of talent identification systems within the Australian sport system.

At the youth level, the talent pathway to becoming an AFL player begins to emerge through regional development squads that have the dual purpose of developing individual player's abilities and preparing teams to participate in state championships at under-14 level and above. The delivery of this player development pathway is supported by community clubs, state-based academy programs, a national academy that is delivered with the support of the AIS, the hosting of national under age championships and state leagues. The AFL identifies five stages to an AFL player's development, followed by the maturation and retirement stages.

- Fundamental Stage (5–11 years): AFL Junior, where the focus is on participation and learning fundamental movement and game skills. The program is well-structured and fun. The emphasis is on the overall development of the participant's fundamental motor skills and physical capacities using game-related, skill-development activities. This is a critical period for motor skill development. Correct running and jumping, and basic game skills should be taught, and participation in a range of sports encouraged for all-round development. Simple rules and ethics are also introduced.

- Sampling Stage (12–14 years): AFL Junior/Youth, where the objective is learning all the fundamental skills of the game and developing basic physical capacities, while continuing to develop all-round sports skills. Players learn how to train and consolidate the basic skills of the game. They are introduced to technical and tactical skills, including positional skills and basic performance-enhancing techniques (e.g., warm-up, cool-down, nutrition, hydration, recovery, goal-setting). This is a critical period for physical and skill development. The focus of training is on learning rather than competing, and a balance between training and playing is struck. Participants should continue to play a range of sports for their all-round development. This stage also includes initial identification for regional development squads.
- Identification Stage (15–16 years): AFL Youth, where the objective is developing higher-level skills of the game and physical capacities. Optimise the development of fitness, individual, positional and team skills. Develop higher-level competition skills and provide appropriate competition to enhance learning and the opportunity to be identified for talent pathway programmes. At this age initial selection into state talent development programmes including the AIS-AFL Academy are introduced.
- Specialising Stage (17–18 years), where the objective is developing higher-level skills of the game and physical capacities. Optimise the development of fitness capacities and individual, positional, team and competition skills. For talented players, selection into state and national talent development programmes, including the AIS-AFL Academy, continues. This includes the provision of an optimum competition programme for player development that also provides opportunities to be drafted to the AFL TAC Cup or state league competition.
- Investment Stage (19–22 years), where the objective is to complete development of all higher-level skills and capacities required for optimum performance. This is the final stage of development, where the focus of the training is on completing a player's development and optimising performance. For talented players, the refinement of physical, technical, tactical, mental and ancillary capacities is completed in the professional club environment.

Changes in practice for elite youth sport

A number of sport development practices have been adapted to ensure they support elite youth development and programs in Australia, notably coaching, competition structures, and athlete career and education support services. The increased emphasis by the ASC and AIS on talent identification and transfer schemes and the increased focus on funded NSOs to deliver high performance outcomes has, in turn, increased the professionalization required among coaches at all levels of sport. The National Coaching Accreditation Scheme (NCAS) is Australia's system of training and accrediting coaches, with more than 70 sports participating. The NCAS includes a set of generic coaching principles, which all coaches learn, as well as sport-specific coaching principles – skills, techniques, strategies and approaches to a particular sport, including age-appropriate coaching techniques. The ASC has been instrumental in developing policies to improve child protection, specifically keeping them safe from physical, sexual or emotional harm. Coaches are required by state or territory law to undergo a national criminal history check to determine their suitability for working with children.

The competition structures of many sports have been designed to provide talented junior athletes opportunities to access structured daily training environments and to play against better athletes more often. For example, the AFL TAC cup structure for Australian Rules football under 16 and 18 competitions in Victoria has become the major source of AFL draftees with more players recruited to the AFL from the TAC Cup than from any other competition throughout Australia. The TAC Cup also provides an opportunity for talented country players to play in a very high standard competition without having to relocate to Melbourne and for providing quality young players, not only to the AFL, but also to the senior VFL competition and local country and metropolitan football (AFL Victoria, 2016, no page). This competition structure has evolved over many years in response to changing demands for elite youth development pathways in football.

The increasing demands on elite youth athletes in the Victorian Institute of Sport (VIS) to devote more time for training, strength and conditioning, recovery, competition and preparation have led to the development of the athlete career and education (ACE) programme and its successor, the Personal Excellence Programme (PEP). The PEP is one example of a sport organisation seeking to assist its athletes achieve a balance between life activities and sport performance, with a focus on increasing overall well-being. As the VIS (2016, no page) states: 'By partnering with Personal Excellence athletes are able to progress their dual careers in sport and life by building professionalism, accountability, resilience, integrity and responsibility. This is achieved by gaining access to personal and professional development, career and education opportunities, and support networks to assist in making more informed decisions'. The PEP delivers programmes in response to the individual needs and aspirations of athletes in areas such as:

- Career Guidance, Counselling and Employment Preparation
- Educational Guidance
- Assistance with building Support Networks
- Transition Support
- Support to access the Elite Athlete Counselling Support program

- Assistance within the Elite Athlete Friendly University Network (EAFU)
- Fully Funded Personal Development and Training.

(VIS, 2016, no page)

Similar holistic athlete-centric programmes have been created by NSOs to cater for elite youth athletes who need to continue to balance the demands for their sporting careers with education and family commitments.

Conclusion

This chapter has described the role of successive national governments in Australia in developing policies for elite youth sport development, and highlighted how government policy has flowed through to practice in a number of sports. It has explored the talent identification pathways in place in the Australian sport system and how sports have structured coach development and competition pathways to support elite youth athletes. In conclusion, I wish to highlight four challenges for the achievement of elite youth sport outcomes for governments, sport organisations and individuals before making some observations regarding the degree of policy convergence evident for elite youth sport policy in Australia.

First, there seems to be a widely held belief among policy makers that the overall capacity of the Australian sport system to support additional participants to enhance the talent pool from which elite youth athletes will emerge is appropriate. In other words, that there are enough qualified coaches, club based volunteers, officials, sport science staff, facilities and appetite for growth among sport providers to service this larger talent pool. As previous reviews commissioned by governments (i.e., the Crawford Report from 2008) and academic analyses (i.e., Hoye & Nicholson, 2011) have highlighted, this belief may be overly optimistic.

Second, there is enormous competition between sports to secure the best elite youth athletes. Australia is unique in that there are four national football codes, cricket, basketball, netball, and golf and tennis pathways, in addition to the other Olympic and Commonwealth Games sports actively recruiting athletes. For Australian elite youth athletes, there is a myriad of choices, many of them offering lucrative careers in domestic leagues, and this competition shows no signs of abating.

Third, as highlighted by both current national sport policy frameworks, participation rates for Australian youth in traditional forms of organised sport continue to decline. In conjunction with the previous challenge, this means that NSOs are confronted with a diminishing pool of athletes from which to draw elite youth talent.

Fourth, the ability of a national level sport policy to be able to exert meaningful action on many of the building blocks of a robust elite youth sport development system in Australia remains questionable. Given the nature of the federated model of government and the positioning of the ASC/AIS and sport policy within the health portfolio at the federal level, it makes it difficult for government to effectively influence all the requisite policy elements for an effective elite youth sport development programme – mandatory physical education in schools, coordinated national facility development, coordinated investments between federal, state and local governments, and control over more commercially focused sporting codes not dependent on federal funding.

As noted in earlier chapters of this book, one of the themes in recent sport policy analyses has been the degree of convergence in national systems (Bergsgard et al., 2007, De Bosscher, 2007; De Bosscher et al., 2009; Houlihan, 2012; Nicholson, Hoye & Houlihan, 2011). There is certainly evidence of this in the Australian policy system related to elite youth sport with targeted investments in sports likely to deliver Olympic and Commonwealth Games medals, a national sport talent draft and transfer program, the adoption of a structured tiered talent development system (FTEM) and the central role of NSOs for the delivery of elite youth sport outcomes with specific sport science and other support being provided by a network of specialist institutes.

In relation to Houlihan's (2012) seven dimensions of the policy process that could illustrate policy convergence, the motives for elite youth sport support in Australia seem to mirror those of other Western systems – increasing the talent pool and targeting specific sports for short-term gains in international success. The agenda and associated discourse for elite youth sport is also to deliver elite success on the world stage and in so doing, reinforce the value of sport for a nation – enhancing national pride, provision of role models for participants, influencing the health of the general population. The inputs and implementation measures used in Australia also seem to mirror those adopted in the UK and Canada, suggesting a degree of policy convergence between at least these countries. The momentum for elite youth sport policy elements in Australia, while not being a discrete policy in itself, certainly seems to be strong in 2016 and is embedded in the current Winning Edge strategy. Whether these have any real impact remains to be seen.

References

AFL Victoria (2016). *History of the TAC Cup [online]*. Available from www.foxsportspulse.com/assoc_page.cgi?c=1-3020-0-0-0&sID=159878 [Accessed 1 February 2016].

Australian Institute of Sport. (2016) *The AIS Sports Draft [online]*. Available from www.ausport.gov.au/ais/australias_winning_edge/ais_sports_draft/faqs Accessed 1 February 2016].

Australian Sports Commission. (1994) *National Junior Sport Policy: A framework for developing junior sport in Australia*. Canberra: Australian Sports Commission.

Australian Sports Commission. (2012) *Australia's Winning Edge 2012-2022*. Canberra: Australian Sports Commission.

Australian Sports Commission. (2014) *Junior Sport Framework [online]*. Available from www.clearinghouseforsport.gov.au/knowledge_base/sport_participation/community_engagement/junior_sport_framework [Accessed 1 February 2016].

Australian Sports Commission. (2015) *Play. Sport. Australia*. Canberra: Australian Sports Commission.

Bergsgard, N.A., Houlihan, B., Mangset, P., Nodland, S.I. & Rommetvedt, H. (2007) *Sport policy; a comparative analysis of stability and change*, Oxford: Butterworth-Heinemann.

De Bosscher, V. (2007) *Sport policy factors leading to international sporting success*, Brussels: VUBPRESS.

De Bosscher, V., De Knop, P., van Bottenburg, M., Shibli, S. & Bingham, J. (2009) Explaining international sporting success: an international comparison of elite sport systems and policies in six countries, *Sport Management Review*, *12*, 113–136.

Green, M. (2007) 'Olympic glory or grass roots development? Sport policy priorities in Australia, Canada and the United Kingdom, 1960-2006', *International Journal of the History of Sport*, *24*(7): 921–953.

Houlihan, B. (2012) Sport policy convergence: a framework for analysis, *European Sport Management Quarterly*, *12*(2), 111–135.

Hoye, R. & Nicholson, M. (2009). Australia. *International Journal of Sport Policy*, *1*(2), 229–240.

Hoye, R. & Nicholson, M. (2011). Australia. In M. Nicholson, R. Hoye & B. Houlihan (Eds), *Participation in Sport: International Policy Perspectives*. London: Routledge, pp. 223–237.

Hoye, R., Nicholson, M. & Houlihan, B. (2010). *Sport and Policy*. Oxford: Elsevier Butterworth-Heinemann.

Nicholson, M. & Hoye, R. (2011). Sport Policy in Australia. In S. Georgakis & K.M. Russell, (Eds), *Youth Sport in Australia*. Sydney: Sydney University Press, pp. 45–59.

Nicholson, M., Hoye, R. & Houlihan, B. (Eds) (2011). *Participation in Sport: International Policy Perspectives*. London: Routledge.

Play by the Rules (2016). *Play by the Rules* [online] Available at www.playbytherules.net.au/ [Accessed 1 February 2016].

Victorian Institute of Sport. (2016) Personal Excellence Program [online]. Available from www.vis.org.au/athlete-services/personal-excellence/ [Accessed 1 February 2016].

Chapter 16

New Zealand

Michael P. Sam

With a population of only 4.3 million inhabitants, New Zealand is a small state with big sport ambitions. It has had a successful sporting past, particularly in relation to rugby – consequently sport is an important part of New Zealand national identity (Scherer and Jackson 2010). The development of elite sport (often referred to as high performance sport) has closely followed the trajectories of other nations but given its geographical isolation in the South Pacific, New Zealand demonstrates a number of adaptions and divergences in terms of policies and organisational structures.

One notable contextual difference is that professional sport is a fairly recent phenomenon, and grew quickly in New Zealand. Rugby was first professionalised in 1995 and since that time, broadcasting revenue has enabled New Zealand athletes to be part of professional trans-Tasman (Australia-NZ) leagues in cricket, basketball, netball and football. Where New Zealanders are reputed to have only two degrees of separation (Sam 2015a), it means citizens are very likely to 'know someone who knows someone' being paid as a professional athlete, coach or elite support personnel. In short, sport appears as a viable career option in the eyes of youth and their families.

Over the past two decades, high performance sport has featured prominently in the political landscape. State involvement has been evident in financial support towards sailing syndicates for the America's Cup, in the country's hosting of the 2011 Rugby World Cup, and co-hosting of the 2015 Cricket World Cup. Though having a lesser appetite for elite youth competitions, New Zealand recently hosted the FIFA U20 World Cup in 2015, thanks in part to central and local government support. At $58 million per year, NZ Government investment into high performance (predominantly Olympic) sport has also grown substantially in the last 15 years, with more funding per capita than larger Commonwealth counterparts Canada ($62 million CAD) and Australia ($170 million AUD). New Zealand agencies have thus endeavoured to expand medal performance outputs. After 15 years of development, the elite sport system has become more centralised and targeted. Centralisation has been most evident in the government's investment in rowing and track cycling and the state-supported development of their respective training centres. Targeted investment, which is effectively funding distributions based on the likelihood of medal winning performance, has been one of the principle drivers of elite sport reforms (Sam 2015b).

New Zealand is distinctive by virtue of its broad state-sector reforms that began after the mid-1980s. While geographically distant from the UK and USA, New Zealand was held in high regard within the 'Washington consensus' because of its rapid adoption of neoliberal doctrines. Among the many changes, the Government privatised state-owned enterprises, deregulated markets (e.g., telecommunications, energy) and reorganised government ministries and departments along corporate lines (Scott *et al.* 1990; Shirley 1990). Nearly 30 years after reforms were instituted, they remain an important legacy for the way in which youth sport is structured. This is particularly true with respect to the marketisation of the education sector and the introduction of a competitive model for secondary school curriculum delivery. Since the late 1980s, schools have competed with one another for enrolments, underpinned by a market model intended to increase the performance of schools and to provide consumer choice. The emergence of 'sport academies' from the late 1990s owes much to these developments (Pope 2002).

The New Zealand sport system

New Zealand's central government interest in sport began in earnest in 1985 through its commissioning of a public inquiry. The ensuing report, 'Sport on the Move' resulted in the establishment of the Hillary Commission for Recreation and Sport, an arm's length agency. Youth featured highly in this report for the same reasons that appear in virtually all documents of this era, namely the importance of character building, general health and wellbeing (Sports Development Inquiry Committee 1985). Germane to the present discussion is that *Sport on the Move* marked the beginnings of the shift from physical education to coaching, a shift that would later be replaced with another paradigm shift: from coaching to talent identification.

Elite sport remained out of direct governmental reach until 2001, when the NZ Sports Foundation (a private charitable trust) was disestablished and recast within the ambit of a new crown agency, Sport and Recreation NZ (SPARC). While quickly gaining traction after the perceived failures at the Sydney Olympic Games, high performance sport remained decentralised and operated via regionally-based academies. From 2005, SPARC explicitly shifted its funding model from 'entitlement' (i.e., block funding to organisations) to 'investment' (i.e., contracts). The details and outcomes of this shift are discussed elsewhere (Sam 2012; Sam and Macris 2014); however, the central agency's advancement of performance budgeting has unashamedly come to reflect an ethos of 'rewarding the winners and punishing the losers' (see High Performance Sport New Zealand 2013). For some successful Olympic sports, this has meant a rapid increase in budgets enabling investment into pre-elite levels and the development of youth elite programmes. For example, whereas in 2004 Rowing NZ supported 13 U23 athletes in two boat classes, by 2014 it listed 34 U23 athletes in 10 boat classes (Rowing NZ 2014). Not all targeted sports, however, have been able to generate sustained success. For Swimming NZ, the lack of medals has resulted in a string of external reviews aimed at generating change and while it is unclear how these changes have played out among its youth ranks, there are proposed changes to its youth competitive structures (Swimming NZ 2015a).

The increasing focus on elite sport is perhaps best underscored by the most recent central level changes. In 2011, shortly after SPARC was rebranded as 'Sport NZ', the latter created a 'subsidiary' agency dedicated to elite services. The new organisation, High Performance Sport New Zealand (HPSNZ), would be overseen by a separate external board of Government appointees. The emphasis on elite sport has grown, from initially occupying approximately 40 per cent of the total sport expenditure (in 2002) to exceeding 60 per cent of the total sport budget (in 2013). Budgeted expenditure on elite sport in 2013/14 was NZD \$58.2 million, against the NZD \$19.2 million allocated to community sport (sport-for-all).

Talent identification policies, plans and programmes

While youth sport has been the focus of government agencies for decades, talk of *elite* youth sport is fairly recent. For the most part, the subject of elite youth sport has been encapsulated in policy under the term 'talent identification'. In 2003 SPARC commissioned a Taskforce on Talent Identification and Development, in response to the apparent decline of New Zealand sport performances internationally. As one Taskforce member highlighted, 'there was some sort of recognition that whilst we were putting a huge amount of effort and influence at the elite end, our ability to influence the next tier down was somewhat limited' (Archer 2008: 65). The final report, entitled 'Linking Promise to the Podium' (2004) proposed 'that Kiwi athletes with potential talent should be identified and placed on appropriate development pathways' (TID Taskforce 2004: 7). While the report indicated the need for more systematic mechanisms and pathways, it stopped short of advocating anthropometric testing as with Australia's Talent Search programme. The report was significant from the standpoint that it departed explicitly from the belief that talent would rise 'naturally' and by extension it signalled increasing misgivings about the capacity of arm's length control for those purposes. Good coaching, while inarguably valuable, was not enough by itself.

Despite the increased interest, central agencies and national governing bodies continued to eschew talent identification, particularly when established by third party organisations. The Peter Snell Institute (named after the famed middle-distance runner) was an independent charitable trust formed in 2000 along the lines of the Australian Talent Search initiative (Archer 2008). Institute representatives went to secondary schools, testing promising athletic youth on a number of measures. In the ensuing years, the organisation provided small scholarships for young athletes to offset the costs of travel, coaching and sports medicine. During the same period, SPARC had established its own funding scheme for young elite athletes – Prime Minister's Scholarships – grants to allow promising athletes to pursue tertiary study. While the Snell Institute reported some successes, it failed to be fully accepted and integrated into the existing sport system and was disestablished in 2009 (NZPA 2009).

Whole-of-sport plans thus became one of the main coordinating mechanisms to bring youth through to the elite levels. Most of the major sports now have 'Talent Development Pathways', ostensibly to encourage talented youth to remain with the sport through their teenage years. While some pathways appear to be more sophisticated than others, they all share the same basic elements, each illustrating the various age-group progressions and where development should ideally take place (e.g., university, club, regional centre, etc.). It is only in recent years that elite youth talent identification and development has come to the fore in government agency policy.

Pathway to Podium (P2P)

The formalisation of youth elite sport has become an explicit strategic aim for Sport NZ and HPSNZ. Partly such formalisation has been in response to the rapid growth of a core of youth elite in sports like rowing but partly also, interest in this area has come from the perceived failure of some sports to 'transition' talented youth to world championship level. Established in 2013/2014 'Pathway to Podium' (P2P) is a 'nationwide talent development programme helping emerging athletes (usually in their late teens) and coaches be better prepared for the demands of a life in high performance sport' (HPSNZ 2015). One of P2P's precursors was the Talent Xcelerator programme, a programme designed to bridge the gap between up-and-coming athletes and the standards required at the high-performance level, and to fast-track them on a performance pathway. The P2P programme currently operates via 14 regional hubs, and targets 12 sports (athletics, bike, canoe-racing, equestrian, hockey, netball, Paralympics, rowing, rugby 7s, swimming, triathlon and yachting). Approximately 350 pre-elite athletes and 150 coaches are selected to participate each year and it is expected that athletes will spend 1–3 years in the P2P programme. It provides for a range of workshops on topics such as nutrition, mental skills development, and 'athlete life' skills including time management and media relations.

Like the Long Term Athletic Development model (LTAD), P2P is both a programme and a rhetorical device. Captured by the slogan *'it takes a village to raise a child, it takes a system to develop an athlete'* (Chiet and Sport New Zealand 2015: 5), it symbolically links the community sport (sport-for-all) and elite policy spheres. Importantly, this implies a systemic need for coordination and alignment. As one Sport NZ official put it:

> For our Sporting System to give the current and next generation of talented athletes the best chance to succeed, those messages in our system need to be aligned (coaches in club, school and regional / national settings, other key individuals and organisations supporting the athlete).
>
> (Chiet and Sport New Zealand 2015: 5)

HPSNZ states that the goal is for athletes to win medals 9–10 years after starting their P2P journey. Athletes in this area are thus deemed to be 'pre-elite' and it is suggested that the P2P programme helps in achieving medal targets in part because it allows officials to better understand elite athletes at this age.

> The P2P programme has given us access to a new cohort of athletes we previously did not have within the AD [athlete development] system. From them we are able to identify gaps in their learning and physical progression – which we can then look to address at an earlier age – while also informing the system of potential gaps.
>
> (Chiet and Sport New Zealand 2015: 11)

Indeed the P2P has enabled the gathering of new data on this pre-elite cohort. Among the findings of HPSNZ's 'Athlete Profile' survey of 163 athletes, P2P athletes were not yet in danger of specialising too early, with many taking part in multiple sports through intermediate and secondary school. Another finding from the survey relates to the 'most significant challenges to progressing in sport'. The most frequently cited challenge from respondents was 'managing multiple commitments', followed by 'lack of financial support', 'mental obstacles', and 'injury'. Paradoxically but perhaps unsurprisingly (given P2P's goal of preparing youth for a career as an elite athlete) the fifth most frequently cited challenge was 'uncertainty whether my future involves elite sport'. Taken together this type of survey data is invaluable for signalling systemic issues that might otherwise be overlooked.

Exemplars of NZ youth sport

To better understand the prominence of elite youth sport, the following section outlines three exemplar sports: swimming (an early peak performance sport); rugby (a professional sport); and rowing (an Olympic sport).

Swimming

Up until 2012, swimming was a Sport NZ 'targeted sport' but its status was downgraded due to the sport's inability to generate Olympic and World Championship medal performances. Unlike some other high profile individual sports (e.g., rowing, track cycling), swimming has no elite youth training divisions such as U18, U21, etc. There are, however, proposed changes in this direction. Swimming NZ has proposed a new competitive pathway that includes the introduction of a 'NZ youth championship' competition (for males 16–18 years and females 14–16 years) in addition to the existing NZ age group championships (male 13–15 years, female 12–13 years). According to Swimming NZ, the new pathway's focus on age and gender developmental differences marks a departure from strict performance thresholds that characterise the current structures (Swimming NZ 2015a).

Swimming is principally organised through clubs. While young swimmers compete in intra and inter-school events, schools play only a small role in the pathway for typical youth elite swimmers. As reported elsewhere, swim training is intensive for elite youth. While training regimens vary between New Zealand clubs, a 'typical' regimen for elite youth swimmers includes between six and ten swimming training sessions per week (with each training session lasting between 1.5 hours and 2.5 hours). In addition, elite youth swimmers may complete up to three gym sessions per week. Similar to other individual sport programmes, there are substantial costs involved to train and compete at this level. Costs include fees for coaching, pool entry, affiliations (club, regional, national), meets, events and camps, as well as travel and accommodation. While it is unknown the extent to which costs are offset through community lottery grants, fundraising and sponsorship, it is estimated that youth elite training and competing can cost between $4–6000 NZD per year.

Elite youth swimmers typically 'rise through the ranks' in the club system until they are selected for talent identification programmes by their regional associations. They are then selected for, and participate in, Swimming NZ programmes such as the 'North Island Regional Age Group Camp'. At the very top level is the National High Performance Centre programme. Swimming NZ operates two high performance centres: the National High Performance Centre in Auckland and the Wellington Regional High Performance Centre. While the former is supported and operated by HPSNZ, the latter programme is a partnership between the local club, Swimming

NZ, the regional sport association (Swimming Wellington), city council and a charitable trust. This centre offers a second option to swimmers to train outside of Auckland (Swimming NZ 2015b).

As of 2014/15, swimming had 24 'Pathway to Podium' athletes. Many of New Zealand's youth elite swimmers are based at one of the two centres, with others training overseas as part of US university athletics programmes. While few in number, US-based swimmers have been among the most high profile, bringing criticism to Swimming NZ and HPSNZ for its apparent 'failures' to produce elite swimmers through the Auckland high performance centre (see swimwatch.net). Regardless of their locales, all athletes are required to have performance plans approved by the national body to receive NZ funding. The Swimming NZ 'Junior Pinnacle Events' are the Youth Olympic Games, World Junior Championships, Youth Commonwealth Games, and Junior Pan Pacific Championships. For all four events, athletes range in age between 14 and 18 years of age. While not strictly a youth event, the Oceania Swimming Championships attracts New Zealand team members ranged in age between 14 and 28 (with most New Zealand swimmers aged between their late teens and mid-twenties).

Rugby (commercial sport)

Rugby is New Zealand's most high-profile professional sport. The sport's national governing body, the New Zealand Rugby Union oversees 14 provincial unions, each with its own elite academy in charge of the identification and development of young players. A typical progression is as follows. After being selected for the U16 representative team, and playing in the regional tournament, players are ranked on a national scale at the under-17 level. From here the academy selects approximately 20 players for an 'Elite Schools Academy Squad'. The players in the national rankings are automatically selected for this squad, and any other selections are made via scouts attending school rugby matches. The players in this squad have multiple resources to develop them into elite senior rugby players, including: three morning trainings per week, access to conditioning and skills coaches and nutritional advisers.

In recent years, secondary schools have become an increasingly important source of talent development. The NZRU views schools as the 'first rung on the high performance ladder… introducing young players to the culture and environment of New Zealand's national teams.' Indeed, professional (Super Rugby) franchises are purportedly recruiting directly from high schools (Paul 2015). Sky Television's broadcasting of schools rugby has raised the profile of this level, further affirming rugby as a career for youth. One of the most prevalent issues here is the establishment of rugby academies at some schools. There is immense variability in the governance of these academies and their recruitment practices. Coaches can be teachers or contracted from local clubs. Some programmes may offer scholarships for overseas students wishing to become boarders and/or in the case of private schools, they may offer tuition waivers. This helps athletes from disadvantaged backgrounds to gain entry into prestigious schools while also raising the possibility that foreign-born players may eventually be granted residency and NZ citizenship.

As platforms for player development these academies cannot be viewed outside the context of the competitive nature of schools and the importance of their status and reputation. Winning is important and as such sport development and educational goals are in tension. The recruitment of players into academies (as with adult elite clubs) is based around the depth in particular positions and larger schools have been accused at various times of 'poaching' talent from elsewhere (Cleaver 2015a). In explaining the growing disparities in talent between schools analysts point to some schools that have set up their academies as professional franchises, with succession plans that include targeted recruitment. As significant as these issues are, the sustained success of international-level youth rugby (e.g., the NZ U20, Junior All Blacks) is undeniable.

Rowing (Olympic)

Rowing is arguably New Zealand's most successful Olympic sport. It has one of the most comprehensive high performance programmes, aided principally by Sport NZ funding. In 2014, $6.5 million of Rowing NZ's 8.6 million total revenue came from Sport NZ (Rowing NZ 2014). The national governing body selects athletes for the U23 World Rowing Championship, U21 Trans-Tasman competition and the Junior World rowing Championships held each year. While Rowing NZ's development pathway is presented as a linear progression, there is substantial overlap of youth athletes competing in Junior, U21, university and U23 ranks. It is not unusual that an athlete move from Junior U18 to U23 in subsequent years. Many of Rowing NZ's athletes took up the sport in secondary school, with the average age starting competition at 15 years old (HPSNZ 2015). According to one report, rowing relies 'almost solely on schools to provide and nurture talent' and the 'vast majority of New Zealand's elite rowers will go straight from school into either regional or national high performance centres' (Cleaver 2015b). Rowing NZ confirms that 79 per cent of its total database consists of U19 rowers (NZ Secondary Schools Rowing Association 2015).

The number of junior athletes considered elite has remained relatively stable over the last decade – 19 junior athletes in 2004, and 22 athletes in 2015 while its U23 athletes have doubled. While Rowing NZ's high performance centre is in Cambridge, the organisation maintains four 'regional performance centres' in part to facilitate the link between tertiary study and the elite pathways. In 2015, Rowing NZ named 22 athletes to take part in the 2015 World Rowing Championship. According to Rowing NZ, 'Junior representation is considered an important part of the Rowing New Zealand high performance pathway'. Indeed, the junior team trains at Lake Karapiro (Rowing NZ's Zealand High Performance Centre) for eight weeks in mid-winter, requiring many of the athletes to relocate to the town of Cambridge. As the juniors prepare and train, they continue their secondary school studies at a local school and are accommodated at Lake Karapiro (Rowing NZ 2015).

Secondary School Sport Academies

New Zealand sport development occurs predominantly via its club system. Increasingly, however, schools are taking an active role in operating competition structures, particularly in relation to team sports. In sports like football, talented youth will play in both secondary school competitions and in more traditional club competition structures. However, the emergence of secondary school sport academies over the past 15 years has added a new dimension to youth elite sport.

The creation of sport academies has its foundations in the 1989 Education Act that promulgated devolved and decentralised school administration through locally elected boards of trustees. Initially introduced as a means of maintaining student motivation, sport academies have grown alongside changes in wider societal views about commercialised sport and the acceptability of sport as a viable career path. To the extent that sport academies are initiated and developed locally, their design and operations vary according to their environments. Pope (2002), for example, documents a surfing academy that aims to create a pathway to professionalism while ensuring academic qualifications and vocational training.

Sport NZ is certainly aware of potential issues arising from the proliferation of secondary school sport academies. According to its survey of youth elite athletes in the P2P programme, 31 per cent were part of a secondary school sport academy. The reported experiences were mixed, reflecting the numerous possible models, and permutations. On their effects, Sport NZ interpreted the variability as 'polarising approaches' that is, the sport academies variously added to, or reduced the athlete's time commitments. 'In some schools,' Sport NZ reported,

> the academies looked to reduce the workload on the athlete by helping them with planning and time management, allowing them to complete their sport specific training during school hours, or giving them time to do homework thus freeing up time after school for training. In other schools they added to the workload by adding several additional generic training sessions to an already overworked young athlete.
>
> (p.23)

272 Michael P. Sam

Secondary schools thus appear to have the potential to provide some of the best assurances of pastoral care for young athletes, though with a propensity for sport to gain an increasing emphasis. According to one report, rowers in a high school U18 programme were expected to train 17–20 hours per week 'to stay competitive' including five two-hour sessions (Cleaver 2015). That this might lead to overtraining and understudying is a concern shared by multiple organisations but these organisations are to some extent complicit in the issue. Indeed it is becoming clear that youth elite sport is developing its own political economy driven by schools, parents, events rights holders, paid coaches and talent development officers employed by the national governing bodies. As academies have emerged, so too have indications that school sport development is being increasingly outsourced. Indeed the percentage of teachers coaching school sport has been in decline since 2005 (NZSSSC 2012), perhaps owing to the higher expectations around coaching and performance.

In contrast, University sport holds a negligible status within the high performance system though historically, university rugby clubs such the University of Otago's were responsible for many developing *All Blacks* in the pre-professional era. Rowing is seeing a resurgence in this area backed by Rowing NZ's desire to retain athletes and integrate its high performance ethos into university clubs. Some universities have embraced closer links with sport by offering scholarships yet these efforts remain linked with university marketing and promotions efforts rather than attempts to establish inter-collegiate sport development per se. One reason inter-university sport has not taken root is because scholarships binding tertiary study with sport are centrally distributed/administered by Sport NZ and HPSNZ through the Prime Minister's Scholarships. This has permitted young athletes to pursue different types of study, including vocational training while also enabling more flexibility in relation to where they choose to study.

Emerging themes, issues and dilemmas

Coaches remain a fundamental pillar in elite youth sport development. The emergence of the P2P programme and the data it generates are almost certainly going to translate into more refined coaching practices for elite youth. HPSNZ recognizes explicitly that coaches are central to the youth environment and that educating coaches is important to understanding talent. More pointedly, the agency recognizes that with the average age of specialisation at between 14 and 16 years, the quality of coaches at this stage of development deserves particular attention. At the same time, the implication of this age of specialisation (at least in HPSNZ targeted sports) is that training environments and competitive structures are equally important (Chiet and Sport New Zealand 2015). However, confounding such conclusions is that the same data suggests specialisation is principally influenced by the athletes experiencing success. Thus, it is unclear if there is a tradeoff in terms of introducing elite platforms (and *more* competitive conditions) at the same time athletes are developing these motivations and identities around success.

Certainly one implication arising from the need for better coaching and quality competitive environments around youth elite sport is the increased financial investment that this requires. More expertise at regional levels implies the need for more professionals in this space which inherently means more investment on the part of organisations and clubs. That costs will be passed on to athletes and their families is a reasonable speculation given it has long been acknowledged that family incomes have a significant bearing on the careers of young elite athletes (Baxter-Jones and Maffulli 2003). Indeed these pressures are apparent in HPSNZ's survey of youth elite athletes. Despite the probability of this cohort already consisting of athletes from higher socio-economic backgrounds, 14 per cent of those surveyed cited 'lack of financial support' as a significant challenge to succeeding in their sport (Chiet and Sport New Zealand 2015).

Well intentioned as P2P may be, it is somewhat ironic that the programme's workshops and training contribute an additional time demand on athletes, when it is recognised that 'managing multiple commitments' is one their biggest challenges. 'Mental obstacles' also appeared in the aforementioned survey as a challenge to success but what that means is unclear. The potential for athlete burnout or dropout is one possible interpretation, hence why athlete welfare remains at the forefront for sports like swimming and rowing particularly as it relates to heavy training. The NZ Secondary Schools Rowing Association, for example, noted that that lightweight rowing for juniors remained a concern with 'another report of anorexia this year' and in 2015, it instituted a limit on the number of events school age rowers could enter at championship regattas (NZSSRA 2015). An equally pressing question, however, is with regards to how youth elite sport structures might inadvertently decrease the pool of athletes in that particular sport. For example, while not focusing on the youth elite ranks per se, there is evidence of high (70 per cent) dropout rates in schools rowing (Beattie 2014).

The introduction of state-sponsored programmes such as 'Pathway to Podium' aimed at pre-elite youth athletes are notable for their interest in pastoral care. P2P recognizes the specific challenges youth face in pursuing high performance sport along with other school and family commitments. In addition, it offers career counselling and a place for youth to discuss the commercial/legal aspects of their sporting careers. Young athletes are increasingly asked to sign performance contracts that while more symbolic than legally binding, signal an increasingly formal relationship between athletes and their organisations. Some of these 'contracts' are hardly new, such as when school coaches demand their athletes maintain a level of academic performance or demand that athletes commit exclusively to their sport. But the proliferation of academies (formed either within schools, facilities or charitable trusts) means that athletes are also becoming the property of these organisations. The slogan that 'it takes a village' [to develop athletes] is undoubtedly credible but to the extent that the survival of village organisations relies on drawing legitimacy from young athletes, we may just as likely see parochialism as collaboration.

The most common theme emerging from discussions around elite youth sport is the need for systemic alignment. This is generally a view from the top, that is, from the perspective of Sport NZ and the national governing bodies. Whether the development pathway includes regional talent programmes, clubs, high performance centres or secondary school academies, the issue is how these can best be coordinated. It is often take for granted that geographically centralised structures are more effective however, club structures in individual sports such as swimming or gymnastics often have their own professional coaches. Thus the challenge for these NSOs is to demonstrate alignment while not overstepping the boundaries of autonomous organisations that have long shared the responsibility of developing youth elite. Accordingly, one of the ways to achieve alignment is to create new competition structures. NZ Football, for example, has prioritised the alignment of existing youth leagues and the creation of new national leagues for U15/U16 age groups. NZ Football suggests that the realignment of current talent development pathways is necessary for providing a blueprint that can directly influence player profiling, identification and programme design (New Zealand Football 2015). It is hard to imagine that the developments around youth elite sport will not have substantial effects on the broader system. As with the emergence of secondary school sport academies in rugby, these are showing signs of distorting other competition structures as well. In 2014, a private school with a tennis academy withdrew from the inter-school competition because other teams were not sufficiently competitive. Labelled as a victim of its own success, the college was accused of denigrating the competition by pulling out (Burnes 2014).

Concluding remarks

The organisational and managerial emphasis on elite youth sport has emerged only recently in New Zealand. In large part, the growth of programmes and structures, and the expansion of age-group national competitions, has been a by-product of the emphasis on high-performance structures more generally. As elite sport budgets have grown, there has been a corresponding increase in the level of services and their 'reach' into pre-elite levels. Elite youth sport is thus the latest 'field' to receive attention by central agency officials and yet in this case, it appears to be an area in which the state's ambitions are to cultivate and tame rather than initiate and lead.

To an extent this is because the 'horse has already bolted'. Sport development officers in their respective sports have long needed to demonstrate the effectiveness of 'junior development' programmes as proof of their adherence to 'whole-of-sport' planning and 'talent identification' pathways (Bloyce and Smith 2009). For over a decade, secondary schools have likewise boasted of their programme's connections to national sport pathways and/or links with professional franchises. New national leagues and competitions for youth are encouraged by all stakeholders and in instances where regional associations or school sport academies can afford to hire professional coaches, it follows that these individuals have to justify their time in employment, hence more practices/trainings per week and longer seasons (owing to off-season development 'camps'). While not discussed above, parents are arguably also complicit in legitimising the emphasis on high level youth sport. In wanting the best for their children, they are as much consumers of talent development programmes as the sports themselves. Where the status of being 'elite' requires a growing commitment in terms of time and money, it may also translate into more difficult choices around where to live and where to study.

In terms of its systemic impact, the increasing importance accorded to youth elite sport might arguably translate into an attendant demand for earlier specialisation at levels immediately below the elite youth level. With its already small economies of scale, New Zealand faces the prospect of organisations trying to recruit at younger and younger age groups in order to capture their 'markets' and retain their talent. The view that it may be 'too late' to take up a new sport at the age of say 13 years may become more common as a result, doing little to leverage the benefits of participating in multiple sports. In the longer term, it seems almost inevitable that the performances of youth athletes will become closely monitored by central sport agencies and NSOs, as markers of a 'sustainable' system. Thus the evolution of elite youth competition, talent identification and development should not be underestimated for the simple reason that the policies and strategies enabling the preparation of youth at that level will have profound effects.

Acknowledgment

I would like to acknowledge Mr Timothy Dawbin for his contribution as well his useful insight into an earlier draft of this chapter.

References

Archer, H. M. (2008) *Linking policy to the process: An examination of the formulation of New Zealand's talent identification and development policy.* Master of Physical Education, University of Otago.

Baxter-Jones, A. and Maffulli, N. (2003) Parental influence on sport participation in elite young athletes. *Journal of Sports Medicine and Physical Fitness*, *43*(2): 250.

Beattie, R. (2014) *The experiences of adolescents rowing in New Zealand: An insight into the influences of attrition in school rowing.* Master of Sport and Exercise, Auckland University of Technology.

Bloyce, D. and Smith, A. (2009) *Sport Policy and Development: An introduction*, Routledge.

Burnes, C. (2014) *College Sport: St Kents opts out of A1 tennis comp* [Online]. Auckland: New Zealand Herald. Available: www.nzherald.co.nz/news/print. cfm?objectid=11217862 (Accessed 6 May 2014).

Chiet, A. and Sport New Zealand (2015) *Talent: Understanding and building the system to best support our athletes of the future* [Online]. Sport New Zealand. Available: www.sportnz.org.nz/assets/connections2015/com2015-Alex-Chiet. ppt (Accessed 22 April 2015).

Cleaver, D. (2015a) *NZ Schoolboy rugby under investigation* [Online]. Auckland: New Zealand Herald. Available: www.nzherald.co.nz/sport/news/article.cfm?c_ id=4&objectid=11513431 (Accessed 15 September 2015).

——(2015b) *How to raise a sports champion - Too much time spent on sport* [Online]. Auckland: New Zealand Herald. Available: www.nzherald.co.nz/sport/ news/article.cfm?c_id=4&objectid=11444278 (Accessed 7 May 2015).

High Performance Sport New Zealand (2013) *Targeted investment proves winning formula* [Online]. Wellington: HPSNZ. Available: www.hpsnz.org.nz/news-events/targeted-investment-proves-winning-formula (Accessed 12 August 2014).

New Zealand Football (2015) *The Whole of Football Plan* [Online]. Wellington: New Zealand Football. Available: www.ebookonline.co.nz/doc/national_player_ development_framework/ (Accessed 2 October 2015).

Nz Secondary Schools Rowing Association (2015) *2015 AGM Draft Minutes* [Online]. Lake Karapiro: NZSSRA. Available: www.schoolrowing.org.nz/nzssra. php?page=B31.

Nzpa (2009) *Snell sports institute shuts for lack of cash* [Online]. Auckland: New Zealand Herald. Available: www.nzherald.co.nz/sport/news/article.cfm?c_ id=4&objectid=10557502 (Accessed 19 February 2015).

Paul, G. (2015) *How to raise a sports champion – Super Rugby sides scouting schools* [Online]. Auckland: New Zealand Herald. Available: www.nzherald. co.nz/news/print.cfm?objectid=11444271 (Accessed 8 May 2015).

Pope, C. C. (2002) Plato makes the team: the arrival of secondary school sport academies. *Waikato Journal of Education*, 889–100.

Rowing Nz (2014) 128th Annual Report. Cambridge: Rowing NZ.

——(2015) *New Zealand Junior Rowing Team to test out Rio Olympic course* [Online]. Cambridge: Rowing NZ. Available: www.rowingnz.kiwi/ Story?Action=View&Story_id=113 (Accessed 23 November 2015).

Sam, M. P. (2012) Targeted investments in elite sport funding: Wiser, more innovative and strategic? *Managing Leisure*, 17(2): 206–219.

Sam, M. P. and Macris, L. I. (2014) Performance regimes in sport policy: exploring consequences, vulnerabilities and politics. *International Journal of Sport Policy and Politics*, 6(3): 513–532.

Sam, M. P. (2015a) Sport policy and transformation in small states: New Zealand's struggle between vulnerability and resilience. *International Journal of Sport Policy and Politics*, 7(3): 407–420.

— (2015b) Big brother and caring sister: Performance management and the athlete's entourage. *In:* Andersen, S. S., Houlihan, B. and Ronglan, L. T. (eds.) *Managing Elite Sport Systems: Research and practice.* London: Routledge, pp.16–30.

Scherer, J. and Jackson, S. J. (2010) *Globalization, sport and corporate nationalism: The new cultural economy of the New Zealand All Blacks*, Peter Lang.

Scott, G., Bushnell, P. and Sallee, N. (1990) Reform of the core public sector: New Zealand experience. *Governance: An international Journal of Policy and Administration*, 3(2): 138–167.

Shirley, I. (1990) New Zealand: The advance of the new right. *In:* Taylor, I. (ed.) *The social effects of free market policies: An international text.* New York: St-Martin Press, pp.351–390.

Sports Development Inquiry Committee (1985) Sport on the move: Report to the Minister of Recreation and Sport. Wellington: Government Print.

Swimming Nz. (2015a) *Proposal of new competitive pathway* [Online]. Swimming New Zealand. Available: www.swimming.org.nz/visageimages/High%20Performance/SNZ%20-%20Proposal%20New%20Competitive%20pathway.pdf (Accessed 1 December 2015).

——(2015b) *High performance centre programme* [Online]. Auckland: Swimming NZ. Available: www.swimming.org.nz/article.php?group_id=438 (Accessed 1 December 2015).

Tid Taskforce (2004) Linking promise to the podium: Talent identification and development in New Zealand. Wellington: Sport and Recreation New Zealand.

Chapter 17

Conclusion

Elsa Kristiansen, Milena M. Parent and Barrie Houlihan

The opening chapter placed the question of convergence in youth elite sport systems at the heart of the review and suggested a framework for analysing the extent and nature of convergence. At first glance, the 15 countries explored provide substantial evidence of convergence despite the variations in political system, culture and history. Before discussing the patterns found in the countries reviewed in this collection, it is valuable to take a step or two back and consider the factors affecting the development of elite sport systems as a way of exploring the scope for variation and innovation. As is the case in so many areas of both commercial and public policy, the aspirations of organizations, the policies they adopt, and the impact of those policies are affected by the interplay of exogenous international or global pressures as well as domestic factors (such as resources, culture, political interests).

Any discussion of exogenous pressures needs to be wary of the casual use of the concept of globalization, where it is used as a simplistic explanation of complex processes. However, to exaggerate the capacity of national sport systems to insulate themselves from economic, social and cultural forces beyond their territorial boundaries would be equally naive. One of the central problems with explorations of globalization is determining the depth of penetration of exogenous economic and cultural factors. For example, it could be argued that the recent rapid growth in the popularity of soccer at the youth level in the United States is a relatively superficial effect of globalization as the underlying organizational and financial basis of sport is unchallenged and indeed reinforced by the cultural import. In order to explore the significance of exogenous factors on the development of elite youth sport systems, we suggest three factors are of particular importance: cultural globalization, commercialization and governmentalization.

Analyses of a range of public policy areas, including welfare (Deacon, 1997), the economy (Simmons & Elkins, 2004), education (Ozga & Lingard, 2007) and the environment (Busch & Jörgens, 2005), all identify the increasing importance of the role and influence of international policy actors in shaping domestic policy. In business sector studies, similar conclusions have been drawn from analyses of the impact of globalization on, for example, regulation (Vogel & Kagan, 2004), human resource management (Quintanila & Ferner, 2003) and structure (Radice, 2000). Although there are some actors, such as the International Monetary Fund, the European Union and the Organisation for Economic Cooperation and Development, whose influence is evident in many business sectors and areas of public policy, each policy sector and area has a cluster of more specialist international actors. Sport is a particularly good example of this phenomenon, as domestic sport is affected by the decisions of a vast array of international actors, including the international federations (IFs), the International Olympic Committee (IOC), the World Anti-Doping Agency (WADA), the Court of Arbitration for Sport (CAS), sponsors and the major broadcasting organizations. With regard to elite youth sport, the development of youth championships have added momentum to the strong domestic pressures to identify and develop talent for the senior competitions. Utilizing Lowi's (1972) typology of policy instruments – distribution, redistribution, regulation and organization – it is easy to see how these international actors have influenced the development of elite youth development systems. For example: access to the considerable financial resources of the IOC by national Olympic committees (NOCs) is conditional on support for IOC policies such as the Youth Olympic Games; and, the establishment of age-related competitions by the IFs not only provides a regulatory and organizational framework for youth competition, but also generates an expectation regarding the nature and pace of youth development. The very few countries, such as Norway, which formally or informally opt to withstand these forces, find themselves under considerable internal pressure to conform, often on the grounds of the potential damage to the country's prospects at the senior level. While the significance of international actors should not be underestimated, it is important not to exaggerate their reach and capacity (Scholte, 2005; Hirst & Thompson, 1999). Acknowledging the vagueness of the concept of globalization and the disputes over the significance of exogenous actors, it is possible to argue, in relation to elite youth sport, that: 1) globalization should be regarded as a multi-layered and multi-directional process mediated by domestic factors, such as education and youth welfare policies and youth employment prospects; 2) the analysis of the significance of cultural globalization must acknowledge the varying depth of social embeddedness of cultural values towards sport, education and child welfare; 3) the impact of globalization on elite youth talent identification and development (TID) policy within individual countries will vary due to the differential 'reach' of global forces and the variability in 'response' in different countries; and 4) while the political and cultural dimensions retain a degree of autonomy from economic processes in relation to youth sport, the intensification of economic interests (particularly from broadcasters and event organizers) at the senior competitive level to affect the youth TID processes in many sports as they seek to preserve their attractiveness to broadcasters.

The second pressure leading to convergence in youth elite sport, commercialization, has three dimensions, the first of which is the transformation of many sports events and clubs into valuable brands and commodities. While few youth sport events or young athletes are valuable brands, the latter are the foundation for sustained brand attractiveness of sports, senior events and club teams. The extensive academy system in football and the early recruitment of athletes in elite junior squads in many Olympic sports is an attempt by those sports and clubs to maintain and enhance their value as commodities for fans and for the international media. The second dimension relates to the growth of sport as a source of profit for non-sports businesses through, for example, sponsorship and broadcasting. Successful youth elite development systems are essential for delivering value to sponsors and broadcasters. The final dimension is the growth of sports-related businesses such as sportswear and equipment manufacturers (Slack et al., 2005; Amis & Cornwell, 2005) for whom the youth market is important.

Commercialization is, in many countries, reinforced by the third source of pressure – governmentalization, which refers to the intervention by government not only in the design and delivery of elite youth sport systems, but also in shaping the values that underpin the systems. Two sets of often mutually reinforcing values are evident in many of the countries in the collection – nationalism and commercialism – with the former providing the rationale for public investment and the latter moulding the culture of the system around values of entrepreneurialism, audit, targets and the efficient use of (young human) resources. Although the promotion of values by the state is an important aspect of governmentalization, by far the more tangible aspect is the design, resourcing and strategic organization of elite systems. Referring again to Lowi's (1972) typology of government policy instruments the development of elite youth sport systems provides, in many countries in this collection, evidence of: distribution (of political legitimacy of involvement of young children in sport, of financial resources and of facilities and expertise); redistribution (of time in the curriculum/school day to allow for more training); regulation (of children's participation in high level competitive sport; of youth coaches and of the interconnection of education and sport talent development); and organization (through the provision of specialist agencies, events and school physical education curriculum).

While cultural globalization, commercialization and governmentalization are ubiquitous elements of the context for contemporary youth elite sport, the ways in which individual countries and, to an extent, individual sports, respond to these elements varies considerably as the previous chapters have demonstrated. Partially independent of these exogenous elements, a second process is in operation, as there is clear evidence most countries with ambitions for elite sporting success engage in extensive policy learning from each other, lesson drawing, and policy transfer (Bergsgard et al., 2007; Green, 2007; de Bosscher, De Knop, & van Bottenburg, 2009b). As Rose (2005, p.16) makes clear, policy transfer is preceded by learning and lesson-drawing: 'A lesson is the outcome of learning: it specifies a programme drawing on knowledge of programmes in other countries dealing with much the same problem.' Lesson-drawing, according to Rose, 'expands the scope for choice in the national political agenda, for it adds to proposals generated by domestic experience the stimulus of examples drawn from foreign experience' (2005, p. 23). Importantly, he also argues lesson-drawing 'accepts the contingency of public policy' and what might work in one country might face considerable obstacles in being applied in a different domestic cultural, political and social context. The attempts by Brazil to transplant a youth development system has encountered substantial problems due in part at least to a highly fragmented polity, the dominance of football, and the instability in public finances. Similarly, in the UK, the importation of elite youth development models from countries such as Australia have been mediated by a social context in which wealth and class are major factors in determining access to elite sport opportunities (Holt, 1992; Birley, 1995; Mason, 1980). All the countries in this volume have distinctive histories, which mediate policy transfer and domestic policy innovation; and, as will be explored in more detail below, it is easier to transfer or adopt some aspects of elite youth TID (for example, the aspiration for elite youth success) than others (such as the allocation of resources). However, while not wishing to understate the degree of variation, it is the similarities between the countries which are most striking, with the variation often being in the progress in system development. The degree of similarity might, as already suggested, be the consequence of policy learning and transfer, mimetic isomorphism, but it might also be the consequence of the characteristics of the policy objective the countries are trying to achieve, that is, greater elite sport success. In other words, it may be the policy routes to elite sport success are very limited with the consequence that, irrespective of the political system, cultural traditions and social structure elite youth sport systems tend to follow a similar design, not simply because it is optimal for the problem to be solved, but because the alternatives are so far from optimal. As Freeman (1985, p. 469) noted in relation to general policy-making:

> The idea that distinctive and durable national policymaking styles are causally linked to the policies of states asserts that 'politics determines policy'. The policy sector approach argues, in contrast, that the nature of the problem is fundamentally connected to the kind of politics that emerges as well as the policy outcomes that result. ... it suggests that 'policy determines politics.'

Policy variation and convergence

'Omnes viae Romam ducunt' or 'all roads lead to Rome' may be debated after reading of the variety of youth sport policy and management paths presented in the previous chapters. Table 17.1 provides a synthesis of the information by country. It demonstrates some similarities, such as in structures (for example, between the Commonwealth Countries), as well as the push for innovation and for elitism in youth sport. However, it also highlights the variety of means used to have 'successful' elite youth sport programmes.

The increasing number of youth competitions and the global pressure to succeed have resulted in a redesign of many nations' talent development systems (Barreiros, Cote & Fonseca, 2014; De Bosscher, Brockett & Westerbeek, 2016), and also in an increased focus on the particular circumstances of the young athlete. However, the attempts to design efficient and effective youth TID systems have not always been successful as evidence suggests that early selection for a national youth development squad does not automatically result in an athlete reaching the senior squad or even staying in the sport. Barreiros and colleagues (2014) found that only one third of early selected athletes became successful athletes at the senior level. One frequently reported explanation for the failure to convert promising young athletes to high-achieving seniors is the tension between sporting ambitions and educational qualifications and their non-sport or post-elite sport career ambitions. Consequently, many countries seem to be adapting their elite youth sport management to accommodate young athletes' dual career aspirations (De Bosscher et al., 2016; EU, 2012). There are a number of examples where the management of education, learning and/or dual careers could be seen, such as in the cases of England/the UK, France, and Norway. To wit, in a thematic analysis of the chapters using the qualitative data analysis software Leximancer, we found schools to be the fifth most important theme, and education to be a sub-theme within athletes, the third most important theme. The top two themes were, understandably, development and sport.

Integration of education and sport development was often sought through the establishment of complex systems, which include high performance centres or secondary school academies (some nations such as China from primary school and onwards), regional talent programmes and clubs. The coordination of these agencies is a substantial management challenge and is often compounded by the distribution of responsibilities between the central and sub-national governments which is a particular problem in countries such as Brazil, Belgium, the UK and Germany, which have either federal or devolved government structures. According to De Bosscher and colleagues, 'the answer to what is the best system seems to lie in how centralized and decentralized approach can be combined' (2016, p. 528).

Table 17.1 Key policy features and structures

Country	Youth Sport Policy features	Youth Management structures
United Kingdom	Focus on limited number of sport; early specialisation; efforts to protect young athlete welfare, but variable	Hierarchy of sports clubs; youth academies; formal performance pathways; bespoke competition calendar
The Netherlands	Focuses on a few sports, late recognition of the importance of sport, focus on talent recognition and development	Local sports clubs, sports schools, special fund for elite athletes, centralized system
Germany	Sport autonomy and fragmented system of different competencies of governmental and non-governmental organizations	Sports clubs first, supplementary training, The German Sports Youth, talent identification – state support for elite youth sport
Russia	From 'physical culture' and state approach to new national policy programs targeting youths	Sport training system: regional clusters, basics; centres of Olympic preparation; and federal centres
Norway	Talent protection and variation between the national federations talent development programmes (federation autonomy)	Sport schools, parent and club dependency for success
France	'Sport, Youth and association' (grassroots sport and elite sport focus)	Centres for Elite Excellence and Centres for Young sporting talents. Sport specific
Canada	Decentralized (10 provinces, 3 territories), variations across jurisdictions. CSP 2012 and LTAD are key for decision-making regarding the national sport system	Combination of public, non-profit and for-profit organizations, clubs and leagues, with some overlap between jurisdictions
United States of America	Sport autonomy and fragmented system, focus on college sport and emphasis on individual achievement. Few policies affect youth sports directly other than Title IX and those from sport governing bodies	A combination of public, private and not-for profit sport organizations – and without federal involvement
Brazil	Isolated actions before 2000, recently a series of youth sport policies have been initiated (still in infancy)	Federal government instigated a national training network (285 Sports Initiation Centres in 263 municipalities)
South Africa	Legacy of Apartheid affects current policy; an increase in early talent identification and development, mass sport participation is costly	Priority sports in schools, provincial sport academies – municipalities important stakeholder, skewed gender balance

Table 17.1 continued

Country	Youth Sport Policy features	Youth Management structures
China	Youth sport department, 9-year compulsory school – but competitive training may start as early as 5–6 years old. Focus on athlete welfare	Government-run sport system, where the sport schools are important for success besides national and provincial sport systems
India	Focus on a healthy lifestyle, but also to increase access to sports facilities and training – and encourage young athletes by implementing programmes	Central government influenced, and regional training centres are being set up
South Korea	Rights as student-athletes: the 'Guarantee Policy of Study Rights' concerning student-athletes' welfare, Sport Vision 2018	Sports schools, NEST (public organization in talent development), KOSTASS identification system
Australia	National Junior Sport Policy (1994), Junior Sport Framework (2014), Winning Edge (2012–2022), and Play.Sport.Australia (2015) have and continue to shaped youth sport policy. Federated model. Emphasis of growing participation rates for health benefits and increase of talent pool. Focus on support of elite athletes	A mix of non-profit, public and for-profit sport organisations, clubs, teams and leagues
New Zealand	Recent formalization of youth elite sport, P2P with regional programmes	Centralized and targeted elite sport system, most successful sports have better youth elite sport programmes

The chapters also point to a strengthening in the belief among national governing bodies (NGBs) that ever earlier specialization is a prerequisite for eventual elite success, as previously pointed out by Hodges and Williams (2012). This specialization is formally embedded in the community sport programmes (grassroots sport, sport-for-all) in most countries, best expressed by Sam when describing the New Zealand's system with their slogan that 'it takes a village to raise a child, it takes a system to develop an athlete' (see Chapter 16). However, as the English/UK and Canadian chapters (see Chapters 2 and 8) point out, early specialization does not necessarily lead to later, continued success at the senior elite level.

The Chinese have had a clear focus on elite, especially Olympic, sporting success and an effective system since the early 1990s, while for other countries in this book, the establishment of systematic approaches to elite youth development is a recent change in sport policy and priorities (e.g., India, Brazil and South Africa). As Hong (Chapter 14) points out, when describing the development in South Korea, effective systems might have the positive side effect of stimulating the discussion and implementation of policies to protect young student-athletes' rights as has been the case in case in Norway and the UK. However, the concern with protecting the interests of young athletes might also be the result of a concern to protect the investment made by NGBs and governments in developing young athletes and preventing burnout and/or dropout. Some research suggests it is the most talented athletes who are more likely to be the ones to burn out (e.g., Brenner, 2007) or become injured (e.g., Bahr, 2014) due to over-ambition for their developmental stage, due in part to the dominant culture within the national system.

An effective system also seems to require a certain size of country. Although most countries tend to prioritize a few sports, 'it is doubtful that the narrowing of priorities in a large country distorts their sporting systems to the same degree' as in a small country (Sam, 2016, p. 538). However, as shown in this book and as reported in de Bosscher et al. (2009), population size is not the only factor that matters; the interplay with other equally important factors, such as the political economy and stability, also have an impact on the sport system in the respective countries. In Chapter 13, Chelladurai and Nair emphasized the increasing interest in India in youth sport resulting in the development of policies in recent years. In a country of India's size, to see the results of promoting a sporting culture among youth will be interesting to follow over the next few decades. Although the Indian chapter touches upon a changing level of interest, the Brazilian and South African chapters focus on a lack of structure as a hindrance for elite youth sport. In Chapter 11, Burnett explained that the current South African system does not facilitate elite sport development, as the recent policy focuses more on mass sport participation programmes in local communities. As she emphasized in her chapter, 'The social transformation of elite sport is currently the main drive with resources allocated to achieve the targets, inclusive of having "ethnic blacks" and "girls/women" featuring in elite teams' (Chapter 11, p. 172). South Africa is a good example of a country where the culture of international sporting achievement was deeply ingrained in the popular culture. Unfortunately, during the apartheid years, that same sporting culture was used as a basis for cultural and racial differentiation and for white South Africans an indication of social superiority. Few countries had such a distorted sporting culture; although, there are very few countries where there is not some association between sport and social differentiation (class, caste, status and wealth). For most countries in this collection, the most striking distinction is between those countries such as Australia, New Zealand, France and the UK, where elite sport achievement is integral to popular culture (and indicated by an extensive network of competitive sport clubs) and those where a culture of elite sporting achievement in Olympic sports (such as China, South Korea, Brazil (with the exception of football) and India (with the exception of cricket)), is promoted/imposed by the state and has only limited organic relationship with popular culture. For many countries, an elite sport culture must be learned; and it is often the values associated with nationalism (whether national rivalry or nation-building, for example in South Africa), economics (neo-liberal individualism, as in New Zealand and the UK) and religion (for example, Calvinism in the Netherlands and in Norway) that drive or (as in the case of Calvinism) impede the pursuit of elite sporting success. Central to the promotion of elite success values and to the facilitation of effective TID systems is the role of schools and particularly sports schools. It is to these organizations that we now turn.

The role of sport schools

The role of the sport schools is mentioned and discussed in almost every chapter. In China, they are considered 'the main sites of cultivating elite youth athletes' (see Chapter 12); in other countries such as Norway and the Netherlands, they are gaining importance and in Germany cooperation between schools and clubs is considered vital for success (see Chapter 4). Although their positioning in the development of young athletes is comparable, their funding, organization, relationship to their respective NOCs as well as to NGBs differs considerably. Former communist countries and China are known for their effective state-run and centralized talent selection and development programmes, often including sport boarding schools. From the chapters in this book, it seems these countries continue to have a systemic advantage. However, as Xing reports in Chapter 12, the perpetuation of the old Chinese system of focusing on training at the expense of education, is under pressure due to the other career opportunities available in the expanding Chinese economy. In recent years, it has proved increasingly difficult to attract young people to attend sport schools as their parents see attending a sports school as foregoing an effective academic education. The declining popularity of sports schools is forcing the issue of the effective management of young athletes' dual career on to the policy agenda. The problem of balancing sporting and educational ambitions is not confined to China. In Chapter 3, Elling and Reijersberg noted top sport athletes had lower school academic performance than athletes performing at a lower level, which was partly explained by the pressure that training requirements place on academic study time. The tension between education and sport training was evident in almost all countries in this collection, with the formula for overcoming the tension and enabling the successful management of a dual career proving elusive. Both national context and the characteristics of the sport (for example, whether the sport is an early peak sport) will determine how the young elite athletes balance school and sports. In general, athletes rate the support they receive as insufficient. In the recent SPLISS investigation, only 27 per cent of athletes viewed their support (e.g., training schedules, medical support services, equipment etc.) as sufficient (De Bosscher et al., 2016). The role of parents is added into this elite youth sport context. With less sport funding and an increasingly decentralized system, parental resources (economic and knowledge) will become increasingly critical for young athletes, as many of the support networks are parent led (Bloom, 1985). Youth elite sport has become a career, which has resulted in a corresponding increase in the level of services required by young athletes and the extension of those services into pre-elite levels.

The cultural significance and management of the sports

The differences within a country are easily apparent when undertaking a comparison between early peak sports, commercial sports and major national sports (see Table 17.2). While Table 17.2 should be read with a critical eye, it is interesting to note how much more extensive the support infrastructure available is to athletes within the commercial sport/national sports. Many of the larger, more popular sports have extensive hierarchical and nationwide, while the less popular sports or those in the less densely populated countries rely more heavily on the school system and on periodic regional/national development camps. In addition, in smaller countries such as the Netherlands and New Zealand, fewer sports tend to be prioritized for public funding. However, an increasingly common feature of elite youth sport systems irrespective of the wealth, geographical size or population of the country is the use of performance indicators, especially previous or predicted medal Olympic success as the basis for government funding. The overall effect of the need by NGBs to be able to justify public financial support is to increase the emphasis on the development of effective TID

Table 17.2 Differences between early peak, commercial and national sports

	Early peak sport	Commercial sport	National sport
Management characteristics	Regional training centres and local clubs	National league system – opt for professional careers	League system and national age graded teams
	Child protection vs adequate training load	National team system – very early talent identification	Larger pool of athletes makes it easier with a structured development system
	Large training volume at a young age	Semi-professional options for younger players	Schools' more active role in team sport
		Voluntary system at grassroots level, but often peripheral to youth TID	
Resources and support system	More parent dependent because of high costs	Club/commercial scholarships	Private academies/ sport schools are significant
			Professionalization and training centres
Consequences and outcome	Sacrifice of social life	Different opportunities for women and men because of revenues – high participation	Cultural significance and national support despite international size
	Harder to get elite status	Attitude problem towards education among talents	Success is a national priority

processes and to treat young talented athletes as resources – factors of production.

Several countries mentioned swimming and diving as an *early peak sport* (South Africa, China, New Zealand, the Netherlands, England), together with figure skating (Norway, Canada), and gymnastics (Germany, France, the United States). In general, it is considered beneficial by the NGB to start early with training if senior success is to be achieved; the nature of the training – its intensity, duration and structure – that is considered appropriate and publicly acceptable varied deeply between the countries. While Chinese athletes might become a full-time athlete at age 10, Norwegians cannot compete nationally (or internationally) before the age of 13. The early specialization sports also start competing internationally at a young age, facing a more performance-oriented environment. This may be perceived as damaging for some young people, especially with regard to their education and social development, and consequently the quality of and easy access to emotional, educational and economic support is vital. In this respect the role of parents is of crucial importance not only in the role as a facilitator of involvement in a youth elite system and as a support network, but also as a legitimiser of the emphasis on high-level youth sport. The entire family must often commit (time, money and other resources) to a certain lifestyle in order for the young athlete to succeed; however, parents may unintentionally add pressure.

More often than not, chapter authors discussed a male team and/or contact sport as the major *commercial sport* in a country, such as football/ soccer (Norway, The Netherlands, France, South Korea, England), rugby (South Africa, New Zealand), field hockey (Australia), ice hockey (Canada) and basketball (Germany and the United States). These sports highlighted a wide gap between what male and female athletes can do and earn within commercial sports. An exception to this would be the South Korean example of women's golf – a huge success due to the high numbers of players in the LPGA. Nevertheless, it seems clear there are significant gender differences in talent development for commercial sports. Even if women's football is growing in both popularity and quality at the international/elite level, it remains far behind the men's game in terms of the sophistication of the talent identification, development and training support.

The greatest variety was of course in the examples of *national/Olympic sports*. The sports range from football (Canada) to swimming (United States), speed skating (the Netherlands), judo (France), cycling (South Africa), cricket (India), cross-country skiing (Norway), rowing (New Zealand), netball (United Kingdom), archery (South Korea), Australian Rules Football (Australia), and track and field (Germany). We can see that popular sports are not always found in the form of professional/commercial leagues. Finally, some chapters, such as Russia, pointed to uniform sport development pathways for sport in their country, offering little leeway for implementation specificity and not differentiating significantly between early peak, commercial, and national sports. In contrast, other chapters (e.g., Brazil) drew attention to the extensive variation in the maturity of TID systems outside the commercial sports and the challenges that countries with ambitions for Olympic success face in establishing a TID system from scratch.

Dimensions of convergence

In Chapter 1, we suggested that in order to examine claims for convergence in elite sport systems and in the youth TID element of those systems, it was important to unpack the concept of convergence and consider seven distinct dimensions. Such an analysis would, we argued, provide a more nuanced foundation for comparison between countries. Taking each dimension in turn, it is clear there is strong evidence of convergence, but the countries are from being convergent.

1   **Motives.** As mentioned in Chapter 1, it is quite possible for governments, sports federations and commercial clubs and leagues to exhibit similar interest and enthusiasm for youth sport TID and to design similar development systems yet have divergent motives. In most of the countries in this collection, there is substantial government involvement in the early peak sports and in the sports of national importance. The most obvious motive for the investment of public funds in sport is to boost or reinforce national identity – a motive which is well established in countries such as New Zealand, Australia and Russia and emerging strongly in India and Brazil. The importance of nationalism is also evident in relation to commercial sports, which have often achieved their commercial value due to their association with national identity. However, nationalism is complemented by commercialism and reflected, for example, in the willingness of commercial clubs (most clearly in English Premier League football and Indian Premier League cricket) to recruit foreign stars, often with the consequence of marginalizing home-grown youth players. It was only in a small number of countries, most notably England/UK, Norway and South Korea, where child protection was evident as a governmental motive; and in the cases of England/UK and South Korea, the motive was generated by scandal.

2   **Agenda and aspirations.** 'Agenda' referred to the presence of issues related to youth sport within the decision-making processes of government and the acceptance by government of a need to respond. 'Elite youth sport' rarely appeared on the agenda of government as a discrete issue, as it was usually subsumed under the broader issue of international sporting success and elite athlete development. However, when the issue did appear, it was most often in relation to the establishment and/or regulation of sport schools. Although, as mentioned earlier, there was considerable variation in the nature of sports schools the prevalence of specialist sports schools was notable. The other issue was bullying and other forms of abuse.

If the agenda showed a degree of convergence, the response to the issues raised was more varied with the countries which have sports schools often expressing an aspiration the schools should manage the dual career of young athletes effectively but few exercising regulatory authority in relation to the operation of the schools. Where there was a greater degree of policy convergence was in relation to the importance of training coaches in the particular skills of working with young athletes; although, this was more often the policy of the NGBs than that of government.

3   **Contextualizing discourse/ideology/values.** Contextualizing discourses for policy interventions in relation to elite youth sport are often the product of deeply rooted values and beliefs about child welfare and development, competitive sport, education and the acceptable activities for young boys and girls. These values are part of the deep structure of a society and can impose significant constraints on policy. The most evident discourse was that of nationalism, which provided the fundamental justification for policy intervention. However, nationalism was often intertwined with other discourses such as the Calvinist distaste for promoting elitism (Norway and the Netherlands), market liberalism, which constrained to a limited extent government intervention (New Zealand), the autonomy of sport which also provided a constraint on government intervention, and the priority of educational achievement (evident in many countries, those less obvious in some commercial sports such as football in England).

4   **Inputs** referred to the mix of resources (e.g., finance, expertise and administrative capacity) and the source of resources (whether from the public, commercial and/or not-for-profit sector) which contributed to the development and maintenance of elite youth sport systems. The most significant resource provided by almost all governments was legitimacy for the incorporation of young people into elite development systems. However, the range of other resources provided varied considerably, ranging from China at one extreme, where the elite sport system was almost wholly state funded and organized, to the more neo-liberal countries, such as New Zealand and the UK, where governments provide funding, but rely substantially on non-governmental bodies (clubs and their NGBs) to provide the expertise and organizational capacity.

5   **Implementation** refers to the selection of instruments and delivery mechanisms; and it was suggested in Chapter 1 that it is often in relation to these dimensions that the clearest examples of convergence are found. A clear majority of countries in this collection shared the following characteristics in relation to the choice of instruments relying heavily on: financial incentives (public subsidies to NGBs and often to clubs); a contractor–client relationship with delivery agents with an accompanying set of penalties for poor performance; and financial and social rewards for successful athletes. There was also substantial commonality regarding delivery mechanisms with academies preferred by the commercial sport, the heavy reliance on sports schools and a hierarchy of clubs, regional training events/camps reinforced by a hierarchy of domestic competitions.

6   **Momentum** referred to the intensity of commitment by powerful policy actors (governments, commercial sports clubs, etc.) to the expressed aspirations and their continued commitment of resources beyond the

initial phase of the policy process. With regard to this dimension, there was considerable variation, with countries such as India and Brazil finding it difficult to move from the policy as aspiration stage to the policy as action stage. Other countries, such as England/UK, Russia and New Zealand, had mature elite development systems supported by undiminished political and commercial commitment and momentum. Others still, including Australia, Norway and South Korea, had exhibited varying degrees of equivocation in relation to the commitment to elite sport in general and elite youth sport in particular.

7   **Impact** referred to convergence in policy effects. It could be argued the intense attention paid over the last 30 years or so to youth TID has had only a limited impact on the historic success of countries in international sport (the rise of China in the Olympic medal tables being the only major exception). However, impact can be assessed at other levels apart from medal success. For example, there has been much greater convergence in the incorporation of children more systematically into the elite development process, successfully turning children into a factor of production and changing the purpose of sport from being a resource for the holistic development of children into one where children are a resource for the political ambitions of governments and commercial ambitions of business.

In conclusion, convergence and divergence are both at play in national elite youth sport systems. Nevertheless, there does not seem to be one best way to approach the issue and many factors need to be considered when designing, implementing and analysing elite youth sport. As such, researchers would do well to take an interdisciplinary or multi-disciplinary approach to studying elite youth sport, combining policy, management, ethics, philosophy, and psychology to name but a few key fields involved. In a similar vein, policy makers, as difficult as this may be, will have to balance the desires of the government with child welfare and the longer-term needs of the youth, as well as consider the capacity and motives of sport organizations when designing and implementing policies affecting elite youth sport.

References

Amis, J. and Cornwell, T. B. (Eds.) (2005). *Global Sport Sponsorship*. Oxford: Berg.

Bahr, R. (2014). Demise of the fittest: are we destroying our biggest talents? *British Journal of Sports Medicine*, 48, 1265–1267.

Barreiros, A., Cote, J. & Fonseca, A. M. (2014). From early to adult sport success: Analysing athletes' progression in national squads. *European Journal of Sport Science*, 14, S178–S182.

Bergsgard, N.A., Houlihan, B., Mangset, P., Nødland, S.I. and Rommetvedt, H. (2007)*Sport Policy: A comparative analysis of stability and change*, Oxford: Butterworth-Heinemann.

Birley, D. (1995) *Land of Sport and Glory: Sport and British society, 1887-1910*, Manchester: Manchester University Press.

Bloom, B. S. (1985). *Developing Talent in Young People*, New York: Ballantine.

Brenner, J. S. (2007). Overuse Injuries, Overtraining, and Burnout in Child and Adolescent Athletes. *Pediatrics, 119*(6), 1242–1245.

Burnett, C. (2010). *Delivery for the Sport Industry by South African Universities*, Johannesburg, South Africa: University of Johannesburg.

Busch, P. O. & Jörgens, H. (2005). The international sources of policy convergence: explaining the spread of environmental policy innovations. *Journal of European Public Policy, 12*(5), 860–884.

Csikszentmihalyi, M., Rathunde, M. & Whalen, K. (1993). *Talented Teenagers: The roots of success and failure*, New York: Cambridge University Press.

Deacon, B. (1997). *Global Social Policy: International organizations and the future of welfare*, London: Sage.

De Bosscher, V., Brockett, C. & Westerbeek, H. (2016). Elite youth sport policy and dual career support services in fifteen countries. In K. Green & A. Smith (Eds), *Routledge Handbook of Youth Sport* (pp. 521–534). Oxon, NY: Routledge.

De Bosscher, V., De Knop, P., van Bottenburg, M., Shibli, S. & Bingham, J. (2009a). Explaining international sporting success: An international comparison of elite sport systems and policies in six countries. *Sport Management Review, 12*.

De Bosscher, V., De Knop, P. & van Bottenburg, M. (2009b). An analysis of homogeneity and heterogeneity of elite sports systems in six nations. *International Journal of Sports Marketing and Sponsorship, 10*(2), 7–27.

EU. (2012, September 28). EU Guidelines on Dual Careers of Athletes. European Union. Retrieved from http://ec.europa.eu/sport/library/documents/dual-career-guidelines-final_en.pdf

Freeman, G.P. (1985). National styles and policy sectors: Explaining structured variation, *Journal of Public Policy, 5*(4), 467–96.

Green, M. (2007). Policy transfer, lesson drawing and perspectives on elite sport development systems, *International Journal of Sport Management and Marketing, 2*(4),

Hirst, P. and Thompson, G. (1999). *Globalisation in Question: The international economy and the possibilities of governance*, Cambridge: Polity.

Hodges, L. J. & Williams, A. M. (2012). *Skills Acquisition in Sport: Research, theory and practice*, London: Routledge.

Holt, R. (1992). Amateurism and its interpretation: The social origins of British sport. *Innovation: The European Journal of Social Science Research, 5*(4), 19–31.

Houlihan, B. & Green, M. (Eds.). (2008). *Comparative Elite Sport Development: Systems, structures and public policy*, Oxford, UK; Burlington, MA: Butterworth-Heinemann.

Kristiansen, E. (2016). Walking the line: How young athletes balance academic studies and sport in international competition. *Sport in Society.* http://doi.org/10.1080/17430437.2015.1124563

Lowi, T.J. (1972). Four systems of policy politics and choice, *Public Administration Review, 32*, 298–310.

Mason, T. (1980). *Association football and British society 1863-1915*. Harvester, Brighton.

Ozga, J., & Lingard, B. (2007). Globalisation, education policy and politics. *The RoutledgeFalmer reader in education policy and politics*, 65–82.

Quintanilla, J. & Ferner, A. (2003). Multinationals and human resource management: between global convergence and national identity. *International Journal of Human Resource Management*, *14*(3), 363–368.

Radice, H. (2000). Globalization and national capitalisms: theorizing convergence and differentiation. *Review of International Political Economy*, *7*(4), 719–742.

Rose, R. (2005) *Learning from Comparative Public Policy: A Practical Guide*, London: Routledge.

Sam, M. (2016). Youth sport policy in small nations. In K. Green & A. Smith (Eds), *Routledge Handbook of Youth Sport* (pp. 535–542). Oxon: Routledge.

Scholte, J. A. (2005). 2nd edn. *Globalization: A critical introduction*, Basingstoke: Palgrave Macmillan.

Simmons, B. A. & Elkins, Z. (2004). The globalization of liberalization: Policy diffusion in the international political economy. *American Political Science Review*, *98*(01), 171–189.

Slack, T., Silk, M. L. & Hong, F. (2005) Cultural contradictions/contradicting culture: Transnational corporations and the penetration of the Chinese market. In M.L. Silk, D.L. Andrews and C.L. Cole (eds.) *Sport and Corporate Nationalisms*, Oxford: Berg, pp. 253–274.

Vogel, D. & Kagan, R. A. (2004). *Dynamics of Regulatory Change: How globalization affects national regulatory policies* (Vol. 1). University of California Press.

Index

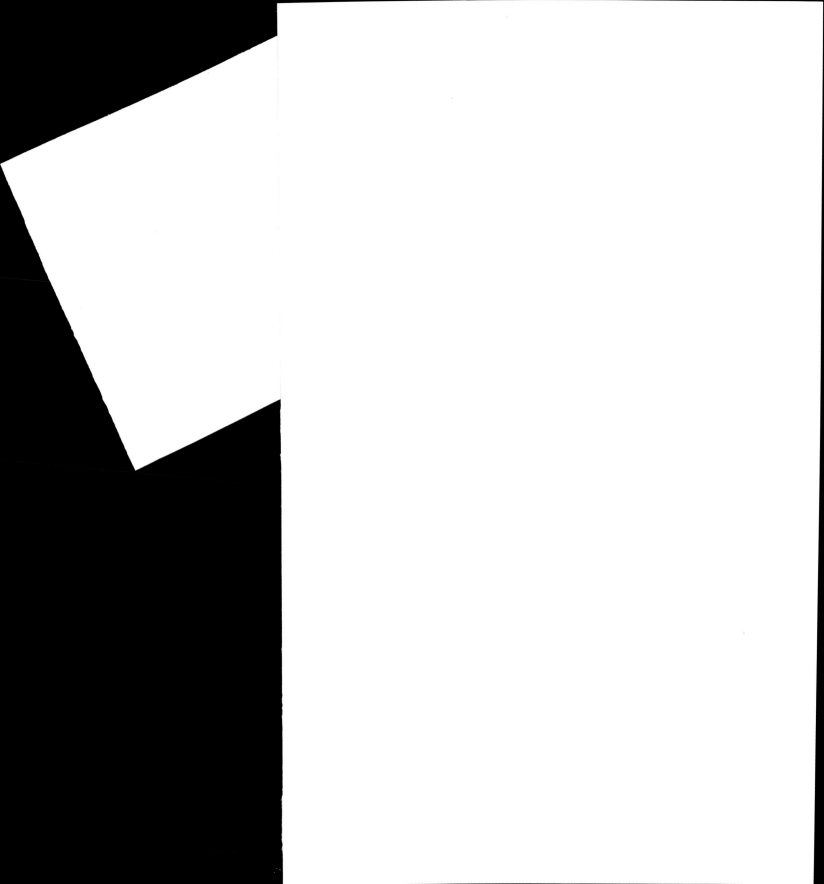

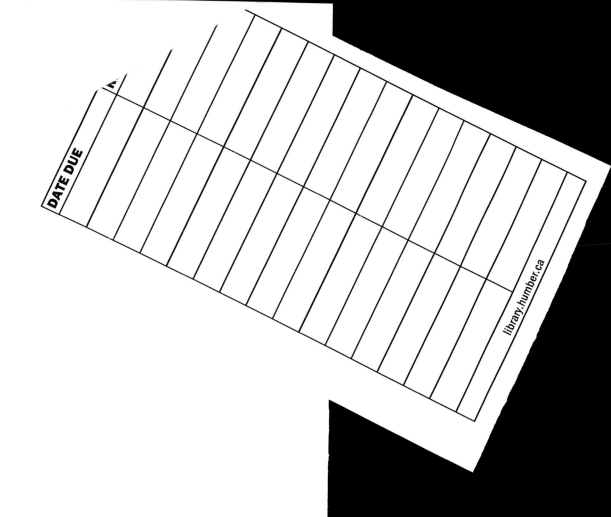